Evidence: Investigation, Rules, and Trials

WEST LEGAL STUDIES

Options.

Over 300 products in every area of the law: textbooks, CD-ROMs, reference books, test banks, online companions, and more—helping you succeed in the classroom and on the job.

Support.

We offer unparalleled, practical support: robust instructor and student supplements to ensure the best learning experience, custom publishing to meet your unique needs, and other benefits such as West's Student Achievement Award. And our sales representatives are always ready to provide you with dependable service.

Feedback.

As always, we want to hear from you! Your feedback is our best resource for improving the quality of our products. Contact your sales representative or write us at the address below if you have any comments about our materials or if you have a product proposal.

Accounting and Financials for the Law Office • Administrative Law • Alternative Dispute Resolution • Bankruptcy • Business Organizations/Corporations • Careers and Employment Civil Litigation and Procedure • CLA Exam Preparation • Computer Applications in the Law Office • Contract Law • Court Reporting • Criminal Law and Procedure • Document Preparation • Elder Law • Employment Law • Environmental Law • Ethics • Evidence Law • Family Law • Intellectual Property • Interviewing and Investigation • Introduction to Law Introduction to Paralegalism • Law Office Management Law Office Procedures Legal Nurse Consulting • Legal Research, Writing, and Analysis • Legal Terminology • Paralegal Internship • Product Liability • Real Estate Law • Reference Materials • Social Security Sports Law • Torts and Personal Injury Law • Wills, Trusts, and Estate Administration

---

West Legal Studies
5 Maxwell Drive
Clifton Park, New York 12065-2919

For additional information, find us online at:
www.westlegalstudies.com

Evidence: Investigation, Rules, and Trials

First Edition

BENJAMIN H. FRISCH

THOMSON
DELMAR LEARNING

Australia Canada Mexico Singapore Spain United Kingdom United States

THOMSON
DELMAR LEARNING

WEST LEGAL STUDIES

Evidence: Investigation, Rules, and Trials

Benjamin Frisch

Vice President, Career Education Strategic Business Unit:
Dawn Gerrain

Director of Learning Solutions:
John Fedor

Managing Editor:
Robert Serenka, Jr.

Acquisitions Editor:
Shelley Esposito

Editorial Assistant:
Melissa Zaza

Director of Content and Media Production:
Wendy Troeger

Senior Content Production Manager:
Glenn Castle

Art Director:
Joy Kocsis

Technology Project Manager:
Sandy Charette

Director of Marketing:
Wendy E. Mapstone

Channel Manager:
Gerard McAvey

Marketing Coordinator:
Erica Conley

Cover Design:
Dutton & Sherman Design

Library of Congress Cataloging-in-Publication Data

Frisch, Benjamin H.
  Evidence : investigation, rules, and trials / by Benjamin H. Frisch.
    p. cm. -- (West legal studies)
  ISBN 1-4180-1692-6
  1. Evidence (Law)--United States. 2. Legal assistants--United States--Handbooks, manuals, etc. I. Title.
  KF8935.Z9F755 2008
  347.73'6--dc22

2007024572
ISBN 13: 978 1-4180-1692-0

NOTICE TO THE READER

Dedication

In memory of my grandfather, Myer R. Shark,
a tireless advocate for the little guy.

Contents

CHAPTER 4 Discovery: Getting Evidence Through the Court
System 75

Preface

I wrote this book to provide paralegal students and professors with a text that is truly written for them. This book will help paralegals improve their attorneys' practices by focusing on the paralegal's role, from interviewing clients and witnesses to investigating cases through formal discovery and informal processes. Each chapter will discuss the complex law of evidence in language that nonlawyers can understand, without sacrificing important coverage. This book will be useful to paralegal and criminal justice students, and anyone else who wants to learn the basics of finding evidence and getting it admitted into or excluded from court.

FOLLOW A CASE FROM START TO FINISH

Evidence: Investigation, Rules, and Trials follows the path of a case from initial client interview through investigation, trial, and appeal. After an introduction to evidence, the text covers informal investigations, including interviewing the client and witnesses. Next we examine the formal discovery process and introduce the courts and evidence rules. Then we can dive into the rules of evidence, starting with relevance. Hearsay, exceptions to hearsay, and opinion testimony follow. Next we cover pretrial matters such as motions in limine and preparing a trial notebook. The penultimate chapter concerns trials, and finally we look at the future of evidence.

Discussions and examples from criminal practice are included where appropriate throughout this text.

I hope you find this book to be practical, not overly technical in explaining the concepts, thorough but not too complex, and as much fun to read as an author can make a textbook on his favorite subject. Wherever possible, I tried to utilize an example that would prove interesting.

FEATURES

Evidence does not exist in a vacuum. I wrote this text to show how evidence is analyzed in the context of the case it supports. To create that context, this text uses a recurring feature called ***Passim Case***, a fictional civil case involving identity theft. In *Fields v. Prairie Bank*, students will learn to apply otherwise abstract concepts to a concrete case, while considering which evidence is admissible and completing projects related to the burgeoning problem of identity theft.

PASSIM CASE **FIELDS V. PRAIRIE BANK**

When something is cited throughout a legal document it can be referred to in an index as "Passim." Throughout the text you will be learning about evidence by looking at a fictional case. It will help you understand the concepts involved in gathering evidence and evaluating its admissibility. That way you will not need to learn these things in a vacuum. You will read an overview of the case and learn more about it in each chapter.

Bench Briefs appear liberally throughout the text to continue building a real-life framework for the law of evidence. Bench Briefs include documents and transcripts from real cases, examples from real-life experience, ethics alerts, and relevant excerpts from movies, television, and novels.

BENCH BRIEF ENTERTAINMENT NOTE

In the following scene from the screenplay for *My Cousin Vinny*, Mona Lisa Vito is an unemployed hairdresser, yet she is qualified as an expert on auto repair.

D.A. JIM TROTTER: Ms. Vito, what is your current profession?

LISA: I'm an out-of-work hairdresser.

D.A. JIM TROTTER: An out-of-work hairdresser. In what way does that qualify you as an expert in automobiles?

LISA: It doesn't.

[she indicates that her training is from working on cars her whole life]

D.A. JIM TROTTER: Now, Ms. Vito, being an expert on general automotive knowledge, can you tell me . . . what would the correct ignition timing be on a 1955 Bel Air Chevrolet, with a 327 cubic-inch engine and a four-barrel carburetor?

MONA LISA VITO: No, it is a trick question!

JUDGE CHAMBERLAIN HALLER: Why is it a trick question?

MONA LISA VITO: 'Cause Chevy didn't make a 327 in '55, the 327 didn't come out till '63. And it wasn't offered in the Bel Air with a four-barrel carb till '64. However, in 1964, the correct ignition timing would be four degrees before top-dead-center.

D.A. JIM TROTTER: Well . . . uh . . . she's acceptable, Your Honor.

End-of-Chapter Assignments provide opportunities for review and further study. There are review questions and projects as well as legal research projects. Most paralegal students will study legal research in a separate course. To complement that learning, this text offers end-of-chapter opportunities for students to practice their legal research skills at varying levels of difficulty. Students may perform book or Internet research to complete such easy tasks as locating a case by citation and briefing it, medium difficulty tasks such as locating sample interrogatories or a form, and more difficult research tasks such as original legal research and writing a memo.

Evidence: Investigation, Rules, and Trials is rich in features that will ease the learning process now and serve as valuable references later.

- *Learning Objectives* in checklist form at the beginning of each chapter
- *Definitions* of important legal terms boxed and highlighted in the margins for easy reference.
- *Cases* carefully excerpted and boxed for easy reference, with discussions of what the student can gain by studying each case
- *Ethics Alerts* provided where appropriate and included in Bench Briefs
- *Summaries* that wrap up the salient points of each chapter
- *Helpful Web Sites* listed at the end of each chapter for reference or to aid further study

A COUPLE OF NOTES REGARDING AUTHOR'S LICENSE

Some cases are tried to the court without a jury, and some are tried to a judge in a *bench trial*. Rather than saying "fact finder" or "judge or jury" throughout the textbook, I have chosen simply to use the word *jury*. The same rules apply to court trials as to jury trials, although a judge might be less persnickety about what evidence comes in when it is he or she who is determining the facts.

I have included some short excerpts from cases, and where they cite something within them, I have typically deleted the citation without stating "citation omitted."

SUPPLEMENTS PACKAGE

- This complete learning package includes an **Instructor's Manual** with sample tests and ideas for using the *Passim Case* to build class discussion, legal role-playing, individual or group projects, and research assignments. The Instructor's Manual is also available online at *http://www.westlegal-studies.com* in the Instructors Lounge under Resource.
- **Online Companion™.The Online Companion™** Web site can be found at *http://www.westlegalstudies.com* in the Resource section of the Web site. The Online Companion™ contains objectives, lists of key terms, lecture notes, and practice quizzes.
- Visit our **Web site** at *http://www.westlegalstudies.com*, where you will find valuable information specific to this book, such as hot links and sample materials to download, as well as other West Legal Studies products.
- **Westlaw®**, West's online computerized legal system, offers students "hands-on" experience with a system commonly used in law offices. Qualified adopters can receive 10 free hours of Westlaw. Westlaw can be accessed with Macintosh and IBM PC and compatibles. A modem is required.

About the Author

Benjamin H. Frisch graduated in 1993 from the University of North Dakota School of Law, where he was an editor on the law review and represented the school in two national competitions. He has 14 years of experience as an attorney in a variety of settings including solo and small firm litigation practice in suburban Minneapolis, and as a prosecutor in rural Minnesota. Currently, he is a Westlaw Reference Attorney assisting other attorneys, law students, judges, paralegals and paralegal students, law librarians, and others who are conducting legal research. He has served as an instructor at the Minnesota School of Business in the paralegal program, teaching litigation and family law.

Acknowledgments

I would like to thank the Thomson sales representative for the Minnesota School of Business, Charlene Rutt, who introduced me to this opportunity. Additional thanks go to Shelley Esposito and her team, who saw enough value in the book proposal to approve it, and to Shelley's invaluable assistant at Delmar Learning, Brian Banks.

Really instrumental in making this a far better book than I could have written by myself was my developmental editor, Mary Clyne. Without her the book would have been short in more ways than I can count.

Together with the publisher, I would like to thank the following reviewers for their valuable contributions:

Elizabeth Church
Lake State University, MI

John DeLeo

Timothy Hart
College of the Sequoias, CA

Craig Hemmens
Boise State University, ID

Elizabeth Mann
Greenville Technical College, SC

Kristine Mullendore
Grand Valley State University, MI

Hal Turk
Auburn University, AL

Linda Carnes Wimberly
Eastern Kentucky University, KY

Juris Pro was courteous enough to let us use a screen shot of their software and they wanted us to let you know about them: "Built by litigation attorneys, JurisPro is a free, national directory of expert witnesses in over 4000 areas of expertise. Once you come to JurisPro's website (www.JurisPro.com) you can view and download the expert's full CV, see the expert's photos, hear the expert speak through streaming audio, learn the expert's background as an expert witness (e.g.: how many times has the expert testified for the plaintiff or defense), access the expert's website, contact the expert's references, read their articles, and contact the expert directly. There are no referral fees of any type from JurisPro—the experts have paid to list in the site. If you cannot find the expert you are looking for online, please contact JurisPro at 888-905-4040, or info@JurisPro.com. The attorneys at JurisPro will help locate an expert witness for you from their internal database of over 75,000 experts, without any charge. The ABA, Legal Technology Resource Center, states: 'JurisPro should be among your first stops for finding an expert witness on the internet.'"

Most of all, I would like to thank my wife, Ione Ansel, for her extraordinary patience with this and other projects and my odds hours, and for her dedication to and love for our family.

CHAPTER 1

Importance and Basics of Evidence

"Jack, can you prove that Harrison
stabbed you in the back?"

Courtesy CartoonStock.com.
www.CartoonStock.com

■ OBJECTIVES

❏ Identify the paralegal's role in working with evidence
❏ Explain the importance of evidence
❏ Summarize the litigation process
❏ List the tasks that a paralegal may be responsible for throughout
   the litigation process
❏ Recall the four major sources for evidence research
❏ Identify methods for conducting legal research regarding evidence
❏ Analyze ethical issues in working with evidence
❏ Examine paralegal ethics and attorney ethics as they relate to para-
   legals and litigation
❏ Identify the roles of the different players in the court system and
   law office

WHY STUDY EVIDENCE?

Evidence is a fun and important subject. It is the basis for lawyers'
objections at trial. It is the material lawyers use to prove their cases. The
evidence that is gathered, admitted, and considered is often what
decides a case or causes it to settle for more or less money, or reach a plea
bargain that is more or less favorable. Paralegals help gather evidence,
organize it, and research whether it is likely to be admitted in court.

THE PARALEGAL'S ROLE IN WORKING WITH EVIDENCE

The process of finding evidence and determining whether it might be admissible at trial begins long before the lawyers first address the jury. Paralegals assist at every step.

After an incident occurs, the potential plaintiff looks for an attorney to take the case. A paralegal may be responsible for fielding calls from potential clients, who may include defendants. Before filing suit, the lawyer is required to make a preliminary investigation to make sure that the suit is not frivolous. Otherwise, the attorney could be subject to sanctions for filing a bad-faith claim. The paralegal might conduct this investigation.

Before a civil suit is filed, a **summons** and **complaint** must be drafted. After the suit is served, the defendant files an **answer**. It might contain a **counterclaim** or a **cross-complaint**. A paralegal could help to draft any of these documents or arrange for the documents to be served. After the complaint is served, the parties conduct discovery. The paralegal may draft interrogatories and requests for production of

■ SUMMONS
A notice that the defendant is being sued and has a limited amount of time to answer the suit.

■ COMPLAINT
A pleading that starts a lawsuit, notifying the defendant of what he or she is being sued for and making demands for relief.

■ ANSWER
A defendant's pleading that replies to and defends against a complaint.

■ COUNTERCLAIM
A claim by the defendant against the plaintiff.

■ CROSS-COMPLAINT
A claim by a defendant against a co-defendant.

BENCH BRIEF   ETHICS ALERT

As a paralegal you may receive calls from people who are looking for a lawyer to handle their case. This is the first point at which you must be careful not to practice law. It is illegal in every state for nonattorneys to practice law. Therefore, be sure not to provide advice on what steps to take.

The best practice is to first screen the potential client to find out if the case is one in which the attorney or firm for whom you are working could be interested. If the firm handles family law exclusively and the client has a personal injury matter, for example, your attorney may not want to spend time meeting with the person. The potential client is certain to have a lot of questions. However, it is better to try to get the person to come into the office for a meeting because making that effort means he or she is more likely to be serious about retaining an attorney. It also avoids the potential for crossing the line into offering legal advice. At the meeting, or after it, the attorney can recommend what action to take.

documents, arrange depositions, organize the material that comes in, and help analyze what might be **admissible** or **inadmissible** in court.

In criminal cases the procedure is similar. The prosecutor obtains an indictment from a grand jury or files a written complaint. A paralegal may draft a complaint. The defendant enters a plea at an initial appearance. The parties exchange information, and the paralegal may participate in this process.

Determinations of what might or might not be admissible often require legal research. There are four major places to find information on whether a given item of evidence would be admissible: evidence rules, statutes, cases, and **secondary sources** such as *Federal Evidence* by Mueller and Kirkpatrick. Many of these materials can be found online at http://westlaw.com, elsewhere on the Internet, or at a law library.

A researcher would rely on **primary law** such as the rules of evidence, the statutes, and the cases in the jurisdiction where the case is pending. If nothing can be found that is specific to the jurisdiction in question, the researcher may look to other jurisdictions. If the state adopted the Federal Rules of Evidence (FRE) the researcher may look at federal cases or consider sister states. Failing that, the researcher will turn to secondary sources including treatises and law reviews.

To find rules of evidence it is useful to know the overall structure of the rules. For example, under the FRE, rules relating to relevance are numbered in the 400s, and rules relating to hearsay are in the 800s. (See Exhibit 1–1.) States adopting the FRE often adopt something close to this numbering format. Nebraska, for example, has Rule 401 at section 27-401 in its statutes. So if a researcher wanted to know what the rules have to say about a relevance topic, a good place to start might be just to browse the rules in the 400 range.

ADMISSIBLE
Material that may be considered by the jury or judge when rendering a verdict.

INADMISSIBLE
Material that the judge or jury may not consider when rendering a verdict.

SECONDARY SOURCES
Items that interpret, analyze, or summarize primary law but lack the force of law, such as treatises, encyclopedias, and law review articles.

PRIMARY LAW
Material that is a direct source of the law, such as constitutions, statutes, cases, and rules.

EXHIBIT 1–1	HOW THE RULES ARE ORGANIZED
FRE NUMBERS	**TOPIC**
100s	General
200s	Judicial Notice
300s	Presumptions
400s	Relevance
500s	Privileges
600s	Witnesses
700s	Opinion
800s	Hearsay
900s	Authentication and Identification
1000s	Contents of Writings, Recordings and Photographs
1100s	Miscellaneous

To do that on Westlaw for the Federal Rules of Evidence, click on Site Map. Under Find a Document, click on the Table of Contents link. At that page click the plus sign for U.S. Material, then the plus sign for Federal Material (Primary & Secondary) and then the link for Federal Rules of Evidence (See Exhibit 1–2).

In addition to rules, statutes often address evidence topics separately. For example, many privileges are established by statute. Case law can shed light on what the rules and statutes mean. The cases with the most value as a **precedent** are from the highest courts that have dominion over the jurisdiction. For example, in federal court, cases from the U.S. Supreme Court would be best, followed by the relevant circuit court of appeals, followed by district court cases. In state court, cases from the highest court of the state would be best, followed by an intermediate court of appeals (if there is one), followed by trial court cases.

■ **PRECEDENT**
How courts have previously addressed a legal issue.

THE BASICS OF EVIDENCE

What follows is an overview of evidence, what it is, what it is needed for, the difference between direct and circumstantial evidence, and judicial notice and stipulations.

What Is Evidence?

Evidence is testimony, objects, test results, expert and nonexpert opinions, and anything else that can be gathered and offered at court to prove or disprove a case. In a date rape case, the only evidence may be the testimony of the alleged victim. In the income tax evasion case against mobster Al Capone, the evidence was testimony and receipts for a series of purchases that, combined, exceeded the income he reported to the Internal Revenue Service.

Examples of interesting things that have been admitted into evidence include:

- e-mails
- 911 call transcripts
- thermography results (a test to verify pain claims by taking heat measurements in the body)
- blood
- semen
- matched-pair test results (for example, two comparable renters of different races try to rent the same apartment to check on possible discrimination)
- compositional analysis of trace elements in bullet lead
- mitochondrial DNA test results
- hair
- pollen
- a company's own database of consumer complaints against its product

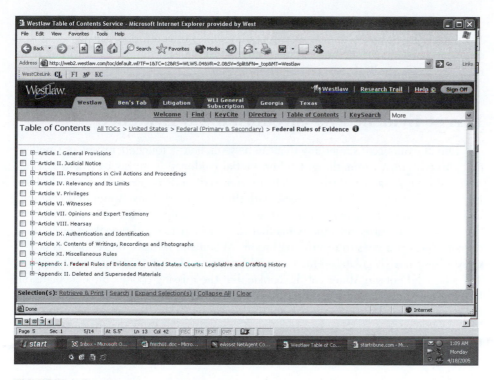

EXHIBIT 1–2   Federal Rules of Evidence Tables of Contents

Things that are not evidence include:

- what the lawyers say or ask
- material that has been stricken from the record
- information obtained by jurors outside the courtroom
- jury instructions

Material that is admitted for a limited purpose is evidence only for that topic and may not be considered for other issues.

How Does an Attorney Use Evidence?

An attorney tries to get favorable evidence admitted into court and tries to keep out unfavorable evidence. To win a case, the party with the **burden of proof** must produce enough evidence on every element of its claim in order to prove it. For example, the elements of a civil negligence claim are (1) a duty owed to plaintiff (2) breached by the defendant (3) where the breach is the actual and legal cause of (4) damages. To win such a case, the plaintiff must prove all four things by a **preponderance of the evidence**. The plaintiff will try to prove the elements by introducing evidence.

■ **BURDEN OF PROOF**
The degree to which a party must prove its case in order to win.

■ **PREPONDERANCE OF THE EVIDENCE**
Evidence for and against a contention results in the point being more likely true than not true.

■ **MOTION IN LIMINE**
A motion made outside the presence of the jury, usually before trial, to exclude evidence as inadmissible.

Material that does not violate evidence rules through its admission is admissible. Evidence that violates evidence rules is inadmissible. If an attorney suspects that the opposing party may try to get inadmissible material into evidence, the attorney may make a **motion in limine** or an objection.

Direct Evidence vs. Circumstantial Evidence

Direct evidence is something that can be seen, heard, touched, tasted, or smelled that directly proves something. Circumstantial evidence is indirect evidence. That means it requires a logical step to go from what is directly perceived to a conclusion. For example, suppose there is a house with three-year-old twins, Abner and Zachary, and a babysitter. The babysitter brings two chocolate chip cookies and puts them on the counter. The sitter tells the twins that they are not to eat the cookies until after dinner. The sitter goes to use the bathroom. When she returns, one cookie is gone. Only Abner has chocolate on his face and fingers, and he is wearing a guilty smirk. The sitter did not see Abner eat the cookie, but the missing cookie, the chocolate on his face and fingers, and his guilty smirk are all circumstantial evidence that he ate the cookie. Direct evidence that he ate the cookie would be Zachary's testimony that he saw Abner eat it, or Abner's admission that he ate it, or the babysitter's testimony that she saw him eat it.

COURT STRUCTURE

There are two types of courts and two main court systems in the United States. The two types of courts are trial and appellate, and the two main systems are federal and state. Trial courts are where judges and juries hear evidence through witness testimony and the admission of exhibits and then render a verdict or decision. This is the place where decisions are made about whether evidence is admissible or not. Appellate courts review decisions made at the trial court. An appeals court may indicate that evidence that was admitted should not have been admitted, or the other way around, and order a new trial or alter the decision of the trial court.

Federal courts hear cases only under limited circumstances. For example, a case that involves a question arising under federal law or the U.S. Constitution could be heard in federal court; another example would be a case in which the plaintiff and defendant are from different states and the amount in controversy is more than $75,000. If federal courts do not have jurisdiction, then the case is heard in state court. Certain types of cases are heard only in state court, such as divorce, violation of state criminal laws, and real estate ownership disputes.

Things Other Than Evidence That Can Be Used to Prove a Case

In addition to evidence, the **fact finder** can also consider material of which the court takes **judicial notice**, and any **stipulations** that the parties make.

ETHICAL ISSUES FOR PARALEGALS

Attorneys must follow ethics rules or face discipline such as censure, suspension of license, or disbarment. Since paralegals are not licensed, they are not subject to such discipline. However, a paralegal's conduct can get the attorney who is supervising him or her in such trouble. For example, if an attorney allows his or her paralegal to practice law, perhaps by appearing in court or drafting a contract from scratch, the attorney could be disciplined for facilitating the unauthorized practice of law.

Ethics in the Law Office

Intuitively, one might think that attorney ethics would be simple, that they would simply say "Do your best to advocate for your client without breaking the law. Avoid conflicts of interest. Have truthful advertising." The reality is, however, that it gets complicated. For example, some of the rules conflict. Attorneys are required to zealously advocate for their clients, but they must abide by the law, follow other ethics rules such as candor with the court, and refrain from presenting false testimony.

Unauthorized Practice of Law

The first step in avoiding the unauthorized practice of law is to make it clear to those with whom you are dealing that you are a paralegal, not an attorney. This includes potential and actual clients, other attorneys, witnesses, and court or administrative agency personnel. A paralegal should not enter into an attorney-client relationship, set fees for legal services, state legal opinions or give legal advice, or go to court or an administrative hearing for a client unless the court authorizes such appearances.

■ **FACT FINDER**
The jury in a jury trial, the judge in a trial without a jury.

■ **JUDICIAL NOTICE**
Something the court accepts as true that is commonly known or easily proven to be true even if no evidence is presented on the point.

■ **STIPULATION**
An agreement between the parties that the jury is to take certain facts as proven.

BENCH BRIEF NOTE

Some states have adopted the Model Rules of Professional Responsibility. Others have adopted the Model Rules of Professional Conduct.

NATIONAL ASSOCIATION OF LEGAL ASSISTANTS MODEL STANDARDS AND GUIDELINES FOR THE UTILIZATION OF LEGAL ASSISTANTS GUIDELINE 1

Legal assistants should:

1. Disclose their status as legal assistants at the outset of any professional relationship with a client, other attorneys, a court or administrative agency or personnel thereof, or members of the general public;

2. Preserve the confidences and secrets of all clients; and

3. Understand the attorney's Rules of Professional Responsibility and these Guidelines in order to avoid any action which would involve the attorney in a violation of the Rules, or give the appearance of professional impropriety.

NATIONAL ASSOCIATION OF LEGAL ASSISTANTS MODEL STANDARDS AND GUIDELINES FOR THE UTILIZATION OF LEGAL ASSISTANTS GUIDELINE 2

Legal assistants should not:

1. Establish attorney-client relationships; set legal fees; give legal opinions or advice; or represent a client before a court, unless authorized to do so by said court; nor

2. Engage in, encourage, or contribute to any act which could constitute the unauthorized practice law.

States and even federal districts and circuits differ on what constitutes the unauthorized practice of law, and on their definition of who is a paralegal. For example, states differ on whether or not it constitutes the unauthorized practice of law for a paralegal to put on a legal seminar. Some factors that some states take into account when considering whether an activity constitutes the unauthorized practice of law include whether legal work is preparatory, such as research, investigation, or drafting of forms, versus the actual creation of legal documents, and how closely the paralegal is supervised by an attorney. Some states allow paralegals to conduct client interviews, file forms and motions, and give advice, while others find that these activities constitute the unauthorized practice of law. It is important to find out what is allowed in your jurisdiction.

> **NATIONAL ASSOCIATION OF LEGAL ASSISTANTS MODEL STANDARDS AND GUIDELINES FOR THE UTILIZATION OF LEGAL ASSISTANTS ° GUIDELINE 3**
>
> Legal assistants may perform services for an attorney in the representation of a client, provided:
>
> 1. The services performed by the legal assistant do not require the exercise of independent professional legal judgment;
>
> 2. The attorney maintains a direct relationship with the client and maintains control of all client matters;
>
> 3. The attorney supervises the legal assistant;
>
> 4. The attorney remains professionally responsible for all work on behalf of the client, including any actions taken or not taken by the legal assistant in connection therewith; and
>
> 5. The services performed supplement, merge with and become the attorney's work product.

It is important to make sure that your work is being properly supervised. Work done by an unsupervised or improperly supervised paralegal may result in a suit for a refund or a malpractice suit against the paralegal or attorney.

For example, in the following case, an "independent paralegal" failed to properly fill out papers to have a sheriff execute a judgment. The plaintiff was seeking money from the paralegal for ruining the judgment. The court found that the judgment was still good and then proceeded to address the paralegal's conduct.

> **CASE**
> **SUSSMAN V. GRADO, 746 N.Y.S.2D 548 (N.Y. DIST. CT., 2002)**
>
> In response to the Court's question: "Do you work under the authority of an attorney?" The defendant answered: "I'm an independent. I assist the general public. I assist attorneys with work. And Mr. Sussman came to me of his own free will and asked me to do this work for him."
>
> *(continues)*

CASE
SUSSMAN V. GRADO, 746 N.Y.S.2D 548 (N.Y.DIST.CT., 2002) *(continued)*

To this Court, there is a difference between assisting someone to fill out a form and preparing a form on a subject with which the "assistance" is unfamiliar. Instead of referring this plaintiff to an attorney, the defendant allegedly asked three (3) attorneys about what a turnover order was ("none of them had ever heard of it") and called the Sheriff's office who informed her that "they needed something to direct the bank to research it's files and find out the assets of the debtor." **"So I prepared for Mr. Sussman the turn over order that you're looking at."** (emphasis in original)

When asked by the Court how she got the form, the defendant answered: "I patterned it based upon what I know of other orders petitioning money from the court."

A turnover proceeding is a common procedure in the collection of outstanding judgments. The defendant has, in this Court's opinion, crossed the line between filling out forms and engaging in the practice of law by rendering legal services. . . . This Court finds that the defendant used independent judgment on a subject with which she had insufficient knowledge. As indicated above, the defendant did not follow proper procedure with respect to the turnover proceeding. Failure to comply with CPLR 5225 and/or 5227 prevented the Court from issuing a turnover order. . . .

Regardless of her intentions to help the plaintiff, this independent paralegal operated without the supervision of an attorney. She tried to create a legal document without the required knowledge, skill or training. As a result the plaintiff may have lost the ability to execute against two bank accounts. Just as a law school graduate, not admitted to practice law, cannot undertake to collect overdue accounts on behalf of prospective clients, so is an independent paralegal barred from attempting to collect a judgment.

This Court finds that the actions of the defendant constituted a deceptive act "likely to mislead a reasonable consumer acting reasonably under the circumstances," and that "the acts or practices have a broader impact on consumers at large." Such action by the defendant in accepting the task to prepare a turnover proceeding when she was not qualified or legally able to prepare the necessary papers violated section 349 of the General Business Law. Here, the Court finds that the accepting of the assignment was misleading in a material respect to the consumer and that the consumer was injured—he was unable to collect his judgment from the two restrained bank accounts. Accordingly, the Court finds that the plaintiff is entitled to treble damages, Gen. Bus. Law 349(h), in the sum of $135.00.

In addition, the Court is sending a copy of this decision to the New York State Attorney General's Office for consideration in his discretion as to whether any action should be taken against the defendant pursuant to sections 476-a(1) and/or 485 of the Judiciary Law.

The court found that a paralegal is practicing law if the paralegal attempts to collect a judgment. Note that she tried to create a form from scratch. The question might be a bit more nebulous if she had filled out the blanks on a preprinted form.

According to the National Association of Legal Assistants Model Standards and Guidelines for the Utilization of Legal Assistants, here are some things that paralegals can do (except as provided by statute, court rule or decision, administrative regulation, or attorney's rules of professional conduct).

NATIONAL ASSOCIATION OF LEGAL ASSISTANTS MODEL STANDARDS AND GUIDELINES FOR THE UTILIZATION OF LEGAL ASSISTANTS GUIDELINE 5

Except as otherwise provided by statute, court rule or decision, administrative rule or regulation, or the attorney's rules of professional responsibility, and within the preceding parameters and proscriptions, a legal assistant may perform any function delegated by an attorney, including, but not limited to the following:

1. Conduct client interviews and maintain general contact with the client after the establishment of the attorney-client relationship, so long as the client is aware of the status and function of the legal assistant, and the client contact is under the supervision of the attorney.

2. Locate and interview witnesses, so long as the witnesses are aware of the status and function of the legal assistant.

3. Conduct investigations and statistical and documentary research for review by the attorney.

4. Conduct legal research for review by the attorney.

5. Draft legal documents for review by the attorney.

6. Draft correspondence and pleadings for review by and signature of the attorney.

7. Summarize depositions, interrogatories and testimony for review by the attorney.

8 Attend executions of wills, real estate closings, depositions, court or administrative hearings and trials with the attorney.

9. Author and sign letters providing the legal assistant's status is clearly indicated and the correspondence does not contain independent legal opinions or legal advice.

Conflicts of Interest

Conflict of interest rules seek to prevent attorneys from having their loyalty and advocacy pledged to different sides in a conflict. Attorneys cannot be on both sides of a case, nor can they undertake representation against a former client where the new case is a related matter. Conflict of interest rules have been applied to paralegals, such as where a paralegal switches firms and ends up working on the other side of a case on which the paralegal has previously worked. However, under Indiana law, conflict of interest rules do not apply to paralegals. Many states have adopted the American Bar Association Model Rules of Professional Conduct, so this chapter provides some of those model rules.

> **AMERICAN BAR ASSOCIATION MODEL RULES OF PROFESSIONAL CONDUCT 1.7**
>
> (a) Except as provided in paragraph (b), a lawyer shall not represent a client if the representation involves a concurrent conflict of interest. A concurrent conflict of interest exists if:
>
>   (1) the representation of one client will be directly adverse to another client; or
>
>   (2) there is a significant risk that the representation of one or more clients will be materially limited by the lawyer's responsibilities to another client, a former client or a third person or by a personal interest of the lawyer.
>
> (b) Notwithstanding the existence of a concurrent conflict of interest under paragraph (a), a lawyer may represent a client if:
>
>   (1) the lawyer reasonably believes that the lawyer will be able to provide competent and diligent representation to each affected client;
>
>   (2) the representation is not prohibited by law;
>
>   (3) the representation does not involve the assertion of a claim by one client against another client represented by the lawyer in the same litigation or other proceeding before a tribunal; and
>
>   (4) each affected client gives informed consent, confirmed in writing.

■ **CHINESE WALL**

The isolation of an attorney or paralegal with a conflict of interest so that he or she does not have access to the file or written or oral discussions about the conflicting case.

Note that conflicts can occur with former clients. Whether a conflict exists with a former client depends upon whether the new case is on the same matter or a related matter. At large firms, a paralegal or attorney who has a conflict of interest can be isolated from the case through the use of a **Chinese Wall**. A client can consent in writing to the representation as long as the attorney is not on both sides of the same case, the representation is not prohibited by law and the lawyer believes that it is possible to be a zealous advocate for both clients.

Duty of Confidentiality

An attorney has a duty of confidentiality to the attorney's current and former clients. This duty extends to paralegals and other office staff, which means both that the attorney may discuss confidential matter with staff, and that staff are bound by the confidentiality requirement.

AMERICAN BAR ASSOCIATION MODEL RULE OF PROFESSIONAL RESPONSIBILITY 1.6

(a) A lawyer shall not reveal information relating to the representation of a client unless the client gives informed consent, the disclosure is impliedly authorized in order to carry out the representation or the disclosure is permitted by paragraph (b).

(b) A lawyer may reveal information relating to the representation of a client to the extent the lawyer reasonably believes necessary:

(1) to prevent reasonably certain death or substantial bodily harm;

(2) to prevent the client from committing a crime or fraud that is reasonably certain to result in substantial injury to the financial interests or property of another and in furtherance of which the client has used or is using the lawyer's services;

(3) to prevent, mitigate or rectify substantial injury to the financial interests or property of another that is reasonably certain to result or has resulted from the client's commission of a crime or fraud in furtherance of which the client has used the lawyer's services;

(4) to secure legal advice about the lawyer's compliance with these Rules;

(5) to establish a claim or defense on behalf of the lawyer in a controversy between the lawyer and the client, to establish a defense to a criminal charge or civil claim against the lawyer based upon conduct in which the client was involved, or to respond to allegations in any proceeding concerning the lawyer's representation of the client; or

(6) to comply with other law or a court order.

In other words, do not discuss cases you are handling with people outside the office.

PASSIM CASE **FIELDS VS. PRAIRIE BANK**

Practice confidentiality. When you discuss the Passim Case with your friends or family who are not in this class, do not discuss the names of the client or the bank.

> ### BENCH BRIEF ETHICS ALERT
>
> Speaking of confidentiality, keep in mind that e-mail is not a very secure method of communication. Missouri requires attorneys to notify all e-mail recipients about the lack of security for e-mail communications. The notice must tell recipients that an e-mail may be copied and held by various computers along its path through the Internet, and that e-mail may be intercepted by improper access to the sender's computer, the recipient's computer, or computers through which the e-mail passes. Clients must consent to receive e-mail communications from their attorneys.

Ethics and Evidence

Additional ethics rules apply to evidence issues.

Presentation of False Testimony

A lawyer has a duty not to present false testimony.

Two American Bar Association Model Rules of Professional govern the presentation of false testimony, Rule 4.1(a) and Rule 8.4(c) and (d):

> ### AMERICAN BAR ASSOCIATION MODEL RULE OF PROFESSIONAL CONDUCT 4.1(A)
>
> In the course of representing a client a lawyer shall not knowingly:
>
> (a)   make a false statement of material fact or law to a third person; . . .
>
> #### Official Comment from the A.B.A.
>
> A lawyer is required to be truthful when dealing with others on a client's behalf, but generally has no affirmative duty to inform an opposing party of relevant facts. A misrepresentation can occur if the lawyer incorporates or affirms a statement of another person that the lawyer knows is false. Misrepresentations can also occur by partially true but misleading statements or omissions that are the equivalent of affirmative false statements.

> ### AMERICAN BAR ASSOCIATION MODEL RULE OF PROFESSIONAL CONDUCT 8.4 (C) AND (D)
>
> It is professional misconduct for a lawyer to:
>
> (c)   engage in conduct involving dishonesty, fraud, deceit or misrepresentation;
>
> (d)   engage in conduct that is prejudicial to the administration of justice;

Here is what happens to a lawyer who violates those rules. In the following case, a prosecutor knowingly presented false testimony in a capital murder case.

> **CASE**
> **IN RE PEASLEY, 90 P.3D 764 (ARIZ. 2004)**
>
> Peasley's intentional elicitation of false testimony against two defendants in a capital murder trial in 1993, re-presentation of the same false testimony in the 1997 retrial of one of the defendants, and exploitation of that false testimony in the closing argument in both trials, could not have been more harmful to the justice system. The credibility of the criminal justice system relies heavily on the integrity of those who work in the system. Moreover, a prosecutor has the added duty to see that justice is done. A prosecutor who deliberately presents false testimony, especially in a capital case, has caused incalculable injury to the integrity of the legal profession and the justice system. In such a circumstance, the public's interest in seeing that justice has been fairly administered has been violated in a most fundamental way. Peasley's misconduct has severely undermined the public's trust and confidence in Arizona's criminal justice system. Therefore, in this case, "[a]ny sanction less than disbarment would be an inappropriate statement of what the bar and this court should and would tolerate."

Since the lawyer presented false testimony, knew he was doing it, did it more than once, and did it in cases where the defendants' lives were at stake, the court disbarred him.

Duty of Confidentiality

Attorneys are required to protect a client's confidences. That means lawyers are not allowed to reveal information that is even tangentially related to the representation without the client's consent.

Duty to Preserve Evidence

A lawyer has a duty as an officer of the court not to destroy, allow the destruction of, lose, or otherwise **spoliate** evidence. A lawyer who intentionally destroys evidence may be prosecuted for obstruction of justice. He or she may also be liable for advising a client to destroy evidence. Some courts have even held that attorneys have a duty to the opposing party to instruct their clients not to destroy evidence. Prosecutors have a duty to preserve **exculpatory** evidence.

> **AMERICAN BAR ASSOCIATION MODEL RULE OF PROFESSIONAL CONDUCT 1.6(A)**
>
> A lawyer shall not reveal information relating to the representation of a client unless the client gives informed consent, the disclosure is impliedly authorized in order to carry out the representation...

■ **SPOLIATE**
To intentionally destroy, alter, or conceal evidence favorable to an opponent.

■ **EXCULPATORY**
Tending to show that the defendant is not guilty, or is guilty of a lesser charge.

PASSIM CASE   FIELDS VS. PRAIRIE BANK

We will pretend that you and a few classmates have just landed your first jobs out of paralegal school. You are working for a small plaintiffs' personal injury firm located in the imaginary State of Eden. Your friend and classmate Charlie is working for the local county attorney. Charlie and a few other acquaintances may bring aspects of their cases to you for your advice.

Your attorney has a client who was the victim of identity theft. Peter Fields first discovered a problem with his credit when he went to refinance his house. He thought he had excellent credit but he was turned down because he owed money on several credit cards he did not know he had. What Mr. Fields has not been able to determine for sure is how his identity was compromised. He was very careful with his personal information, however, so he is confused as to how someone obtained credit in his name and ruined his credit. He has spent a lot of time trying to clean up his credit and he wants justice.

Unlike most people, he had identity theft insurance through the IDO Insurance Company. He suspects the thief was a worker at Prairie Bank, where he has done his banking for many years, or someone who otherwise had access to their files. The bank has a general business insurance policy with a rider that covers theft of customer data through All-Farms Insurance.

The county attorney Charlie is working for is considering filing criminal charges. Therefore, during the first portion of the text, you will be gathering evidence, and later you will be learning whether various items of evidence would be admissible in a criminal or a civil case. You will learn details of the case as we progress through the text.

During your investigation, some facts that you find may contradict other facts. This is a normal part of any investigation and it is also a little bit of author's license to tweak the facts to make a point or two.

The State of Eden has adopted the Federal Rules of Evidence.

ROLES OF DIFFERENT PEOPLE IN THE COURT SYSTEM

This section contains a brief overview of the roles different people play in the court system.

Lawyer

Lawyers are advocates for their clients and officers of the court. They must zealously advocate for their clients without breaking the law or ethics rules. They provide legal advice, draft documents, and appear at depositions and at court. A prosecutor is a lawyer who represents the state (or the people of the state or the commonwealth, or the District of Columbia, or the federal government) in criminal cases. A prosecutor has an extra duty to seek justice.

Paralegal

The role of a paralegal will vary greatly from job to job. However, as a general rule, paralegals assist attorneys through legal research, drafting documents, interviewing clients and witnesses, investigating cases through formal and informal processes, arranging depositions, organizing material for trial, and attending trials.

Law Clerk

A law clerk is usually a second- or third-year law student or a recent graduate who has not yet passed the bar. Law clerks conduct legal research and draft legal arguments or memoranda.

Judge

Judges make oral and written rulings on the law and sometimes on the facts. They try to speed cases along the procedural process and otherwise deal with large case volumes. Judges are almost always former attorneys. Some are elected, others are appointed, and a few obtain or retain their seat on the bench through a combination of methods.

Court Reporter

A court reporter takes down verbatim what is said at a deposition or during a trial, usually using a stenograph machine, and prepares a transcript of what was said. Some court reporters work for themselves or for an agency and mostly take depositions, others work for the clerk of court or for the judge and mostly take down trial testimony.

Peace Officer

Police officers, troopers, and sheriff's deputies have varying roles. Police officers and troopers investigate crimes and accidents and may issue tickets and citations, make arrests, apply for search warrants, conduct searches, reconstruct accidents, and testify at trials. Sheriff's deputies may do some of those things; they may also serve as bailiffs, jailers, and process servers, and help collect civil judgments by seizing assets, conducting evictions, and the like.

ABOUT IDENTITY THEFT

Identity theft is a rapidly growing problem costing individuals and businesses billions of dollars. Nearly one out of 10 Americans were victimized in the past five years, according to a survey by the Federal Trade Commission. MasterCard and Visa estimated their identity theft fraud losses at $114.3 million in 2000, and the General Accounting Office contends that the losses of those companies is closer to the $1 billion range. Costs to individuals whose identities are stolen average $500, with more serious victims paying an average of $1,200. One in four U.S. households have experienced identity theft in the past five years. Identity theft victims spend an average of 30 hours resolving the problem, with more serious victims spending about twice that amount of time restoring their credit. Social security numbers are very useful for identity thieves because the numbers are used for so many things, such as car rental, patient identification, and credit applications.

How to Protect Yourself from Identity Theft

- Prevent dumpster diving by shredding important personal information such as bank statements and receipts. Or avoid receiving such information in the mail at all by doing your bill paying and banking online.

- Remove yourself from mailing lists.

- Use a separate e-mail address to give out to Web sites that might send you spam. Use another e-mail address for close friends and relatives and do not disclose it.

- Do not put your home address on luggage. Pay up front at hotels and do not leave an imprint of your card at the reception desk.

- Do not click on links sent to you in e-mails from people you do not know, even if it sounds or looks as if it is from a legitimate web site.

- Empty your Internet browser cache regularly.

- Use strong passwords with numbers, uppercase and lowercase letters, and characters mixed together, such as CubsFan#1. Never use the password "password."

- At an ATM, make sure that no one is looking over your shoulder.

- Run a spyware checker on your computer in case someone has installed keylogging software that keeps track of your keystrokes.

- If you move, have your mail forwarded for at least a year. Otherwise, someone may fill in your name on the junk mail you receive from credit card companies.

(continues)

ABOUT IDENTITY THEFT *(continued)*

- Avoid carrying important information in your wallet, such as PINs for ATM and credit cards, and social security numbers. Consider keeping your driver's license or I.D. card out of your wallet, since it has your address on it.

- Get all of your boxes of check blanks delivered to your bank rather than your home address. Do not mail checks from your home mailbox. Use a U.S. Postal Service receptacle.

- When ordering new credit cards or renewing expired credit cards, make sure the card comes within the time it is estimated for the card to arrive. If it is not received by then, contact the credit card company to see if the card was mailed.

- Cancel credit cards that you do not use.

- Place passwords on all accounts. Do not use your mother's maiden name.

- Check your credit reports with the three major credit bureaus:

Equifax – http://www.equifax.com
To order your report, call: 800-685-1111 or write:
P.O. Box 740241, Atlanta, GA 30374-0241

Experian – http://www.experian.com
P.O. Box 2002, Allen TX 75013

Trans Union – http://www.transunion.com
To order your report, call: 800-888-4213 or write:
P.O. Box 1000, Chester, PA 19022

What to Do If You Are an Identity Theft Victim

From the Federal Trade Commission Web site:

- Place a fraud alert on your credit reports, and review your credit reports.

- Contact the creditors (for example, credit card companies, phone companies and other utilities, and banks and other lenders) to close any accounts that have been tampered with or opened fraudulently. Ask to speak with someone in the security or fraud department of each creditor, then follow up in writing. It is particularly important to notify credit card companies in writing.

- File a report with your local police.

- File a complaint with the FTC. The FTC maintains a database of identity theft cases which are used by law enforcement agencies for investigations.

SUMMARY

Evidence is an important subject for paralegals because paralegals assist at every step of the evidence-gathering and presentation process. They may conduct interviews with potential clients and witnesses, draft documents such as complaints, discovery requests, and answers, and conduct legal research regarding the admissibility of evidence. Evidence can be just about anything that an attorney can use to try to prove the elements of the case. In addition to admitted evidence, information may come in at the trial through stipulations and judicial notice.

■ KEY TERMS

admissible	exculpatory	primary law
answer	fact finder	secondary sources
burden of proof	inadmissible	spoliate
Chinese Wall	judicial notice	stipulation
complaint	motion in limine	summons
counterclaim	precedent	
cross-complaint	preponderance of the evidence	

■ HELPFUL WEB SITES

http://www.consumer.gov
http://www.identitytheft.org
http://www.privacyrights.org
http://www.westlaw.com
http://www.findlaw.com
http://www.paralegals.org
http://www.nala.org
http://paralegal.westlaw.com
http://lawschool.westlaw.com

■ REVIEW AND DISCUSSION QUESTIONS

1. What things might a paralegal do to help gather evidence and make it ready for trial?
2. If you want to know if a particular item of evidence will be admissible, how would you go about the legal research?
3. Pick a case that has recently been in the news. What kinds of direct and circumstantial evidence might the case involve?
4. Identify some things that could be admitted by judicial notice in a court in your state but not in a court in another part of the country.
5. Why might a party agree to stipulate to something in a hard-fought case?

6. How do attorney ethics rules apply to paralegals?

7. What special duty does a prosecutor have?

8. In your state, how do the courts title criminal cases, State v. , People of the State v. , Commonwealth v. , or District v. ?

9. How does the role of a paralegal differ from that of an attorney?

■ LEGAL RESEARCH PROJECTS

1. Get a copy of a case that is excerpted in this chapter and read all of it. Brief the case by providing a summary of the facts, the legal issue, the holding, and the court's reasoning.

2. Obtain a copy of the attorney ethics rules for your state and read them. Indicate which rules apply most to paralegals and summarize them.

3. Find an attorney or paralegal ethics case in your state or a neighboring state. Brief the case by providing a summary of the facts, the legal issue, the holding, and the court's reasoning.

For additional resources, visit our Web site at www.westlegalstudies.com

Investigating Cases Outside the Court System

"Loose mortar, no warning signs - Mr Dumpty, you are a victm of gross negligence."

Courtesy of CartoonStock.com.
www.CartoonStock.com

■ OBJECTIVES

- ❏ Explain the importance of investigating a case
- ❏ Analyze different methods for obtaining information relating to a case
- ❏ Outline how to investigate a case
- ❏ Compare the advantages and disadvantages of different methods of investigating a case
- ❏ Organize an investigation file
- ❏ Make a tickler system
- ❏ Characterize resources that are available on the Internet

IMPORTANCE OF FACT INVESTIGATION

A rule of civil procedure requires an attorney to investigate a case before filing a suit. In federal court, Rule 11 requires attorneys to personally sign all pleadings and indicates that by signing the pleadings, the attorney acknowledges having made a good-faith investigation into the law and facts of the case. If the case is thrown out as frivolous, the attorney and party can be held liable for attorney fees, costs, and sanctions. Rule 11 underwent major amendments in 1983 and 1993. Some states still base their rule on the original version, others follow the 1983 version, and still others have kept their rule parallel to the current federal rule by adopting the 1993 version. Georgia, for example, allows sanctions along the lines of Rule 11 if the court "finds that an attorney or party unnecessarily expanded the proceeding by other improper conduct, including, but not limited to, abuses of discovery procedures." Ga. Code Ann., § 9-15-14. Minnesota has a statute that basically extends Rule 11 to written motions or other papers submitted to court. Minn. Stat. § 529.211.

FEDERAL RULES OF CIVIL PROCEDURE 11

(a) Signature. Every pleading, written motion, and other paper shall be signed by at least one attorney of record in the attorney's individual name, or, if the party is not represented by an attorney, shall be signed by the party. Each paper shall state the signer's address and telephone number, if any. Except when otherwise specifically provided by rule or statute, pleadings need not be verified or accompanied by affidavit. An unsigned paper shall be stricken unless omission of the signature is corrected promptly after being called to the attention of the attorney or party.

(b) Representations to Court. By presenting to the court (whether by signing, filing, submitting, or later advocating) a pleading, written motion, or other paper, an attorney or unrepresented party is certifying that to the best of the person's knowledge, information, and belief, formed after an inquiry reasonable under the circumstances,

  (1) it is not being presented for any improper purpose, such as to harass or to cause unnecessary delay or needless increase in the cost of litigation;

  (2) the claims, defenses, and other legal contentions therein are warranted by existing law or by a nonfrivolous argument for the extension, modification, or reversal of existing law or the establishment of new law;

  (3) the allegations and other factual contentions have evidentiary support or, if specifically so identified, are likely to have evidentiary support after a reasonable opportunity for further investigation or discovery; and

  (4) the denials of factual contentions are warranted on the evidence or, if specifically so identified, are reasonably based on a lack of information or belief.

(c) Sanctions. If, after notice and a reasonable opportunity to respond, the court determines that subdivision (b) has been violated, the court may, subject to the conditions stated below, impose an appropriate sanction upon the attorneys, law firms, or parties that have violated subdivision (b) or are responsible for the violation.

  (1) How Initiated.

    (A) By Motion. A motion for sanctions under this rule shall be made separately from other motions or requests and shall describe the specific conduct alleged to violate subdivision (b). It shall be served as provided in Rule 5,

(continues)

FEDERAL RULES OF CIVIL PROCEDURE 11 *(continued)*

but shall not be filed with or presented to the court unless, within 21 days after service of the motion (or such other period as the court may prescribe), the challenged paper, claim, defense, contention, allegation, or denial is not withdrawn or appropriately corrected. If warranted, the court may award to the party prevailing on the motion the reasonable expenses and attorney's fees incurred in presenting or opposing the motion. Absent exceptional circumstances, a law firm shall be held jointly responsible for violations committed by its partners, associates, and employees.

(B) On Court's Initiative. On its own initiative, the court may enter an order describing the specific conduct that appears to violate subdivision (b) and directing an attorney, law firm, or party to show cause why it has not violated subdivision (b) with respect thereto.

(2) Nature of Sanction; Limitations. A sanction imposed for violation of this rule shall be limited to what is sufficient to deter repetition of such conduct or comparable conduct by others similarly situated. Subject to the limitations in subparagraphs (A) and (B), the sanction may consist of, or include, directives of a nonmonetary nature, an order to pay a penalty into court, or, if imposed on motion and warranted for effective deterrence, an order directing payment to the movant of some or all of the reasonable attorneys' fees and other expenses incurred as a direct result of the violation.

(A) Monetary sanctions may not be awarded against a represented party for a violation of subdivision (b)(2).

(B) Monetary sanctions may not be awarded on the court's initiative unless the court issues its order to show cause before a voluntary dismissal or settlement of the claims made by or against the party which is, or whose attorneys are, to be sanctioned.

(3) Order. When imposing sanctions, the court shall describe the conduct determined to constitute a violation of this rule and explain the basis for the sanction imposed.

(d) Inapplicability to Discovery. Subdivisions (a) through (c) of this rule do not apply to disclosures and discovery requests, responses, objections, and motions that are subject to the provisions of Rules 26 through 37.

■ **CLASS ACTION**
A lawsuit involving such a large number of plaintiffs who have suffered similar wrongs by the defendant(s) that it would be inefficient to have many cases; therefore one person or a small group represents the class of injured people.

■ **CLASS REPRESENTATIVE**
The named and lead plaintiff who serves as a representative of the class in a class action suit.

In the following case, the plaintiff's attorney filed a **class action** suit against every pharmaceutical employer in Puerto Rico, including some defendants who did not have manufacturing facilities in Puerto Rico, and failed to indicate for which defendant his **class representative** worked. Despite being given several chances to amend the pleadings, and despite being warned that he was running the risk of being sanctioned, the plaintiff's attorney still failed to properly investigate the case.

CASE

DIAZ V. ADCHEM PHARMA OPERATIONS, 2005 WL 2397489 (D. P.R. 2005)

Before the Court are . . . defendants Motion for Rule 11 Sanctions . . . and plaintiff's opposition thereto . . . The present lawsuit was filed on June 1, 2004 by Salvador Piñero Díaz . . . and others . . . against 20 pharmaceutical Companies in Puerto Rico . . . alleging violations of the Fair Labor Standards Act, the Family and Medical Leave Act, [and] Puerto Rico wage and hour laws. The Complaint was filed as a "class action." . . . Nowhere in the Complaint did Piñero-Díaz identify which of the 20 companies included as defendants was his employer . . .

Of critical importance is the fact that . . . plaintiffs did not include any specific factual allegation in support of the generalized statement in the case's caption and at paragraph 4 of the Amended Complaint that there were other individuals "similarly situated." . . .

Co-defendants filed a Motion for Sanctions Under Rule 11 . . . The Motion for Sanctions argued that plaintiffs' counsel's insistence on advocating claims against them under the FLSA, FMLA and various local statutes was unwarranted by existing law and contrary to the mandate of Rule 11 . . . the Court noted plaintiffs had failed to meet their burden of establishing that the putative class members were similarly situated under the FLSA. The Court noted "plaintiff have done nothing more than identify some 31 individuals who, we can only assume worked [for any one of four (4) different employers bearing the Bristol name], and the mere listing of names . . . " [a]t the time the original Complaint was filed and subsequently, plaintiffs' counsel knew he had no basis to include in the Complaint the Manatí, Mayagüez and Humacao subsidiaries, not to mention Lilly, SB Pharmco and the rest of the named defendants.

The Court finds the efforts described by Mr. Rodríguez-García extremely sparse and, it must be noted, rather preocupating. As it appears from the evidence brought to the Court's attention by Mr. Rodríguez-García himself, as well as representations made in previous motions, he sought to sue a large part of the Puerto Rico pharmaceutical industry for alleged FLSA, FMLA and Act 379 violations on the basis of (1) unspecified information obtained from inquiries made to the Pharmaceutical Industry Association in Puerto Rico, (2) unspecified research conducted during the course of the Warner Lambert litigation and (3) the statements of two unnamed Lilly employees who did not retain his services and are not named plaintiffs in the instant case. Notably, other than the aforementioned averments, plaintiffs' counsel failed to provide any affidavits setting forth factual pre-filing research.

In sum, the Court finds that in filing the instant action . . . attorney Rodríguez-García violated the mandate of Rule 11 . . .

The Court agrees with co-defendants, and finds that the conduct displayed by the attorney for plaintiffs is sanctionable, his pre-filing failed and legal inquiry was grossly

(continues)

> ## CASE
> ### DIAZ V. ADCHEM PHARMA OPERATIONS, 2005 WL 2397489 (D. P.R. 2005)
> *(continued)*
>
> inadequate ... Consequently, after a careful review of the evidence submitted the Court finds that defendants SB Pharmco and Eli Lilly are entitled to $8,000 each in attorney's fees for work performed in this case. As to Bristol-Manatí, Bristol-Humacao and Bristol-Mayagüez ... the amount hereby imposed in sanctions is $4,000 to be divided among them.

The court found that there was an egregious lack of investigation and ordered the plaintiff's attorney to pay $20,000 in legal fees to the defendants.

Another reason to thoroughly investigate a case prior to bringing suit is to get a head start before the opposing party is put on notice of being sued. Likewise, a defendant who anticipates the possibility of a suit can be better prepared to defend it if an investigation is done soon after the incident rather than after a suit is served. Finally, an attorney may wish to investigate a case in order to see if it is worthwhile to pursue, especially if it is a **contingency fee** case.

■ **CONTINGENCY FEE**
A fee based upon whether a recovery is made on behalf of the client and the size of the recovery, if any.

GETTING EVIDENCE

A good (and obvious) source for evidence is the client, or potential client. Get whatever documentation he or she has, as well as the names, addresses, and phone numbers of any witnesses.

Lay Witnesses

An investigator may locate lay witnesses through the client by examining documents, and by talking to witnesses that the investigator already knows about through these sources.

Expert Witnesses

The client may lead the investigator to an expert. For example, a plaintiff in a personal injury case may seek expert testimony from a treating physician, therapist, chiropractor, or the like. Some firms also have experts upon whom they frequently rely for particular types of cases. Westlaw has **databases** of expert witnesses. For example, the Expert Resume database contains resumes of expert witnesses, including education, training, licensure, professional memberships, prior cases where they were retained as a consultant or expert and the results obtained, area of expertise,

■ **DATABASE**
A searchable collection of data. A synonym of source.

and information on the fees charged by the expert. Another example is Profiler (profiles of expert witnesses), which has information regarding the amounts of verdicts and settlements obtained in cases in which the expert testified. Abstracts of expert witness testimony are available in the National Expert Transcript Service database. On the Internet you can find free resources for finding expert witnesses. (See Exhibits 2–1 and 2–2.)

These sites typically allow a visitor to search for an expert on a particular topic, or in a geographic area. Depending upon the expert's area of expertise, rules in your **jurisdiction** regarding what has to be disclosed to the opposing party in terms of expert consultations and procedures for retaining an expert vary somewhat. Typically, some preliminary investigation is first made into whether the expert's area of expertise will be helpful in examining the case. An agreement is reached for what the expert will do, material is sent to the expert, and the expert conducts an investigation. The expert will then issue an oral or written report to the attorney regarding the expert's thoughts on the case.

In some jurisdictions, the opposing party will be able to learn through discovery that the expert was consulted, and the nature of the expert's opinion about the case. In other jurisdictions, as long as the party does not plan to call the expert at trial, the consultation and opinion need not be disclosed. This is important in cases where the expert's opinion is at odds with what the party is trying to prove. For example, if

■ **JURISDICTION**
The location where a case may be brought, such as federal court or state court.

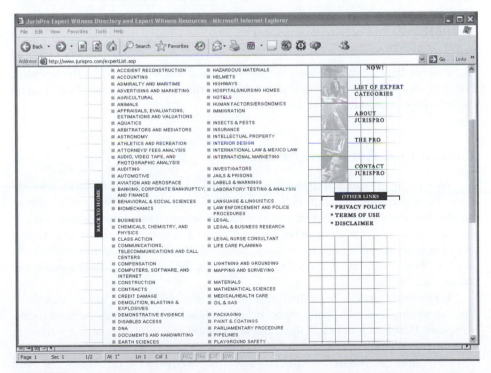

EXHIBIT 2–1   Courtesy of the Jurispro Expert Witness Directory. http://www.jurispro.com.

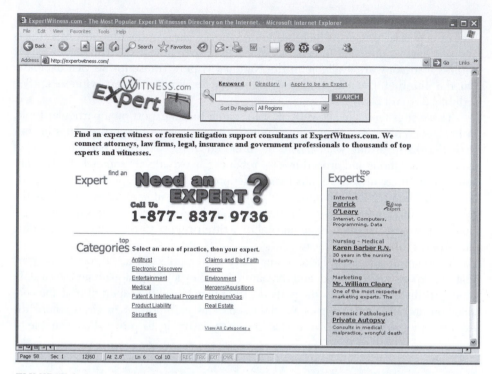

EXHIBIT 2–2   Expertwitness.com screen shot

■ **TESTATOR**

The person signing a will and designating the disposition of his or her property upon death.

the attorney hopes to prove that a last will and testament was signed by the **testator**, but the expert thinks it is a forgery, it would be harmful if the other side knew that an expert who was consulted held that opinion.

Crime and Accident Scenes

As a paralegal you will probably never go to a crime scene. However, you will have the opportunity to obtain police reports and you should be aware of what goes on at crime scenes. For crime scenes that require crime scene investigation, such as murder, the police first set up a perimeter in order to control the scene by letting in or out only people who need to be there. Next, **criminalists** process the scene, look-ing for fibers, hair, blood and other bodily fluids, bullet casings, fingerprints, tire prints, and the like.

■ **CRIMINALIST**

A person who investigates crime either at a crime scene or in a crime lab.

Like crimes, accidents are investigated by peace officers. The officer may do as little as writing a simple police report or as much as making a computerized recon-struction. How much depends upon the investigator's skill set, available technology, and the severity of the accident.

As a paralegal, you may get police reports and the results of criminalist tests and findings through your own requests. Your job may also entail sending them to the opposing attorney. To get the most complete version of a police report, you may need to have your client sign a release; otherwise you may be able to get only the public version of the report, which could be quite cursory and not all that useful. For example, in a rape case, the public version may just say there was an attempted rape at such and such an address on a particular date. If you are representing the rape victim and she signs a release, you would be able to see a summary of her statement, which officers investigated the case, and much more detail about the case.

Real police work is much more mundane and detail oriented than the way it is usually depicted on television. In the movie *Insomnia*, Ellie is an eager young cop who has just made detective. She is investigating the shooting of another officer. Consider how methodical she is in going about her business.

BENCH BRIEF ENTERTAINMENT NOTE

INSOMNIA

From a script by Hillary Seitz, available at http://www.simplyscripts.com/.

(At the beach. We see nothing but fog. A VOICE comes through.)

ELLIE: . . . and it was at this point that Detective Dormer headed towards the noise . . .

> *(Ellie emerges from the fog. Carrying the map and talking into a small tape recorder. She's climbing over the rocks, wearing a windbreaker a couple sizes too big.)*

> *(A uniformed officer follows, carrying a camera. She turns to him.)*

ELLIE: Remember, Kepp, shoot everything . . .

> *(back to the tape recorder)*

> . . . wherein he discovered the wounded Detective Farrell Brooks, having been shot in the vastus externus of the upper left thigh . . .

> *(She climbs over the same bank Will Dormer climbed two evenings before. Finds . . . another uniformed officer, hanging out and smoking.)*

ELLIE: Francis!

> *(He looks up. Pimples on his chin.)*

FRANCIS: What?

ELLIE: You're supposed to be Farrell. Shot in the thigh and writhing in pain.

FRANCIS: C'mon, Ellie. What's it matter?

ELLIE: Accuracy. That's what.

> *(points to the ground)*

> Now get down.

(continues)

An episode of *CSI* can demonstrate how television can be unrealistic in its portrayal of criminal investigations. For example, in the first-season episode "Table Stakes" the investigators are looking into the death of an exotic dancer whose body is found floating in a mansion pool. Everything happens faster in the show than in real life. The autopsy is done that night. This usually takes at least a few days, and final results can take months pending toxicology results. The DNA testing on the show takes place the day after the crime, including matching markers for degree of biological relationship, but such testing and matching usually takes weeks or months, depending upon the type of testing and the backlog at the lab. Then when the crime is quickly solved, instead of doing separate interviews with the suspects where they are persuaded to confess, the police lay out all of their evidence to both suspects at the same time.

BENCH BRIEF   ENTERTAINMENT NOTE *(continued)*

BRASS: On behalf . . . of the State of Nevada my apologies. You've been cleared of all charges.

PATRICK HAYNES: *(amused)* It took three of you to tell me that?

BRASS: But . . . on behalf of the State of Texas you're under arrest. You're being extradited for the murder of Lana Grimshaw.

PATRICK HAYNES: I slept with her, but I didn't kill her.

CATHERINE: Huh. Just like with Lacey Duvall.

PATRICK HAYNES: Absolutely.

(The door opens and AMANDA HAYNES is escorted in by an OFFICER. She walks into the room.)

GRISSOM: Mm-hmm. Now I see it.

PATRICK HAYNES: *(shakes his head)* What? See what?

GRISSOM: The family resemblance.

(CATHERINE turns around to look at the HAYNES'.)

GRISSOM: Donnie and Marie—brother and sister—I've got the DNA to prove it.

(AMANDA HAYNES swallows. PATRICK gets to his feet and walks toward AMANDA.)

GRISSOM: Let me tell you what else I can prove. Your sister, killed Lacey Duvall.

. . .

AMANDA HAYNES: *(to PATRICK)* You're surprised? Look at your face. You never made a mistake until you met her.

PATRICK HAYNES: You killed Lacey because I told her about us?

AMANDA HAYNES: I had no choice. We were partners. You can't grift me, Chad.

Private Investigators

A private investigator can find people and find out about people. A private investigator can conduct a **skip trace** to try to locate a person such as a debtor, defendant, or witness.

Private investigators can also find out about people, such as whether or not they are hiding assets or exaggerating an injury, and with whom they are associating. In the following **workers' compensation case**, the claimant was caught doing activities he alleged that he could not perform.

- **SKIP TRACE**
A search for a person whose location is unknown.

- **WORKERS' COMPENSATION CASE**
A case in which employees injured on the job collect on the employer's insurance policy for injured workers rather than sue the employer.

CASE
BEAUBIEN V. DAIMLERCHRYSLER CORP., 2002 WL 869937
(MICH. CT. APP. 2002)

Plaintiff appeals by leave granted the order of the Worker's Compensation Appellate Commission (WCAC), reversing the magistrate's open award of benefits. We affirm . . .

Plaintiff began working for defendant as a general laborer on the assembly line in 1972. He worked at a variety of jobs for about five years before being assigned the job of installing windshields, which job he held for the remainder of his employment. Plaintiff was required to lift the windshield, properly situate it and then secure it. Plaintiff testified that each windshield weighed about forty pounds, and that he had to install approximately one windshield per minute. Although plaintiff was able to continue performing his specific job, he began to experience difficulty with his back sometime in 1979. In September, 1992 while carrying a windshield, plaintiff slipped on an oily floor and fell about two to three feet into a pit on the assembly line.

On the advice of a friend, he saw Dr. Herkowitz, who eventually performed spinal fusion surgery in August 1993. Plaintiff was off work for about six months before returning with restrictions against twisting, bending or heavy lifting. Notwithstanding plaintiff's specific limitations, defendant placed him back on the line installing windshields. Plaintiff admitted that after the surgery, the numbness in his leg was gone, although he still experienced pain in his middle back.

In May, 1994 plaintiff fell into a pit a second time. When Dr. Herkowitz was unable to treat him further, plaintiff went to see several other doctors on his own. Plaintiff testified that he was on and off disability for two weeks to several months at a time. Although defendant sent plaintiff to a "work hardening" program in 1996, plaintiff claimed that he could not tolerate the pain . . .

Plaintiff filed a petition for hearing claiming work-related disability to his back, legs, and other body parts and areas. At the hearing, plaintiff testified that he could not return to regular work because it would cause too much pain. Although plaintiff conceded that he can do limited amounts of bending, twisting and lifting, he estimated that he could only work for about ten minutes at a time before he would need to take a break and relieve his back . . .

[Defendant] also offered the testimony of a private investigator, who in turn produced five videotapes comprising nine hours of surveillance. The videotapes apparently show plaintiff bending, stooping, working around the house, hammering, climbing ladders, and lifting something described as a long wooden pole approximately fifteen feet long and weighing two hundred pounds, without any apparent difficulties . . .

We find the videotape evidence is compelling and overwhelming[ly] refutes plaintiff's testimony that he is restricted in his everyday activities. Videos one and four, in particular,

(continues)

CASE
BEAUBIEN V. DAIMLERCHRYSLER CORP., 2002 WL 869937
(MICH. CT. APP. 2002) *(continued)*

reveal plaintiff consistently bending and twisting. We agree with defendant that the most significant video evidence is video one in which plaintiff can be seen pulling and lifting what appears to be a very large piece of heavy wood to the top of a motor home without any assistance in addition to climbing up and down a ladder. Video three shows plaintiff constantly bending, often on all fours, and hammering over a long period of time without any sign of physical discomfort. The video evidence clearly indicates that plaintiff could and can do far more than what he related to Dr. Shapiro.

The court found in favor of the employer, relying on the videotape produced by the private investigator.

The Internet

Many investigatory resources are available on the Internet free or for a small fee.

For-Fee Resources

There are private investigation sites that claim to allow users to search for FBI records, credit reports, unlisted phone numbers, e-mail and street addresses, and more (see Exhibit 2–3).

Just typing a person's name into a search engine such as Google can produce interesting information about a person. Unless the name is quite unusual, it might or might not be the person for whom you are looking. For example, putting in the name Max Winter, aiming to get the former Minnesota Vikings owner, might pull up information about a writer by the same name. Another search engine may have results for the right person. At http://www.privateye.com you can learn a person's name and address for free, and for a modest fee, age, possible current address, up to a 20-year address history, phone numbers, bankruptcies, tax liens and judgments, property ownership, possible relatives, possible roommates, aliases/maiden names, neighbors, marriages and divorces, D.E.A. registrants, and Web site ownership. (Complete Web addresses for this and other sites are found at the end of the chapter.)

Westlaw Resources

Westlaw has a number of databases that can help with an investigation (see Exhibit 2–4). Some of them, such as those containing full social security numbers, are accessible only to highly qualified users such as certain government agencies (for example, law enforcement and Homeland Security). Such entities must qual-

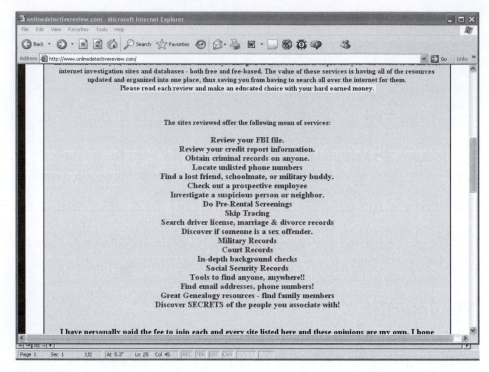

EXHIBIT 2–3 Cyber Detective screen shot

ify to have an account through a review process. The Personal Profile Database has information regarding individuals, including their current and former addresses, people associated with those addresses, possible relatives, and motor vehicles. Public records databases include driver and vehicle records, real property records (which include a link to find out the value of a residential property), and a way to search for people with name, address, phone number, or social security number. Westlaw also has criminal records, jury verdicts and settlements, newspaper articles, scholarly articles in legal and nonlegal journals, voter registration records, case law, statutes, and newspaper and magazine articles. There are also databases for locating and finding out about expert witnesses.

Lexis-Nexis

■ **SOURCE**

A searchable group of data. A synonym of database.

Lexis-Nexis has more than 36,000 **sources**, including data similar to what is on Westlaw. It has some material that Westlaw lacks, such as public records from a few foreign countries, just as Westlaw has some material that Lexis-Nexis lacks, such as concealed weapons and concealed carry permits and sex offender records.

Here is what Lexis-Nexis has to say about itself on its Web site: "The Lexis® service, the first commercial, full-text legal information service, began in 1973 to help legal practitioners research the law more efficiently. The companion Nexis® news

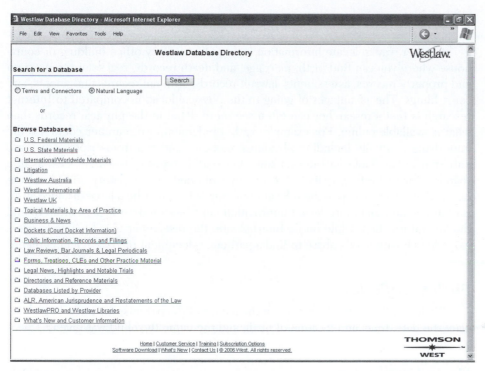

EXHIBIT 2-4   Westlaw Database Directory screen shot

and business information service launched in 1979 to richen research with recent and archival news and financial information. Since that time, the service has grown to become the largest news and business online information service, including comprehensive company, country, financial, demographic, market research and industry reports. Providing access to thousands of worldwide newspapers, magazines, trade journals, industry newsletters, tax and accounting information, financial data, public records, legislative records, data on companies and their executives makes the LexisNexis® service an indispensable tool for gathering information and providing accurate answers."

You can see the databases that are available on Westlaw at http://directory.westlaw .com/ and on Lexis at http://w3.nexis.com/sources/. Both companies also offer free sites: http://lexisone.com and http://findlaw.com.

Other Subscription Providers

Smaller and generally less expensive legal research providers include http://versulaw.com, http://jurisearch.com, http://loislaw.com, http://www.itislaw.com, and https:// www.fastcase.com. There are also Web sites for searching public records, such as http://knowx.com, http://peoplesearch.com, http://switchboard.com, http://law.com and http://www.whitepages.com.

Public Records

Another way to locate information is to go to a county office building or courthouse where you can find birth, marriage, and death records, real estate transaction and property records, assessments, lawsuit records, criminal records, judgments, and court filings. The advantages of going to the physical location compared to Internet research is that a researcher can often see more detail in the physical records than what is available online. For example, with a judgment, a researcher could see the underlying court file including pleadings, motions, and trial transcripts, which are only sparsely available on Internet sites. For certain types of research, such as title searches for real estate, visits to the recorder of deeds is mandatory. The disadvantage is that an actual trip to the relevant building, which may be a large distance away, is required, and a lot of irrelevant information must be sorted through in order to find the key information, while on an Internet site, the researcher may be able to use a word search within a database to find a particular document or part of a document.

Birth Certificates

Birth certificates typically contain the names of the parents; the attending physician; the date, time, and location of birth; and the name the child was given.

Death Certificates

Death certificates usually have the name of the deceased, the cause of death, the name of the attending physician, and the day and time of death.

Marriage Records

Marriage records indicate the names of the partners, the date and county of the marriage, and whether the ceremony was civil or religious.

Real Estate Assessor Records

Real estate assessor records often contain the address of the property, the legal description, parcel number, lot size, land value, improvement value, real estate taxes, number of rooms, number of bathrooms and bedrooms, and other information about the property such as amenities, whether or not the basement is finished, when it was last sold, and the price.

Real Estate Transaction Records

Real estate transaction records indicate name and address of the buyer of the property, parcel number, name and address of the seller, date of sale, and sale amount. Sometimes mortgage and financing information is also provided.

Motor Vehicle Records

Motor vehicle records include the name and address of the owner; the license plate number and vehicle identification number; when the plates expire; make, model, and year of the vehicle; and how long the owner has been the registrant.

Freedom of Information Act and State Equivalents

A researcher can get a government agency to give information simply through a request letter. This tool is more frequently utilized by journalists and other writers but is available to anyone.

The agencies may withhold information under exceptions such as trade secrets and personnel files. The agencies are required to provide information regarding who to contact to make a request under the Freedom of Information Act, and many of them have Web sites with this information. (See Exhibit 2–5.) Each state has its own equivalent to the federal Freedom of Information Act, although they may call it by a different name. Some states have separate statutes requiring open meetings.

Weather Reports

In a car accident, slip-and-fall case, or other case involving something happening outdoors, the weather at the time of the incident can be important. Weather information is available through the National Weather Service, http://www.weather.com, and newspapers.

---

5 U.S.C.A. 552(A)(2)

Each agency, in accordance with published rules, shall make available for public inspection and copying

(A) final opinions, including concurring and dissenting opinions, as well as orders, made in the adjudication of cases;

(B) those statements of policy and interpretations which have been adopted by the agency and are not published in the Federal Register;

(C) administrative staff manuals and instructions to staff that affect a member of the public;

(D) copies of all records, regardless of form or format, which have been released to any person under paragraph (3) and which, because of the nature of their subject matter, the agency determines have become or are likely to become the subject of subsequent requests for substantially the same records; and

(E) a general index of the records referred to under subparagraph (D);

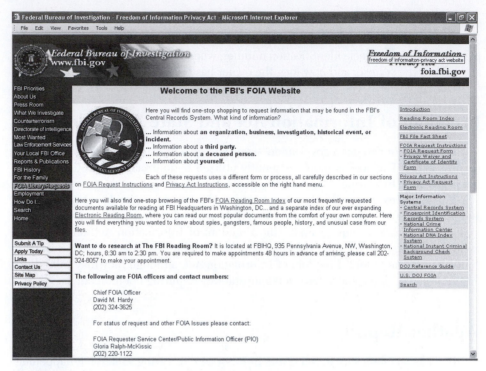

EXHIBIT 2–5   FBI's Freedom of Information Web site screen shot

Videotapes

A number of types of videotapes can come into evidence. There are elaborate reenactment tapes that try to recreate the incident underlying the case, day-in-the-life tapes that show how an injury has affected a plaintiff, and tapes shot at the time of the incident such as those from security or surveillance cameras.

Because of the advent of television crime shows, juries may expect parties to present elaborate reenactment tapes. At least one jury has convicted a person of lesser charges because they expected to see a computerized reenactment. The *Star Tribune* (Minneapolis) reports that a Dakota County jury convicted a man of misdemeanor reckless driving rather than criminal vehicular homicide even though the prosecutor was sure he had a solid case (see Bench Brief). The expectation that juries will be presented with high-tech evidence in every case is being called the **CSI effect**. Such tapes are very expensive to produce and may not be appropriate in every case.

■ **CSI EFFECT**
A jury's unreasonable expectation that science or technology should be presented in every case.

BENCH BRIEF

"CSI EFFECT" LEAVES FINGERPRINT ON TWIN CITIES COURTROOMS

© **Star Tribune December 1, 2005**

by Paul Gustafson

Dakota County authorities thought their felony case against a driver charged with criminal vehicular operation was solid. But jurors knocked it down to a misdemeanor, convicting the defendant of reckless driving instead.

Then they told the prosecutor they were disappointed with the case.

"They wanted to see a computerized reenactment," said Phil Prokopowicz, chief deputy county attorney. "It was something they expected."

Prokopowicz said he fears the recent case is an example of what prosecutors across the country are calling the "CSI effect": Juries filled with growing numbers of crime-drama devotees demanding the same high-tech, slam-dunk proof of guilt that their TV heroes produce every week.

No one has proved the effect, but the huge audiences that popular dramas such as "CSI: Crime Scene Investigation" are drawing are worrying some prosecutors so much they have begun changing their courtroom tactics.

Judges and attorneys around the Twin Cities say prosecutors are now routinely asking questions about the television shows during jury selection—and at times striking prospective jurors from serving on trials because of the perceptions they say the crime dramas are causing.

Because of the "CSI" shows, some prosecutors contend, more jurors believe every crime scene yields forensic evidence that offers conclusive scientific proof of innocence or guilt, almost instantly.

When selecting jurors, Hennepin County Attorney Amy Klobuchar said, prosecutors are now trying to explain "that real life is not like a TV show . . . and that just because there is no DNA evidence does not mean that there is not substantial other evidence sufficient to prove our case."

Even so, some prosecutors say they are asking police and crime labs to do more testing for fingerprints and DNA evidence out of concern that jurors expect to see more of it at trials.

Forensic scientists at the Minnesota Bureau of Criminal Apprehension (BCA) also say they are getting more requests from prosecutors to testify about why fingerprints and DNA evidence cannot be recovered at every crime scene—and why they don't always yield conclusive proof.

Klobuchar said there's great new pressure to provide "negative forensic evidence."

(continues)

BENCH BRIEF *(continued)*

Prosecutors say they are feeling more compelled to call such witnesses because defense attorneys are arguing more often that key evidence was not tested.

"You see more [defense] arguments like, 'Sure, they have an eyewitness, but they never did a DNA test on the handle of the weapon,' " Prokopowicz said.

It's possible that the new expectations jurors have for seeing high-tech forensic evidence at trials may be more the result of how much prosecutors have relied on it in recent years—and not a "CSI effect," said Ramsey County Attorney Susan Gaertner.

When DNA evidence was new to the courtroom 15 years ago, Gaertner said, prosecutors had difficulty explaining its value to jurors, or getting them to pay close attention to it.

But that's all changed, she said, and the new trend is not necessarily troubling.

"Jurors' acceptance of [new] scientific evidence and what it can tell them about a case is a good thing," Gaertner said. "The problem, obviously, is if their expectations are Hollywood-like rather than reality-based."

What's undeniably true, judges and lawyers say, is that prosecutors now routinely ask prospective jurors about their TV viewing habits.

Criminal defense attorney Anthony Torres said recent jury selections have convinced him that " 'CSI' is the most-watched program on television. It seems three-fourths of the prospective jurors have viewed it."

But Torres and Diane Wylie, president of National Jury Project Midwest, a jury-selection consulting firm, said that long before the popular crime shows, defense attorneys asked in court whether authorities had performed enough forensic tests.

Both said they've seen no proof of the "CSI effect."

Hennepin County District Judge Kevin Burke also said his recent trial experience has convinced him that shows like "CSI" have many fans, but that most prospective jurors seem to know "they are entertainment, and not the real stuff."

But Anoka County Attorney Robert Johnson said new courtroom campaigns to counter a potential "CSI effect" are forcing prosecutors and law enforcement officials to try to predict how much forensic evidence a jury will demand—without overtaxing their labs and budgets.

"We may say a forensic test is not relevant to us, and that we have proof beyond a reasonable doubt," Johnson said, "but it may be relevant to the jurors."

Meanwhile, some crime-scene investigators are also wondering if law enforcement officials are watching the shows too much.

Frank Dolejsi, lab director at the Bureau of Criminal Apprehension in Minnesota, said he heard recently that Wisconsin officers investigating the suspicious death of a man whose body was found along a highway asked a crime lab to do DNA tests on 100 cigarette butts on the roadside.

"If we did examinations on every possible item that might be found at a crime scene," Dolejsi said, "our backlog would be worse than it already is."

Another type of tape is one that is shot during an incident, such as the video of the Rodney King beating, a sporting event, a clip shown on *America's Funniest Home Videos*, or a surveillance tape. The length of time that a business keeps a surveillance tape varies, so be sure to ask for one as soon as you find out that you need it. If the business is unaware that an incident occurred, it may be erased as soon as two days later. If the tape goes against the business, and it is destroyed intentionally, that may be considered destruction of evidence if the business is made aware of the incident and the tape is requested.

One question with videotapes is whether to edit the tape and, if so, when? Presenting raw, unedited tape to a jury may not be possible if the court rules part of the tape inadmissible. It may also be a waste of time to watch eight hours of tape when the incident spanned only a few minutes or less. It may be possible to just queue up the tape to the key moment, but what if the equipment operator fails to turn it off or turn down the volume during the inadmissible segment? The decision of how and whether to edit will be case-specific and may be dictated by the court. The camera operator can decide to turn the camera off or to start recording again, or it may be edited on an editing machine either before it is given to the opposing party, or before it is presented to the jury. Opposing parties should be informed of the edits so that they can request the unedited tape if they so desire.

Audiotapes

In some jurisdictions, it is not illegal to tape a conversation as long as one of the participants knows that it is being taped. In these jurisdictions, an individual may tape a conversation between himself or herself and another person. Or a third party can tape a conversation as long as one of the participants is aware that it is being recorded. On the other hand, when neither person knows they are being taped, that is considered wiretapping and is illegal. In other jurisdictions, it is illegal to tape a conversation unless all parties know that it is being taped. It is illegal for anyone to record a conversation to which the recorder is not a party without the consent of one of the participants. The government must obtain a wiretap search warrant in order to make a tape recording of a suspect.

Tape recordings are ubiquitous. Callers to businesses are frequently warned that their call may be recorded or monitored to assure quality service. Answering machine and voice mail messages are recorded, as are 911 calls.

Computers and Data

It is best to have a professional handle retrieval of computers and electronic data. It is possible for an untrained person to accidentally compromise the data or the machine. (This is covered in more depth in Chapter 4.)

Medical Records

Medical professionals and their staff must be careful to comply with federal law when providing medical records. The Health Insurance Portability and Accountability Act (HIPAA) imposes privacy and security regulations on health plans, health care providers, and health care clearinghouses. Violations of the act can result in penalties of up to $250,000 and a prison sentence of up to 10 years.

Therefore, it is important to respect their need to have releases signed in order to release medical records and to talk to personnel from your office regarding the case. They may require the patient/client to sign a written waiver allowing your attorney to access the data.

---

42 U.S.C.A.1320D-6. WRONGFUL DISCLOSURE OF INDIVIDUALLY IDENTIFIABLE HEALTH INFORMATION

(a) Offense

A person who knowingly and in violation of this part—

(1) uses or causes to be used a unique health identifier;

(2) obtains individually identifiable health information relating to an individual; or

(3) discloses individually identifiable health information to another person, shall be punished as provided in subsection (b) of this section.

(b) Penalties

A person described in subsection (a) of this section shall—

(1) be fined not more than $50,000, imprisoned not more than 1 year, or both;

(2) if the offense is committed under false pretenses, be fined not more than $100,000, imprisoned not more than 5 years, or both; and

(3) if the offense is committed with intent to sell, transfer, or use individually identifiable health information for commercial advantage, personal gain, or malicious harm, be fined not more than $250,000, imprisoned not more than 10 years, or both.

BENCH BRIEF

HIPAA OR HIPPA OR HIPPAA

Courts and commentators often incorrectly spell the acronym HIPAA. When conducting online searches, it is a good idea to use all spellings because of the frequency of this mistake.

BENCH BRIEF

HORSES

Imagine having a case involving horses and not knowing anything about them. To learn you could go for a horseback ride, attend a horse convention or rodeo, visit with a large-animal veterinarian, go to the library and read about horses, talk to experts, talk to people in your personal network such as friends, neighbors, former classmates, and family, and watch a documentary about horses.

Other Sources

Be creative when conducting an investigation. There are a number of sources that are either nontraditional or more general, such as public libraries, law libraries, the Better Business Bureau, news reporters, court personnel (including clerks and court reporters), expert witness directories, your network of fellow paralegals and former classmates, and legal education seminars.

ORGANIZING AND CONDUCTING THE INVESTIGATION AND PRESERVING EVIDENCE

Keeping organized during the investigation phase of a case will make things easier later on and will save time in the long run.

The best way to get and stay organized is to start with a plan for the investigation. The first step is to consider what you already know, and the source and reliability of that knowledge. For example, a potential client enters your office wearing a neck brace and walking with crutches and a cast on her leg. She says she was hurt in a car versus bike accident. You can be more sure that her leg is actually hurt than that her neck is actually sprained, since an x-ray can verify her broken bones, but it is more difficult to substantiate a soft-tissue neck injury. She could be exaggerating the injury for effect. Basics such as age, address, and names are generally trustworthy.

Second, you should think about the goals of the investigation and write out a plan for how to achieve those goals. Weigh all the different potential sources of information and consider which ones would be prudent to use for the case. Keep in mind that the plan needs to be flexible. Keep perspective on how much the case might be worth, and how much time and effort are available for the investigation because of other duties and cases. A typical slip-and-fall case with a broken bone is probably worth less than a product liability case that results in partial paralysis and may take less time to investigate.

■ **BOUTIQUE**

A specialty firm limited exclusively to one or two areas of practice.

BENCH BRIEF

PRESERVING EVIDENCE

Imagine working at a **boutique** personal injury firm as a paralegal. One of your cases involves a broken bicycle, which you have in your office. What might you need to do? Attach a giant note to the bicycle, declaring that it is not trash. Otherwise, the cleaning service may consider it trash and throw it away. Having physical or documentary evidence discarded, even by accident, could be a devastating blow to a client's case.

Be quick and thorough. It is important to act quickly lest evidence disappear or be altered. For example, if photographs are needed, it is important to take them as near in time to the event as possible so that they accurately portray the scene or item in question; otherwise, they may not be admissible. Take multiple photos to increase the probability of good results.

Use a tickler system to stay on task; make sure that deadlines are not missed and that important tasks do not get lost in the shuffle and hustle-bustle of a busy law office. Suppose an investigator makes a phone call to a potential witness and leaves a message. The tickler system can be used to follow up with the witness in a few days or a week if the call is not returned; otherwise it may suddenly become urgent. There are manual tickler systems that use cards for months, days, and years in the future. If something needs to get done next month, a reminder card is placed in the file for that month. If it needs to be followed up on in three days, the reminder card is placed in the spot for three days from now. Tickler cards stay in the system until the task is completed. There are computerized tickler systems available for litigation. However, a basic system could be set up using general office calendar software such as Microsoft Outlook. The tickler system should remind you a few business days in advance of something tremendously important, such as an answer to a complaint that is due or a statute of limitations that is running.

BENCH BRIEF

WHEN NATURAL DISASTERS STRIKE EVIDENCE

Hurricane Katrina wreaked havoc on the evidence that was available to try many cases in New Orleans. Evidence rooms were flooded, witnesses were scattered, and archived court files were damaged. In response, the governor declared "a court holiday" for about two months to give the justice system a chance to catch up. Defendants who were jailed without formal charges or a chance to appear in court argued that their constitutional rights were violated by the circumstances. The courts gave prosecutors deadlines by which to file charges or release the defendants. All parts of the justice system were operating out of makeshift space.

COLLECTING A DEBT AND PERFORMING BANKRUPTCY INVESTIGATIONS

Debtor-creditor law investigations involve finding assets and following the Fair Debt Collection Practices Act.

Finding and Recovering Assets

If your clients win cases as plaintiffs, all they actually win are pieces of paper that say the defendants owe them money. That piece of paper is valuable only as a tool to collect the debt. Having a **judgment** against a debtor allows the creditor to search for assets through formal court discovery processes (see Chapter 4). Before obtaining the judgment it usually would have been improper to ask the defendant questions about the defendant's assets, but now such questions are allowed because they are relevant to collecting the debt. Additional places to look for assets include many of the public records listed above, particularly the real estate and motor vehicle sources, and asset databases. Techniques to be used include wage garnishment, attachment of bank accounts, and liens on real estate, motor vehicles, boats, and recreational vehicles.

■ **JUDGMENT**
A legal document issued by the court at the end of the case that declares each party's legal obligations, such as owing the other party money.

Fair Debt Collection Practices Act

Anyone who collects a debt as a professional must follow the federal Fair Debt Collection Practices Act (FDCPA). Although it is directed primarily at collection agencies, it applies to all those who collect a debt that is not owed to them. Therefore, it applies to law firms engaged in collecting consumer debts. It protects the consumer from harassment such as repeated phone calls, letters, lies, and threats. It requires debt collectors to give a **mini-Miranda warning** when calling a debtor on the phone or writing the debtor a letter. There are attorneys who handle FDCPA cases by suing creditors who break the rules. The debtor does not need to suffer damages in order to recover damages and attorney fees.

■ **MINI-MIRANDA WARNING**
A warning that the "debt collector is attempting to collect a debt and that any information obtained will be used for that purpose."

Bankruptcy Investigations

Under recent reforms to the bankruptcy code, bankruptcy attorneys are now more responsible for the completeness and accuracy of information submitted on their debtor clients' bankruptcy petitions and schedules. This means that attorneys cannot simply take their debtor clients' word for what their assets and liabilities are.

In the following case, a judge warns of what could happen if inaccurate schedules are filed.

CASE
IN RE MCKAIN, 325 B.R. 842 (BANKR. D. NEB., 2005)

These contested matters arise from the debtor's failure to list certain assets in her bankruptcy schedules, or to properly amend the schedules after she became aware of the unlisted property. The problem appears to be the result of a mistake or miscommunication, rather than fraudulent intent. The situation, however, is important for debtors and their attorneys to be aware of, as slightly different facts could cause a significantly different outcome. At the outset, it should be made clear that Mr. Blackwell did not represent the debtor at the time of the events that led to this trial. He became involved in the case about three months after it was filed. The problem stems from an intentional delay between the time the debtor provided her schedule information to her attorney and the time the petition and schedules were filed. This eight-month delay was a result of the debtor's counsel's desire to resolve certain child custody and child support issues before filing the bankruptcy case. However, the bankruptcy schedules were prepared and filed without updating the information originally provided by the debtor.

In the period between submitting information for the schedules in July 2003 and the bankruptcy petition and schedules actually being filed in March 2004, the debtor received child support payments and state and federal income tax refunds, and created a lien on her car. Upon the advice of her attorney, she held onto the child support and tax refund checks until her § 341 meeting, when the trustee requested them and she turned them over to him . . .

The parties bring before the court the larger issues of what standard of care debtors and their attorneys should be held to and the extent to which a trustee may reasonably rely on and act on information provided in bankruptcy schedules . . .

The trustee is also concerned about the debtor's affirmative response to his standard § 341 meeting question of "do the schedules that you've filed accurately set out a complete list of all your debts and all your assets, to the best of your knowledge?" He is correct that debtors should not simply or automatically answer "yes" to that question, particularly when they are aware that the schedules are not accurate or that circumstances have changed since the schedules were filled out. Ideally, the trustee should not have to ferret out the necessary information. He should be able to reasonably rely on the documents provided when reviewing the case, and debtors and their counsel should be keenly aware of their duty in that regard.

I am cognizant that, in general, attorneys are busy and have many matters competing for their attention, and that debtor's counsel in this case filed this petition sooner perhaps than he had anticipated. Nevertheless, they have to conduct their business in light of the debtor's counsel standards set out above or the bankruptcy system will quickly become unworkable. Both the debtor and her attorney share the responsibility for the

(continues)

> **CASE**
> **IN RE MCKAIN, 325 B.R. 842 (BANKR. D. NEB., 2005)** *(continued)*
>
> current situation. They each had a duty to make sure the schedules and statement of affairs were correct, and they each dropped the ball. This issue takes on even greater significance in light of the Bankruptcy & Consumer Protection Act of 2005, most of which takes effect in October 2005. Under the provisions of the new law, counsel's signature on a petition constitutes a certification that the attorney has no knowledge, after an inquiry, that the information in the schedules filed with the petition is incorrect. Attorneys may be subject to assessment of a civil penalty for signing a document without conducting a reasonable inquiry into the underlying facts.

The court did not find fraud; rather it reminded attorneys of the consequences of filing inaccurate court documents.

SUMMARY

Investigating a case is important because it helps the attorney and client avoid sanctions for filing frivolous claims, get a head start on the opposition, and determine whether or not it is worthwhile to take on a case. Good sources for investigations include the client; lay and expert witnesses; police reports; private investigators; the Internet (including free and subscription sites); and public records, including birth and death certificates, marriage records, real estate assessor and transaction records, and motor vehicle records. Anyone can utilize the federal Freedom of Information Act and state equivalents to get information from public agencies. Weather reports are useful in certain cases. Paralegals can be creative in finding sources other than those listed in this chapter. In collecting a debt, be aware of the Fair Debt Collection Practices Act, and note that additional resources may be available to you. In handling a bankruptcy, it is important to file accurate petitions and schedules.

■ KEY TERMS

boutique	CSI effect	skip trace
class action	database	source
class representative	judgment	testator
contingency fee	jurisdiction	workers' compensation case
criminalist	mini-Miranda warning	

■ HELPFUL WEB SITES

http://directory.westlaw.com
http://w3.nexis.com/sources/
http://www.westlaw.com
http://www.lexis.com
http://www.versuslaw.com
http://www.catalaw.com
http://www.ilrg.com
http://www.loislaw.com
http://www.deponet.com
http://www.findlaw.com
http://www.jurispro.com
http://www.expertwitness.com
http://www.expertlaw.com
http://www.privateye.com
http://www.google.com
http://www.lycos.com
http://www.dogpile.com
http://www.metacrawler.com
http://www.excite.com
http://www.mapquest.com
http://www.weather.com
http://www.ncdc.noaa.gov
http://www.knowx.com
http://www.jurisearch.com
http://peoplesearch.com
http://switchboard.com
http://whitepages.com
http://www.spj.org

■ REVIEW AND DISCUSSION QUESTIONS

1. What must an attorney do to avoid Rule 11 sanctions?
2. What is the first technique you would use to investigate our Passim case?
3. How would you organize the file for our Passim case?
4. What is the rule in your jurisdiction on providing information about expert witness consultations to the opposing party?
5. How can a person investigating a case get a more complete copy of a police report?
6. How can a private investigator help investigate a case?
7. What free resources available on the Internet would be particularly useful for investigating our Passim case?

8. How could you use a subscription service such as Westlaw or Lexis to investigate our Passim case?

9. What can an investigator learn from public records?

10. What does your state call its equivalent of the federal Freedom of Information Act? Is there a separate statute for open meetings?

11. How does the Fair Debt Collection Practices Act apply to a law firm collecting a debt?

■ LEGAL RESEARCH PROJECTS

1. Find a legal dictionary such as *Black's Law Dictionary* and read the definition of one of the words or phrases that is defined in this chapter. How does the dictionary definition differ from the one in the textbook?

2. Visit one of the helpful Web sites listed in this chapter. Summarize what you found.

3. Go to your local courthouse or county government building and see what you can find out about a local public figure such as a politician or sports figure. What real property does this person own? How much does the person pay in property taxes? What is his or her property's assessed value? Are there any judgments against the person? Is the person a party to a lawsuit? Was the person married or divorced in the county? Where does the person live?

For additional resources, visit our Web site at www.westlegalstudies.com

"So, let's get this straight Goldilocks, You sat on Baby Bears chair, it collapsed and you've had pain in your back ever since"

Courtesy CartoonStock.com.
www.CartoonStock.com

CHAPTER 3

Witness and Client Interviews

■ OBJECTIVES

❏ Identify the communication dynamics of an interview
❏ Recall that listening is a skill
❏ Explain the role of nonverbal communications in interviews
❏ Prepare for an interview
❏ Construct good interview questions
❏ Role-play how to build rapport with an interviewee
❏ Discuss how to set up an interview
❏ Demonstrate how to interview a witness
❏ Summarize and analyze an interview
❏ Identify factors involved in interviewing special witnesses

COMMUNICATION THEORY

There is a whole field of study that examines the dynamics and intricacies of communication. A student could take a college course on the communication theory and dynamics of various types of interviews. Even doctoral degrees are offered in communications. Being a lawyer requires a high level of communication skill, as attorneys must be able to interview, negotiate, speak in public, orate in court, as well as be excellent listeners. Communication skills are also important for paralegals as they conduct interviews and interact with attorneys and with clients, whose emotional involvement in the case sometimes clouds their ability to listen well.

Communication theory is the study and analysis of how people exchange information among themselves. Laswell's Maxim says that communication is "who says what to whom in what channel to what effect." It is a recently developed field that merges the study of speech communication, rhetoric, and journalism and includes small- and large-group communication, cultural and language barriers, technology, policy, and legal issues. Marshall McLuhan said that "the medium is the message," meaning that the way a message is conveyed is much more important than the content of the message. Verbal communication is the transfer of information utilizing words. Most communication occurs nonverbally. Studies vary as far as the percentage, but between 65 and 93 percent of a message is actually conveyed via tone of voice, gestures and facial expression, or anything else that is not stated through words. However, when something is heard or seen that does not convey information, emotion or context, it is considered noise. Anything that interferes with communication is noise.

BENCH BRIEF INTERVIEW

INTERVIEW OF PRINCE CHARLES

Throughout this chapter, we will be sampling excerpts of interviews. Here is an interview that was aired on the CBS program *60 Minutes* where Steve Kroft interviewed Prince Charles. Kroft does a good job of listening and following up on the answers, and the prince really listens to the questions and gives answers that are responsive.

KROFT: What is the most difficult part of your job, besides dealing with people like me?

PRINCE CHARLES: Yes, exactly. Oh, dear. Well, the most important thing is to be relevant. And so—I mean, it isn't easy, as you can imagine. Because if you say anything, people will say, it's all right for you to say that. It's very easy to just dismiss anything I say. So what I've—I mean, it's difficult. But what I've tried to do is to put my money where my mouth is as much as I can, by actually creating like here, models on the ground.

KROFT: You are in many ways the public advocate for the traditional. What are the great parts of Great Britain that are worth preserving, besides the monarchy?

PRINCE CHARLES: Well, there's an awful lot of things that are worth preserving. I mean, the trouble, I always feel, in today's world is that we abandon so many things unnecessarily, I believe, so often it's in the interest of, you know, efficiency. If you

(continues)

make everything over-efficient, you suck out, it seems to me, every last drop of what, up to now, has been known as culture. We are not the technology. It should be our—you know, our slave, the technology. But it's rapidly becoming our master in many areas, I think.

KROFT: Are you trying to stop progress?

PRINCE CHARLES: No, not at all. I'm just trying to say that we ought to redefine the way in which progress is seen. Is it progress to rush headlong into upsetting the whole balance of nature? Which is what I think we're beginning to do. You know, if you look at the latest figures on climate change and global warming, they're terrifying. Terrifying.

KROFT: How do you deal with (government employees who think you're meddling)? How do you walk that line?

PRINCE CHARLES: Well, years of practice, perhaps.

KROFT: Does it get you in a spot of trouble from time to time from certain people?

PRINCE CHARLES: Oh, inevitably. But it seems to be part and parcel of the thing. I mean, if I wasn't, I think, doing these things, I'd be accused by people like you, doing nothing with my life.

KROFT: Anybody ever tell you to tone it down a little bit?

PRINCE CHARLES: Oh yes, of course. But, I mean, I think the proof is in the pudding. And I think, you know, all the things they try to tell me to tone down over the years, if you look now, though, you'll find they're fairly mainstream.

Communication Theory As Applied to Interviews

■ DYADIC COMMUNICATION

Two people talking.

A pair of people is called a dyad. Therefore, two people talking is **dyadic communication**. Person A says something that is received by Person B. Person B says something that is received by Person A. Each person is supplying feedback to the other.

Usually, dyadic communication is proximate, informal, and simultaneous. Two people who are talking usually are standing or sitting close to one another rather than standing at opposite goal lines of a football field. Messages are not generally prepared in advance. The participants quickly switch back and forth between sending and receiving messages.

An interview is an example of dyadic communication; however, it has a particular purpose. In a job interview, the applicant's purpose is to secure a job offer and to find out if he or she would like to accept a job offer from the employer; the employer's purpose is to evaluate the applicant and determine whether to make an offer of employment to the applicant. In a legal interview, the client is seeking help with a legal problem and the paralegal is seeking to find out the facts. If an attorney is conducting the interview, the attorney is also seeking to identify the legal issues, to be retained by the client, and to determine whether the attorney wants the case, and to render advice.

Another communication concept that applies to interviews is noise. A number of factors can cause noise in an interview. First, the environment where the interview takes place can interfere if it is too cramped, too lavish, uncomfortably hot or cold, or too messy. The interviewee should be comfortable and the setting should be professional. The interview should begin on time and should be conducted without interruptions or distractions such as sounds from machines or other conversations. The client and interviewer should be seated close together without the barrier of a desk between them (see Exhibit 3–1). For example, sit on the same side of a conference table, or in client chairs on the same side of a desk (see Exhibit 3–2).

A second factor that can cause noise is state of mind. For most clients, the trip to an attorney's office is probably not something they are looking forward to. Rather, the topic they need to meet about may be rather unpleasant, such as divorce, bankruptcy, or identity theft. A client may have a negative view of attorneys through lawyer jokes or "war stories" from their friends' or relatives' cases and may have developed the impression that lawyers are untrustworthy, money-grubbing scum. They may expect to be charged an excessive fee for something they detest being involved with in the first place. The attorney's or paralegal's state of mind can also negatively impact the communication. Perhaps the interviewer is sick to death of handling family law matters but feels the need to keep handling them for economic

Attorney / Paralegal

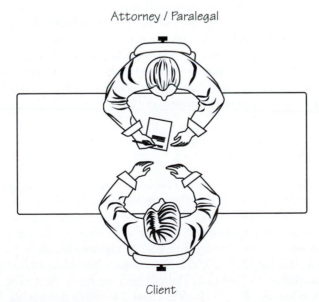

Client

EXHIBIT 3–1   Bad Interview setup

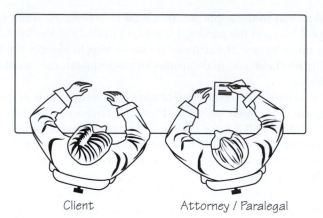

Client   Attorney / Paralegal

EXHIBIT 3–2   Good Interview setup

reasons, and here the client represents yet another divorce case, and it looks like an ugly one to boot; or perhaps the interviewer is ecstatic about winning an appeal or getting a raise. In any of these cases, one's mind is not on the task at hand. To avoid this problem, take a few moments before the interview to compose yourself. Prepare an outline of the topics that need to be covered.

A third factor that can cause noise in an interview is differences between the client's and the interviewer's social, racial, economic, religious, or educational status, or upbringing, gender, or sexual orientation. If a female, elderly, white, rich, straight, Catholic, former schoolteacher with a master's in English is being interviewed by a male, young, gay, black, immigrant musician for whom English is a second language, there might be some preconceived notions that cause distrust or miscommunication. To avoid this type of noise, be aware of the differences and try to be sensitive to them by avoiding stereotypes, cliches, and trigger words or phrases.

Other potential noise sources include legal jargon or other technical words, or words that are beyond the grasp of the particular client. Clients can have varying levels of education, vocabulary, and intelligence. This type of noise can be avoided by adapting your vocabulary to the interviewee.

LISTENING

We hear whenever we are awake. People hear music, conversation, the radio, or the TV, but that does not mean that they are listening. Listening is a skill. There are people who study and teach listening. There is an International Listening Association. The average person listens well only 25 percent of the time, recalls half of what was said during a 10-minute presentation an hour after it, and recalls only a quarter of it after two days. People listen at 125 to 250 words per minute but think at 1,000 to 3,000 words per minute, according to HighGain (http://highgain.com/). According to Wikipedia (http://en.wikipedia.org/), people speak at about 200 words per minute. That makes it easy to drift off into thoughts or daydreams instead of paying rapt attention.

"I said your son doesn't listen well in class..."

EXHIBIT 3–3   *Courtesy CartoonStock.com. www.CartoonStock.com*

Listening Is Important

Companies have found that good listening avoids waste and increases sales. Interviewee comfort levels can be increased through listening. Listening is important for paralegals because they need to communicate professionally with attorneys, experts, clients, witnesses, deputy court clerks, process servers, and others.

BENCH BRIEF

A college professor taught a television magazine course where students produced a monthly television show. One of his students arranged an interview with the football coach, who, unbeknownst to anyone at the show, was fired on the day of the interview. The coach was professional and gracious enough not to cancel the interview. The student was nervous and wrote his questions out word for word.

STUDENT: Coach, thanks for coming in today. (*looking at his notes for the first of 10 questions that he has written out, and reading it*) I know it was kind of a disappointing season with only four wins. What do you plan to do to improve the offense next season?

(continues)

BENCH BRIEF *(continued)*

COACH: Well, unfortunately, I won't be around next year. I've just been fired, which is unfortunate because I was really looking forward to working with this great group of kids. (*The student is still looking at his notes.*)

Next year's class was the first one that I recruited entirely and they learned a lot during my tenure. I'll miss working with them during their senior season, and I'm sure they'll have a lot of success, but that's part of this business and I just wish them all the best.

STUDENT: What about the defense?

Lessons: (1) Do not be married to your notes. (2) Listen to the answers. (3) Ask follow-up questions based upon the answers.

Listening is also important for everyone involved in a trial. The attorneys need to listen to the jurors during jury selection so that they can pick a good jury, and to the witnesses so that they can ask good questions. The judge needs to listen to the trial so that he or she can make just rulings. Since the whole purpose of having a trial is to develop the truth, jurors need to pay close attention to the evidence so that they can render a good verdict.

Listening Is a Skill

Active listening is listening with a purpose to make sure that the listener is hearing the same thing that the speaker is saying. The listener listens to the words spoken, watches for nonverbal clues, and paraphrases or gives feedback to what the speaker said. For example, a student may say to a librarian, "I got in trouble at school and now I need to write a paper. We're studying Africa, and I like animals so I'm looking for a book on an African animal like lions, elephants, tigers, or whatever." If the librarian is an active listener, the librarian will repeat, "So you're looking for a book about a large animal that originates from Africa?" And the patron may say, "No, it doesn't have to be a large animal. It could be a snake or an ant. It just has to be something cool and from Africa." Feedback may also include commenting on the speaker's perceived emotion. For example, a paralegal may say to someone going through a divorce, "I bet that made you really angry."

BENCH BRIEF

TEN IRRITATING LISTENING HABITS

1. Interrupting the speaker.

2. Not looking at the speaker.

3. Rushing the speaker and making the speaker feel that the speaker is wasting the listener's time.

4. Showing interest in something other than the conversation.

5. Getting ahead of the speaker and finishing his or her thoughts.

6. Not responding to the speaker's requests.

7. Saying, "Yes, but . . . ," as if the listener has made up his mind.

8. Topping the speaker's story with "That reminds me . . ." or "That's nothing, let me tell you about . . ."

9. Forgetting what was talked about previously.

10. Asking too many questions about details.

From *Listen Up* by Larry Barker and Kittie Watson (St. Martin's Press, 2000)

Here is another example of a good interview featuring good questions that are based upon the answer to the previous question, and answers that are very responsive to the questions.

BENCH BRIEF   INTERVIEW

INTERVIEW OF RICHARD PRYOR BY LARRY KING
CNN, December 10, 2005, 2005 WLNR 19911690

KING: You licked an addiction to cocaine, didn't you?

PRYOR: No, you never lick that.

KING: Are you still an addict?

PRYOR: Always.

KING: But you haven't used it in . . .

(continues)

BENCH BRIEF INTERVIEW *(continued)*

PRYOR: I haven't used it.

KING: How were you able to stop using it?

PRYOR: Getting away from the people that had it, and cleaning up my life, in a sense. You know, I mean, drugs will kill you, you know? That's the truth of it.

KING: You write very, I guess, emotionally, about that fire incident. Was that the hardest thing to write in the book?

PRYOR: Yeah. It was hard for me to face that person.

KING: Who did that?

PRYOR: Yeah. You know . . .

KING: Why did he do that?

PRYOR: Because he wanted to die. He wanted to just say, 'What the hell?' You know, 'Let's go.' You know, and God said, 'No, sorry, you don't get to call the shots on that. I'll tell you when you get to go. But I'll give you a little something to take with you.'

KING: Hey, Rich.

PRYOR: What?

KING: What was it like to be on fire?

PRYOR: What was it like?

KING: What was that like?

PRYOR: First, it was scary and petrifying and awesome. You know, fires—it looks—you know, a fire looks red and stuff? But it's really orange and white. I didn't know that until after it was over. I said, 'Wait a minute, this is not—this is fire, but it don't look like it.' And . . .

KING: But the pain must be . . .

PRYOR: Excruciating is the word. You know, because when that guy wiped me in the hospital, the guy was giving me a shower, and they have them little brushes, things, and the guy said—he showed it to me first, said, 'Look, this is a sponge, right?' I said, 'Yeah.' But I had no idea what that would do.

KING: Pain?

PRYOR: Yeah. I didn't have any idea.

INTERVIEWING A CLIENT

An attorney or paralegal interviewing a client or potential client has a number of goals. First, impress the client that he or she has found the right lawyer/law office for the case. Second, find out if the client's case is one the firm wants to undertake.

Third, find out the status of the case and the client's overall version of what happened. Fourth, educate the client about what would happen if he or she goes forward with the case. Fifth, let the client know what needs to be done to retain the attorney or firm. If the lawyer is conducting the interview, the lawyer may discuss fee arrangements; however, paralegals may not do so.

The first impression garnered by the client during the interview will impact the entire case. The initial interview should establish a good working relationship between the client and the paralegal. The client should get over any initial fear of working with a law firm, get comfortable exchanging information, and get some idea of what legal issues are involved in the case. Unless the client is home-bound or hospitalized, the interview should be conducted in the firm's offices, preferably in a conference room unless the paralegal's or attorney's office is neat and tidy enough. If it is a family law matter, or something else that may generate emotion, have facial tissue available in the room.

Sometimes clients will appear with a friend or family member. If the nonclient's presence will ease the client's mind, the person may attend the meeting. However, his or her presence will jeopardize the attorney-client privilege, and the client should be made aware of this fact so that the nonclient can be excused when sensitive material is discussed.

In the next Entertainment Note, a criminal defense attorney is having an initial interview with a woman who may be charged with murder.

BENCH BRIEF   ENTERTAINMENT NOTE

BODY OF EVIDENCE

Script by Brad Mirman, from the Second Draft located at http://www.imsdb.com/scripts/Body-of-Evidence.html

DULANEY: Miss Lawson, I'm Frank Dulaney.

(*She raises the cigarette to her lips. DULANEY notices despite her outward composure her hand is shaking.*)

REBECCA: (*nervously*) Are you going to represent me?

DULANEY: There are no charges against you. I'm here to decide if I'm going to represent you should that occur.

(*beat*)

Did you kill him?

(*REBECCA appears hurt by the question.*)

REBECCA: You don't waste any time, do you?

(*DULANEY doesn't answer. He studies her—his eyes probing hers.*)

(*continues*)

REBECCA: *(continuing)* Do you think I did it?

DULANEY: I don't know. That's why I'm asking you.

REBECCA: You must have some feeling. Some immediate impression. A young, attractive woman, involved with an older man who leaves her everything in his will. And the things that went on in that house. Such wild sex. What kind of picture does that paint?

DULANEY: Not a very good one I'm afraid.

REBECCA: And that's exactly what the jury will see when they look at me. That's why I need a very good lawyer, Mr. Dulaney.

DULANEY: You're assuming the District Attorney is going to file charges.

(REBECCA's anxiety begins to surface. She feigns a weak smile.)

REBECCA: He'll file. He's an ambitious man. Ambitious men build their careers on the bodies of others.

DULANEY: You still haven't answered my question.

(She takes a long drag of her cigarette before answering. She looks at Dulaney. Displaying emotions is not something that comes easily. Tears well up in her eyes.)

REBECCA: *(emotionally)* I loved him. A big part of my life has been torn away from me, Mr. Dulaney. A part I can never get back—and on top of that people are saying that I am somehow responsible for it. They've taken everything that is good and caring about two people in love and made it dirty.

(A single tear streams down her check. She knows what he wants to hear her say—and she resents having to say it.)

REBECCA: No—I didn't kill him.

What is unrealistic about this interview is the complete failure to establish a rapport before starting the interview, and that a criminal defense attorney would not ask the client whether she did it or not because it could compromise the attorney's ability to call the defendant to the stand. If the defendant says, "I did it but I want to testify in my own behalf and lie and say I didn't do it," then the attorney might have to withdraw.

Starting the Interview

Go get clients from the waiting room, where they should not have been kept waiting long. Introduce yourself, shake hands, and have them follow you to a private room, either your office (if it is neat enough) or a conference room. First impressions are important, and if you take them into an office cluttered with files and file boxes piled ceiling high, the clients may wonder if you are too busy to handle their case.

When meeting people for the first time, small talk is important in order to develop a rapport. They may have some anxiety about lawyers. They may be apprehensive about the cost of representation, so it may be advisable to tell them right away that you want to get to know them a little bit before "starting the clock." Discuss the weather, sports, or something else innocuous. Avoid political discussions. Be careful with humor, which can be a useful tool but can also unexpectedly offend. Clients may be anxious, upset, scared, grieving, overwhelmed, or some combination of these things. Get background information about clients such as full name, address, phone number, e-mail address, and how they found your firm. The firm should have an initial client interview data sheet so that important information is not forgotten. Other important data to obtain includes the name, address, and phone number of a person who will always know where they are so that you can locate clients if they move and fail to inform the firm. If the case is a divorce, many firms have multipage questionnaires that cover all the information needed to process the initial documentation. Often clients will take the form, fill it out, and return it. Beyond getting the basic information about clients, avoid taking copious notes, at least at first, as this interferes with the establishment of rapport. If your firm ends up with the case, you will have plenty of time to gather detailed information later.

Clients may have questions about you, your lawyer, and the firm. Be sure to answer honestly. A client who lies or exaggerates can cause problems later on in the representation, so it is important to be truthful. They may also have questions about what the procedure is for their case, or what you think the result will be. Avoid answering these questions, as they are apt to remember any predictions or what they perceive to be promises of success, and if the case does not go their way, those words may come back to haunt you.

Avoid Giving Legal Advice

Explain to them that you are a paralegal, not an attorney, and that you cannot give legal advice. After a paralegal is in practice for a while, he or she may be certain of the answer to common questions. No matter how obvious it seems, if answering the question would cause the person to take action that would change their position on a case, exercise or waive a right, or decide to do or not do something, the best practice is to indicate that you need to consult with your attorney. Suppose, for example, that a major league baseball player wanted to avoid paying child support. You probably do not even need much of a legal education to know the answer to that question. Still, you can quickly indicate to the attorney the question and proposed answer, and go back to the client (or prospective client) and say, "I consulted with the attorney and we don't think that the court is going to agree to waive your child support obligation since you are making $1,100,000 a year."

The following would constitute legal advice:

- "When the lease ends, you become a month-to-month tenant at the old rental rate, so you can plan on staying there."
- "You can sign the contract; it protects all your rights."
- "If she won't let you have visitation, you should just pick the kids up from school a little bit early on a Friday and keep them for the weekend."
- "You can fire that employee because we're an at-will employment state."
- "The tax consequences of giving her the exemptions aren't worth the effort of fighting her about it."
- "You shouldn't testify at the suppression hearing because the prosecutor can impeach you with that testimony later at trial."
- "It's a bad idea to flee the state to avoid having your wages garnished."
- "Waiting period waivers are granted only in cases where a doctor will certify that the waiting period will cause a nervous breakdown."
- "We can offer them a discount if they settle now and then go back to the old higher demand if they don't agree to the discounted offer."
- "We will have to file the case in Renville County because that is where venue lies."
- "The family debts are subject to equitable distribution, which means you could get stuck with her medical school loans."

BENCH BRIEF ETHICS ALERT

In some jurisdictions, it is considered the practice of law, and therefore improper, for a paralegal to meet alone with a prospective client. Find out what the rule is in your jurisdiction before meeting alone with a prospective or new client.

Conducting the Interview

Get the Facts

■ **NO-FAULT DIVORCE**
Divorce granted as long as the marriage is irretrievably broken, without trying to determine which spouse is the root cause of the failure of the marriage.

After establishing a rapport, find out the facts. What happened? How to handle this aspect of the interview is quite dependent upon the type of case. In a divorce, it usually does not matter why the marriage failed, as most states have **no-fault divorce**. In a personal injury action, it is extremely important to find out exactly how the accident happened. The particular case may also dictate how to focus the fact questions. For example, the interview for a divorce case with no children involved but a major dispute about a family-owned business would be very different than a projected all-out custody and visitation battle. Have in mind what you need to know and try to guide the client to focus on that information. Even what looks to you like a plain old business contract dispute can be emotional for a client. The plaintiff may have been a long-time customer with whom the client has socialized. The client may attempt to go off on an irrelevant, time-wasting tangent. Try to gently steer the interview back to the relevant topics.

Ask Open-Ended Questions

Be sure to ask **open-ended questions.** An open-ended question is one that cannot be answered with a "yes" or a "no" or some other single word or short phrase. "What happened next?" is open ended. "Did you tell the police?" is not. "Where did you go next?" is open ended but "Have you ever been to First Avenue?" is not. It is better to ask open-ended questions because they are more likely to garner information, they give you a chance to hear about the case from the client's perspective, and they prevent you from displaying assumptions or putting words into the client's mouth. See Exhibit 3–4 for more examples.

■ **OPEN-ENDED QUESTION**

A query that cannot be answered with a single word or phrase.

EXHIBIT 3–4   OPEN-ENDED VS. CLOSE-ENDED QUESTIONS

OPEN-ENDED	NOT OPEN-ENDED
"What did the President know and when did he know it?" Senator Howard Baker (regarding President Nixon and Watergate)	"Are you now or have you ever been a member of the communist party?" Members of the House Un-American Activities Committee (to various witnesses)
"You inherit five million dollars the same day aliens land on the earth and say they're going to blow it up in two days. What do you do?" Veronica in the movie *Heathers*	"Are you running for something?" President Nixon (to Dan Rather)
"Why does man kill? He kills for food. And not only food: frequently there must be a beverage." Woody Allen	"No sir, Mr. President, are you?" Dan Rather (to President Nixon)
"Why isn't there a special name for the tops of your feet?" Lily Tomlin	"The whole problem can be stated quite simply by asking, 'Is there a meaning to music?' My answer would be, 'Yes.' And 'Can you state in so many words what the meaning is?' My answer to that would be, 'No.'" Composer Aaron Copland
"If winning isn't everything, why do they keep score?" Vince Lombardi	"You've got to ask yourself one question: 'Do I feel lucky?' Well, do ya, punk?" Clint Eastwood as "Dirty" Harry Callahan
"Why do you have to be a nonconformist like everybody else?" James Thurber	"What's another word for thesaurus?" Comedian Steven Wright
"After I'm dead I'd rather have people ask why I have no monument than why I have one." Cato the Elder	"Do women know about shrinkage?" George Costanza on *Seinfeld*

Avoid Leading Questions

Try to avoid leading questions. **Leading questions** suggest an answer. For example, "you recycle, don't you?" is a leading question. To ask the same question without leading, say "Do you recycle?" It is better to get the information from the witness rather than giving them your assumptions and having them repeated back to you.

Have an Outline

It may be productive to have an outline for the interview going into it, so that you ask about all the major topics that should be covered. An outline can be chronological or topic or issue based. The outline will vary from practice area to practice area. Do not get married to your outline; rather, use it to make sure all the needed topics are addressed.

Take Good Notes

One technique to get good notes on the interview is to dictate out loud in the client's presence a memo regarding the meeting. The client will be impressed with your attentiveness and can make any necessary corrections.

Ending the Interview and Assessing It

At the end of the interview, let the client know what the next step is. This may vary depending upon firm or attorney policies, type of case, the stage that the case is at, whether the firm would be pursuing or defending the case, and the client's desires. The firm may not automatically accept the client's case. If it is a contingency fee case, the firm may decide that the likelihood of recovery and damages are too small to justify taking the risk of time and expenses. The firm may determine that there is a conflict of interest (although the best practice is to determine if there is a conflict before the initial meeting). The firm or attorney may determine that they lack the time or resources to pursue the matter. If the firm would be initiating the case, it may be concerned about a statute of limitations. If the firm would be defending the case, it would be concerned about filing a responsive pleading by the deadline, or obtaining an extension to answer. If the case has already started and the client is dissatisfied with his present counsel or has been handling it himself, there may be other deadlines. The client may be meeting with additional firms before deciding to go ahead with your firm, or to go ahead with the case at all.

Some firms provide free initial consultations. Others charge for the consultation only if they are retained. Still others charge for such consultations. If it is free and time is up, be sure to show the client that you value your time by pointing out that the free period has run out and you will now begin to charge. Do it diplomatically, but be firm.

Following the interview, write a memo to the attorney regarding what the client said about the case, any legal issues about which the client is concerned, any other legal issues that you are aware of, the status of the case, and your overall impression of the client and case.

PASSIM CASE FIELDS V. PRAIRIE BANK

Client Interview Memo

I met with potential client Peter Fields today who obtained the name of our firm from the Bar Association lawyer referral service. He wants to sue Prairie Bank for identity theft. He does all his banking and finance at the bank. He has no accounts anywhere else. He's banked there his whole life, going back to when his mom started a saving account for him when he was 7 years old.

Recently, he went there to see about getting his house refinanced. He first talked to Anne, a teller. She pointed out that he might have some problems since he had credit cards that had large balances that had never had a payment on them on his credit report. Anne talked to a lady he believes to be the teller supervisor, the teller supervisor told a man who he thought was a banker, and the banker must have talked to Dave, the Branch Manager, as Peter got called into his office. The Branch Manager gathered information from Peter, and promised an investigation. Peter agreed to let them take his finger prints.

Peter blames the bank for his identity theft because he is very careful about his personal information. He routinely shreds credit card applications, and anything else that has personal data on it. He figures he can always get copies of what he needs if he really needs it, and he says he's a disorganized slob so he would have trouble finding a bank statement if he kept them. He works at a small company as an accountant and he does the payroll himself so no one there has access to his social security number. He is sure that he did not apply for the credit cards that were in his name.

He wants help getting the credit card companies to forgive the debt and clean up his credit rating and he wants to sue the bank. He has spent a lot of time trying to clean up his credit himself. Because he could not refinance his house immediately, he missed out on a business opportunity. He closed his accounts at the bank and took his business elsewhere because he no longer feels comfortable there. However, his credit rating really took a hit from the unpaid credit cards.

He seemed like a nice guy and I think that he would make a good witness. I told him that I would discuss the case with you and that someone from the office would be following up with him regarding whether we would take the case and, if so, under what terms.

INTERVIEWING A WITNESS

Witness interviews are used to gather information about the case. This section addresses informal witness interviews as opposed to depositions, which are covered in Chapter 4. It may be surprising to know that witnesses favorable to the other side may be informally interviewed, although they may also decline to talk to you. You must properly identify yourself to them in terms of your name and for whom you are working.

■ **COACH**

To influence the content
of a witness's testimony.

BENCH BRIEF ❗ ETHICS ALERT

To **coach**, woodshed, or horseshed witnesses is to steer their statements and testimony to fit your client's case. This is not proper. However, the line between advocating, helping to phrase something, and overtly influencing testimony can be nebulous. A suggestion can be made regarding how to phrase something. For example, in the move *The Verdict* the expert witness is advised to say "she threw up in her mask" rather than "She'd aspirated vomitus into her mask . . ." However, later the attorney placed words in the doctor's mouth by saying, " . . . You brought thirty years of medical experience to bear. Isn't that what you did? . . . A patient riddled with complications, questionable information on her, on her admitting form . . . to save her and to save the baby." That might be considered improper coaching.

In reviewing the following deposition transcript, a court agreed that the following exchange was improper coaching:

Defense Attorney: Now, let me ask you, in the few minutes we have remaining before we break for this part one of your deposition, the reason the GPWS system didn't give an alert at any of the places that you said it should have, is there any part in your report where it says that the reason is?

Witness: Yes.

Defense Attorney: Where?

Witness: I think that is the second item in there. The second item discusses that.

Defense Attorney: Any other places besides item 2, or is that it?

Witness: Item 2.

Defense Attorney: I am not trying to encourage you to have more, I certainly don't want you to. I just want to be certain I extract it.

Plaintiff Attorney: I want to make sure, too. I mean, Glenn, if your whole report goes to that—

Defense Attorney: Objection. I think this is improper coaching of the witness.

Plaintiff Attorney: I'm sorry. I don't want to coach him either.

Defense Attorney: Let's just not even do this.

Plaintiff Attorney: I want to make sure the witness understands the question.

Defense Attorney: I don't want you to make sure anything about the witness. He can answer this question that is pending.

Plaintiff Attorney: Let me note an objection, and I will let it go. Object to the form of the question.

Witness: Item 2, item 3, item 4, I think discuss that, and, in general, you know, item 5 goes toward the systematic disregard of standard practices.

The witness took the lawyer's hint and expounded upon how additional sections of the report supported his position. Wilson v. Sundstrand Corp., 2003 WL 22012673 (N.D. Ill. 2003).

Starting the Interview

As with client interviews, an important first step is to establish rapport. Witness interviews are less likely to take place in your office. You may need to visit witnesses at their home or place of employment. It is preferable to meet in person (although you may also find yourself on the phone), as you may get nonverbal cues from meeting them in person that will help you assess their credibility. Let them know the purpose of the interview.

If you do not already have all of a witness's contact information, such as full name, snail mail and e-mail addresses, phone numbers, employer, age, and date of birth, get it.

Conducting the Interview

In addition to using open-ended, nonleading questions, additional techniques may be needed to keep witnesses talking. When witnesses finish an answer, silence may cause them to continue on, giving more information than they intended. Silence can be uncomfortable, and witnesses may try to fill it. You can also give a sort of verbal nudge such as "uh-huh" or "go on" or "please continue." If the answer is not really responsive to your question, try asking the same question again, or repeat back the part of the answer that was responsive, and then ask the original question again.

For example, in our case, we might have an interview with Anne, the bank teller, along this line.

PASSIM CASE **FIELDS V. PRAIRIE BANK**

Paralegal: Do you recall the day that Peter Fields came to the bank originally to complain about his identity being stolen?

Anne: Well, he was agitated. He was a regular, but we have so many customers, I wouldn't have recognized him outside of the bank. One time, I was out to dinner with my family and a customer stopped by, and you know how when you see someone out of context, you might not recognize them? Like, if I saw him in the bank, I'd of gone, 'Oh, hi Mr. Johnstone' but when I saw a customer that was a semi-regular guy in a restaurant he had to tell me where he knew me from.

Paralegal: So, you might recognize him if you saw him in the bank. Do you recall the day that he originally came in to complain about his identity being stolen?

Ask one question at a time rather than asking compound questions that cram more than one question into a question, such as "Tell about your new book, where you got the idea, what it's about, and whether you think there's a good chance Hollywood will make a movie out of it." The witness may have difficulty remembering all of the questions, and you may not remember that the second or third questions were not answered.

It is also important with witness interviews to have an outline of the topics that you want to cover. However, do not be stuck to your outline. Follow up on answers to your questions.

In the following interview excerpt, a police officer conducts an interview with a witness. Jerry Lundegaard is an unscrupulous car salesman at his desk when Marge, a visibly pregnant police chief, comes to interview him about a car that she thinks might have been stolen from his dealership and used in a triple homicide. See how his answers and demeanor might change him from a witness to a suspect.

BENCH BRIEF ENTERTAINMENT NOTE

FARGO

Screenplay by Joel and Ethan Coen, available at http://www.imsdb.com/scripts/Fargo.html/

MARGE: Mr. Lundegaard? Sorry to bother you again. Can I come in?

JERRY: Yah, no, I'm kinda—I'm kinda busy—

MARGE: I unnerstand. I'll keep it real short, then. I'm on my way out of town, but I was just—

Do you mind if I sit down? I'm carrying a bit of a load here.

JERRY: No, I—

(*But she is already sitting into the chair opposite with a sigh of relieved weight.*)

MARGE: Yah, it's this vehicle I asked you about yesterday. I was just wondering—

JERRY: Yah, like I told ya, we haven't had any vehicles go missing.

MARGE: Okay, are you sure, cause, I mean, how do you know? Because, see, the crime I'm investigating, the perpetrators were driving a car with dealer plates. And they called someone who works here, so it'd be quite a coincidence if they weren't, ya know, connected.

JERRY: Yah, I see.

MARGE: So how do you—have you done any kind of inventory recently?

JERRY: The car's not from our lot, ma'am.

MARGE: But do you know that for sure without—

JERRY: Well, I would know. I'm the Executive Sales Manager.

MARGE: Yah, but—

JERRY: We run a pretty tight ship here.

(continues)

BENCH BRIEF 🎬 ENTERTAINMENT NOTE *(continued)*

MARGE: I know, but—well, how do you establish that, sir? Are the cars, uh, counted daily or what kind of—

JERRY: Ma'am, I answered your question.

(*There is a silent beat.*)

MARGE: . . . I'm sorry, sir?

JERRY: Ma'am, I answered your question. I answered the darn—I'm cooperating here, and I . . .

MARGE: Sir, you have no call to get snippy with me. I'm just doin' my job here.

JERRY: I'm not, uh, I'm not arguin' here. I'm cooperating . . . There's no, uh—we're doin' all we can . . .

(*He trails off into silence.*)

MARGE: Sir, could I talk to Mr. Gustafson?

(*Jerry stares at her.*)

MARGE: . . . Mr. Lundegaard?

(*Jerry explodes.*)

JERRY: Well, heck, if you wanna, if you wanna play games here! I'm workin' with ya on this thing, but I . . .

(*He is getting angrily off his feet.*)

Okay, I'll do a damned lot count!

MARGE: Sir? Right now?

JERRY: Sure right now! You're darned tootin'!

Ending the Interview and Assessing It

At the end of the interview, you can ask if there is anything else witnesses want to tell you or that they think you should know. Following the interview, write up a summary of what the witnesses said, assess their credibility, and note any other impact you think what they had to say will have on the case.

SPECIAL INTERVIEWEES

Certain individuals require special treatment during an interview, for example, children and people for whom English is not their native language.

Children

Children are impressionable. They have been known to say what an adult has told them to say, even unintentionally. In perhaps the most famous case, wild allegations of massive abuse of children at a pre-school later turned out to be false.

BENCH BRIEF

MCMARTIN PRESCHOOL

Daily Breeze (Torrance, CA) A1 (October 30, 2005) 2005 WLNR 17588738

In an interview and apology in the *Los Angeles Times Magazine*, one of the children who claimed to be abused in the infamous McMartin pre-school case admitted that he lied. Kyle Zirpolo states that, after initially denying that anything had happened to him, he was pressured by investigators to change his story. He said he remembered feeling uncomfortable about questions regarding touching, and that when he said such things did not happen, the interviewers told him that they knew these things did happen. He said if he gave an answer he did not like, they would ask him again until he gave the answer they wanted. They told him he was intelligent and that he could help the other children who were too scared.

He said that he lied because he thought that his parents wanted him to, in order to protect his younger siblings. He said that he made up details of satanic rituals by describing details in the actual church that he and his family attended, such as describing an alter or describing a satanic priest the same way as a Catholic priest except he changed the color of the clothing to red.

He understood the importance of telling a consistent story. That is why he was among the 41 children chosen to testify to the grand jury from the 360 who claimed to be abused. He understood the importance of being consistent and he tried hard to keep his lies consistent.

About a year after the trial was over he tried to tell his mother that he had lied. He said that when he was about ten years old, he made an attempt to tell his mother that nothing inappropriate had occurred. His mother did not believe him.

Kyle Zirpolo as told to Debbie Nathan, I'm Sorry, Los Angeles Times Magazine, October 30, 2005 page 10

It takes special training to be able to interview a child regarding sexual or physical abuse. Having an improperly trained person conduct the interview can forever taint the child's testimony. Therefore, do not conduct such interviews yourself unless you first get training on interviewing potentially abused children.

In any interview with a child, it is ultra-important to avoid leading questions due to the propensity for children to try to seek adult approval with their answers. Modify your vocabulary and questions to make them appropriate for the child's age.

Other Difficult Witnesses

Witnesses who do not speak fluent English or are hostile may also require special treatment. For people uncomfortable talking about a serious subject in English, it is important to get a translator for the interview. It is the responsibility of the firm to locate and pay for the translator.

Try to be empathetic with hostile witnesses. You will still try to establish a rapport. Try to find some common ground. Identify why they are hostile. Ask open-ended questions. If they decline to talk to you, do not threaten them, but let them know that you can take their deposition and subpoena them.

BENCH BRIEF ENTERTAINMENT NOTE

BLADE RUNNER

From an early draft of the screenplay by Hampton Fancher (1980) available at http://www.dailyscript.com/scripts/Blade-runner_early.html

(Dekhard is looking for some escaped humanoid robots. Taffey is a criminal but not the type that Dekhard is after.)

DECKARD: Taffey Lewis?

TAFFEY: Yes?

DECKARD: Can I come in?

(There is a pause lasting the time it takes Taffey not to think of a way to say no. The door opens and Deckard enters.)

TAFFEY: Excuse my niece there . . . She's studying for an exam.

(Deckard takes the Identikit hard copies our of his pocket and pushing some junk out of the way, fans them out on the table.)

DECKARD: I'd like you to take a look at these pictures.

TAFFEY: Of course.

(Taffey bends down really close, peering at the pictures from about two inches away.)

TAFFEY: You see I lost my contacts a couple of days ago around here somewhere and my sight is a little . . . What am I supposed to be looking for?

(continues)

DECKARD: Do you recognize any of them?

(He stops at Zhora.)

TAFFEY: This one looks familiar, but I don't know. Naw. There's one came in today looks a little like this one but . . .

DECKARD: What did she want?

TAFFEY: Who?

DECKARD: The girl that doesn't look like that girl.

TAFFEY: Nothing. She wanted to know about suck night.

DECKARD: What night?

TAFFEY: I didn't know if I wanted to handle her—I already got a snake act. But my partner goes down there to the Opera House on suck night to book the good ones.

DECKARD: What's suck night?

TAFFEY: That's what we call in the trade, audition free-for-alls and most of it sucks. But I don't think that's her.

DECKARD: You talking about the Opera House on the Main?

(Taffey nods. Deckard goes to the door and turns.)

DECKARD: Book the good ones for where?

TAFFEY: Lots of places. The tours, the clubs, the Silicone shows, private parties.

DECKARD: What shows?

TAFFEY: Silicone Valley. Lots of these science guys never leave that place. We book two shows a month in there. Those big time techs and bio-guys might be real high zoners up here, but when it comes to the arts, they like it loud and lewd.

Expert Witness Interviews

■ **ATTORNEY WORK PRODUCT**
Material prepared for litigation that is protected from disclosure by the attorney-client privilege.

An investigator may need to find an expert witness to support a client's case, and in so searching, may have a chance to speak with an expert. The goals would be to determine the expert's area of expertise and whether it matches the case at hand, to assess the expert's credibility and ability to talk to a jury in layman's terms about his or her field of expertise, and possibly to learn the expert's preliminary opinion about the client's case. These interviews will usually take place over the phone. Both the expert and the law firm must consider ethical concerns when conducting the interview. Each side may have confidentiality concerns, and the law firm may have to protect the **attorney work product**. Releases may need to be signed, particularly if the expert is a medical professional.

SUMMARY

Interviews are dyadic communication. The most important part of an interview is listening to the answers, and active listening is fundamental. A lot of communication occurs nonverbally, such as through facial expression. Client interviews are a way to make a first impression on the client. First, establish a rapport. Use open-ended, nonleading questions. Write a summary for your attorney after the interview. Witness interviews are an informal way to get information on a case. Be careful when interviewing children not to ask leading questions.

■ KEY TERMS

attorney work product	dyadic communication	no-fault divorce
coach	leading question	open-ended question

■ HELPFUL WEB SITES

http://www.cornerhousemn.org
http://www.listen.org
http://www.highgain.com

■ REVIEW AND DISCUSSION QUESTIONS

1. Conduct an interview with a classmate or relative about an incident in which he or she was involved.
2. If you could interview the actual identity thief in our case, what would you ask?
3. What are some barriers to communication?
4. What do you think Marshall McLuhan meant when he said that the medium is the message? To what extent do you think that he was correct?
5. Who are some good interviewers on TV or radio? Who are some bad interviewers in the media?
6. What things can cause noise in an interview?
7. How does a client interview differ from a witness interview?
8. What is the first step in any interview?
9. What types of questions should be asked? What types of questions should be avoided?
10. How should you end interviews?
11. What should you do after an interview?
12. Describe the line between preparing a witness and improperly coaching a witness.
13. Conduct a mock-client interview with a classmate who is pretending to be Peter Fields.

■ LEGAL RESEARCH PROJECTS _____

1. Find a list of questions for an initial-client interview in a personal injury case. How could you adapt it for the Passim case?

2. Find an expert witness checklist or questionnaire.

For additional resources, visit our Web site at www.westlegalstudies.com

4

Discovery: Getting Evidence Through the Court System

"We object to the term 'snail mail'."

Courtesy CartoonStock.com.
www.CartoonStock.com

■ OBJECTIVES _____

❏ Construct a set of interrogatories and requests for production of documents
❏ List the various methods of discovery that are available through the legal system
❏ Relate how depositions work
❏ Characterize legal issues that can come up with discovery, such as privileges, trade secrets, and discovery abuse
❏ Differentiate civil and criminal discovery
❏ Examine how discovery differs under the modern federal approach

PURPOSE AND IMPORTANCE OF DISCOVERY

In the previous two chapters, we considered how to obtain information outside of official court processes. Here we examine the formal court processes that are collectively known as discovery.

Purpose of Discovery

The purpose of discovery is for each side to gather information and material that it might be able to use to prove its case, and to narrow the issues that might be in dispute at the trial. A movie or television show such as *Perry Mason* or *Matlock,* where information suddenly appears in the middle of a trial, is unrealistic in this regard. Once in a great while some new scintillating tidbit will surface, but by the time a case is ready for trial, all sides that are properly prepared should know all about the evidence that the opposition has at its disposal to present.

Prior to the adoption of discovery rules, parties were required to do their own investigations. The only notice that they had regarding the other side's case was the complaint or answer. In the mid 1940s the Federal Rules of Civil Procedure were adopted. These rules established the discovery system that is widely used in most states and, until very recently, was used in federal court for civil cases. Under this system, each party can send discovery requests to the other side. The opposition will reply with the information requested. If the system works as it was designed, judges do not get involved in the discovery process. Information simply flows back and forth until the discovery deadline passes. If there is a dispute, the parties go to court and get the judge to make a ruling. Initially, most states adopted civil procedure rules that were similar to the federal rules. However, the trend has been for states not to adopt amendments analogous to the federal rules. Therefore, discovery rules have started to vary quite a bit from state to state, or even among different districts within states.

In 1993 the Federal Rules of Civil Procedure were amended to require parties to disclose, without first receiving a request, basic information such as potential witnesses, documentary evidence, damages, and insurance. Later, each party is to identify any expert witness that it might utilize and provide a detailed report, and then to indicate what evidence it intends to offer at the trial. The goal of these amendments was to speed up the discovery process. It appears that only Utah has adopted the 1993 federal approach to discovery.

Typically, the court issues a schedule early in the case that establishes a discovery deadline. By this date, depositions must be completed. Interrogatories, requests for production of documents, and requests for admissions must be sent out but need not be answered by the deadline. Some courts may have a local rule that establishes the deadlines.

Importance of Discovery

Discovery is important because it is a good source for evidence; information obtained through it can lead to settlement of a case or victory at trial. Also, requesting the other side to answer a discovery question can obtain information regarding its perspective on the case and the evidence that it has. A discovery question can commit the opposition to a factual position that is useful in framing a trial strategy.

Who Pays?

Generally, each party is responsible for covering its own costs of litigation, including the costs of discovery. It can take time and money to copy all the documents requested in discovery, fly a witness in for a deposition, extract data from a computer system, or pull archived files. However, when a discovery request is unduly burdensome, the court may order the requesting party to pay the cost.

What Is Discoverable?

Anything that is **reasonably calculated** to lead to the discovery of admissible evidence is subject to a discovery request. A party cannot go on a fishing expedition, looking for speculative material. However, it can seek material that would not be admissible, so long as it might lead to the discovery of evidence that would be admissible.

Since most states follow the old version of the Federal Rules of Civil Procedure regarding discovery, this chapter features rules from several states as examples.

> ### MINNESOTA RULE OF CIVIL PROCEDURE 26.02. DISCOVERY, SCOPE AND LIMITS
>
> Unless otherwise limited by order of the court in accordance with these rules, the scope of discovery is as follows:
>
> (a) In General. Parties may obtain discovery regarding any matter, not privileged, which is relevant to the subject matter involved in the pending action, whether it relates to the claim or defense of the party seeking discovery or to the claim or defense of any other party, including the existence, description, nature, custody, condition and location of any books, documents, or other tangible things and the identity and location of persons having knowledge of any discoverable matter. The information sought need not be admissible at the trial if the information sought appears reasonably calculated to lead to the discovery of admissible evidence.

A court may consider some discovery requests **overbroad**. For example, if a party asks for all documents rather than specifying which type, or asks for documents covering a long period that goes beyond the scope of the case, the court may issue a **protective order**.

■ **REASONABLY CALCULATED**
Having any possibility that the question will result in the discovery of admissible evidence.

■ **OVERBROAD**
Beyond the appropriate scope. It can refer to discovery as well as to statutes, constitutional law, or court orders.

■ **PROTECTIVE ORDER**
A court order limiting or prohibiting conduct that would otherwise violate a right or be unduly burdensome.

In the following case, the court limited a discovery request to a nonparty that it considered overbroad.

CASE
WIWA V. ROYAL DUTCH PETROLEUM CO., 392 F.3D 812 (5TH CIR. 2004)

We find, however, that, as written, the subpoena's document request is overbroad. Oteri challenges the subpoena's request for all documents that relate to his dealings with the Nigerian government. Oteri has dealt with the Nigerian government for more than twenty years, even after he moved to the United States. This information clearly falls under the subpoena's request but is irrelevant to Kiobel's claim. Further, Oteri is correct in his assertion that the document request in the subpoena seeks personal information irrelevant to Kiobel's claim. For example, the subpoena, as worded now, encompasses personal information—such as Oteri's tax forms—that are irrelevant to Kiobel's claim. We therefore limit the substantive document request to corporate documents that (1) pertain solely to Oteri's position as security coordinator at Shell *and* (2) relate to Shell's alleged interactions with the Nigerian government and its treatment of the Ogoni.

Further, the subpoena requests all documents to which Oteri has "access." Oteri contends that the term "access" is overbroad because Federal Rule of Civil Procedure 34 requires only the production of documents in the "possession, custody, or control" of the person to whom the subpoena is directed. Oteri argues that the term "access" encompasses documents that he does not have under his "possession, custody, or control." We agree. The phrase "to which he has access" is overbroad; it would require the retrieval of documents from Nigeria—documents not under Oteri's custody, control, or possession, but to which he could conceivably have access by virtue of his prior position with Shell. We therefore limit the documents request in the subpoena to documents within Oteri's custody, control, or possession.

We also limit the temporal scope of the subpoena. Kiobel maintains that she requests only "documents concerning Mr. Oteri's contacts with the Nigerian government and military during a specific time period." Although the absence of a time frame in the subpoena belies Kiobel's contention, she notes that in her letter dated May 23 . . . she "specifically referenced Mr. Oteri's knowledge derived from his position as 'security coordinator' for Shell in Nigeria during the relevant period of the Complaint and his knowledge regarding Shell's complicity with the Nigerian government and military." Accordingly, we limit the document request to the period alleged in Kiobel's complaint and to the information described in the May 23 letter. We are satisfied that these modifications remedy the overbreadth of the subpoena's document request.

The court limited the document request by date, and whether or not the respondent had direct control over the requested documents.

TYPES OF DISCOVERY

Parties can obtain discovery on anything reasonably calculated to lead to the discovery of admissible evidence. In other words, even if something will not be admissible, it may still be subject to a legitimate discovery request. The federal rule indicates, "Parties may obtain discovery regarding any matter, not privileged, that is relevant to the claim or defense of any party, including the existence, description, nature, custody, condition, and location of any books, documents, or other tangible things and the identity and location of persons having knowledge of any discoverable matter." Fed. R. Civ. P. 26(b)(1). On the other hand, sound policy reasons back the rules of evidence that may exclude material from being admissible.

In the following case, the court considers which party should have the burden of proof regarding whether or not something is discoverable.

CASE
VARDON GOLF CO., INC. V. BBMG GOLF LTD., 156 F.R.D. 641
(N.D. ILL. 1994)

When an item is inadmissible as evidence at trial because of an exclusionary rule, the question then becomes whose burden it is to establish that the item is reasonably calculated to lead to the discovery of admissible evidence. Those courts placing the burden on the proponent of discovery follow *Bottaro v. Hatton Associates,* 96 F.R.D. 158 (E.D.N.Y. 1982) . . . . The *Bottaro* court held that because Congress intended to exclude certain items of evidence, the burden should be placed upon the proponent of discovery to make some "particularized showing" of a likelihood that admissible evidence will be generated by discovery of the information.

We believe that the *Bottaro* approach represents the proper course. The policies underlying exclusionary evidentiary rules have an equal if not stronger basis in our policy as the policies favoring sweeping discovery. The more logical approach to reconciling these divergent policies follows the path of *Bottaro.* To place the burden of proving that the evidence sought is not reasonably calculated to lead to the discovery of admissible evidence on the opponent of discovery is to ask that party to prove a negative. This is an unfair burden, as it would require a party to refute all possible alternative uses of the evidence, possibly including some never imagined by the proponent.

(continues)

> ## CASE
> ## VARDON GOLF CO., INC. V. BBMG GOLF LTD., 156 F.R.D. 641
> ## (N.D. ILL. 1994) *(continued)*
>
> We think, however, the *Bottaro* court overstated the nature of the proponent's burden. The Federal Rules of Civil Procedure do not speak to a "particularized showing," but to what is "reasonably calculated to lead to the discovery of admissible evidence." Therefore, we hold that where information sought in discovery would not be admissible due to an exclusionary rule in the Federal Rules of Evidence, the proponent of discovery may obtain discovery (1) by showing that the evidence is admissible for another purpose other than that barred by the Federal Rules of Evidence or (2) by articulating a plausible chain of inferences showing how discovery of the item sought would lead to other admissible evidence. The proponent may do this by simply articulating what kind of information it reasonably expects to find in the documents sought and how this will lead to other admissible evidence. The proponent need not show that the information expected is in fact in the items sought, but need only articulate why it is reasonable to believe that information of that nature would be revealed were discovery permitted.
>
> . . . Vardon's Second Set of Interrogatories seeks information relating to settlement negotiations between Vardon and Dunlop. Dunlop has objected to the question on the grounds that [Rule of Evidence 408] makes evidence relating to settlement negotiations inadmissible to prove the validity of the claim or its amount. Vardon counters that evidence of settlement negotiations is admissible on the question of a reasonable royalty. We view Vardon's argument as ignoring the obvious: that the amount of a reasonable royalty does relate, as a matter of fact, directly to the amount of a claim. This being the case, settlement evidence would be barred under [Rule 408]. Additionally, Vardon has made no showing that the settlement evidence is reasonably calculated to lead to discovery of other admissible evidence. Accordingly, since the interrogatory seeks inadmissible evidence, and since Vardon has made no showing that the interrogatories are reasonably calculated to lead to discovery of other admissible evidence, Vardon's motion to compel will be denied.

The court concluded that the party trying to obtain the discovery must show that it is reasonably calculated to lead to the discovery of admissible evidence, and that discovery of settlement negotiations would not lead to the discovery of admissible evidence.

Interrogatories

■ **INTERROGATORY**

A written question sent to a party that must be answered in writing, under oath.

Interrogatory is a fancy word for question. In discovery, it is a written question asked of a party that the other party must answer, unless it has a valid objection. Interrogatories may be sent only to another party. The other party then has 30 days to supply written, sworn answers to the interrogatories.

TEXAS RULE OF CIVIL PROCEDURE 197.1

A party may serve on another party—no later than 30 days before the end of the discovery period—written interrogatories to inquire about any matter within the scope of discovery except matters covered by Rule 195. An interrogatory may inquire whether a party makes a specific legal or factual contention and may ask the responding party to state the legal theories and to describe in general the factual bases for the party's claims or defenses, but interrogatories may not be used to require the responding party to marshal all of its available proof or the proof the party intends to offer at trial.

PASSIM CASE FIELDS VS. PRAIRIE BANK

Sample Interrogatories from Plaintiff to Defendant

1. Please list any employees at the bank who had access to my social security number or other personal data that could be used to steal my identity.

2. List any experts that you consulted on this case, including their address and telephone number, regardless of whether or not you intend to call the expert as a witness.

3. List any third-party entities or people who have access to my social security number or other personal data that could be used to steal my identity.

4. Describe any security measures that you presently have in place to protect your customers against identity theft.

5. Identify any changes to account security procedures that you have made since my identity was stolen.

In some jurisdictions, there is a limit on the number of interrogatories that may be asked. This has led to gamesmanship about how to write the interrogatories and how to count the number of questions. For example, look at this interrogatory and think about whether it should count as one interrogatory or more. If more, how many?

    (1) For each witness you intend to call, list their

      (a) name

      (b) address, and if not at the same address for the last five years, provide five years of address history

      (c) work and home phone number

      (d) place of employment

      (e) job title and if at this position for less than a year, job history for the last five years

      (f) expected subject of their testimony

Is it one interrogatory? Or is it six (a–f)? Or is it eight (a–f plus two parts to questions 1b and 1e)? Some interrogatories will even define words and the definitions will end up making what seems like one interrogatory into more. For example, before listing the actual questions, the interrogatories may list definitions such as "Identify means, with respect to a person, their name, address, phone number, and occupation." Then if the interrogatory is simply "Identify your witnesses," that could arguably count as four interrogatories.

In the following case, the court tries to determine how many interrogatories were asked.

CASE
BANKS V. OFFICE OF SENATE SERGEANT-AT-ARMS, 222 F.R.D. 7
(D.D.C. 2004)

By his Order of January 5, 2004, Judge Kennedy restricted the parties in these three consolidated cases to 30 interrogatories. Before that Order had issued, plaintiff served two sets of interrogatories. According to plaintiff, the first set of interrogatories was comprised of nineteen questions and the second eight, for a total of twenty-seven. S.A.A. sees it differently, insisting that one question in the first set (number 8) and seven in the second set (numbers 1–6 & 8) contained subparts and, when those subparts are counted as separate interrogatories, plaintiff has propounded many more interrogatories than Judge Kennedy permitted by the January 5, 2004 Order.

When Rule 33(a) was amended to limit the number of interrogatories that can be propounded, the draftsmen appreciated that the numerical restriction could be evaded by "joining as 'subparts' questions that seek information about discrete separate subjects." Therefore, the numerical limitation in the rule is stated as "not exceeding 25 in number including all discrete subparts."

Identifying a "discrete subpart" has proven difficult. While a draconian approach would be to view each participial phrase as a subpart, the courts have instead attempted to formulate more conceptual approaches, asking whether one question is subsumed and related to another or whether each question can stand alone and be answered irrespective of the answer to the others. But . . . this is anything but a bright-line test . . .

Perhaps a more pragmatic approach . . . would be to look at the way lawyers draft interrogatories and see if their typical approaches threaten the purpose of the rule by putting together in a single question distinct areas of inquiry that should be kept separate.

The first and most obvious example is the combining in a single interrogatory of a demand for information and a demand for the documents that pertain to that event. Clearly, these are two distinct demands because knowing that an event occurred is entirely different from learning about the documents that evidence it occurred. Thus, a demand for information about a certain event and for the documents about it should be counted as two separate interrogatories.

(continues)

CASE

BANKS V. OFFICE OF SENATE SERGEANT-AT-ARMS, 222 F.R.D. 7

(D.D.C. 2004) *(continued)*

Lawyers, sensitive to the numerical restriction, also subdivide interrogatories so that after they introduce a topic, they demand to know in detail all the particulars about it, frequently introducing their specific demands with the phrase "including but not limited to." Thus, they may ask their opponent to state whether a particular product was tested and then demand to know when the tests occurred, who performed them, how and where they were conducted and the result. In such a situation, all the questions relate to a single topic, testing, and it would unfair and draconian to view each of the demands as a separate interrogatory. This approach ends, however, the moment the interrogatory introduces a new topic that is in a distinct field of inquiry. Thus, in the "testing" example, asking how the results of the tests were used in any advertising about the product's fitness for a particular purpose would have to be viewed as a separate interrogatory.

After reviewing the interrogatories at issue, I find myself agreeing with SAA as to interrogatory 8 of the first set and interrogatories 2, 5, 6, and 8 of the second set, insofar as these interrogatories first demand information and then demand the documents pertaining to it.

I also find, however, that SAA is arguing in favor of using the draconian approach of counting every subdivision of an interrogatory as a separate question. I rejected that method as unfair. For example, in objecting to interrogatory 4 of the second set, SAA insists that asking about what duties plaintiff was given or had taken away is distinct from asking who added them or took them away. Those two topics are too intimately and logically connected to have to be divided into two separate questions.

The court rejected the approach of counting every subpart of a question as a separate question, instead focusing on whether the subpart is inherently related.

When interrogatories are answered, the party answering them first repeats the question and then gives the answer. For example, with our interrogatory example from above, when the bank answers the interrogatory, it will look something like this:

(1) For each witness you intend to call, list their
   (a) name
   (b) address, and if not at the same address for the last five years, provide five years of address history
   (c) work and home phone number
   (d) place of employment
   (e) job title and if at this position for less than a year, job history for the last five years
   (f) expected subject of their testimony

Answer
(a) Joe Schmolina
(b) 101 Bank Place

(c) 555-121-BANK
(d) Prairie Bank
(e) Bank President
(f) Bank procedures

(a) Mary Teller
(b) 101 Bank Place
(c) 555-121-BANK
(d) Prairie Bank
(e) Head Teller
(f) Teller procedures

The answer is signed under oath so that false answers would be perjury.

Requests for Production

According to the Federal Judicial Center, requests for production of documents are the most frequently utilized discovery tool, used in 84 percent of cases. Attorneys may request copies of documents or things. These are generally sent along at the same time as the interrogatories, usually as part of the same document. It may be titled "Plaintiff's Interrogatories and Requests for Production of Documents." Usually, the request is for copies of documents.

KENTUCKY RULE OF CIVIL PROCEDURE 34.01

Any party may serve on any other party a request (a) to produce and permit the party making the request, or someone acting on his behalf, to inspect and copy any designated documents (including writings, drawings, graphs, charts, photographs, phono-records, and other data compilations from which information can be obtained, translated, if necessary, by the respondent through detection devices into reasonably usable form), or to inspect and copy, test, or sample any tangible things which constitute or contain matters within the scope of Rule 26.02 and which are in the possession, custody or control of the party upon whom the request is served; or (b) to permit entry upon designated land or other property in the possession or control of the party upon whom the request is served for the purpose of inspection and measuring, surveying, photographing, testing, or sampling the property or any designated object or operation thereon, within the scope of Rule 26.02.

PASSIM CASE **FIELDS VS. PRAIRIE BANK**

In our case, requests might be made by Fields for records of all the transactions made by the identity thief, any surveillance tape that identified the thief, bank records regarding Fields's complaint of identity theft, and records of the activity on the Fields account during the time in question.

Occasionally, a mistake will be made and material that should not be disclosed is disclosed. For example, in one case a secretary sent a copy of an expert report to the other side with hand-written notes made by the attorneys on the report. Zapata v. IBP, Inc., 175 F.R.D. 574 (D. Kan., 1997). The court used a five-factor test to determine whether the **work product privilege** had been waived: "1. The reasonableness of the precautions taken to prevent inadvertent disclosure; 2. The time taken to rectify the error; 3. The scope of discovery; 4. The extent of disclosure; and 5. The overriding issue of fairness." This test is called the middle test, but there are two other approaches that other courts have adopted. One is that privilege is never waived by inadvertent disclosure, and the other is that disclosure automatically waives the privilege.

Depositions

A **deposition** is a hearing where a witness's testimony is transcribed by a court reporter. It typically takes place in a conference room of a law office with the lawyers, parties, court reporter, and occasionally a paralegal present, but the judge is not present. Usually, depositions of parties are taken, and less frequently, witnesses. To set up a deposition for a party, the attorneys usually discuss a mutually convenient time, and often each side takes the other party's deposition during the same time frame, such as the same day. If the **deponent** is a witness, the party desiring to take his or her deposition should serve the witness with a subpoena. If the party wants the witness to bring documents or material, the witness should be served with a **subpoena duces tecum**. If the deponent is another party, the party's lawyer should be served with a notice of deposition.

■ **WORK-PRODUCT PRIVILEGE**
A rule that allows a party to withhold information that was created by an attorney in anticipation of or during litigation.

■ **DEPOSITION**
A hearing usually held outside of the courtroom to record the testimony of a witness or party.

■ **DEPONENT**
A person whose deposition is being taken.

■ **SUBPOENA DUCES TECUM**
Court order to appear and produce specified things, usually documents.

PASSIM CASE   FIELDS VS. PRAIRIE BANK

NOTICE OF ORAL DEPOSITION OF PETER FIELDS AND SUBPOENA DUCES TECUM

TO: Peter Fields, by and through their attorney of record, _____
[attorney/firm/address]

PLEASE TAKE NOTICE that in accordance with Rule 114 of the State of Eden, the oral deposition of Peter Fields will be taken by Defendant to be used as testimony at trial of this case before a duly certified court reporter commencing on January 7, 2008 in the offices of Holstein and Ball.

A subpoena duces tecum is issued in accordance with Rule 114.2(b)(5) of the Eden Rules of Civil Procedure requiring the witness to bring and produce at the deposition the documents identified in the attached Exhibit "A."

Respectfully submitted,
[signature block]

A deposition does more than provide an opportunity to gather evidence. It also gives lawyers a chance to see how deponents perform as witnesses, how much they know, and what they will say. It really helps to evaluate a case to see how witnesses perform. Also, it locks deponents into their testimony so that if they try to change their story when they testify at the trial, the deposition transcript can be used to impeach them. Furthermore, if a deponent is not available to testify, the transcript can be read to the jury. Depositions also have the advantage of affording flexibility to ask follow-up questions and are more spontaneous, since they are in person.

PASSIM CASE

Deposition Excerpt of Anne, a Prairie Bank Teller

01 **Q** Were you working at the bank on July 7, 2003?

02 **Q** I don't recall.

03 **Q** If you signed teller slips and deposit slips with that

04   date, would that be an indication to you that you

05   worked that day?

06 **A** Yes.

07 **Q** Do you recall seeing someone in your teller line that

08   raised your suspicion about a bank customer?

09 **A** No.

10 **Q** Do you know the customers by sight?

11 **A** Sometimes. The regular ones I do.

12 **Q** Was Peter Fields a regular customer?

13 **A** He was a semi-regular.

14 **Q** If someone other than Peter Fields came into the bank

15   claiming to be him, would you know it?

16 **A** I think so. But we have a lot of customers and I'm

17   not that good at names and faces.

18 **Q** Is that why the bank has security procedures for

19   identifying customers attempting to make withdrawals?

20 **A** Correct.

Depositions may also be used to record testimony when it is known in advance that a witness will be unavailable at the trial or as a professional courtesy to doctors. The deposition will be recorded by a court reporter and a videotape technician. For example, in a personal injury suit, the defendant's medical expert and the plaintiff's treating physician may testify in this manner, thereby saving them a trip to court and avoiding a disruption to their always busy patient schedules. Then at trial, the videotape can be played.

Objections may be made by attorneys at depositions; however, since the judge is not present, no ruling is made. Generally, objections are noted for the record and witnesses answer the questions, unless their attorney instructs them not to answer due to a privilege, or to enforce a court-imposed limitation on the deposition. It is possible for a judge to get involved in a dispute about how a deposition is proceeding, but judges tend to discourage such mid-deposition phone calls, preferring to let the attorneys resolve matters on their own.

Usually, the attorneys are quite professional in a deposition. However, in the following case the court addresses a situation where an attorney behaved badly during a deposition.

CASE
FREEMAN V. SCHOINTUCK, 192 F.R.D. 187 (D. MD. 2000)

Defendants . . . have filed a motion to preclude one of the plaintiff's expert witnesses, Grace Ziem, M.D., from testifying at trial, because, they contend, she failed to comply with this Court's order of October 15, 1999, allowing the Defendants additional time to depose Dr. Ziem. In this order, the Court found that when originally deposed by the Defendants, Dr. Ziem's answers often were evasive, incomplete, and non-responsive. Accordingly, Defendants were given additional time to depose Dr. Ziem, and Plaintiff's counsel was warned that if she failed to give proper answers the Court would consider additional sanctions, including ordering that she not be permitted to testify at trial, as allowed by Fed.R.Civ.P. 37(b)(2)(B). Defendants contend that when Dr. Ziem was redeposed on January 18 and 19, 2000, she violated this Court's order, and, as a sanction, she should not be permitted to testify at trial . . . . For the reasons stated below, Defendants' motion is denied, and sanctions will be entered against Defendants' attorney, Mr. Brandon M. Gladstone, for his unprofessional conduct during the resumption of the Ziem deposition.

During the seven hours of the first day of Dr. Ziem's renewed deposition, January 18, 2000, Defendants' counsel repeatedly and flagrantly was insulting to Plaintiff's counsel and

(continues)

CASE
FREEMAN V. SCHOINTUCK, 192 F.R.D. 187 (D. MD. 2000) *(continued)*

Dr. Ziem . . . . Additionally, Defendants' counsel made antagonistic and hostile comments throughout the first day of the deposition . . . .

Defendants' counsel also was sarcastic throughout the deposition. Finally, Defendants' counsel frequently made threatening comments to the deponent and Plaintiff's counsel during the deposition.

Viewed as a whole, the conduct of Defendants' counsel during the first day of the deposition was appallingly unprofessional and discourteous, suggesting that he took the Court's orders allowing him additional time to depose Dr. Ziem, and ordering her to be responsive, as license to do whatever he wanted during the deposition. No one expects the deposition of a key witness in a hotly contested case to be a non-stop exchange of pleasantries. However, it must not be allowed to become an excuse for counsel to engage in acts of rhetorical road rage against a deponent and opposing counsel, using an order of the court as the vehicle for the abuse. While isolated acts of discourtesy or loss of temper can be expected, even from the best of counsel, and excused by the court, systematic and deliberate abuses such as displayed by Defendants' counsel during Dr. Ziem's deposition cannot go unsanctioned as they are destructive of the very fabric which holds together the process of pretrial discovery—cooperative exchange of information without the need for constant court intervention.

The court sanctioned the offending attorney and witness by barring the witness from testifying in the case. Also, note that the goal of the court with regard to discovery is to have the parties exchange information without the supervision of a judge. If parties were constantly looking to the court for answers during discovery, it would be a large drain on limited judicial resources.

Depositions via Written Questions

It is also possible to conduct a deposition using written questions. The party desiring to do so sends written questions to the witness, with copies to all other parties. Other parties may serve cross-examination questions, and the party requesting the deposition can then send redirect questions, and finally other parties can send re-cross questions. After all the questions are served, the witness answers them, theoretically in front of a stenographer, but in actual practice the witness probably works on the answers with his or her attorney and signs them in front of a notary public. This method is somewhat impractical in that all the questions, including what would be live follow-up questions at a live deposition or at a trial, are asked in advance. An example of a case where this rule was used involved an ill witness who lived out of town and who wanted to invoke his Fifth Amendment right against self-incrimination. Gatoil, Inc. v. Forest Hill State Bank, 104 F.R.D. 580 (D. Md.1985).

Requests for Admissions

Requests for admissions can be used to reduce discovery costs by establishing facts that are costly or difficult to prove. One party can ask another to admit some fact or application of law or admit that a document is genuine. The request cannot be solely to admit a matter of law. Requests can be made for undisputed facts or facts crucial for the case. Requests should call for a "yes" or "no" answer. The responding party can admit, deny, qualify, object, or claim a lack of knowledge; however, a failure to respond to a request for an admission can constitute an admission. Once something is admitted, it is conclusively established for the case and no further proof is required. Admissions made in one case are for that case only and may not be used for other cases.

Electronic Data Discovery and Computer Forensics

A new and quickly developing area of discovery is getting information from devices that store data, such as computers. Data from e-mails, Web pages, word processing, instant messaging, and handheld devices, as well as computers and servers, are subject to discovery. According to *Computer Technology Review*, 93 percent of corporate documents are created electronically and only 30 percent of those are ever printed out on paper. Large cases can involve billions of documents and several gigabytes of data stored on cache memory, magnetic disks (hard drives or floppy disks), optical disks (DVDs or CDs), magnetic tapes, cellular phones, personal digital assistants such as BlackBerry devices, voice mail, and digital copy systems.

BENCH BRIEF

NETFLIX, INC. CLASS ACTION SETTLEMENT AGREEMENT

In late 2004 and 2005, the parties conducted extensive discovery. Defendant produced, and Class Representative reviewed, approximately 100,000 pages of documents. Both parties served and answered interrogatories. Defendant deposed Class Representative. Class Representative deposed Netflix, Inc. through five of its employees over the course of seven days. Class Representative also deposed a third party.

It is well settled that electronic data and data compilations are discoverable and should be treated the same way as a request for documents that reside in a file cabinet. In some cases electronic production of documents may be required such that mere production of printed copies is insufficient. Copies of files may not be sufficient as bit-by-bit images may be required. This is because **metadata** can be lost. Backup tapes must be produced if relevant. A requesting party has been granted access not only to business data, but to the opposition's personal computer hard drive. Data and data compilations must be preserved so that the requesting party has access to deleted files.

"Technically, e-mail messages are permanently recorded since 'most e-mail programs keep copies of every message a user ever wrote, every message the user ever received, and every message the user deleted.' Although some e-mail services may offer the possibility of 'shredding' an e-mail message, arguably the equivalent of actually deleting it, the e-mail file may still be retrievable using certain software. 'A deleted file is really not a deleted file, it is merely organized differently.'" State v. Townsend, 57 P.3d 255 (Wash. 2002) (Bridge concurring).

■ **METADATA**
Data about data, such as the author, time, and date of a file.

BENCH BRIEF

EMBARRASSING E-MAILS

"Can I look forward to my waning years signing checks for fat people who are afraid of some silly lung problem?" (E-mail from a Wyeth-Ayerst administrator that later came back to haunt the company during fen-phen litigation.)

"It's a piece of [expletive deleted]" (Merrill Lynch analyst Henry Blodget's e-mail to a colleague when talking about 24/7 Media, an Internet company that Merrill Lynch rated as a buy, which cost the investment firm millions in a settlement with the New York attorney general when the e-mail was discovered.)

"We strongly suggest that before you leave for the holidays, you should catch up on file cleaning." (Frank Quattrone, an executive at Credit Suisse First Boston (CSFB) just after an investigation was announced. A colleague had suggested the language in a note, saying "Today it's administrative housekeeping. Tomorrow, it could be improper destruction of evidence.")

Reports and data normally generated in the ordinary course of business are subject to discovery. However, a discovery request cannot require the responding party to create new reports.

There are companies such as Kroll Ontrack that can make a forensic examination of a data-containing device and retrieve the information, even if someone has tried to delete the data. Parties can be ordered to turn over raw computer data for the other side to process. There are also software programs that can help organize electronic discovery such as Mobius.

BENCH BRIEF

COMMON MISTAKES IN COMPUTER FORENSICS

Kroll Ontrack Continuing Legal Education Seminar, March 2005

- Boot the computer / Access Files
- Open a hard drive outside of a clean room
- Failure to perform analysis of an image
- Failure to create a sector-by-sector image
- Failure to Maintain chain of custody

BENCH BRIEF ETHICS ALERT

It is possible to unintentionally **spoliate** electronic evidence. Through the regular use of a computer, important data may disappear. Courts have entered severe sanctions against parties who have allowed the spoliation of electronic evidence, including fines, unfavorable jury instructions, prohibiting witnesses from testifying, and even default judgment. In short, attorneys and paralegals have a duty to make sure that all electronic sources of discovery are located and searched to comply with discovery requests.

■ **SPOLIATE**
To destroy, hide, or damage evidence intentionally.

BENCH BRIEF

COMMON MISTAKES IN ELECTRONIC DATA COLLECTION

Kroll Ontrack Continuing Legal Education Seminar, March 2005

- Failing to have a plan
- Failing to prioritize the data
- Neglecting to conduct thorough interviews
- Ignoring key data locations and file types
- Doing a do-it yourself data collection (or having the company's information technology department do it themselves)
- Failing to properly image files
- Ignoring alternative file names
- Failing to maintain chain of custody

Costs for electronic discovery are evaluated and assessed differently than other discovery costs. A federal court in New York, which had previously issued an opinion on this topic that had been considered the gold standard by several other courts, articulated an improvement on its own test to determine which party should pay for the cost of electronic discovery. It announced a seven-factor test designed to balance the importance of the evidence sought against the cost of producing it.

CASE
ZUBULAKE V. UBS WARBURG LLC, 217 F.R.D. 309 (S.D.N.Y., 2003.)

1. The extent to which the request is specifically tailored to discover relevant information;
2. The availability of such information from other sources;
3. The total cost of production, compared to the amount in controversy;
4. The total cost of production, compared to the resources available to each party;
5. The relative ability of each party to control costs and its incentive to do so;
6. The importance of the issues at stake in the litigation; and
7. The relative benefits to the parties of obtaining the information.

(continues)

> **CASE**
> **ZUBULAKE V. UBS WARBURG LLC, 217 F.R.D. 309 (S.D.N.Y., 2003.)** *(continued)*
>
> …Whenever a court applies a multi-factor test, there is a temptation to treat the factors as a check-list, resolving the issue in favor of whichever column has the most checks. But "we do not just add up the factors." When evaluating cost-shifting, the central question must be, does the request impose an "undue burden or expense" on the responding party? Put another way, "how important is the sought-after evidence in comparison to the cost of production?" The seven-factor test articulated above provide some guidance in answering this question, but the test cannot be mechanically applied at the risk of losing sight of its purpose.

The Federal Rules of Civil Procedure were amended in December 2006 to deal with electronic discovery. The amendments require a meeting among the parties to discuss electronic data discovery, limit discovery of electronic information to that which is readily accessible, allow objections in certain circumstances, and prohibit sanctions where data was lost due to routine deletion.

According to an American Bar Association survey of experienced corporate counsel, meetings to discuss electronic discovery among counsel were only occurring about 25 percent of the time prior to the amendments. When they did occur, however, the parties were able to resolve how to conduct the electronic discovery 90 percent of the time. Parties apparently often agreed to produce data in multiple formats including paper, searchable and nonsearchable PDF, and as stored in the ordinary course of business.

PROBLEMS WITH DISCOVERY

A number of problems can arise during discovery. Sometimes responding parties provide incomplete answers, refuse to turn over requested information, or raise a privilege as a defense to a request. Parties may make requests that go beyond what would be appropriate for the case, or go too far considering the amount at stake and the burden of complying with a request. Also, either side may let the heat of battle get to them and step out of bounds by being unprofessional or by abusing the discovery process.

Continuing Duty to Disclose

Parties have a continuing duty to update their discovery responses so that if a party finds a mistake or omission, or something changes, it needs to alert the other parties. In addition to a discovery deadline, some courts may also have a deadline for supplementing discovery replies.

> ### FEDERAL RULE OF CIVIL PROCEDURE 26(E)
>
> **Supplementation of Disclosures and Responses.**
>
> A party who has made a disclosure under subdivision (a) or responded to a request for discovery with a disclosure or response is under a duty to supplement or correct the disclosure or response to include information thereafter acquired if ordered by the court or in the following circumstances:
>
> (1)   A party is under a duty to supplement at appropriate intervals its disclosures under subdivision (a) if the party learns that in some material respect the information disclosed is incomplete or incorrect and if the additional or corrective information has not otherwise been made known to the other parties during the discovery process or in writing. With respect to testimony of an expert from whom a report is required under subdivision (a)(2)(B) the duty extends both to information contained in the report and to information provided through a deposition of the expert, and any additions or other changes to this information shall be disclosed by the time the party's disclosures under Rule 26(a)(3) are due.
>
> (2)   A party is under a duty seasonably to amend a prior response to an interrogatory, request for production, or request for admission if the party learns that the response is in some material respect incomplete or incorrect and if the additional or corrective information has not otherwise been made known to the other parties during the discovery process or in writing.

A party that fails to supplement its discovery replies as required may be sanctioned by having the evidence that was not supplemented excluded.

Privileges, Protections, and Abuse

Certain discovery requests may be problematic due to privileges that prohibit a party from answering the request or question. When a party determines that a privilege prohibits it from answering a discovery request, it can state an objection to the question on that basis and refuse to answer. The most common privileges that are asserted during discovery include the attorney-client privilege, and its close relative, the work product privilege.

A party may also move the court for a protective order, either to try to avoid having to answer questions based upon privilege, or to have the court protect sensitive information such as trade secrets. If a trade secret is relevant to the case, the court may order the party to disclose, but also order the requesting party to keep the information confidential.

Both parties seeking discovery and those responding to it are capable of discovery abuse. The requesting party may seek information that is not reasonably calculated to lead to the discovery of admissible evidence or that is overbroad and burdensome to produce. The responding party may not respond, or may respond with reams of irrelevant data in a sort of needle-in-the-haystack response, or may respond in a vague and unhelpful manner.

When a party does not respond properly (or at all), or raises a privilege, the requesting party may make a **motion to compel**. This motion typically asks the court to order the responding party to respond properly and to pay attorney fees incident to making the motion. Before filing such a motion, the attorneys for each side should try to discuss and iron out their differences.

A privilege that applies directly to paralegals is the attorney-client privilege. The attorney-client privilege protects attorneys from having to reveal information about their clients. In the following case, a law firm is disqualified because it hired away a paralegal who had been working on the other side of a case.

■ **MOTION TO COMPEL**

A motion requesting the court to order another party to answer a discovery request.

CASE
IN RE COMPLEX ASBESTOS LITIGATION, 232 CAL. APP. 3D 572 (CAL. APP. IST. 1991).

Attorney Jeffrey B. Harrison . . . appeal[s] from an order disqualifying the Harrison firm in nine asbestos-related personal injury actions. The appeal presents the difficult issue of whether a law firm should be disqualified because an employee of the firm possessed attorney-client confidences from previous employment by opposing counsel in pending litigation. We hold that disqualification is appropriate unless there is written consent or the law firm has effectively screened the employee from involvement with the litigation to which the information relates . . . .

Michael Vogel worked as a paralegal for the law firm of Brobeck, Phleger & Harrison (Brobeck) from October 28, 1985, to November 30, 1988.

During most of the period Brobeck employed Vogel, he worked on settlement evaluations. He extracted information from medical reports, discovery responses, and plaintiffs' depositions for entry on "Settlement Evaluation and Authority Request" (SEAR) forms. The SEAR forms were brief summaries of the information and issues used by the defense attorneys and their clients to evaluate each plaintiff's case. The SEAR forms were sent to the clients.

Vogel attended many defense attorney meetings where the attorneys discussed the strengths and weaknesses of cases to reach consensus settlement recommendations for each case. The SEAR forms were the primary informational materials the attorneys used at the meetings. Vogel also monitored trial events, received daily reports from the attorneys in trial, and relayed trial reports to the clients. Vogel reviewed plaintiffs' interrogatory answers to get SEAR form data and to assess whether the answers were adequate or further responses were needed.

In 1988, Vogel's duties changed when he was assigned to work for a trial team. With that change, Vogel no longer was involved with the settlement evaluation meetings and

(continues)

CASE
IN RE COMPLEX ASBESTOS LITIGATION, 232 CAL. APP. 3D 572
(CAL. APP. 1ST. 1991). *(continued)*

reports. Instead, he helped prepare specific cases assigned to the team. Vogel did not work on any cases in which the Harrison firm represented the plaintiffs ...

Brobeck gave Vogel two weeks' notice of his termination, though his termination date was later extended to the end of November ....

A critical incident involving Vogel's activities at Brobeck first came to light during the hearing. Brobeck's computer system access log showed that on November 17, 1988, Vogel accessed the computer records for 20 cases filed by the Harrison firm. On the witness stand, Vogel at first flatly denied having looked at these case records, but when confronted with the access log, he admitted reviewing the records "to see what kind of cases [the Harrison firm] had filed." At the time, Vogel had no responsibilities for any Harrison firm cases at Brobeck. The date Vogel reviewed those computer records was very close to the time Vogel and Harrison first spoke. The access log documented that Vogel opened each record long enough to view and print copies of all the information on the case in the computer system.

The case information on the computer included the SEAR form data .... Vogel, Harrison, and the other two witnesses from the Harrison firm denied that Vogel ever disclosed any client confidences obtained while he worked for Brobeck. However, Harrison never instructed Vogel not to discuss any confidential information obtained at Brobeck .... During the course of the hearing, the Harrison firm terminated Vogel on August 25, 1989 ....

Absent written consent, the proper rule and its application for disqualification based on nonlawyer employee conflicts of interest should be as follows. The party seeking disqualification must show that its present or past attorney's former employee possesses confidential attorney-client information materially related to the proceedings before the court .... Once this showing has been made, a rebuttable presumption arises that the information has been used or disclosed in the current employment .... To rebut the presumption, the challenged attorney has the burden of showing that the practical effect of formal screening has been achieved. The showing must satisfy the trial court that the employee has not had and will not have any involvement with the litigation, or any communication with attorneys or coemployees concerning the litigation, that would support a reasonable inference that the information has been used or disclosed. If the challenged attorney fails to make this showing, then the court may disqualify the attorney and law firm.

The court disqualified the paralegal's firm from handling the cases.

BENCH BRIEF   Ethics Alert

The work-product doctrine applies to documents prepared in anticipation of litigation or for trial. It provides qualified immunity to discovery so that documents that are work product need to be disclosed only when there is a substantial need and there is no other way to get the information.

In a New York case, a paralegal had taken notes on some documents that were produced as part of a discovery response. However, the party that produced the documents blocked out the notes, citing the work-product privilege because the notes were made for litigation on another case. Also, the court noted that the work of a paralegal is subject to the work-product doctrine. Therefore, the court upheld the claim of work product and the disclosing party did not have to turn over the notes. Fine v. Facet Aerospace Products Co., 133 F.R.D. 439 S.D.N.Y., 1990.

Other privileges that might be the basis for an objection to a discovery request or the basis for a protective order include patient-doctor, patient-therapist, clergy-parishoner, and spousal privileges.

Sanctions

Occasionally, discovery abuse gets bad enough that the court may find it necessary to sanction the offending party. In the following case the court imposes a severe sanction on a party that did not sufficiently answer some discovery questions.

CASE

COMPAQ COMPUTER CORP. V. ERGONOME INC., 387 F.3D 403

(5TH CIR. 2004)

On March 26, 2001, the district court held Ergonome, Inc., Brown, and Mowrey in contempt of court for failing to respond adequately to Compaq's discovery requests. While the court declined at that time to find that Brown was the alter ego of Ergonome as a matter of law, the court cautioned that if the discovery was not provided within thirty days, it would be "prepared to do so in light of Defendants' long history of filibuster and delay on the matter." ...

First, any sanction must be 'just'; second, the sanction must be specifically related to the particular 'claim' which was at issue in the order to provide discovery. Based on the facts and circumstances surrounding the district court's decision, we conclude that the

(continues)

> ### CASE
> ### COMPAQ COMPUTER CORP. V. ERGONOME INC., 387 F.3D 403
> ### (5TH CIR. 2004) *(continued)*
>
> sanction was "just." Compaq struggled for well over two years to obtain sufficient alter ego discovery from Brown and Ergonome. Brown and Ergonome engaged in abusive practices for the sole purpose of frustrating Compaq's ability to extract the discovery. The district court was not alone in its assessment of the delaying tactics. In denying Ergonome's third petition for writ of mandamus, this court warned that "[t]he mandamus petition is arguably frivolous and would entitle the opposing party to attorneys' fees." Additionally, the bankruptcy court found that Ergonome's suggestion of bankruptcy was filed solely to avoid potential liability in the Compaq litigation. The entire egregious course of overlitigation and discovery abuse is among the worst we have seen.

A concurring judge noted that the result of the sanction was to impose personal liability on an individual defendant for $2.8 million in attorney fees.

DISCOVERY IN CRIMINAL CASES

Discovery in criminal cases is generally somewhat analogous to the modern federal civil discovery rules in that an almost automatic exchange of information occurs, except that the defendant determines whether or not to invoke the discovery rule that causes the exchange. The defendant typically makes a request for the government to disclose its evidence. This request requires the government to disclose the content of any statement the defendant made to a law officer, including copies of any written statements, the defendant's grand jury testimony (if there was any, which there usually is not), a summary of any expert witness testimony the government intends to present in its **case in chief**, and the defendant's prior criminal record. The defendant must also be allowed, upon request, to "inspect and to copy or photograph books, papers, documents, data, photographs, tangible objects, buildings or places, or copies or portions of any of these items, if the item is within the government's possession, custody, or control" if the item is relevant, or part of the evidence the government intends to produce, or the item belongs to the defendant. Fed. R. Crim. P. 16. The government is not required to turn over witness statements until after the witness has testified at trial.

There is a price that the defendant pays in making the discovery request, however, because upon doing so, the government is entitled to receive reciprocal discovery from the defendant (as long as the government complies with the defendant's discovery request). The government must be allowed to "inspect and to copy or photograph books, papers, documents, data, photographs, tangible objects, buildings or places, or copies or portions of any of these items . . . the results or reports of any physical or mental examination and of any scientific test or experiment . . ." if the defendant has possession or control over them and the defendant intends to use the

■ **CASE IN CHIEF**
The portion of a party's case in which it calls witnesses and presents evidence. It excludes rebuttal witnesses.

EXHIBIT 4–1   Table comparing discovery aspects of the federal civil discovery rules, both before and after they were amended and federal criminal discovery rules.

	OLD FEDERAL DISCOVERY RULES	NEW FEDERAL DISCOVERY RULES	FEDERAL RULES OF CRIMINAL PROCEDURE
Followed by most states	Yes	No	Yes
Automatic initial discovery requirements	No	Yes	No, but requests are usually standard
Defendant owes reciprocal discovery	No	No	Yes
Depositions	Yes	Yes	Rare
Requests for admission	Yes	Yes	No
Interrogatories	Yes	Yes	No
Requests for production	Yes	Yes	No

EXHIBIT 4-1   Table comparing discovery aspects of the federal civil discovery rules, both before and after they were amended and federal criminal discovery rules.

material during the defendant's case in chief. Fed. R. Crim. P. 16. Also parallel with the government's disclosure duty is the requirement that the defendant turn over a statement regarding his or her expert witnesses' testimony. The defendant is not required to disclose "reports, memoranda, or other documents made by the defendant, or the defendant's attorney or agent, during the case's investigation or defense" or statements made to the defendant or his attorney, or witness statements.

As with civil discovery, the parties in a criminal case also have a continuing duty to disclose new material evidence that they encounter while the case is pending. (See Exhibit 4-1 for a comparison of civil and criminal discovery.)

Therefore, it is typical for each side to exchange information such as names, addresses, and telephone numbers of witnesses. The prosecutor may request information regarding a defendant's planned alibi defense and any alibi witnesses. The defendant must also notify the prosecutor of certain defenses such as mental illness or that the defendant was acting with the authorization of a public official. Depositions are generally taken in criminal cases only to preserve evidence in exceptional cases, or if the parties agree. There are no requests for admission or interrogatories in criminal cases.

There is no constitutional right for a defendant to receive discovery, but the state has a duty to turn over **exculpatory evidence** to the defense. This is called the **Brady rule**, named after the U.S. Supreme Court case *Brady v. Maryland*, which held that a prosecutor violates the defendant's constitutional rights under the Due Process Clause when the government fails to disclose material evidence favorable to the defendant. Brady v. Maryland, 373 U.S. 83 (1963).

■ **EXCULPATORY EVIDENCE**
Material that tends to negate one or more elements of a crime.

■ **BRADY RULE**
A rule derived from a United States Supreme Court case that requires a prosecutor to disclose to the defense evidence that is favorable to the defendant.

SUMMARY

The discovery process is an important way to get evidence for a pending case and to find out what evidence the other side has available to present. Information can be gathered through a variety of discovery techniques such as depositions, interrogatories, requests for production of documents, and requests for admissions. The goal of the discovery process is a free-flowing exchange of information among the parties without court supervision. Anything that is reasonably calculated to lead to the discovery of admissible evidence is subject to a discovery request. A request that goes beyond that limit is subject to a protective order. A lot of discovery now seeks information stored on electronic equipment such as computers and BlackBerry devices. Parties can go too far in what they are asking for, and they can be too lax in their responses. Abuse of the process can result in sanctions, which can include awards of attorney fees. Sometimes a party will have a legitimate objection to a discovery request, such as a privilege, and may move for a protective order.

■ KEY TERMS

Brady rule	interrogatory	reasonably calculated
case in chief	metadata	spoliate
deponent	motion to compel	subpoena duces tecum
deposition	overbroad	work-product privilege
exculpatory evidence	protective order	

■ HELPFUL WEB LINKS

http://www.krollontrack.com/

http://www.nala.org/

http://www.mobius.com/

http://www.josephnyc.com/

http://www.uscourts.gov/rules/newrules6.html

■ REVIEW AND DISCUSSION QUESTIONS

1. What are the advantages and disadvantages of using discovery as a method of finding evidence?

2. What is the most effective method of discovery?

3. Write interrogatories and requests for production of documents to Prairie Bank.

4. Are there limits in your state for the number of interrogatories that can be asked? Are there other limits on discovery? Are there local rules within your state that affect discovery?

5. The lawyer you are working for wants you to handle the discovery in a case involving data from a computer with a damaged hard drive. What steps are you going to take to preserve the data? What things are you going to avoid?

6. How many interrogatory questions are in the following? Why do you reach that conclusion?:

   For each bank account that you have had access to during the past three years, indicate the (a) bank, (b) account number, (c) current balance, (d) interest payments received, (e) any deposits or additions, and (f) any withdrawals, checks, or other reduction in the funds available.

7. What can an attorney learn from a deposition?

8. What factors are considered when determining which party pays for the costs of discovery?

9. How do discovery rules differ between civil and criminal cases?

10. What are some significant differences between the modern federal discovery rules and the original version?

11. What discovery tools are available in your state?

12. What are some ways to manage a large amount of electronic data?

13. What is the best discovery tool and why?

14. When does the work-product doctrine apply to paralegals?

15. If you switched from working for the law firm representing our client to working for the firm representing the other party, what would the new firm have to do?

16. How does discovery in criminal cases differ from civil cases?

17. What are the differences between criminal discovery, the first version of the Federal Rules of Civil Procedure governing discovery, and the modern amendments to those rules?

■ LEGAL RESEARCH PROJECTS

1. Get a copy of one of the cases excerpted in this chapter and read all of it. Brief the case by providing a summary of the facts, the legal issue, the holding, and the court's reasoning.

2. Find a list of interrogatories for a personal injury case and adapt it for the Passim case.

3. Find a case in your jurisdiction regarding a discovery dispute and brief it by providing a summary of the facts, the legal issue, the holding, and the court's reasoning.

For additional resources, visit our Web site at www.westlegalstudies.com

CHAPTER 7

Courtesy CartoonStock.com.
www.CartoonStock.com

CHAPTER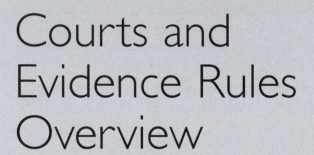

Courts and Evidence Rules Overview

■ OBJECTIVES _____

❏ Diagram a *big picture* of the court system
❏ Recall an overview of the rules of evidence
❏ Identify how a court might keep evidence in or out
❏ Analyze whether the rules of evidence will apply to a tribunal
❏ Analyze whether the rules of evidence will apply at a particular stage of a case
❏ Examine rules of evidence regarding foundation and chain of custody
❏ Summarize how facts can be established without evidence through judicial notice, admissions, and stipulations

OVERVIEW OF THE COURT SYSTEM

There are two main sets of courts, federal and state. Certain cases belong in each court.

Federal Courts

Federal courts are courts of limited jurisdiction. There must be something special about a case in order for it to be brought to federal court. For example, it could be a border dispute between states, or it could involve a question of federal law, or it could be a suit where all the defendants live in a state other than the one where the plaintiff lives and the amount in controversy exceeds $75,000. Therefore, there are no divorce, probate, or real estate title disputes in federal court. For a criminal case to be brought in federal court, it must arise under a federal criminal statute, or occur on federal or tribal land. Patent and bankruptcy cases are always federal. Two of the most frequently filed civil cases in federal courts are product liability and other torts, and employment discrimination, according to the Judicial Business of the United States Courts, *Annual Report of the Director, 2000–2004*, Table C–2A.

Federal courts are divided into 94 districts. Each state has at least one district, while large states such as California and New York have several. Each district has district court judges who are appointed by the president and confirmed by the Senate and receive lifetime appointments. Those judges may choose to hire magistrate judges who do "a staggering volume of judicial work" Peretz v. United States, 501 U.S. 923, 928-29 n. 5 (1991). However, magistrate judges do not have lifetime appointments and serve only eight-year terms. Decisions of the district court may be appealed to one of the 13 federal courts of appeal, which are made up of the First through the Eleventh Circuits, the District of Columbia Circuit, and the Federal Circuit (see Exhibit 5–1).

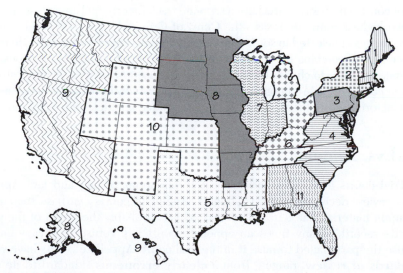

EXHIBIT 5–1   The 13 Federal Courts of Appeal

The U.S. Supreme Court is the highest court in the land. It hears border and water disputes between states, appeals from federal circuit courts of appeal, and cases raising federal constitutional questions. It is the court of last resort. Except for when it has original jurisdiction in a dispute, it is free to accept or decline to hear cases as it sees fit. Out of the approximately 8,000 cases that come before it annually, the Supreme Court issued only 83 to 91 opinions per year between 1999 and 2003, according to the Judicial Business of the United States Courts, *Annual Report of the Director, 2000–2004*, Table A–1.

State Courts

State courts are courts of general or residual jurisdiction. Any case that cannot be brought in federal court is brought in state court. Most cases are filed in state court. Conservative estimates place domestic relations cases such as divorce at between 25 and 30 percent of state court civil cases, while some authorities say it is more than half, according to Catherine J. Ross, "The Failure of Fragmentation: The Promise of a System of Unified Family Courts," 3 *Family Law Quarterly* 3, 6 and n. 8 (Spring 1998).

State court systems have various quirks and differences. For example, in most states, the Supreme Court is the state's high court. However, in New York, the Supreme Court is the trial-level court and the highest court in the state is the Court of Appeals. Most states follow English common law, but Louisiana follows both English common law and a civil code originally based upon French law.. Some states have intermediate courts of appeal such as the Minnesota Court of Appeals; other states have only one appellate court, such as the Supreme Court of North Dakota. Some states have various specialty courts that hear only certain types of cases such as family, probate, or criminal cases (see Exhibit 5–2), while other states have only one type of court. The Texas courts have a separate track for criminal appeals so that there are two highest courts in Texas—the Court of Criminal Appeals and the Supreme Court. Judges are elected in some states, appointed in others, and in still others there is some type of combination such as initial appointment followed by elections.

States are free to choose their own rules of procedure, evidence, and a structure for their court system. Additionally, some rules may vary by location within a state, such as in California where there are separate rules and fee schedules for many counties.

Trial vs. Appeal

Trial courts hear cases and make determinations of fact and law. Appellate courts review decisions of the trial court. Appellate courts can base their review only upon material that is in the **record**. This is probably the origin of the phrase "for the record." Many times an appellate court will refuse to review an issue because the party failed to raise it in the trial court. Appellate courts have varying **standards of review**, ranging from a **clearly erroneous** standard to **de novo**. Questions of fact are generally given a clearly erroneous review, while questions of

■ RECORD
Material that was compiled in the trial court, including transcripts of witness testimony, exhibits, and filings.

■ STANDARD OF REVIEW
A measure of how much deference an appellate court will give to a ruling or finding of a trial court.

■ CLEARLY ERRONEOUS
A standard of review that gives a very high level of deference to the trial court's ruling. Unless there was no support for the holding in the record, the trial court's ruling will stand.

■ DE NOVO
A standard of review that gives no deference to the trial court's ruling. The appellate court decides the issue for itself, without regard for how the trial court ruled.

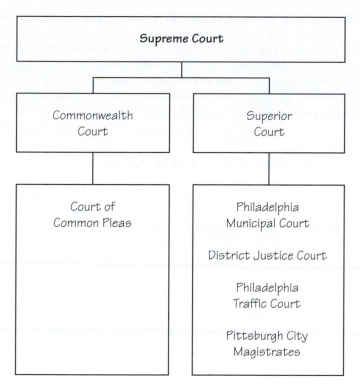

EXHIBIT 5–2   The Pennsylvania court structure divides cases by topic among different types of courts

law are generally reviewed de novo. Because appellate review is limited to that which is on the record, it is extremely important to enter on the record anything that a party would want an appellate court to see. Sometimes a trial court's ruling that evidence should not be admitted will cause the party offering it to make an **offer of proof** in order to protect the record.

OVERVIEW OF THE RULES OF EVIDENCE

Now that we have covered how evidence is gathered, it is time to learn how to find out if evidence is admissible. The rules of evidence, and sometimes other laws, govern what is admissible and inadmissible. If something is admissible, the court will let it into evidence. If the evidence is testimony, and if it is admissible, the jury will hear it and may consider it. If the evidence is a document, the jury may bring the document into the deliberation room and look at it. If it is an item such as a weapon they may look at that as well.

If something is inadmissible, the judge will try to keep the evidence out of the hearing or sight of the jury. The judge may take precautions to avoid exposing the jury

■ **OFFER OF PROOF**
Placing excluded evidence on the record, outside the presence of the jury.

■ **ORDER IN LIMINE**

(pronounced lim'-in-ee) Court directive not to refer to certain inadmissible evidence.

■ **OBJECTION**

A protest by an attorney that a question calls for, or an exhibit or testimony is, inadmissible material.

■ **SUSTAINED**

A ruling by the judge that an objection was proper and that the question should not be answered, or the evidence should not be admitted.

■ **OVERRULED**

A ruling by the judge that an objection was not valid so that the question can be answered or the evidence or testimony considered.

■ **FOUNDATION**

Evidence about evidence that establishes its admissibility, such as by showing that an item is what it purports to be.

■ **CHAIN OF CUSTODY**

A series of people and movements that caused an object to get from the incident to court, where it is presented as evidence.

to inadmissible evidence by issuing **orders in limine**, warnings to the attorneys, and rulings on objections. If the precautions fail and evidence that the jury should not hear or see is presented, the judge may order the jury to disregard the material.

During a trial, if an attorney makes an **objection** and the judge **sustains** the objection, the question is not answered, or the jury is instructed to disregard the answer. If an objection is **overruled**, the witness may answer the question, or the exhibit may be entered into evidence.

FEDERAL RULES OF EVIDENCE

The Federal Rules of Evidence govern cases heard in federal courts, including bankruptcy courts and district courts. In states that have adopted the federal rules, or follow them, the rules typically apply in their trial courts as well.

History

Prior to the adoption of the federal rules, evidence rulings were based upon case law precedent. However, it was very cumbersome to read many cases in the middle of a trial to learn the current state of the law. So mistakes were made, and rulings were inconsistent. Therefore, an advisory committee was established to draft Proposed Federal Rules of Evidence, which were passed by Congress and became law in 1975.

Where Adopted

Forty-one states have adopted some form of the Federal Rules of Evidence (FRE). (See Exhibit 5–3.) Only California, Georgia, Illinois, Kansas, Massachusetts, Missouri, New York, Vermont, Virginia, and Washington DC have not adopted the Federal Rules of Evidence in some form. Some states that have not adopted the FRE as a whole may have adopted certain portions, or look to them as persuasive authority. States that have not adopted the FRE usually have their own evidence code or rules they have relied upon since before the advent of the federal rules and they have never switched. For both states that have adopted the FRE and those that have not, cases often shed light on how a court will treat the admissibility of evidence.

FOUNDATION AND CHAIN OF CUSTODY

Foundation and **chain of custody** evidence proves that the evidence being offered in court is authentic: that is, the knife being paraded around by the prosecutor is the murder weapon; the voice on the voice mail message being offered belongs to the victim; the checking account statement is really from the bank and really pertains to the defendant's account.

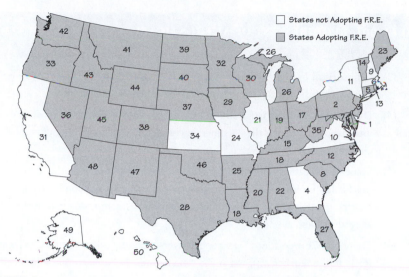

EXHIBIT 5–3   Which States Have Adopted the Federal Rules of Evidence

Foundation

As the foundation of a building supports the building's weight, in the context of evidence, foundation evidence supports the admission of other evidence. Foundation evidence supports the idea that an object is what the person offering it is claiming it to be. For example, suppose a party offers a voice mail message from a woman into evidence by testifying that he knows the woman's voice and that he recognizes it as her voice on the message. That would establish a foundation for the message.

RULE 901. REQUIREMENT OF AUTHENTICATION OR IDENTIFICATION

(a)   General Provision. The requirement of authentication or identification as a condition precedent to admissibility is satisfied by evidence sufficient to support a finding that the matter in question is what its proponent claims.

(b)   Illustrations. By way of illustration only, and not by way of limitation, the following are examples of authentication or identification conforming with the requirements of this rule:

(1)   Testimony of Witness With Knowledge. Testimony that a matter is what it is claimed to be.

(2)   Nonexpert Opinion on Handwriting. Nonexpert opinion as to the genuineness of handwriting, based upon familiarity not acquired for purposes of the litigation.

(continues)

RULE 901. REQUIREMENT OF AUTHENTICATION OR IDENTIFICATION
(continued)

(3) Comparison by Trier or Expert Witness. Comparison by the trier of fact or by expert witnesses with specimens which have been authenticated.

(4) Distinctive Characteristics and the Like. Appearance, contents, substance, internal patterns, or other distinctive characteristics taken in conjunction with circumstances.

(5) Voice Identification. Identification of a voice, whether heard firsthand or through mechanical or electronic transmission or recording, by opinion based upon hearing the voice at any time under circumstances connecting it with the alleged speaker.

(6) Telephone Conversations. Telephone conversations, by evidence that a call was made to the number assigned at the time by the telephone company to a particular person or business, if (A) in the case of a person, circumstances, including self-identification, show the person answering to be the one called, or (B) in the case of a business, the call was made to a place of business and the conversation related to business reasonably transacted over the telephone.

(7) Public Records or Reports. Evidence that a writing authorized by law to be recorded or filed and in fact recorded or filed in a public office, or a purported public record, report, statement, or data compilation, in any form, is from the public office where items of this nature are kept.

(8) Ancient Documents or Data Compilations. Evidence that a document or data compilation, in any form, (A) is in such condition as to create no suspicion concerning its authenticity, (B) was in a place where it, if authentic, would likely be, and (C) has been in existence 20 years or more at the time it is offered.

(9) Process or System. Evidence describing a process or system used to produce a result and showing that the process or system produces an accurate result.

(10) Methods Provided by Statute or Rule. Any method of authentication or identification provided by Act of Congress or by other rules prescribed by the Supreme Court pursuant to statutory authority.

Note that the rule contains illustrations only and that they are not the exclusive way to establish foundation for the items discussed in the rule. In the following divorce case the court considers the foundation of a financial statement.

CASE

IN RE MARRIAGE OF POLSON, 2000 WL 1880483 (MONT. 2000)

The requirement of authentication or identification as a condition precedent to admissibility is satisfied by evidence sufficient to support a finding that the thing in question is what the proponent claims. The District Court ruled that Marcia failed to lay adequate foundation for the admittance of her proposed Exhibit B, a financial statement. Marcia attempted to introduce this proposed exhibit through Andrew's testimony at trial. However, Andrew was not sure if the signature on Exhibit B was his. Further, when Marcia's counsel inquired whether Andrew provided the information contained in proposed Exhibit B to the bank, he replied "I'm not sure that I told the bank anything." In order to use a witness to authenticate a proposed illustration, the witness must testify that the illustration is what it is claimed to be. We agree that Marcia failed to provided an adequate foundation.

The problem here was that Marcia tried to introduce the financial statement through her husband's testimony. If he had testified to what she wanted him to testify, that it was his signature on the document, it might have been admissible. Some things are **self-authenticating**, meaning that foundation evidence is not required in order to make the item admissible. In this manner, a public record or document with a certification or seal, an official government publication or pamphlet, a trade inscription, an acknowledged document such as one that is notarized, commercial paper, something that Congress has designated, or a certified record of regular activity such as a certified business record will not need evidence outside of the item itself in order to be admissible.

■ **SELF-AUTHENTICATING**
Not requiring a foundation in order to be admissible.

RULE 902. SELF-AUTHENTICATION

Extrinsic evidence of authenticity as a condition precedent to admissibility is not required with respect to the following:

(1) Domestic Public Documents Under Seal. A document bearing a seal purporting to be that of the United States, or of any State, district, Commonwealth, territory, or insular possession thereof, or the Panama Canal Zone, or the Trust Territory of the Pacific Islands, or of a political subdivision, department, officer, or agency thereof, and a signature purporting to be an attestation or execution.

(2) Domestic Public Documents Not Under Seal. A document purporting to bear the signature in the official capacity of an officer or employee of any entity

(continues)

RULE 902. SELF-AUTHENTICATION *(continued)*

included in paragraph (1) hereof, having no seal, if a public officer having a seal and having official duties in the district or political subdivision of the officer or employee certifies under seal that the signer has the official capacity and that the signature is genuine.

(3) Foreign Public Documents. A document purporting to be executed or attested in an official capacity by a person authorized by the laws of a foreign country to make the execution or attestation, and accompanied by a final certification as to the genuineness of the signature and official position (A) of the executing or attesting person, or (B) of any foreign official whose certificate of genuineness of signature and official position relates to the execution or attestation or is in a chain of certificates of genuineness of signature and official position relating to the execution or attestation. A final certification may be made by a secretary of embassy or legation, consul general, consul, vice consul, or consular agent of the United States, or a diplomatic or consular official of the foreign country assigned or accredited to the United States. If reasonable opportunity has been given to all parties to investigate the authenticity and accuracy of official documents, the court may, for good cause shown, order that they be treated as presumptively authentic without final certification or permit them to be evidenced by an attested summary with or without final certification.

(4) Certified Copies of Public Records. A copy of an official record or report or entry therein, or of a document authorized by law to be recorded or filed and actually recorded or filed in a public office, including data compilations in any form, certified as correct by the custodian or other person authorized to make the certification, by certificate complying with paragraph (1), (2), or (3) of this rule or complying with any Act of Congress or rule prescribed by the Supreme Court pursuant to statutory authority.

(5) Official Publications. Books, pamphlets, or other publications purporting to be issued by public authority.

(6) Newspapers and Periodicals. Printed materials purporting to be newspapers or periodicals.

(7) Trade Inscriptions and the Like. Inscriptions, signs, tags, or labels purporting to have been affixed in the course of business and indicating ownership, control, or origin.

(8) Acknowledged Documents. Documents accompanied by a certificate of acknowledgment executed in the manner provided by law by a notary public or other officer authorized by law to take acknowledgments.

(continues)

RULE 902. SELF-AUTHENTICATION *(continued)*

(9) Commercial Paper and Related Documents. Commercial paper, signatures thereon, and documents relating thereto to the extent provided by general commercial law.

(10) Presumptions Under Acts of Congress. Any signature, document, or other matter declared by Act of Congress to be presumptively or prima facie genuine or authentic.

(11) Certified Domestic Records of Regularly Conducted Activity. The original, or a duplicate of a domestic record of regularly conducted activity that would be admissible under Rule 803(6) if accompanied by a written declaration of its custodian or other qualified person, in a manner complying with any Act of Congress or rule prescribed by the Supreme Court pursuant to statutory authority, certifying that the record—

(A) was made at or near the time of the occurrence of the matters set forth by, or from information transmitted by, a person with knowledge of those matters;

(B) was kept in the course of the regularly conducted activity; and

(C) was made by the regularly conducted activity as a regular practice.

A party intending to offer a record into evidence under this paragraph must provide written notice of that intention to all adverse parties, and must make the record and declaration available for inspection sufficiently in advance of their offer into evidence to provide an adverse party with a fair opportunity to challenge them.

(12) Certified Foreign Records of Regularly Conducted Activity. In a civil case, the original or a duplicate of a foreign record of regularly conducted activity that would be admissible under Rule 803(6) if accompanied by a written declaration by its custodian or other qualified person certifying that the record—

(A) was made at or near the time of the occurrence of the matters set forth by, or from information transmitted by, a person with knowledge or those matters;

(B) was kept in the course of the regularly conducted activity; and

(C) was made by the regularly conducted activity as a regular practice.

The declaration must be signed in a manner that, if falsely made, would subject the maker to criminal penalty under the laws of the country where the declaration is signed. A party intending to offer a record into evidence under this paragraph must provide written notice of that intention to all adverse parties, and must make the record and declaration available for inspection sufficiently in advance of their offer into evidence to provide an adverse party with a fair opportunity to challenge them.

The rationale for the rule is given by the Advisory Committee note that was written when the rule was first proposed in 1972: "Case law and statutes have, over the years, developed a substantial body of instances in which authenticity is taken as sufficiently established for purposes of admissibility without extrinsic evidence to that effect, sometimes for reasons of policy but perhaps more often because practical considerations reduce the possibility of unauthenticity to a very small dimension. The present rule collects and incorporates these situations, in some instances expanding them to occupy a larger area which their underlying considerations justify. In no instance is the opposite party foreclosed from disputing authenticity." Therefore, it is possible for something that is listed in Rule 902 to not quite meet all the criteria for the item and yet to still be admissible through Rule 901.

PASSIM CASE **FIELDS VS. PRAIRIE BANK**

Peter Fields is a disorganized slob who does not keep his bank statements. Could he still get his bank statements admitted into evidence? He could first try to get the documents by making a request for production of documents to the bank, or by issuing a deposition subpoena duces tecum to the bank for someone to appear with the documents. Then, he could use Rule 902(11) and argue that the statements were kept in the ordinary course of bank business. However, the bank may object on a technicality under the rule, perhaps on the basis that the record is not certified, or that there is no person at the bank with knowledge of the transactions. Then, Fields could still use Rule 901 and argue that the statements are what they purport to be.

In the following case, the court considers whether a party offering a business record needs to have testimony from the person or company that wrote it.

CASE

JAZZ PHOTO CORP. V. UNITED STATES, 353 F. SUPP. 2D 1327, 1359–1360 (FED. CL. 2004)

Plaintiff sought to lay the foundation for the admissibility of the exhibits at issue through the testimony of Messrs. Silvera and Zawodny that the documents were business records of either Photo Recycling or Jazz, and that they qualified for admission under the business records exception to the hearsay rule.

The contention that each and every business document offered into evidence must be separately authenticated by a witness from the entity that prepared the document, however, has no basis in law. . Defendant's narrow reading of the requirement of Fed. R. Evid. 901 essentially would swallow the 803(6) business records exception and prevent most entities from using documents at trial that are germane to the operation of their businesses. Mr. Silvera testified that he is familiar with the documents contained in the business record of Photo Recycling and that the exhibits at issue were in fact business records generated and/or maintained or integrated during the ordinary course of Photo

(continues)

CASE
JAZZ PHOTO CORP. V. UNITED STATES, 353 F. SUPP. 2D 1327, 1359–1360 (FED. CL. 2004) *(continued)*

Recycling's business. Although Mr. Zawodny could not testify definitively that every document within the subject exhibits were "records of operation" maintained by Jazz in the ordinary course of business, he was able to identify the exhibits as business records and explain the contents of each document and their significance to Jazz's business operations.

The witnesses purport that the documents at issue are either business records of Photo Recycling or Jazz. The trial testimony of Messrs. Silvera and Zawodny and the government's consent to waive its hearsay objection in light of Mr. Benum's deposition have, for purposes of Fed. R. Evid. 901, established that the documents are what the proponents claim; therefore, the grounds for any authentication objection have been extinguished.

The court has no reason to question the testimony and circumstantial evidence that these exhibits are actually business records of either Photo Recycling or Jazz or the testimony of the witnesses relating to their reliance on such records. Any questions as to the extent of a witness' personal knowledge of the contents of the business records will be considered by the trier of fact, in this case the trial court, only in determining the credibility of the witness and the weight to be accorded to the solicited testimony.

BENCH BRIEF TRANSCRIPT

FOUNDATION FOR O. J.'S GLOVES

In the following excerpt from the O. J. Simpson criminal trial, Brenda Vemich, a men's gloves buyer for Bloomingdales in 1990, is examined by prosecutor Christopher Darden in an effort to establish part of the foundation for the infamous pair of gloves that were found at the crime scene and at the defendant's home.

People Of The State Of California, Plaintiff V. Orenthal James Simpson, Defendant, Official Transcript, Superior Court, Los Angeles County June 15, 1995 1:32 P.M., page 10–11

Q Looking at the item marked people's 372 for identification, can you tell us what that item is? The item depicted there?

A This is a Bloomingdales receipt . . .

Q Okay. Now, looking at that receipt, there are several numbers on it; is that correct?

A Yes.

Q Can you interpret those numbers for us? . . .

A The "517" represents the department number, seasonal accessories.

Q Now, do you see the no. "222034" at the top upper left?

. . .

(continues)

BENCH BRIEF   TRANSCRIPT *(continued)*

Q   . . . and to go down to the right of the "515," we see the numbers "55."

A   Yes.

Q   What do those numbers indicate?

A   That is the classification number and "55" represents a glove classification.

Q   So that indicates that gloves were purchased?

A   Yes.

Q   Okay. And to the right of the "55" is the no. "953"?

        . . .

A   That is the vendor number and in this case it is Aris Isotoner.

Q   And so based on those three numbers then you can tell that you say there was a purchase in the Men's Accessories Department, seasonal?

A   Seasonal.

Q   Gloves were purchased?

A   Yes.

Q   And that they were Aris gloves?

A   Yes.

Q   To the right of the "953" we see the no. 70268. What is that number?

A   That is the style number of the glove.

Q   . . . And to the right of the "70268" you see the no. "2." what does that indicate?

A   Quantity that were purchased is two, two gloves.

Q   Two pairs of Aris gloves?

A   Yes.

Q   And to the right of the "2" we see the number "$77.00"?

A   Yes. That is the retail for the two pair of gloves.

Q   Okay. And to the right of the "$77.00" we see the no. "30"; is that correct?

A   Yes. And that is thirty percent off.

Q   So that means in the two pairs of gloves were purchased for thirty percent off at $77.00?

A   Yes.

Q   Can you tell us what the regular price of the gloves was?

A   The regular price of gloves of this style is $55.00.

Q   Okay . . Q how many different types of Aris gloves did you sell at $55.00 during December?

A   There was only one Aris glove that I sold at $55.00.

In addition to the receipt, the prosecution established foundation for the gloves with an FBI glove expert, crime scene investigators, detectives, and photographs and videotapes of the defendant wearing the gloves that appeared to be the same, or at least similar.

Chain of Custody

BENCH BRIEF

THE GOLDEN RULE OF HOMICIDE INVESTIGATION

"Never touch, change or alter anything until identified, measured and photographed. Remember that when a body or an article has been moved, it can never be restored to its original position."

Source: Lemoyne Snyder, Homicide Investigation: Practical Information for Coroners, Police Officers, and Other Investigators, *Second Edition (Springfield, Illinois: Charles C. Thomas, 1972), page 36.*

How does the jury know that the object the prosecutor is holding in her hand is the murder weapon? Because the prosecution presents a chain of custody that follows the item from the crime scene to the courtroom.

Say an inexperienced officer arrives at the scene of a murder in a kitchen. There is a knife on the floor next to the victim. He picks it up and places it in a manila envelope that is lying on the kitchen table. He picks up the phone to call his sergeant. Then the sergeant tells him not to touch anything, he is going to call for a homicide investigator. The crime scene investigator takes the envelope containing the knife from the rookie cop and places it into an exhibit container such as a plastic bag or a special envelope. The container will be labeled with such information as the case number, the name or initials of the person bagging it, the date that it was found, and an indexing number for the items at the crime scene. The homicide investigator will then give it to a criminalist at a crime lab for examination for prints and body fluids such as blood. If it is blood, is it animal blood or human? If it is human, what is the blood type: A, B, O, or AB? Rh positive or negative? The knife is then returned to the investigator, who places it in an evidence locker for safekeeping until trial.

Later at the trial, in order to get the knife into evidence, assuming that the defendant will not admit that the knife is *the* knife, the prosecutor must prove it through chain of custody evidence. In this case, she needs testimony from (1) the inexperienced officer, (2) the investigator, and (3) the criminalist

Chain of custody evidence says, "This is the object that I am talking about and I know it is the same object that is important to this case because . . . " In this case, the prosecutor will ask the initial officer, "I'm showing you what's been marked for identification as

Exhibit six. Do you recognize it?" The officer will say where he found the knife, what it looked like, and that he gave it to the investigator. The investigator will testify that he recognizes the knife and the markings that were made on the package that it was in; that he received the knife from the rookie officer, put the knife in the container, and labeled the container; that exhibit six is in the container with the same markings and it appears to be the same knife; and that he gave the item to the criminalist and received it back from the criminalist. Therefore, each person in the chain of custody will testify about what he or she did with the knife and that it appears to be the same knife, until its whereabouts have been accounted for from the day of the crime to the day of trial. Once foundation is established, the prosecutor can say, "Your honor, the state offers Exhibit six." The defense may object on the grounds of foundation, or some other grounds, but unless that objection is sustained, the exhibit can now come into evidence and it can be **published** to the jury.

For chain of custody to be established, each person in the chain must indicate that he or she received the item, what was done with it, and how it was kept safe from being replaced or altered when it was not in that person's possession. In most jurisdictions, a gap in the chain would not render the evidence inadmissible, as long as the item appears to be the same item and has not been modified in a relevant way. Testimony might not be necessary from every person in the chain, or every person who could have had a chance to substitute or alter the item, as long as the prosecution can show it is reasonably certain that no such thing occurred. Therefore, suppose someone at the crime lab in charge of distributing mail took the mailed envelope containing the evidence envelope to the criminalist's lab and handed it to him. The mail distributor's testimony is probably not necessary. However, a minority view holds that if the chain is broken, the item is inadmissible. The majority rule is that if there is some minor or speculative problem with the chain of custody and the court admits the evidence, it affects the weight of the evidence rather than its admissibility. However, if an item is subject to identification, it may not need to go through a chain of custody. For example, say it was a one-of-a-kind knife made by an artist who makes only a single unit of each knife, then a chain of custody might not be necessary.

In the following case, the court considers the impact of a date discrepancy on foundation and lists the ways the foundation was established for cocaine that was purchased from the defendant.

PUBLISHED
Passed around or distributed to the members of the jury (applied to an object or document).

CASE
ARNOLD V. STATE, 617 S.E.2D 169, 177 (GA. APP. 2005)

Arnold next claims that the chain of custody was insufficient to permit the introduction of the cocaine as evidence. He emphasizes that there was a two-day discrepancy between the date upon which the evidence custodian testified he hand-delivered the bagged substance to the GBI crime lab and the date upon which the chemist testified the lab received it. Yet, we find the State adequately met its burden "to show with reasonable certainty that the evidence is the same as that seized and that there has been no tampering or substitution." By the identifying marks on the packaging, it was established through

(continues)

> **CASE**
> **ARNOLD V. STATE, 617 S.E.2D 169, 177 (GA. APP. 2005)** *(continued)*
>
> testimony from several witnesses that the substance which tested positive for cocaine and which was introduced at trial was the substance purchased from Arnold, double bagged by the Narcotics Division investigator, placed in the evidence locker, retrieved and transported to the GBI crime lab, and subjected to testing by that lab. Accordingly, while a small discrepancy between specific dates may exist, the identity of the evidence itself was preserved. "When there is only a bare speculation of tampering [or substitution], it is proper to admit the evidence and let what doubt remains go to the weight."

The court ruled that the evidence should be admitted despite the date discrepancy.

JUDICIAL NOTICE, ADMISSIONS, AND STIPULATIONS

Judicial notice, admissions, and stipulations all have the effect of making a fact true for the purpose of the case without the presentation of evidence of the fact. The court will typically address the jury and indicate that thus and so is the way it is.

Judicial Notice

Courts can take judicial notice of facts that cannot reasonably be disputed, that are general knowledge in the community, or that can easily and accurately be determined by referring to sources whose accuracy cannot readily be questioned.

> **RULE 201. JUDICIAL NOTICE OF ADJUDICATIVE FACTS**
>
> (a) Scope of rule. This rule governs only judicial notice of adjudicative facts.
>
> (b) Kinds of facts. A judicially noticed fact must be one not subject to reasonable dispute in that it is either (1) generally known within the territorial jurisdiction of the trial court or (2) capable of accurate and ready determination by resort to sources whose accuracy cannot reasonably be questioned.
>
> (c) When discretionary. A court may take judicial notice, whether requested or not.
>
> (d) When mandatory. A court shall take judicial notice if requested by a party and supplied with the necessary information.
>
> e) Opportunity to be heard. A party is entitled upon timely request to an opportunity to be heard as to the propriety of taking judicial notice and the tenor of the matter
>
> *(continues)*

> ### RULE 201. JUDICIAL NOTICE OF ADJUDICATIVE FACTS *(continued)*
>
> noticed. In the absence of prior notification, the request may be made after judicial notice has been taken.
>
> (f)   Time of taking notice. Judicial notice may be taken at any stage of the proceeding.
>
> (g)   Instructing jury. In a civil action or proceeding, the court shall instruct the jury to accept as conclusive any fact judicially noticed. In a criminal case, the court shall instruct the jury that it may, but is not required to, accept as conclusive any fact judicially noticed.

If a party provides the court with the required information, it is required to take judicial notice. A court can take judicial notice even if a party does not ask it to do so. In other words, the judge can pipe up in the middle of the trial and say, "Ladies and gentlemen of the jury, I'm going to take judicial notice that Lake Calhoun is connected by bike path, walking path, and street to Lake Harriet." (See Exhibit 5–4 for examples.)

EXHIBIT 5–4

Judicial Notice Not Appropriate	Mandatory Judicial Notice	Discretionary Judicial Notice
Terrazzo floor becomes dangerously slippery when wet	Interstate was a "way" as defined by statute	A small amount of water in a bathtub creates a slippery condition
Newspaper articles	Defendant's testimony during a previous trial	In Texas, the customary royalty in an oil and gas lease is one-eighth of the oil and gas produced
Internal Revenue Service Technical Advisory Memos	Administrative regulations regarding safety inspections of commercial vehicles	In Vermont, snow from February is gone by June
Governor's statement on a radio talk show	Speed schedules for city streets	Window screens are not intended to keep people from falling out of a window
Local ordinance	Statutes from two states were similar	Gasoline is explosive

EXHIBIT 5–4   When is Judicial Notice Inappropriate, Mandatory or Discretionary

The Federal Jury Instruction Guide for civil cases suggests the following instruction to read to the jury at the end of the case: "Although no evidence has been introduced on the subject, the court has accepted as proved the fact that [describe]. You must accept this fact as true for purposes of this case." *Federal Jury Practice and Instructions*, Civil Section 102.20.

Admissions

During the pleading phase, a party may admit something in an answer or answer and counterclaim. During discovery, a party can request another party to admit something and it may be admitted. In these cases, no evidence needs to be presented on the item that was admitted.

The *Federal Jury Instruction Guide* for civil cases suggests the following instruction regarding admissions made during the pleadings phase: "Before the trial began, the parties filed written statements with the court describing their claims and defenses. These statements are known as pleadings. In their pleadings, the parties have admitted certain facts as follows: [Read admissions.] You will take these admitted facts to be true for purposes of this case."

Federal Jury Practice and Instructions, Civil Section 101. 46.

A similar instruction is suggested for those admissions which are made through the discovery phase of the case.

Stipulations

The parties to a case may decide to stipulate to certain facts. That means they agree that the fact finder may assume that those facts are true. The parties will typically agree on a statement to be read to the jury. The parties may chose to do this to cut down on the length and cost of the trial, especially if there is little doubt about the facts to which they are stipulating. For example, in a car accident case the parties may stipulate that it was raining at the time of the accident. Sometimes parties will even stipulate to a major aspect of the case, such as when a defendant admits liability. Defendants may do so in order not to inflame the jury with their bad conduct and attempt to get the jury to focus on the damages.

Back to the gloves in the O. J. Simpson case, the parties stipulated to the testimony of Nicole Simpson's mother. She presumably preferred not to testify because it would have been too emotional. The defense would not have wanted her on the stand and would not have had anything productive to gain by cross-examining her, and the prosecution was probably happy to get her testimony in uncontested. Also, part of her testimony was foundation for the glove.

BENCH BRIEF   TRANSCRIPT

SIMPSON CRIMINAL TRIAL STIPULATION

People Of The State Of California, Plaintiff V. Orenthal James Simpson, Defendant, Official Transcript, Superior Court, Los Angeles County July 6, 1995 2:20 P.M., page 5-6

THE PEOPLE OF THE STATE OF CALIFORNIA, PLAINTIFF IN THE WITHIN ACTION, AND JOHNNIE L. COCHRAN, JR. , COUNSEL FOR DEFENDANT ORENTHAL JAMES SIMPSON, STIPULATE:

Juditha Brown was called as a witness, duly sworn, and testified as follows:

She is the mother of Nicole Brown Simpson, the decedent and named victim in count one of this action. On June 12, 1994, she attended a dance recital where her granddaughter, Sydney Simpson performed. Thereafter, she accompanied her daughter Nicole, granddaughter Sydney, and other family members to the Mezzaluna Restaurant for a post-recital celebration. Upon arriving, she inadvertently dropped the pair of eye-glasses marked as part of the exhibit designated People's exhibit 32, which were intact prior to that point, outside the restaurant. At approximately 9:37 p. m. on June 12, 1994, Juditha Brown telephoned the Mezzaluna restaurant and spoke to an employee named Karen Crawford, who has testified previously in this case. Ms. Brown asked Ms. Crawford to locate the eye-glasses and hold them for pickup at a later time by Nicole Brown Simpson. Ms. Crawford located the eye-glasses and agreed to set them aside for Nicole Brown Simpson. This conversation lasted approximately two minutes.

At approximately 9:40 p. m. , Juditha Brown telephoned her daughter Nicole Brown Simpson, reaching her at her daughter's residence, located at 875 South Bundy Drive, in the City of Los Angeles. Juditha Brown conversed with Nicole Brown Simpson for approximately two minutes. Nicole Brown Simpson stated that she would arrange for the retrieval of Juditha Brown's eye-glasses. This was the last time that Juditha Brown spoke to her daughter Nicole Brown Simpson.

It is further stipulated that Juditha Brown examined the eye-glasses contained in the exhibit marked People's exhibit 32 and testified these were the eye-glasses that she left at the Mezzaluna Restaurant on June 12, 1994 and were the subject of her conversations with Karen Crawford and Nicole Brown Simpson. It is further stipulated that Juditha Brown testified that she was familiar with the handwriting of her daughter Nicole Brown Simpson. Juditha Brown testified that she examined the Bloomingdale's Department Store charge card receipt marked People's exhibit 372 and the copies of that receipt depicted in People's exhibits 372(A) and 372(B) and that the signature "Nicole Brown" on that document appeared to have been written by her daughter Nicole Brown Simpson.

IT IS SO STIPULATED.

JOHNNIE L. COCHRAN, JR.

Attorney for Orenthal James Simpson

MARCIA R. CLARK

Deputy District Attorney

Dated: July 6, 1995

BEST EVIDENCE RULE

It might be better to call the best evidence rule the original document rule. Although a rule requires an original, a subsequent rule then says a copy is treated the same as an original unless there is a valid question about the authenticity or it would be unfair for some other reason.

> ### RULE 1002. REQUIREMENT OF ORIGINAL
>
> To prove the content of a writing, recording, or photograph, the original writing, recording, or photograph is required, except as otherwise provided in these rules or by Act of Congress.

> ### RULE 1003. ADMISSIBILITY OF DUPLICATES
>
> A duplicate is admissible to the same extent as an original unless (1) a genuine question is raised as to the authenticity of the original or (2) in the circumstances it would be unfair to admit the duplicate in lieu of the original.

Therefore, unless there is a legitimate question about a document being altered, copies are admissible. In addition, there are some other circumstances where an original is not required, such as if an original is lost, destroyed, unavailable, or in the possession of another party, or where it is not going to be used to prove something that really matters to the case.

> ### RULE 1004. ADMISSIBILITY OF OTHER EVIDENCE OF CONTENTS
>
> The original is not required, and other evidence of the contents of a writing, recording, or photograph is admissible if—
>
> (1) Originals Lost or Destroyed. All originals are lost or have been destroyed, unless the proponent lost or destroyed them in bad faith; or
>
> (2) Original Not Obtainable. No original can be obtained by any available judicial process or procedure; or
>
> (3) Original in Possession of Opponent. At a time when an original was under the control of the party against whom offered, that party was put on notice, by the pleadings or otherwise, that the contents would be a subject of proof at the hearing, and that party does not produce the original at the hearing; or
>
> (4) Collateral Matters. The writing, recording, or photograph is not closely related to a controlling issue.

■ **BEST EVIDENCE RULE**
A copy of a document is admissible unless valid doubts can be raised regarding its authenticity, or it is unfair.

Certified copies of public records are admissible.

In the following case, the court considers the application of the rule to a videotape that was lost.

CASE
PEOPLE V. JIMENEZ, 796 N.Y.S.2D 232 (N.Y. SUP., 2005)

Defendant was indicted for assault in the first degree, assault in the second degree and assault in the third degree arising out of an altercation between the defendant and Wilfredo Acevedo, the complainant. During the trial, the People offered the testimony of the owner of the store in which the altercation began who, although not a witness to the events, had viewed the videotape of the store's surveillance camera. The owner's testimony was offered to establish what the videotape had showed, the actual tape having been lost by the time of trial . . .

As per the People's offer of proof, after the incident, the owner viewed the laundromat's surveillance videotape but did not preserve it or turn it over to the police and it no longer existed at the time of trial. The People proposed to call the owner and have him testify to what he had observed on the videotape.

The best evidence rule requires production of an original writing where its contents are in dispute and sought to be proven. At its genesis, the rule was primarily designed to guard against mistakes in copying or transcribing the original. In New York, the definition of a "writing" parallels the formulation supplied by the Federal Rules of Evidence and now includes photographs and X-rays as well as motion pictures and videotapes. Thus, the original videotape had to be produced in court before a witness who did not observe the events recorded thereon could testify to what he had observed on the tape.

That said, under a long recognized exception to the best evidence rule, secondary evidence of the contents of an unproduced original may be admitted upon threshold factual findings that the proponent of the substitute has sufficiently explained the unavailability of the primary evidence and that the derivative proof "is a reliable and accurate portrayal of the original."

In Schozer . . . the defendant lost the X-ray of the plaintiff's chest after the defendant's radiologist had reviewed and analyzed it. The Court of Appeals held that the trial court should not have precluded the radiologist's report and testimony without having given the defendant the opportunity of establishing that such testimony correctly reflected all of the contents of the original substantially and with reasonable accuracy.

Here, the videotape no longer existed, its owner, a third party, having failed to preserve it. Its unavailability was therefore explained. Consequently, the admissibility of the owner's testimony as to what it showed turned on whether the People had carried their "heavy burden" of establishing that the witness was able to recount or recite, from personal knowledge, substantially and with reasonable accuracy all of its contents. Schozer, however,

(continues)

> **CASE**
> **PEOPLE V. JIMENEZ, 796 N.Y.S.2D 232 (N.Y. SUP., 2005)** *(continued)*
>
> concerned an X-ray, in other words, one photograph. And while an expert might well be able to recount or recite substantially and with reasonable accuracy all of the pertinent contents of one such photograph, the same cannot be said of the innumerable details of the literally thousands of images that constitute videotape footage. Inevitably, the witness' testimony would be no more than a summary of his interpretation of what he had seen on the tape and not a reliable and accurate portrayal of the original . . . . Based thereon, this Court holds that the best evidence rule precludes a witness from testifying to an altercation he observed on a surveillance videotape in the absence of the tape.

WHEN DO THE RULES APPLY?

The rules of evidence do not apply in all proceedings. Typically, in administrative law hearings and in probation or parole hearings, the rules do not apply. An example of an administrative law hearing is a social security disability benefits hearing. The rules do apply in regular court hearings before a trial court judge. It is best to check in your jurisdiction to see when they apply. However, the court may nevertheless apply the rules even though it is not required to do so.

SUMMARY

Most cases go to state court because federal courts can hear only certain cases. The U.S. Supreme Court is the highest court in the United States. It sits above 13 circuit courts of appeal, and they sit above district courts in 94 districts. The most common type of case in state court is dissolution of marriage. There are differences among state court systems. Trials determine and apply the law to facts; appeals courts review the record and apply the appropriate standard of review to factual findings and legal rulings.

The Federal Rules of Evidence govern federal cases in federal district court. Many states have adopted the Federal Rules of Evidence.

Foundation is evidence about evidence that establishes a basis for admitting the later. It shows that what has been offered is what it purports to be. Chain of custody follows evidence from place to place, demonstrating that the object that is being offered in court as an exhibit is the same item that was used in the crime or found at the crime scene.

Sometimes evidence is not necessary if the parties stipulate, if one party makes an admission, or if something is so well known or obvious that the court takes judicial notice.

The best evidence rule allows copies unless the authenticity of the copy is in dispute and in a few other circumstances. The Rules of Evidence apply in trials, but not in some other proceedings such as administrative proceedings or parole violation hearings.

■ KEY TERMS

best evidence rule	objection	record
chain of custody	offer of proof	self-authenticating
clearly erroneous	order in limine	standard of review
de novo	overruled	sustained
foundation	published	

■ HELPFUL WEB SITES

http://www.ncsconline.org/index.html
http://www.uscourts.gov/

■ REVIEW AND DISCUSSION QUESTIONS

1. What makes a case eligible for federal court?

2. Is your state divided into multiple federal districts? How many are there and which one are you in?

3. What is your state's court structure?

4. What are some quirks in your state's court system?

5. What are some different standards of review for an appellate court?

6. How can a lawyer protect the record?

7. How many states have adopted the Federal Rules of Evidence? Did your state adopt them? Are there any differences between your state's Rules of Evidence and the Federal Rules of Evidence?

8. What is foundation and how can it be established?

9. What is chain of custody? Describe how a chain of custody would follow a shoe found at a crime scene.

10. What things are self-authenticating?

11. Why would a party admit something?

12. What is the effect of an admission or stipulation?

13. What is something that a court could take judicial notice of in your state? In general, what kinds of things can a court take judicial notice of?

14. When do the rules of evidence not apply?

15. When is an original writing needed?

■ LEGAL RESEARCH PROJECTS

1. Find out the federal court district in which you are located, and the circuit court of appeals to which you would appeal.

2. Investigate the makeup of your state's court system. How many judicial districts are there, and which one are you in? Is there an intermediate appellate court? How are judges selected in your state? Has your state recently conducted a study regarding racial or gender bias in the courts? If so, what were some of the key findings?

3. Learn whether your state has adopted the Federal Rules of Evidence. If it has, find out if there are any differences. If it has not, what is used instead and how does it differ from the federal rules?

For additional resources, visit our Web site at www.westlegalstudies.com

OH. THAT SIX MILLION DOLLARS.

Courtesy CartoonStock.com.
www.CartoonStock.com

Relevance

■ OBJECTIVES

- ❏ Contrast relevant and irrelevant evidence
- ❏ Classify evidence as likely to be admissible as relevant, or inadmissible as irrelevant
- ❏ Examine Evidence Rules 401–415
- ❏ Predict when evidence might be so prejudicial that it will not be admitted
- ❏ Differentiate admissible character evidence from inadmissible character evidence
- ❏ Examine Evidence Rules 608–610

INTRODUCTION

An important task for any lawyer involved in litigation is to determine what evidence the **fact finder** will be allowed to hear or consider. Clients may want to tell their lawyers all about the opposing party and what a rotten, despicable person she is. They may wish to discuss, and want the jury to hear, how the defendants are liars who cheat at cards, look down the blouses of teenagers, do not pay taxes, and have extremist political views. However, unless any of that has a bearing on the **material** facts at issue in the case, it is irrelevant.

This chapter will cover when evidence is **relevant**, irrelevant, or relevant but **prejudicial**. If it is relevant, it is admissible unless some other rule keeps it out. For example, if it is relevant but prejudicial, it is not admissible. If evidence is irrelevant, it is not admissible. This chapter will also discuss character evidence and special rules related to relevance.

RELEVANT, IRRELEVANT, AND PREJUDICIAL EVIDENCE

A paralegal can help a lawyer get a case ready for trial, by knowing what information from a client, witness interview, or deposition is likely to become evidence because it is relevant, and what will likely be inadmissible because it is irrelevant or prejudicial. To make this determination, the paralegal must know the rules of evidence that govern relevance.

All Relevant Evidence Is Admissible

Cases are often good demonstrations of how human perception, memory, communication, and credibility can differ strangely. Witnesses at the same event can testify quite differently on the most basic facts. If there are three witnesses, the fact finder could hear up to nine versions of what happened if the witnesses' testimony varies from one another, and each witness's testimony differs from what they said at the time of the incident, the date of their deposition, and at trial. By the time a case gets to trial, several years may have passed. If it were easy to figure out what happened, especially in high-stress, high-speed, traumatic incidents, we would not need trials. Even with instant replay, a simple question of whether the football player's feet were in bounds when he caught the ball can result in three opinions from the announcers, which may or may not match what the referee eventually decides. Jurors cannot decide with absolute certainty what happened. They must rely on what they think probably happened, when they render a decision. So, courts want to let in anything that helps a jury determine what probably happened.

> ### RULE 401. DEFINITION OF "RELEVANT EVIDENCE"
>
> "Relevant evidence" means evidence having any tendency to make the existence of any fact that is of consequence to the determination of the action more probable or less probable than it would be without the evidence.

■ RELEVANT

Tending to make a fact in dispute more or less likely.

■ FACT FINDER

The jury, or if the case is tried without a jury, the judge, determining what happened in the incident or transaction that underlies the case.

■ MATERIAL

Having a logical tie to the facts that matter in a case.

■ PREJUDICIAL

Causing the fact finder to focus on something other than the facts, such as emotion, in reaching a decision.

> ### RULE 402. RELEVANT EVIDENCE GENERALLY ADMISSIBLE; IRRELEVANT EVIDENCE INADMISSIBLE
>
> All relevant evidence is admissible, except as otherwise provided by the Constitution of the United States, by these rules, or by other rules prescribed by the Supreme Court pursuant to statutory authority. Evidence which is not relevant is not admissible.

This rule defines "relevant evidence" as something that makes a fact, which matters more or less likely to be true. If the case is a slip and fall that occurred on a banana peel in a grocery-store produce aisle, and the grocery store has evidence that it was out of bananas on the day of the alleged fall, that might tend to make the plaintiff's claim less likely to be true. If the grocery store kept a log of when its aisles were inspected and the log said the aisles had not been inspected at all that day, that log might make the plaintiff's claim more likely to be true.

This rule means that anything that could shed light on an issue that matters to the outcome of the case is admissible, unless otherwise specified by another rule or a law. Logically then, anything that is irrelevant is not admissible.

For example, in a contract dispute over the sale of carpet, the buyer's medical history would be irrelevant. However, the negotiations the parties engaged in prior to the contract would be relevant. In a landlord-tenant dispute over unpaid rent, the tenant's taste in music would probably be irrelevant, but it might be relevant in a nuisance suit by a neighbor claiming that he was blasting heavy metal music.

BENCH BRIEF ENTERTAINMENT NOTE

HALF MOON AND EMPTY STARS
From a novel by Jerry Spence

In this excerpt from a novel by the famous attorney Jerry Spence, a witness tries to testify about a dream.

"I had this dream," Simon Yellow Dog began.

"Objected to," Mueller said. "Dreams are not evidence."

"Sustained," the judge ruled.

"And this mare fell on me."

"This is irrelevant," Mueller said.

"Sustained. I don't want to hear anything more about your dream, Mr. Yellow Dog," the judge said.

"Them dreams is important," Simon said.

(continues)

In the following civil case for personal injury from an auto accident, the court considers whether a photograph taken during the repair of the car that was in the accident was relevant:

CASE
WILKINSON V. SWAFFORD, 811 N.E.2D 374 (CT. APP. IND. 2004)

Swafford contends that the trial court abused its discretion when it admitted . . . photographs that depicted Wilkinson's vehicle as it was being repaired. Admission of photographs into evidence is left to the sound discretion of the trial court, and we will not reverse that decision except for an abuse of that discretion. To admit a photograph into evidence, a trial court must first determine the photograph is relevant . . . . Swafford had previously tendered a photograph of Wilkinson's vehicle, but Wilkinson sought to admit [the photo] on grounds that it more accurately depicted the damage to her vehicle. Swafford's attorney objected on relevance grounds and argued that the photograph did not depict how her vehicle looked just after the accident. Rather, it depicted the vehicle with the hood raised and with certain portions of the vehicle removed for repair purposes . . . . We agree with Swafford that [the photo] has little, if any, relevance, because it does not reflect how Wilkinson's car looked after the accident.

The court found the photograph irrelevant, since it did not depict the car the way it looked just after the accident. The fact that parts had been removed for repair and that the hood was raised could have confused the jury into thinking that the accident caused the hood to pop open or that the car was more badly damaged than it actually was. Therefore, the court concluded that the trial court should have excluded the evidence on irrelevance grounds.

Otherwise Admissible Evidence Is Prohibited by Another Law or Rule

■ **RAPE SHIELD LAW**
A law designed to prohibit the admission of evidence regarding the sexual history of sexual assault victims.

■ **SUBSEQUENT REMEDIAL MEASURES**
Fixing a safety problem after it becomes apparent.

Another important part of the rule prohibits the admission of otherwise relevant evidence if it is prohibited by some other rule or law. For example, evidence of a sexual assault victim's prior sexual activity is generally not admissible pursuant to **rape shield laws** and Rule 412. Evidence of negotiations in a civil case would be somewhat relevant to show what amount of damages might be appropriate, but to encourage the settlement of cases out of court, Rule 408 makes it inadmissible. To encourage companies to fix safety problems with their products, Rule 407 makes **subsequent remedial measures** inadmissible. There are many other rules and laws that keep out otherwise relevant evidence. Some of these are discussed later in the text.

Prejudicial Evidence Is Inadmissible

A court may be concerned that a relevant piece of information may so inflame the jury that they will not be able to reach a just result if they hear about it.

The most important part of this rule says that relevant evidence may be excluded if it would be prejudicial. The rule provides a balancing test where, on one side of the scale, the court considers how much the evidence tends to prove an important fact; on the other side, it places the likelihood that the evidence will cause the jury to be inflamed because of the evidence and become biased against the other party.

In the next case, the trial court considers whether it is prejudicial to admit evidence that the plaintiff, Gandy, had trace amounts of marijuana in his system after a railroad accident.

RULE 403. EXCLUSION OF RELEVANT EVIDENCE ON GROUNDS OF PREJUDICE, CONFUSION, OR WASTE OF TIME

Although relevant, evidence may be excluded if its probative value is substantially outweighed by the danger of unfair prejudice, confusion of the issues, misleading the jury, or by considerations of undue delay, waste of time, or needless presentation of cumulative evidence.

BENCH BRIEF NOTE

Most lawyers do not have rule numbers memorized; however, Rule 403 is an exception. Most lawyers know off the top of their heads that Rule 403 prohibits the admission of prejudicial evidence.

CASE
ILLINOIS CENT. R.R. CO. V. GANDY, 750 SO. 2D 527 (MISS. 1999)

The Railroad further asserts that the trial judge should have allowed into evidence the deposition of forensic toxicologist Dr. Francis M. Esposito and the proffered testimony of Dr. David T. Stafford, its expert toxicologist. Dr. Esposito's deposition indicates that a trace amount of marijuana metabolites (THC) was found in a urine sample which was taken from Gandy on the date of the accident and tested using gas chromatography and mass spectrometry. Blood tests taken to determine the presence of drugs in his blood stream had proven negative. Dr. Esposito stated in his deposition that the results were such that Gandy would not have been impaired cognitively or mentally at the time of the accident. In a 1996 deposition, Gandy testified that the night before the accident, he had driven around for several hours in a small pick-up truck with a friend who was terminally ill with cancer and who was smoking marijuana as recommended by his doctor in addition to prescription THC tablets. The Railroad, however, proffered that Dr. Stafford would have testified that the THC concentration in Gandy's urine sample was indicative of active consumption of the drug and could not have resulted from passive inhalation . . . .

There is no evidence in the record to support the Railroad's contention that Gandy had any kind of drug problem; rather the record is replete with evidence that he was a responsible, hard-working man, who had a relatively exemplary record over his many years of service with the railroad. The Railroad's mischaracterization of the evidence in its brief illustrates clearly how the danger of prejudice far outweighed any probative value the evidence held. The circuit court therefore did not abuse its discretion in excluding the evidence.

PASSIM CASE FIELDS VS. PRAIRIE BANK

Fields has been a fine, upstanding citizen for the last 15 years. However, prior to that he had a big drinking and gambling problem. He was banned from a Las Vegas casino after getting drunk and swearing profusely at a blackjack dealer. He stormed off and drove drunk, crashing his car. The police arrested him and found some marijuana in his car. This evidence would probably be prejudicial and not admissible because it is old, it has no bearing on this case, and it would cause the jury to focus their emotions on his unsavory background.

CHARACTER EVIDENCE

Character evidence is information about a person's character, personality, or habits. It could tend to portray someone in either a negative or a positive light. Examples of character evidence might be the following:

- a man has season tickets to the Minnesota Timberwolves and has never missed a game
- a woman has a history of exploding into a verbal rage when things do not go her way at work
- a man always has a pre-dinner drink with his wife each weekday and they have done so for the 52 years of their marriage

Character Evidence Is Inadmissible to Prove Conduct

The general rule is that character evidence is inadmissible to prove conduct (exceptions to this rule will be discussed later in this text). The purpose of this rule is to try to get the fact finder to analyze the case based upon the facts rather than upon a popularity contest or a witness's personal history. Imagine what it would be like without the rule.

Who do you think a jury would favor in a sexual misconduct case? An Eagle Scout, church-going Gulf War veteran who was awarded a Purple Heart, and who is married and has three children but got drunk on the night in question? Or a single mother of two kids by two different fathers, who is known for her skimpy clothes and sleeping around? The fear is that the fact finder, especially a jury, would focus on the differences between their backgrounds rather than the facts.

Exceptions

The first exception to the general rule that character evidence is not admissible is for a criminal defendant to offer proof of his or her own good character. For example, if the defendant is accused of perjury, he may offer evidence that he has a reputation for telling the truth. However, by offering such evidence he is **opening the door** to

■ **OPENING THE DOOR**

Asking a question or giving an answer that makes it unfair to exclude otherwise inadmissible evidence.

> **RULE 404. CHARACTER EVIDENCE NOT ADMISSIBLE TO PROVE CONDUCT**
>
> Evidence of a person's character or a trait of character is not admissible for the purpose of proving action in conformity therewith on a particular occasion . . .

BENCH BRIEF   TRANSCRIPT

PROSECUTOR: After you broke the dish, did your husband hit you?

WOMAN: No.

PROSECUTOR: No? Do you recall giving a statement to the police the day of the incident?

WOMAN: Yes.

PROSECUTOR: And it was tape recorded, right?

WOMAN: If you say so.

PROSECUTOR: And in that taped statement you said, "He was yelling at me and I got scared and nervous and I dropped a dish. He hit me really hard in the face and I'm pretty sure I'm going to have a black eye." Right?

WOMAN: If you say so.

the prosecution, so that it can present evidence that shows what a gigantic liar the defendant is.

The second exception is to show a character trait of the victim. In an assault case, if the victim had a reputation for losing her temper in a flash and the defendant was claiming self-defense, evidence of her temper might be admissible.

The third exception is a list of three rules that cover **impeachment**. Rule 608 says that a party may attack the credibility of a witness, even if it is the party who called the witness. For example, in a domestic relations dispute, suppose the battered partner has informed the prosecutor of a desire to no longer go forward and for the case to be dismissed, but the prosecutor goes ahead with the case anyway, and the battered spouse denies or minimizes what happened. The prosecutor may impeach the witness with quotes from the police report. If the defendant denies that he hit the victim, the prosecutor may impeach the victim by comparing the current testimony to the transcript of what the victim said to the police when the victim was first interviewed.

The prosecution might also impeach her, by introducing a photograph of her black eye. It does not matter that the prosecutor called the witness, because the rule specifically says that the attorney may impeach a witness that the attorney called to the stand. Witnesses called by the opposing side may also be impeached. Impeachment can be utilized in civil and criminal cases.

Rule 609 says that, in civil cases, a defendant's felony conviction may be admitted as long as it passes the balancing test in Rule 403, which weighs prejudicial impact against what the evidence tends to prove.

In a criminal case, evidence of a felony conviction may be admitted against the defendant if it is not too prejudicial compared to what it proves, but the balancing test is not done with Rule 403. Evidence that a witness was convicted of a "crime of dishonesty or false statement" may be admitted, even if it was not a felony. Examples of such crimes might include check forgery, perjury, or larceny, and some courts even

■ IMPEACHMENT
Attacking the credibility of a witness, often by showing prior inconsistent testimony or contradictions between the testimony and exhibits.

hold that any form of theft is a crime of dishonesty. However, a judgment is based not upon the title of the crime, but rather upon the facts in the particular case.

In the following case the court considers whether evidence of prior convictions may be admitted to impeach a defendant.

CASE
UNITED STATES V. CARROLL, 663 F. SUPP. 210 (D. MD. 1986).

[t]he government has filed notice of its intention to impeach Carroll in accordance with Rule 609, Federal Rules of Evidence, by introducing evidence of his prior conviction for bank larceny as well as a 1985 conviction for felony theft . . . . Carroll has filed a motion in limine to preclude introduction of these prior convictions.

In his 1984 conviction for bank larceny, Carroll pled guilty to stealing a total of $135,000 from the [Bank]. Carroll described in his handwritten confession a wire transfer scheme with which he was able to obtain $60,000 and $75,000 checks. . . . Carroll told Fox . . . he expected a wire transfer . . . . Later the same day, someone called Mrs. Fox pretending to be an employee in the bank's mailroom and told [Fox] that a wire transfer had come in for Carroll. Fox then issued a check for $60,000, which Carroll picked up. This procedure was later repeated, and Fox issued a $75,000 check . . . .

The government asserts that in the **instant case**, someone . . . called [Fox] and identified himself as Thomas Gilbert . . . . This "Thomas Gilbert," . . . told [Fox] he was expecting a $75,000 wire transfer from California. Shortly thereafter, a person whose voice was similar to that of "Thomas Gilbert" called, identified himself as a mailroom employee and told [Fox] a wire transfer had arrived for Thomas Gilbert. [Fox] alerted . . . law enforcement officials. When Gilbert arrived to pick up the transfer check, he was arrested and during questioning implicated Carroll . . . .

Here, the government argues persuasively that evidence of Carroll's prior conviction indicates that a common scheme was used in both . . . wire transfers, that this scheme is probative of identity, and that it bears on Carroll's knowledge of wire fraud . . . the scheme used in this case is virtually identical to that used [before]. Both involve the same bank, indeed the same bank employee, and the same sequence of contacts . . . . Such similarities in execution of a scheme have served as the basis for Rule 404(b) evidence . . . . The government's proposed evidence also bears on knowledge of the mechanics of wire transfers . . . .

Where the scheme used in the prior crime is identical in virtually every respect with that used in the crime charged, and where it was attempted at the same bank, it is probative of the defendant's common plan or scheme, knowledge and identity. It is clearly offered for reasons other than to show the character or disposition of the defendant, and is thus relevant under Rule 404(b) . . . .

(continues)

■ **INSTANT CASE**

The current case that the court is deciding rather than a previous one or one that it is citing.

> **CASE**
> **UNITED STATES V. CARROLL, 663 F. SUPP. 210 (D. MD. 1986).** *(continued)*
>
> Finally, there is little prospect that introduction of evidence of Carroll's prior conviction would unduly prejudice him. Evidence of a prior conviction would be unlikely to have any inflammatory effect . . . and any prejudice could be countered with an appropriate [jury] instruction. The evidence of Carroll's prior conviction is relevant and probative without being prejudicial and is thus admissible under Rule 404(b).

The Court found that the prior convictions were relevant and were not being offered for an improper purpose. Therefore, it admitted the evidence of the prior convictions.

Methods of Proving Character

If evidence of character is admissible, how can a party prove it? Courts do not wish trials to turn into assessments of a person's entire life history through anecdotes of how he or she helped blind women across the street or stole from an employer. Instead, the general rule is that character must be shown through evidence of reputation, or through opinion according to Rule 405. For example, a witness who knows the person whose character is at issue, perhaps from work or from the community where they live, may testify about reputation. Rule 405(b) says that testimony about specific instances is allowable during cross examination or when "character of a person is an essential element of a charge, claim, or defense." For example, in a defamation case where the plaintiff claims that his reputation as a good hairdresser has been injured by the plaintiff and offers character evidence about what a good hairdresser he is, the defense may counter with specific incidents of hair disasters.

Habits of people or organizations are closely related to character. John Stockman of Jensen & Stockman in Bloomington, Minnesota, handles wills and probate. Whenever a client comes to his office to execute a will, he goes through a script. The questions are the same every time: "Are you at least 18?" (the 70-year-old ladies get a kick out of that question); "Is this your will?" "Does it represent what you want done with your things when you die?" "Are you taking any medication that would affect your ability to make this type of a decision?" Stockman does it this way so that ten years from the time a will is executed, if there is a dispute, he will be able to say that it is his habit to ask these questions, that he always asks these questions in the same order at every will execution ceremony. Presumably, he would not be able to remember a particular will signing, since he does about twenty-five a year. But his testimony about his habit of asking these questions would be helpful to proving the **testator's** intent and state of mind.

■ **TESTATOR**
A person who makes a will indicating what should be done at his or her death.

The routine practices of an organization are also admissible. If nurses staffing a health clinic's nurse line log every call, even if it is a hang-up or transfer, that habit would be admissible to demonstrate that a patient never called the nurse line if there was no call log noting the call.

OTHER RELEVANCE RULES

A few other relevance rules apply to particular situations.

Subsequent Remedial Measures

Rule 407 prevents the admission of subsequent remedial measures. For example, if a company sold a toy-computer mouse including a long cord, and a child was injured by getting the cord wrapped around her neck, the company would wisely shorten the cord or eliminate it from the toy. However, the injured child would not be able to present evidence regarding the design change to the product. Companies might be tempted to claim that their products are safe and that no design changes are needed, if they had to fear evidence of design changes being admitted. The defense would face the plaintiffs' attorneys, arguing, "Even they agree that the mouse was unsafe. After my client was injured, they changed the design."

Settlement Negotiations

Rule 408 precludes the admission of settlement discussions and offers to settle. This is an attempt to encourage settlement. Parties would be reluctant to make offers of settlement, if they knew that the jury would hear about them. Sometimes settlement offers are made to avoid the cost of litigation or out of concern for the victim. However, if jurors hear that the defendant offered the plaintiff money, they might think that the plaintiff's claim has some merit just by virtue of the fact that money was offered. States differ on whether a suit must have been brought before the offer is made, in order for the offer to be inadmissible.

Plaintiff's Medical Expenses

Rule 409 is similar to Rule 408, in that it prevents admission of the defendant paying the plaintiff's medical expenses. Suppose a grocery store had just cleaned the produce section, and there was nothing on the floor just 15 minutes before a plaintiff slipped on a banana peel and fell and broke her hip. Since the plaintiff and her whole family are long-time customers, the store may want to help the plaintiff by paying her medical expenses as a goodwill, public relations, and humanitarian gesture. The store might not take this step, if it had to worry that evidence of paying the plaintiff's medical expenses could be admitted in a suit.

Guilty Pleas and Plea Bargaining

Rule 410 is the criminal equivalent to Rule 408, in that it prevents the admission of withdrawn guilty pleas and plea bargaining discussions.

Insurance

Rule 411 prevents the admission of evidence regarding whether the defendant was insured. If such evidence were admissible, jurors might say, "Oh, that poor plaintiff, a few grand would mean so much to her and it's such a little drop in the bucket to that giant insurance company that is backing the defendant." They might make an award when they would not otherwise be so inclined. The mention of insurance is an easy way for an attorney to make a judge very angry, as just bringing the subject up can be grounds for a mistrial. If mention is made of insurance, the attorney who would like to object must request a **side bar** to raise the objection so that the jury does not hear anything further about insurance.

■ **SIDE BAR**
A conference at the bench among the attorneys and the judge outside of the jury's hearing.

Sexual Assault Victim's Sexual Behavior

Rule 412 makes a sexual assault victim's past sexual behavior inadmissible. The rule is an attempt to protect such victims from an assault on their sex lives and reputations.

When defendants want to introduce evidence of a victim's prior sexual experience, they must make a motion to do so long before the trial ever starts. The court then holds a hearing outside the presence of the jury to determine whether or not to admit the evidence. Evidence of specific sexual conduct the victim has engaged in or that she has a reputation for sleeping around, is not admissible unless it meets one of the exceptions.

PASSIM CASE ⚖ FIELDS VS. PRAIRIE BANK
It would be irrelevant that the bank has a general business insurance policy with a rider that covers theft of customer data through All-Farms Insurance, even if the insurance company was providing the defense.

> ## RULE 412. SEX OFFENSE CASES; RELEVANCE OF ALLEGED VICTIM'S PAST SEXUAL BEHAVIOR OR ALLEGED SEXUAL PREDISPOSITION
>
> (a) Evidence generally inadmissible.—The following evidence is not admissible in any civil or criminal proceeding involving alleged sexual misconduct except as provided in subdivisions (b) and (c):
>
>   (1) Evidence offered to prove that any alleged victim engaged in other sexual behavior.
>
>   (2) Evidence offered to prove any alleged victim's sexual predisposition.
>
> (b) Exceptions.—
>
>   (1) In a criminal case, the following evidence is admissible, if otherwise admissible under these rules:
>
>   (A) evidence of specific instances of sexual behavior by the alleged victim offered to prove that a person other than the accused was the source of semen, injury or other physical evidence;
>
>   (B) evidence of specific instances of sexual behavior by the alleged victim with respect to the person accused of the sexual misconduct offered by the accused to prove consent or by the prosecution; and
>
>   (C) evidence the exclusion of which would violate the constitutional rights of the defendant.
>
>   (2) In a civil case, evidence offered to prove the sexual behavior or sexual predisposition of any alleged victim is admissible if it is otherwise admissible under these rules and its probative value substantially outweighs the danger of harm to any victim and of unfair prejudice to any party. Evidence of an alleged victim's reputation is admissible only if it has been placed in controversy by the alleged victim.

The exceptions include having sexual relations with someone else where that other person could be the source of physical evidence such as semen, blood, or injury. For example, in the Kobe Bryant rape case, evidence was admitted that the underwear the alleged victim had on when she reported the rape the next day had semen from another man on it. Another exception allows evidence that the victim had previous sexual relations with the accused. Finally, there is an exception if the defendant's constitutional rights require the admission of the evidence.

Here is a case where the defendant claimed that he and the alleged rape victim had occasional, consensual sex for up to three years before the incident.

CASE
UNITED STATES V. SAUNDERS, 736 F. SUPP. 698 (E.D. VA. 1990)

Defendant and the alleged victim have known each other since their teen-age years. Defendant testified he had sex with the alleged victim about half a dozen times during the period spanning 1983 to 1987 . . . . The alleged victim, by contrast, denies ever having had sex with defendant, except on the night of the alleged incident . . . the Court must go on to consider whether evidence of a sexual relationship some three years prior to the alleged rape is relevant to consent and, if so, whether the probative value of this evidence outweighs the danger of its unfair prejudicial effect.

The government argues that evidence of a sexual relationship three years in the past is too remote in time to be probative on the consent issue presented here. Put simply, the government argues that just because she may have consented three years ago does not mean she consented on the night in question. There is some force in this argument. Although Rule 412 does not include an explicit timeliness requirement, it seems clear that the temporal element must be taken into account in the weighing process called for in subsection (c)(3). Evidence of an isolated consent to engage in sex with an accused some ten years in the past would likely have no probative value, and more than a little potential for unfair prejudice. By contrast, evidence of consent to sex that is in closer proximity to the alleged rape may be very probative, as in the case of a recent or ongoing intimate relationship. From this, it follows that the application of Rule 412 must include a consideration of the temporal element . . .

This is a manifestly close question, but the Court ultimately concludes that the evidence should be admitted as having some probative value on the consent issue, but little, if any, risk of unfair prejudice. Defendant's claim of a prior sexual relationship with the alleged victim is central to the consent defense. Defendant's version of consensual sex at his home earlier in the evening is far more plausible in light of his claim of a prior relationship with the alleged victim. To be sure, the three-year period in issue here is certainly quite close to the indistinct boundary between some probative value and none . . .

In sum, therefore, defendant's evidence of his prior sexual relationship with the alleged victim is admissible on the issue of consent as provided for in Rules 412(b)(1) and (b)(2)(B). Admitting this evidence strikes a proper balance between protecting rape victims from humiliation or unfair loss of credibility as a result of public disclosure of their prior sexual activities and preserving an accused's right to present relevant, exculpatory evidence.

The court found the prior relationship relevant even though it was three years old.

Prior Incidents of Sexual Assault or Child Molestation

Rules 413 through 415 allow into evidence prior incidents of sexual assault or child molestation committed by defendants accused of those crimes or sued civilly for those acts.

SUMMARY

All relevant evidence is admissible unless it is prejudicial, or some other rule or law keeps it out. Character evidence is generally inadmissible to prove conduct; however there are exceptions for a criminal defendant to show evidence of his good character, or the character of the victim, and any party may impeach a witness. Character evidence may be shown with opinion or reputation testimony. Several other rules govern specific situations.

◼ KEY TERMS

fact finder	opening the door	side bar
impeachment	prejudicial	subsequent remedial measures
instant case	rape shield law	testator
material	relevant	

◼ REVIEW AND DISCUSSION QUESTIONS

Consider whether the following would be admissible in our case. Analyze both the civil and criminal case.

1. The plaintiff is a recovering alcoholic.
2. The bank has a routine of locking all desk drawers.
3. Bank employees undergo thorough background checks when hired.
4. The bank routinely shreds garbage with a cross-cut shredder.
5. The shredder was broken for a month while Peter Fields had an account open.
6. The bank used an outside shredding company to shred its documents. The outside shredding company was sued by another customer for failing to shred and just throwing the material away instead.
7. Peter Fields has a four-year-old D.W.I. conviction.
8. Peter Fields had to register as a sex offender after he was convicted of exposing himself.
9. The president of the bank is a lay pastor at his church.
10. Peter Fields has not voted in the last three elections.
11. Peter Fields previously sued another person as a result of personal injuries suffered during a car accident and received a large settlement.
12. Peter Fields had an insurance policy against identity theft.
13. The F.B.I. has declined to investigate the case.
14. The sheriff's department lacks the resources to investigate the case.
15. Peter Fields shredded all his own documents, had no cleaning service at his home, and had no girlfriend or other person who ever had access to his house or his records.

■ LEGAL RESEARCH PROJECTS

1. Get a copy of one of the cases excerpted in this chapter and read all of it. Brief the case by providing a summary of the facts, the legal issue, the holding, and the court's reasoning.

2. Find a case involving an issue of relevance from your jurisdiction. Brief the case by providing a summary of the facts, the legal issue, the holding, and the court's reasoning.

3. Research and write a memo regarding the circumstances under which a criminal defendant's prior bad acts are admissible.

For additional resources, visit our Web site at www.westlegalstudies.com

Courtesy CartoonStock.com.
www.CartoonStock.com

Hearsay

■ OBJECTIVES

❑ Define hearsay
❑ Contrast the difference between the common definition of hearsay and the legal definition
❑ Identify what is not hearsay because a rule says it is not hearsay
❑ Examine Rules 801, 802, 805, and 806
❑ Recognize hearsay within hearsay and demonstrate how to apply the hearsay rules to each level of hearsay

HEARSAY IS NOT ADMISSIBLE

The general public has a very broad definition of hearsay.

Most people probably think that hearsay is a statement that is heard and repeated, such as a rumor. A rumor can be hearsay, and that is what the word means when it comes to ordinary speech. There is a lot more to it than that, however, when the word is considered a **term of art** and the official rules are considered.

Before we get into the official, legal definition, consider the purpose of keeping hearsay evidence out of court. The purpose of keeping hearsay out of the courtroom is to make sure that cases are decided upon first-hand information rather than rumors or what witnesses heard about an incident. Remember the childhood game of telephone where a group of people whisper a statement from one person to another? By the time it gets back to the original speaker it is hardly ever the same message.

Now it is time to get a little more technical. Here is the official definition from the rules:

RULE 801(C).

HEARSAY

"Hearsay" is a statement, other than one made by the **declarant** while testifying at the trial or hearing, offered in evidence to prove the truth of the matter asserted.

Let us now examine the rule part by part. First, what is a statement? It is an oral, written, or nonverbal assertion. That means that hearsay can be in writing, or it can be a nonverbal gesture such as nodding the head or holding up a hand to an ear in the phone shape with thumb and pinky fingers extended.

The second part of the sentence means that hearsay does not include anything that was said by the witness during the proceeding. Therefore, even if the witness made the statement himself or herself, it could be hearsay if the statement was made outside of court. The third part of the sentence means that the statement is being offered to prove the content of the statement.

This third part of the rule is the first of many holes that are found in the general rule that hearsay is inadmissible. If the party offering the statement can show some purpose in offering it other than proving the content of the statement, it is not hearsay (see Exhibit 7–1).

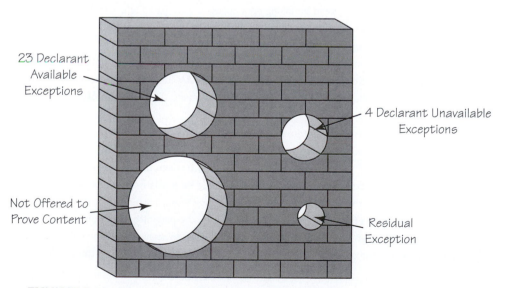

EXHIBIT 7–1   A Small Amount of Hearsay is Actually Inadmissible

23 Declarant Available Exceptions

4 Declarant Unavailable Exceptions

Not Offered to Prove Content

Residual Exception

■ TERM OF ART

A word or phrase that has a special meaning within the jargon of a profession, avocation, or other group.

■ HEARSAY

A statement repeated in court to try to prove the same assertion made in the original statement.

■ DECLARANT

The person whose statement a witness providing hearsay testimony is repeating.

> **BENCH BRIEF**
>
> **NOTE**
>
> If the goal in a case is to prove that a certain blond, rich celebrity is a dummy, the proponent of that concept could offer her statement "they sell walls at Wal-Mart" because the party is trying to show not that Wal-Mart sells walls, but rather that she is an idiot. Oftentimes the party actually wants the statement admitted for the content as well as some purpose other than the content.

In the following case, the court considers potentially harassing statements made to a woman who filed suit for a hostile work environment with regard to whether they were hearsay or not hearsay due to a purpose in offering them other than proving the content of the statements.

> **CASE**
> **NOVIELLO V. CITY OF BOSTON, 398 F.3D 76 (1ST CIR. 2005)**
>
> On October 5, 1999, Barbara DiGirolamo accused the plaintiff of throwing a tampon at a coworker . . . . On October 26, 1999, a coworker shouted that the plaintiff was the "scum of the earth." Another loudly proclaimed, in reference to the plaintiff, "I smell a rat, do you smell a rat?" . . . On December 8, 1999, a new employee told the plaintiff that although he had no problem with her, other coworkers had advised him to "stay away" because she was "trouble." . . . On December 21, 1999, Bernadette Gilardi announced in front of the plaintiff that she would be taking up a collection for [the Defendant] Ortiz . . . . In January of 2000, a tow truck driver told the plaintiff that Gilardi had begun circulating a petition urging management to dismiss the plaintiff, but that he had refused to sign it . . . . The insults and taunting that the plaintiff recounts do not create hearsay problems; those statements are not offered for their truth, but, rather, to show that the words were spoken (and, thus, contributed to the hostile work environment). They are, therefore, admissible . . . .
>
> We note, however, that two statements give us pause. The first is a statement from an unnamed coworker that other employees told him to "stay away" from the plaintiff as she was "trouble." Insofar as the plaintiff is attempting to introduce this statement as evidence of other coworkers' harassing behavior, it is hearsay; its probative value ultimately depends on the truth of the declarant's own unsworn out-of-court utterance. It is, therefore, inadmissible. A similar problem exists with respect to the plaintiff's assertion that a tow truck driver said that Gilardi had been circulating a petition to have the plaintiff fired. Consequently, we cannot consider the content of either statement in analyzing the plaintiff's claims.

The court found that some of the statements were not offered to prove the truth of the matter asserted in them. The plaintiff was not trying to show that she was a tattletale or the scum of the earth. Rather, she was trying to demonstrate that she was the victim of harassing comments and conduct. Therefore, the statements were not hearsay because they were not offered to prove the assertions. However, the court also found that other statements were offered to show that additional employees were harassing the plaintiff, which would support her claim of a hostile work environment. So those other statements were offered to prove their content and were not admissible.

Hearsay is not admissible. This is a general rule that is narrowed quite a bit by aspects of the legal definition, and by exceptions to the rule (which we will discuss in depth in the next chapter).

RULE 802.
HEARSAY RULE

Hearsay is not admissible except as provided by these rules or by other rules prescribed by the Supreme Court pursuant to statutory authority or by Act of Congress.

BENCH BRIEF

THINGS THAT WERE RULED INADMISSIBLE HEARSAY

- statement in hospital record about how an accident happened that was not relevant to diagnosis or treatment
- description over police radio of a suspect as a six-foot white male with a teardrop tattoo
- doctor's testimony about the contents of hospital records that had not been admitted into evidence
- nurse's testimony repeating what rape victim told her
- police officer's testimony about the contents of a tip that drugs were being sold
- testimony from victim of criminal damage to property regarding her insurer's repair cost estimate

WHEN HEARSAY IS NOT HEARSAY

Another part of the rule that defines hearsay excludes from the definition two items that would otherwise be hearsay: prior consistent or inconsistent statements from the witness, and admissions by a party-opponent. These are the second and third holes in the wall that supposedly keep hearsay out.

Prior Consistent or Inconsistent Statement by Witness

By the time a case gets to trial, witnesses may have been interviewed or had their deposition taken. It may take several years for a case to get to trial. During that time, recollections may cloud, or motivations may change. Therefore, witnesses may say something at trial that differs in a significant way from what they said during an interview or deposition. When that happens a witness can be impeached by his or her former statement.

In the following excerpt of testimony from the Microsoft antitrust trial, Microsoft's expert economist Dr. Richard Schmalensee, who is the dean and professor of economics and management at MIT's Sloan School of Management, is impeached with his deposition testimony and earlier trial testimony. He is testifying about price elasticity, which, in the field of economics, means how much a price change will affect demand. In other words, if Microsoft raised the price of its Windows operating system, would people still buy the same number of copies of the operating system (inelastic) or would they buy fewer (elastic). This was important in the trial because if demand was inelastic, that would be a sign that Microsoft had a monopoly.

BENCH BRIEF

TRANSCRIPT

U.S. v. Microsoft Trial Transcript, United States District Court for the District of Columbia June 24, 1999, afternoon session.

Q. And have you attempted to determine what the elasticity was over particular finite ranges, as you use that term?

A. I have done no studies other than sort of looking at elasticities in the literature that we've discussed in this proceeding. There are no additional studies.

Q. When did you look at these estimates of elasticities in the literature?

(continues)

BENCH BRIEF *(continued)*

A. Been doing it since I began my career as an economist. Economists commonly estimate demand elasticities.

Q. Well, when you say—when you said first in your deposition and then again in this
trial in January of this year, no, I have not, nor have I seen estimates in the literature,
was that an accurate answer to my question at that time?

A. Of course, Mr. Boies. You asked, and I stated this throughout, your question is very
precise, it says, to estimate the price elasticity of PC systems, and the answer is no, I
have done no work myself on the price for elasticity for of PC systems, nor have I
seen estimates of that elasticity in the literature. As I indicated, my judgment as to
what's a reasonable elasticity here depends on, is informed by, general estimates for
price elasticities for aggregates, for markets for particular brands. not by detailed
analysis or estimation for this industry.

Q. When you were giving your testimony in October of 1998, you said you didn't think
you knew enough to narrow it from the range of one at the low side to five or six at
the top side; correct, sir?

A. I did say that, though—I did say that, yes.

Q. And you certainly reviewed this literature that you say you have been reviewing since
you started your career, prior to the time that you had this October 1998 deposition; correct, sir?

A. That's correct, Mr. Boies, but I have to say I have never seen an elasticity that high
for anything but a brand. And as I say, the October testimony is doing a very
wide range.

Q. Well, sir, you say you never seen anything. There is an implication there that an elasticity of four or so, or five or six, is just totally implausible. Do you mean to be suggesting that?

A. For this market, yes.

Q. Well, sir, why, then, at your deposition, the October 7th, 1998, deposition on page 75,
76, when you were asked about elasticities for computer systems, did you say what
you said there? Which is that numbers below one are pretty implausible. Numbers
above five and six are pretty implausible, based on elasticities one encountered, but
that's a pretty wide range economically, and I don't think I know enough to narrow it?

A. I think I hadn't [thought] through the issue. For instance, the reason why numbers
below one are pretty implausible has to do with our colloquy—the discussion we
had earlier about the implication for pricing. Elasticities generally, one encounters five

(continues)

BENCH BRIEF *(continued)*

to six, but for PC systems, on further reflection, Cheerios doesn't have an elasticity that high. A demand elasticity of five would mean that an increase in the price of computer systems . . . would cut the demand roughly in half. And frankly, that level of price sensitivity in this market strikes me as implausible. I couldn't prove that it was wrong. I couldn't prove that was wrong in October, but it isn't implausible.

Q. And your explanation to us now as to why you didn't say that back in October and didn't say that in January is that you just hadn't thought about it enough?

A. You didn't ask me that question in January. You asked me the question, had I done additional studies to estimate, and I had not, and I answered that question correctly. I could perhaps have expanded on the answer, but I answered the question you asked.

Q. First, let me go to the deposition, and then I will go back to the trial testimony. In the deposition, it's absolutely clear that what you're saying in the deposition is inconsistent with what you're saying now; correct?

A. The only inconsistency is that—where I say it in lines five and six, I don't know enough to narrow it. I think if you think about it more than I had thought about it in October, it becomes pretty clear that the notion that a ten percent increase in price will cut demand in half for PC's is implausible. I couldn't prove that in October, and it's hard to know exactly what I meant. If I meant that, it's certainly true now, but it's implausible.

Q. Now let me go to your trial testimony, page 39. and there, (reading): "question: and you told me at your deposition that you believe that the elasticity was somewhere between one on the low end and five to six on the high end, you didn't know how to get it into a narrower range. Have you done any work since your deposition to estimate the price elasticity for PC systems? answer: no, I have not, nor have I seen estimates in the literature." Now, do I understand that what you're saying is that you knew at that time that your deposition testimony didn't reflect your current view, but you just didn't want to go beyond a very narrow answer to my question? is that what you're testifying to?

A. Mr. Boies, you're occasionally upset with me when I answered a question you didn't ask. I answered there the question you asked.

Q. And that's sort of what I'm focusing on, sir, whether it's really plausible, to use your words, that you held back here, and you really were simply answering a very narrow question and not putting in context what you now say you knew, which was that your deposition testimony was not completely accurate. Is that plausible, given the way you have answered questions generally?

A. Well, I have certain difficulty in trying to decide what's plausible in one's own behavior, but I think if you look at the direct examination—at the direct examination, my

(continues)

> filed testimony in this case, which clearly shows the state of my thinking on elasticities when that testimony was filed, it seemed to me it spoke for itself. I can't tell you what I had in my mind that day when you asked me that question. Perhaps you had just instructed me to give answers to questions asked. in any case, I did.
>
> Q. The record will show whether you got such an instruction then.

RULE 801(D) STATEMENTS WHICH ARE NOT HEARSAY. A STATEMENT IS NOT HEARSAY IF—

(1) Prior statement by witness. The declarant testifies at the trial or hearing and is subject to cross-examination concerning the statement, and the statement is (A) inconsistent with the declarant's testimony, and was given under oath subject to the penalty of perjury at a trial, hearing, or other proceeding, or in a deposition, or (B) consistent with the declarant's testimony and is offered to rebut an express or implied charge against the declarant of recent fabrication or improper influence or motive, or (C) one of identification of a person made after perceiving the person;

Depositions are the most frequent source of prior statements that meet the Rule 801(d)(1)(A) criteria. Another less common source would be statements during a previous trial.

In addition to prior inconsistent statements, which may be used to impeach a witness, prior consistent statements may be used to bolster credibility by rebutting "an express or implied charge against the declarant of recent fabrication or improper influence or motive." So in a motor vehicle accident case an attorney could show a witness's statement to a police officer and deposition in which she said that the light was red to refute an accusation that she just made up her present testimony.

Finally, if the witness identified a person, that earlier identification is not hearsay pursuant to Rule 801(d)(1)(C). This might occur if a victim identified his or her assailant to a police officer, but at trial is unwilling or unable to identify the defendant. Then the statement to the police that the defendant was the assailant would be admissible.

Admission by Another Party-Opponent

If a party in a case said something that another party wants to come into evidence, it is not hearsay. Note that the statement need not actually be an "admission" along the lines of "OK, OK, I admit it, I killed my wife, but she cheated on me." It does not even have to be incriminating to the party who made the statement or beneficial to the person offering it. It simply has to be something the party said.

> ## RULE 801(D) STATEMENTS WHICH ARE NOT HEARSAY.
> ## A STATEMENT IS NOT HEARSAY IF—
>
> (2) Admission by party-opponent. The statement is offered against a party and is (A) the party's own statement, in either an individual or a representative capacity or (B) a statement of which the party has manifested an adoption or belief in its truth, or (C) a statement by a person authorized by the party to make a statement concerning the subject, or (D) a statement by the party's agent or servant concerning a matter within the scope of the agency or employment, made during the existence of the relationship, or (E) a statement by a coconspirator of a party during the course and in furtherance of the conspiracy. The contents of the statement shall be considered but are not alone sufficient to establish the declarant's authority under subdivision (C), the agency or employment relationship and scope thereof under subdivision (D), or the existence of the conspiracy and the participation therein of the declarant and the party against whom the statement is offered under subdivision (E).

Sony BMG Music Entertainment was caught by the attorney general of New York violating payola laws that prohibit record companies from paying radio stations or disc jockeys to play songs. The case was settled, but had it gone to trial there were a number of memos that would have been admissible under this rule.

BENCH BRIEF

ADMISSIONS

Here are some examples of admissions from the Sony case:

- "I plan on setting up the record with each mix show jock who has a free hand to play what they want @ the station. I would like to ask them their show size and send one Adidas sneaker to them and send the other match when the airplay reaches @ least 10 spins. For the stations who come out (sic) the box with 10 or more spins they will get an autographed pair of Adidas as well as a t-shirt to match."

- "We pay only for the stations designated on our list. We will only pay the amount on the rate sheet for each artist. An add shall be defined, and payment will only be generated, after a station has spun a song for 56 times in a four week period, in the 6 a.m. to 12 midnight daypart."

- "The following are the promotions I did this week … WXXX $750 budget take out of independent fee. Train, Beyonce (sic), Frankie J, increase 5x day from 2x a day."

(continues)

BENCH BRIEF *(continued)*

- "OK, here it is in black and white and it's serious: If a station got a flyaway to a Celine show in Las Vegas for the add and they're playing the song all in overnights, they are not getting the flyaway. Please fix the overnight rotations immediately."

- "WHAT DO I HAVE TO DO TO GET AUDIOSLAVE ON WKSS THIS WEEK?!!? Whatever you can dream up, I can make it happen!!!"

BENCH BRIEF

NOTEWORTHY ADMISSIONS, REAL AND FICTIONAL

- "America's war in the Gulf was prosecuted for the sake of jobs, jobs, jobs." Former U.S. secretary of state James Baker

- "You're goddamn right I did." Col. Jessep in *A Few Good Men* after being asked if he ordered the Code Red

- A Philip Morris memo compares nicotine to cocaine and morphine, and concludes that "the primary reason" people smoke is "to deliver nicotine into their bodies," and says that smokers use nicotine to "change psychological states."

- "She's my sister and my daughter! . .—my father and I, understand, or is it too tough for you?" Evelyn in the movie *Chinatown*

- "I killed Roger Ackroyd." The killer in *The Murder of Roger Ackroyd* by Agatha Christie

- "I shot the sheriff but I didn't shoot no deputy." Bob Marley

- "I'm a loser, baby, so why don't you kill me?" From the song "Loser" by Beck

- "Indeed I did have a relationship with Ms. Lewinsky that was not appropriate. In fact, it was wrong. It constituted a critical lapse in judgment and a personal failure on my part for which I am solely and completely responsible." President William Jefferson Clinton

- "I did a bad thing. There you have it." Hugh Grant regarding being caught with a prostitute

- "I tried to play husband, tried to taste the life of a simple man. But, it didn't work out, so I took a souvenir . . . her pretty head." John Doe in the movie *Seven*

- "I only regret that I have but one life to lose for my country" Nathan Hale's last words before being executed in 1776 for spying on the British

An admission is also not hearsay if the party adopts the statement. A party adopts a statement when it demonstrates a belief in the statement. A party can even adopt an admission through silence if, for example, a forceful denial would be expected if the statement were untrue.

If an admission is made by a party's authorized agent it is not hearsay. The first step is to show that the parties had an agency relationship and, second, whether the statement was made within the bounds of the agency relationship.

In a criminal case, a coconspirator's statement is not hearsay if it is made in furtherance of the conspiracy. Therefore, such statements must be made while the conspiracy is ongoing, and not after its objectives have been completed or the attempt has ended in failure. So an accusation made by one coconspirator alleging the involvement of another coconspirator that is made after the conspiracy is over is still hearsay.

IMPEACHING THE DECLARANT

With hearsay, the declarant is essentially an absent witness who is testifying through the actual witness. Had the declarant been in court, testifying under oath, his or her testimony would be subject to impeachment. This rule allows attorneys to impeach the declarant as well as to support the declarant's credibility.

RULE 806. ATTACKING AND SUPPORTING CREDIBILITY OF DECLARANT

When a hearsay statement, or a statement defined in Rule 801(d)(2)(C), (D), or (E), has been admitted in evidence, the credibility of the declarant may be attacked, and if attacked may be supported, by any evidence which would be admissible for those purposes if declarant had testified as a witness. Evidence of a statement or conduct by the declarant at any time, inconsistent with the declarant's hearsay statement, is not subject to any requirement that the declarant may have been afforded an opportunity to deny or explain. If the party against whom a hearsay statement has been admitted calls the declarant as a witness, the party is entitled to examine the declarant on the statement as if under cross-examination.

PASSIM CASE **FIELDS VS. PRAIRIE BANK**

If the identity thief came into the bank and told the teller a story about how his six-year-old niece was at Children's Hospital, getting a kidney transplant, evidence that no six-year-old had ever received a kidney transplant at Children's Hospital could be used to impeach his credibility. Also, if he told a different sob story to a different teller, that statement would be admissible to impeach him.

The declarant's credibility can be attacked, but if it is attacked, it can be supported. For both supporting and attacking credibility, any evidence that would have been admissible to impeach or bolster the declarant if the declarant had been present and testified would be admissible.

There are some practical differences in impeaching a declarant under this rule, since the declarant is not subject to cross-examination. For example, a prior consistent or inconsistent statement cannot be read to the declarant. However, such statements are admissible.

HEARSAY WITHIN HEARSAY

Hearsay within hearsay may also be called double hearsay, triple hearsay, chain hearsay, layered hearsay, totem pole hearsay, or multiple-level hearsay. It is best illustrated by an example: Suppose Doug has information that comes from Cathy, who received it from Bill, who received it from Alice. If Doug testifies about Alice's information, this would be not only hearsay within hearsay, but hearsay within hearsay within hearsay. This rule indicates that, as long as a hearsay exception applies to each step in the chain, the hearsay is admissible (unless it is inadmissible under some other rule).

If the testimony is "she told me that he said," it is hearsay within hearsay.

Conversely, if no exception applies to a step in the chain, then the testimony is not admissible under the hearsay rule.

In the following murder case, the court considers the admission of hearsay within hearsay within hearsay (triple hearsay).

■ **HEARSAY WITHIN HEARSAY**
A hearsay statement that contains hearsay.

RULE 805.
HEARSAY WITHIN HEARSAY

Hearsay included within hearsay is not excluded under the hearsay rule if each part of the combined statements conforms with an exception to the hearsay rule provided in these rules.

CASE
MCGOFFNEY V. COMMONWEALTH, 2003 WL 22430268 (KY. 2003)

In the days between the Webb's murder and Appellant's arrest, Appellant was in hiding in the company of three friends and relatives: Nicole Bradley (the mother of Appellant's cousin's children), Jerome Owens (Appellant's brother), and Ameisha Harmon (Appellant's former girlfriend). After Appellant's arrest, Lieutenant Mark Barnard of the Lexington Police Department interviewed each of these persons and reported their statements in his official police report.

At trial, the Commonwealth called Bradley, Owens, and Harmon as witnesses and questioned them about what Appellant had told them about the murder. Each witness substantially echoed Appellant's testimony. Each testified that Appellant told him or her that (1) the shooting occurred over a drug dispute; (2) Appellant only began shooting after Webb or the other man had reached for his gun; and (3) Appellant was not sure whether his gunfire actually hit Webb.

Barnard was then called to the stand and questioned about his conversations with Bradley, Owens, and Harmon. In answer to each of these inquiries, Barnard read from his report over Appellant's objection what he had recorded as the statements each witness claimed that Appellant made to that witness . . .

Appellant now claims (1) it was error to allow Barnard to read from his police report; (2) Barnard's testimony as he read from his report constituted inadmissible hearsay . . .

A witness, including a police officer, may not read from a document under the guise of "refreshing his recollection" pursuant to KRE 612.

The trial court characterized the KRE 612 issue as a problem of "form over substance," but that ignores the hearsay implications of reading from a report prepared out of court. Barnard's testimony while reading from his report was hearsay within hearsay within hearsay, or "triple hearsay." Each item of testimony involved an out-of-court statement made by Appellant to the witness which was repeated out of court by the witness to Barnard, and written by Barnard out of court in his report, and then read by Barnard in court. Therefore, the statements were admissible only if "each part of the combined statements conforms with an exception to the hearsay rule provided in [the Kentucky Rules of Evidence]." KRE 805. If Barnard had not read from his report in violation of KRE 612, the problem would have been one of only "double hearsay."

We analyze each layer of the triple hearsay in turn. The first layer (Appellant's statements to the witnesses) is unproblematic. Pursuant to KRE 801A(b)(1), a "party's own statement" which "is offered against a party" is not excluded by the hearsay rule. E.g., Thurman v. Commonwealth, Ky., 975 S.W.2d 888, 893 (1998).

In contrast, most of the mid-level statements (the witnesses' statements to Barnard) do not conform to any hearsay exception. The only exception is Bradley's statement to

(continues)

CASE
MCGOFFNEY V. COMMONWEALTH, 2003 WL 22430268 (KY. 2003) *(continued)*

Barnard that Appellant said that his gunfire did not hit Webb. That declaration was admissible pursuant to KRE 801A(a)(1) as a prior inconsistent statement. Bradley testified at trial that Appellant told her he was not sure if he hit the victim when he fired; that statement was inconsistent with Bradley's report to Barnard that Appellant said he did *not* hit Webb. *Thurman, supra,* at 893. That statement alone survives the first two layers of hearsay. Note that all of the other statements related prior *consistent* statements of Appellant and would not have been admissible even if offered by Appellant.

However, the final layer of hearsay renders all of the statements, including Bradley's statement to Barnard, inadmissible. Barnard's reading from his own report might have been permissible pursuant to KRE 803(5) ("recorded recollection"), but a witness may not utilize KRE 803(5) unless a proper foundation has been laid establishing that the witness "once had knowledge" of the matter in question "but now has insufficient recollection to enable the witness to testify fully and accurately." KRE 803(5). A KRE 803(5) document must also be "shown to have been made . . . when the matter was fresh in the witness' memory and to reflect that knowledge correctly." *Id.* Here, Barnard did not claim that he had an "insufficient recollection to testify fully and accurately." Indeed, he claimed that his memory was sufficient to recall the basics of the interview and he read from the report only to "give you exactly as much information exactly as I can without trying to refer to it just on memory."

Q: Lieutenant Barnard, I noticed that when [the prosecutor] was going over the statements that Mr. Owens and Ms. Harmon made to you, you were looking down at your notes, is that because you didn't of your own recollection recall exactly what they said all this time later? A: No sir.

Thus, the statements were inadmissible under KRE 803(5).

The court went on to rule that admission of the hearsay was harmless error and affirmed the conviction.

PASSIM CASE FIELDS VS. PRAIRIE BANK

When the bank first learned of the situation involving Peter's account, a teller named Anne was the first to know about it. Anne told Betty, the teller supervisor, that someone at the bank might have stolen Peter's personal information. Betty told Charlie, a banker, and Charlie told Dave, the branch manager, who met with Peter. If Dave testified about how the bank first learned of the problem, Dave's testimony would be hearsay within hearsay within hearsay within hearsay within hearsay) (hearsay: If A testified that would be hearsay. If B testified it would be hearsay within hearsay (double). If C testified it would be hearsay within hearsay within hearsay (triple) so when D testifies it is hearsay within hearsay within hearsay within hearsay (quadruple) (A told B, B told C, C told D and D testified).

SUMMARY

Hearsay is a statement not made by the witness during the trial that is offered to prove the statement's content. Certain things that meet this definition are not hearsay because the rule says they are not hearsay. Prior consistent or inconsistent statements, and admissions by opponents (statements made or adopted by opponents, or made by their authorized representatives), are not hearsay. Statements of identification are not hearsay. Hearsay within hearsay is admissible only if each step in the chain of hearsay meets some hearsay exception.

◾ KEY TERMS

declarant   hearsay within hearsay   term of art

hearsay

◾ REVIEW AND DISCUSSION QUESTIONS

1. What is hearsay? How does the common meaning of hearsay differ from the legal definition?

2. Jane testifies that she heard Alice offer John a job in exchange for a sexual favor. Who is the declarant?

3. When is a prior consistent statement admissible?

4. Which of these could be a statement under the hearsay rule?

   a. a wink

   b. a head nod in agreement or disagreement

   c. a hand gesture

   d. an obscene gesture

   e. a facial expression

5. If a company always sends out an e-mail letting people know that someone is leaving the company for other opportunities, but it does not do so when Alex departs the company, is not sending such an e-mail a statement?

6. Why should courts be reluctant to let hearsay evidence in?

7. What types of things are not hearsay even though they meet the initial definition of hearsay in the rule?

8. How do courts determine if hearsay within hearsay is admissible?

▋ LEGAL RESEARCH PROJECTS _____

1. Find and make a copy of the hearsay rule for your state. Does it differ from the federal rule? How does the rule organization for your state differ from the federal rules? Is the numbering system the same?
2. Find a hearsay case from your state. Brief the case by providing a summary of the facts, the legal issue, the holding, and the court's reasoning.
3. Find an example of hearsay from the media, such as a newspaper, magazine, or movie, or from your life, and research and analyze whether the statement would meet the legal definition of hearsay.

For additional resources, visit our Web site at www.westlegalstudies.com

"I'm sorry Perkins, you know perfectly
well there can be no exceptions to our
policy of mandatory retirement at sixty-five."

Courtesy CartoonStock.com.
www.CartoonStock.com

Hearsay Exceptions

■ OBJECTIVES

❏ Identify what is hearsay but is admissible due to a hearsay exception, regardless of declarant's availability

❏ Describe when a witness is unavailable

❏ Analyze when hearsay is admissible because of an exception that applies only when the declarant is unavailable

❏ Explain the catch-all exception to hearsay

❏ Examine Rules 803, 804, and 807

EXCEPTIONS

The qualifications to the hearsay definition in the previous chapter, and the exceptions to the hearsay rule in this chapter, arguably consume the rule. It is a slight exaggeration to say that an attorney who cannot get hearsay evidence admitted is not worth his or her weight in salt and should find another line of work. This chapter covers the 29 exceptions to the hearsay rule.

As a practical matter there is no difference between an exception and a qualification. If something is not hearsay because it is not offered for the truth of the matter asserted in the statement, it comes into evidence. If something is hearsay but it is admissible due to an exception, it is admissible as well.

WHEN DECLARANT IS AVAILABLE

Later in the chapter we will discuss what makes a witness unavailable; in the meantime we will look at the exceptions that do not depend upon the declarant being unavailable. The rule that lists the exceptions when the declarant is available indicates that the following are not excludable as hearsay and then lists 23 exceptions. So when you read the rules in this section, remember that each one is part of a list that begins after the opening sentence of Rule 803; otherwise the exceptions sound like sentence fragments.

Present Sense Impression

The first exception is for **present sense impressions**. The declarant's statement must be made spontaneously so that the declarant lacks an opportunity to develop commentary on the situation that favors the declarant; it must describe what the declarant personally heard, saw, felt, tasted, or smelled; and it must be made while the declarant was sensing it or immediately afterwards.

Examples of admissible present sense impressions would include:

- a 911 transcript where someone says something about what is happening at a crime or fire scene or a medical emergency.
- a pilot's statement captured on a black box regarding a key component failing.
- spontaneous commentary made by a police officer who was taping an open-air drug market.
- "the truck tire is on fire" (just before an explosion).

■ **PRESENT SENSE IMPRESSION**
A hearsay exception for a declarant's spontaneous statement regarding what he or she is seeing, hearing, feeling, smelling or what the defendant just sensed.

RULE 803(1)
PRESENT SENSE IMPRESSION

A statement describing or explaining an event or condition made while the declarant was perceiving the event or condition, or immediately thereafter.

Examples of things that were not considered present sense impressions include:

- long, self-congratulatory memos.
- a complaint about a parking lot attendant made the day after the incident.
- a murder victim's statement of fear regarding her killer stalking her and potentially killing her.
- a letter written two weeks after receiving an earlier letter.

Excited Utterance

Another exception closely related to the first is for excited utterances. In fact, both of these exceptions were classified as **res gestae** exceptions prior to the enactment of the hearsay rules and are still referred to by that name in some states.

In order for a statement to be considered an **excited utterance** there must be a startling event, the statement must be made during the event or just after it so that there is no time to conjure up a lie or an exaggeration, and it must be made when the declarant is still feeling nervous or excited due to witnessing the event. To consider whether there is a sufficient state of excitement, a court may consider such factors as:

- how much stress or excitement the declarant was experiencing when he or she made the statement.
- the time between the event and the statement.
- whether the statement was an answer to a question.
- the age and physical and mental condition of the declarant.
- the nature of the incident and the subject matter of the statement.

The most important factor is the amount of time that elapsed between the incident and the statement. However, courts appear to accept long gaps of time between events and statements when the declarant is a young child who recently was the victim of or a witness to a crime.

Examples of statements that were deemed admissible as excited utterances include:

- a 911 call indicating that a rifle had been fired.
- "okay I think my gyro just quit" said by a helicopter pilot 19 seconds before a crash.
- a school-age sexual assault victim's report of the abuse to an adult.
- a murder victim's statement identifying her killer moments after she was stabbed.

The rationale for the res gestae exceptions is that there is no chance for loss of memory and no time to fabricate a lie because the impression or utterance is being made immediately. However, the rule allows present sense impressions to be admitted not only if they were made at the time of the incident, but also if they were made "immediately thereafter." The rationale for these rules may not be supported by social science studies, which indicate that a lie can be made up and told in less than

■ **RES GESTAE**

A hearsay exception that allows statements into evidence if they were made contemporaneously with the event about which they are concerned.

■ **EXCITED UTTERANCE**

A hearsay exception that allows statements made during or right after an exciting or stressful incident.

RULE 803(2)
EXCITED UTTERANCE

A statement relating to a startling event or condition made while the declarant was under the stress of excitement caused by the event or condition.

one second. But if the rule did not allow statements to be made "immediately there-after," there would be nitpicking arguments about whether a statement was being made while the event was occurring. For example, if someone called 911 because one shot had just been fired and that was the whole incident— a gun was fired to scare someone, no one was hurt, and the shooter left right away— there would be arguments about whether the call was made during the incident, since the call would have to be made after the shot was fired.

State of Mind

The official notes to this rule from the committee that drafted them states, "Exception (3) is essentially a specialized application of Exception (1), presented separately to enhance its usefulness and accessibility." However, there can be mental, emotional, or physical conditions that do not meet this criterion (see the *Kramer vs. Kramer* exhibit below in this section). For a statement to fall under the **state of mind** exception it must be made at the same time as the event, the declarant must not have had time to reflect about the most advantageous thing to say about his or her state of mind, and the statement must be relevant to an issue in the case.

Examples of mental, emotional or physical conditions would include:

- the Wicked Witch in *The Wizard of Oz* saying, "Ohhh—you cursed brat! Look what you've done! I'm melting! Melting! . . . Who would have thought a good little girl like you could destroy my beautiful wickedness!?"

- in *Alien*, when the crew members first wake up from a deep freeze, one saying "Jesus am I cold," and another saying "I feel dead."

- at the beginning of *Beavis and Butt-Head Do America* when Beavis and Butt-Head discover their TV missing, Butt-Head saying, "This sucks more than anything that has ever sucked before."

> ■ **STATE OF MIND**
> A hearsay exception that allows into evidence a statement made by a declarant regarding his or her state of mind.

RULE 803(3) THEN EXISTING MENTAL, EMOTIONAL, OR PHYSICAL CONDITION

A statement of the declarant's then existing state of mind, emotion, sensation, or physical condition (such as intent, plan, motive, design, mental feeling, pain, and bodily health), but not including a statement of memory or belief to prove the fact remembered or believed unless it relates to the execution, revocation, identification, or terms of declarant's will.

BENCH BRIEF   ENTERTAINMENT NOTE

KRAMER VS. KRAMER

From the Revised Third Draft of the screenplay by Robert Benton, based on the novel by
   Avery Corman, available at http://www.imsdb.com/scripts/Kramer-vs-Kramer.html.

In this scene Ted tells Thelma—his neighbor and his wife's best friend—how he feels after
   his wife has just walked out on him.

THELMA: Ted, don't be so hostile.

*(Ted draws himself upright with the dignity of the Ambassador to the Court of St. James. However, dur-
   ing the following, begins pounding the pillows on the couch into shape with real vehemence.)*

TED: Hostile?

(pow)

Me?

(whack)

Thelma, I'm not hostile.

(thud)

I am anything but hostile.

(sock)

But if you want to know what I am. I'll tell you what I am. What I am is, I am hurt. I am
   very hurt. And I just want to know one thing, okay? Just one thing . . . Why? That's all
   I want to know . . . Why?

   Ted's statement, "I am hurt. I am very hurt," is a statement regarding his mental and
emotional state and would be admissible under the state of mind exception.

From real cases, undated notes made after a meeting when the meeting was fresh
in the declarant's mind were among the things found to be admissible under the state
of mind exception. The statement "hold on a minute, there is Justin, he owes me some
money, I want to go see if I can get it" was allowed into evidence to show intent in a
criminal case. On the other hand, a court excluded a statement that indicated the
declarant was scared because it included *why* he was scared. Time is also an important factor for this exception, as courts have ruled that statements made two hours, 20
days, or a year after the event were too remote in time to qualify under the exception.

BENCH BRIEF

EXCITED UTTERANCES

Imagine a home poker game. Six friends are sitting around a table, playing a friendly no-limit Texas Hold'em tournament. Each player puts up $5 and receives 2,000 in chips. Whoever gets all the chips wins all the money. To be cool, all the players call one another by their poker nicknames. Fish is dealt the queen and ten of diamonds and calls the forced 25-chip blind bet. Donkey is dealt two jacks and raises to 100 chips, and PokerPro has two aces so he raises to 300 chips. Fish and Donkey both call, the other players fold. The flop, which consists of three community cards, is the ace of diamonds, the jack of diamonds, and the four of clubs. Donkey and PokerPro both have three of a kind (jacks and aces, respectively), but Fish is one card away from a royal flush, the best possible hand in poker (as long as there is no wild card). Donkey and PokerPro both go all-in, so Fish wisely folds. The next community card is the king of diamonds. Fish says, "[Expletive], I folded the royal flush!" His statement would be an excited utterance.

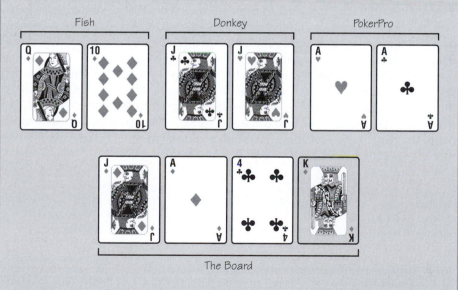

EXHIBIT 8–1   Fish's excited utterance when the final card is dealt is admissible.

Medical Diagnosis or Treatment

If a patient does not tell the doctor the truth, it makes it more difficult for the patient to get the appropriate diagnosis and treatment. That is the rationale for this next exception. Therefore, the critical factor in determining whether a statement will be admitted under this exception is whether it is a statement that a doctor would rely upon in making a diagnosis and setting a course of treatment.

The statement does not have to be made to a doctor; "hospital attendants, ambulance drivers, or even members of the family might be included," according to the official notes to the rule. Cases have allowed statements made to psychologists, psychotherapists, and social workers, but not to a medical interpreter who was talking to the patient in a doctor's office when no doctor was present and the interview was not given in the course of diagnosis or treatment.

RULE 803(4) STATEMENTS FOR PURPOSES OF MEDICAL DIAGNOSIS OR TREATMENT

Statements made for purposes of medical diagnosis or treatment and describing medical history, or past or present symptoms, pain, or sensations, or the inception or general character of the cause or external source thereof insofar as reasonably pertinent to diagnosis or treatment.

> **RULE 803(5)**
> **RECORDED RECOLLECTION**
>
> A memorandum or record concerning a matter about which a witness once had knowledge but now has insufficient recollection to enable the witness to testify fully and accurately, shown to have been made or adopted by the witness when the matter was fresh in the witness' memory and to reflect that knowledge correctly. If admitted, the memorandum or record may be read into evidence but may not itself be received as an exhibit unless offered by an adverse party.

Recorded Recollection

In order for a document to be admitted under this exception, the witness must have personally known about the things noted in the document, the witness must not be able to remember enough about the event to be able to testify completely and accurately, and the record must have been made when the events that are noted in the record were fresh in the witness's mind. Examples of **recorded recollections** that could be admitted include memos, notes, telephone messages, and e-mails. This exception is one of the most widely adopted across jurisdictions, even by those that shy away from allowing evidence of contemporaneous or near contemporaneous writings or statements.

It is easy to confuse this concept with the idea of refreshing a witness's recollection. An attorney may ask a witness who does not recall a detail, "would it refresh your recollection to look at this document?" Then the witness may review the document and say "Now, I remember." In contrast, under the recorded recollection exception, the witness's memory is so lacking that the witness cannot testify about the event, but is willing to swear that a writing is true. When a document is used to refresh recollection, it does not become evidence. In contrast, when a document is deemed admissable under the recorded recollection exception, it is admitted into evidence and becomes an exhibit for the fact-finder to consider.

■ **RECORDED RECOLLECTION**
A hearsay exception that allows into evidence something that was documented by the witness when the event was fresh in his or her mind that the witness can no longer recall.

PASSIM CASE FIELDS VS. PRAIRIE BANK

A record that might be admitted under this exception is a police report written by a law enforcement officer who takes many identity theft reports and does not recall this particular one at all.

Records of Regularly Conducted Activity

Records that are made regularly and systematically as part of running a business are admissible under this exception, as long as the business expects to rely on the records. The word "business" is broadly defined, meaning that it can be almost any sort of entity such as a nonprofit organization, a school, or an association. However, documents prepared for litigation, or in anticipation that there might be litigation, are not admissible under this exception. The person who made the record need not testify to get the record into evidence, as long as someone else such as the records custodian can testify that it was the regular practice of the business to make the record and that the record was made in the ordinary course of business.

Examples of records that have been admitted under this exception include those regarding:

- drug purchases and sales.
- applicants for a firefighter position.
- an autopsy report.
- audit sheets showing the amount of money in a bank teller's drawer.
- freight bills with handwritten notations.

Absence of Entry in Records

When a record that would be admissible under the business records exception is missing, this fact is admissible.

RULE 803(6) RECORDS OF REGULARLY CONDUCTED ACTIVITY

A memorandum, report, record, or data compilation, in any form, of acts, events, conditions, opinions, or diagnoses, made at or near the time by, or from information transmitted by, a person with knowledge, if kept in the course of a regularly conducted business activity, and if it was the regular practice of that business activity to make the memorandum, report, record, or data compilation, all as shown by the testimony of the custodian or other qualified witness, or by certification that complies with Rule 902(11), Rule 902(12), or a statute permitting certification, unless the source of information or the method or circumstances of preparation indicate lack of trustworthiness. The term "business" as used in this paragraph includes business, institution, association, profession, occupation, and calling of every kind, whether or not conducted for profit.

> ### RULE 803(7) ABSENCE OF ENTRY IN RECORDS KEPT IN ACCORDANCE WITH THE PROVISIONS OF PARAGRAPH (6)
>
> Evidence that a matter is not included in the memoranda, reports, records, or data compilations, in any form, kept in accordance with the provisions of paragraph (6), to prove the nonoccurrence or nonexistence of the matter, if the matter was of a kind of which a memorandum, report, record, or data compilation was regularly made and preserved, unless the sources of information or other circumstances indicate lack of trustworthiness.

Thus an inference may be drawn from the absence of a record that would, in the ordinary course of business, have been made had the event in question occurred. The absence of a record that would normally have been kept, had an event occurred, only creates an inference that the event did not occur; it does not prove that the event did not occur. Therefore, it is even more important when offering evidence under this exception that the records be well kept. If records of the activity are not always made by the particular business, the absence of a record does not prove as much as if the records are made every time the activity occurs.

Examples of absent things about which testimony has been allowed under this exception include invoices and written requests for information sent to a retirement plan.

Public Records and Reports

This exception is somewhat similar to the public records exception. It has three subparts. Clause A allows in public records and reports reflecting a public agency's activities, Clause B makes observations and reports of the agency admissible (with the exception of police reports), and Clause C admits, in certain cases, factual findings from reports that an agency was required by law to make. "The exception contains

> ### BENCH BRIEF
>
> #### ABSENCE OF RECORDS
>
> Imagine two incoming call centers. One requires its employees to log all calls, even disconnects and wrong numbers, noting the date, time, and content of the call. At another call center the employees log only important calls. It is up to the call center employees whether or not to log calls. They are encouraged to log calls. If there is no record of a call at the first call center, that means a lot more than if there is no record at the second one.

> ### RULE 803(8)
> ### PUBLIC RECORDS AND REPORTS
>
> Records, reports, statements, or data compilations, in any form, of public offices or agencies, setting forth (A) the activities of the office or agency, or (B) matters observed pursuant to duty imposed by law as to which matters there was a duty to report, excluding, however, in criminal cases matters observed by police officers and other law enforcement personnel, or (C) in civil actions and proceedings and against the Government in criminal cases, factual findings resulting from an investigation made pursuant to authority granted by law, unless the sources of information or other circumstances indicate lack of trustworthiness.

three clauses that divide public records into overlapping categories. Often it makes no difference whether an item fits clause A rather than B or C, or fits two or even all three. But sometimes it does matter, not only because clause C is the only one that reaches material based on outside information, but because the three are subject to different use restrictions and foundation requirements." *Federal Evidence*, 2d, by Christopher B. Mueller and Laird C. Kirkpatrick, § 453 (West).

Just as the word "business" is defined broadly under the business records exception, the phrase "public offices or agencies" is also broadly defined so that quasi-public agencies such as the National Academy of Sciences, which was founded by an act of Congress, are included. Also, independent contractors working for the government have had their documents ruled admissible under this exception. Since public records are considered to be even more reliable than business records, foundational testimony, indicating that the records are ordinarily made in the course of operations of the agency and that this was such a record, is not generally required.

Examples of things that have been admitted under this exception include:

- a computer printout listing the names of people who were deported.
- Intoxilyzer breath test certifications.
- records of conviction.
- an accident report prepared by a public transportation company.

> ### RULE 803(9)
> ### RECORDS OF VITAL STATISTICS
>
> Records or data compilations, in any form, of births, fetal deaths, deaths, or marriages, if the report thereof was made to a public office pursuant to requirements of law.

> ### RULE 803(10) ABSENCE OF PUBLIC RECORD OR ENTRY
>
> To prove the absence of a record, report, statement, or data compilation, in any form, or the nonoccurrence or nonexistence of a matter of which a record, report, statement, or data compilation, in any form, was regularly made and preserved by a public office or agency, evidence in the form of a certification in accordance with Rule 902, or testimony, that diligent search failed to disclose the record, report, statement, or data compilation, or entry.

Records of Vital Statistics

Governments keep records of marriages, births, and deaths, and those records are admissible under this exception.

Examples of things admitted under this section include birth and death certificates. Documents from foreign jurisdictions have also been found admissible.

Absence of Public Record or Entry

A rule analogous to 803(7) makes the absence of a government record admissible.

Examples of things admitted under this exception include a Certificate of Non-Existence of Record that signified an illegal alien status, and testimony that no lien had been filed by a defendant.

Records of Religious Organizations

Personal information from a religious organization is admissible under this rule. The rule is analogous to business records. One notable difference is that there is no requirement for the record to be kept in the ordinary course of business, since it is so unlikely for this type of record to be fabricated.

> ### RULE 803(11) RECORDS OF RELIGIOUS ORGANIZATIONS
>
> Statements of births, marriages, divorces, deaths, legitimacy, ancestry, relationship by blood or marriage, or other similar facts of personal or family history, contained in a regularly kept record of a religious organization.

> ### RULE 803(12) MARRIAGE, BAPTISMAL, AND SIMILAR CERTIFICATES
>
> Statements of fact contained in a certificate that the maker performed a marriage or other ceremony or administered a sacrament, made by a clergyman, public official, or other person authorized by the rules or practices of a religious organization or by law to perform the act certified, and purporting to have been issued at the time of the act or within a reasonable time thereafter.

Birth and baptismal records have been admitted into evidence under this exception. It is not a very commonly used exception.

Marriage, Baptismal, and Similar Certificates

There is an exception for marriage, baptismal, and similar certificates, which is not used very often.

Family Records

There is an exception for records contained in family bibles, family trees, family pictures, and the like.

An example of something admitted under this exception is an old postcard with a note on the back, "Ren Robinson, My Sister, Daughter, Age About 3." This exception is also used infrequently.

Property Records

There is an exception for records of documents affecting property rights.

This exception would allow into evidence deeds, plats, and judgments affecting real estate. This exception is not used very often.

> ### RULE 803(13) FAMILY RECORDS
>
> Statements of fact concerning personal or family history contained in family Bibles, genealogies, charts, engravings on rings, inscriptions on family portraits, engravings on urns, crypts, or tombstones, or the like.

**RULE 803(14) RECORDS OF DOCUMENTS AFFECTING
AN INTEREST IN PROPERTY**

The record of a document purporting to establish or affect an interest in property, as proof of the content of the original recorded document and its execution and delivery by each person by whom it purports to have been executed, if the record is a record of a public office and an applicable statute authorizes the recording of documents of that kind in that office.

Statements in Property Records

There is an exception for statements in documents affecting property rights. This exception differs from the previous exception in that it allows into evidence statements contained within documents that affect property rights.

The official comments to the rule state, "Dispositive documents often contain recitals of fact. Thus a deed purporting to have been executed by an attorney in fact may recite the existence of the power of attorney, or a deed may recite that the grantors are all the heirs of the last record owner." This exception is not often used.

Statements in Ancient Documents

Documents 20 years old or older at the time they are offered into evidence are admissible under this exception. The rationale is that someone who wrote something that long ago would not have foreseen or been thinking about the litigation.

**RULE 803(15) STATEMENTS IN DOCUMENTS AFFECTING
AN INTEREST IN PROPERTY**

A statement contained in a document purporting to establish or affect an interest in property if the matter stated was relevant to the purpose of the document, unless dealings with the property since the document was made have been inconsistent with the truth of the statement or the purport of the document.

**RULE 803(16) STATEMENTS IN
ANCIENT DOCUMENTS**

Statements in a document in existence twenty years or more the authenticity of which is established.

> ## RULE 803(17) MARKET REPORTS, COMMERCIAL PUBLICATIONS
>
> Market quotations, tabulations, lists, directories, or other published compilations, generally used and relied upon by the public or by persons in particular occupations.

Examples of things admitted under this exception include old letters, a service pass for a Nazi concentration camp guard, and the transcript of a statement given during World War II.

Market Reports and the Like

There is an exception for market reports and quotations, lists, commercial publications, and directories upon which either the general public or people in a particular occupation rely. The reason that these are considered reliable is that such things are published by those with motives for accuracy. If a phone book had many errors in it, the phone company would be inundated with complaint calls and people would rely on more accurate sources.

Examples of things admitted under this exception include testimony about a database of vehicle identification numbers; a phone directory; "Gun Trader's Guide;" and "The National Stock Summary." It is not utilized very much.

Learned Treatises

■ LEARNED TREATISE
A hearsay exception that allows an expert witnesses to refer to, and be cross-examined about, a text written for his or her profession.

When an expert testifies, the expert may refer to **learned treatises**, journals, or the like and the opposing attorney may cross-examine an expert using those items as well, even if the expert did not testify from it. With the assistance of the expert, the jury can benefit from the information in a treatise or journal article that is written by and for people in a highly educated profession such as medicine. However, such items standing alone are not generally admissible in most courts due to the risk that a fact finder not educated in the field will misunderstand the treatise. The expert needs to be able to explain and assist in the application of the concepts in the treatise or article in order for it to be admissible. Therefore, the treatise would not be admitted as an exhibit, and jurors would not be able to view it during deliberations. It must be established that the treatise is "a reliable authority," which can be done through testimony, or the court might take judicial notice of a particularly well known authority.

Examples of material admitted under this exception include a videotape produced for doctors by the American College of Obstetricians and Gynecologists regarding shoulder dystocia, a safety manual for fishing vessels, and banking and surgery treatises. In contrast, a Justice Department manual was not considered to be a learned treatise.

> ## RULE 803(18)
> ## LEARNED TREATISES
>
> To the extent called to the attention of an expert witness upon cross-examination or relied upon by the expert witness in direct examination, statements contained in published treatises, periodicals, or pamphlets on a subject of history, medicine, or other science or art, established as a reliable authority by the testimony or admission of the witness or by other expert testimony or by judicial notice. If admitted, the statements may be read into evidence but may not be received as exhibits.

Reputation Concerning Personal or Family History

The next exception is for reputation as to personal or family history. If you have an aunt and uncle who are around the same age as your parents, you assume that they are married, but how do you know? You were probably not at their wedding and probably have not seen their certificate of marriage, but he calls her his wife and she calls him her husband, everyone else in your family says they are married and acts as though they are married, and maybe you once saw their wedding photo album. But in order to testify that they are married you would need this hearsay exception, since you would be testifying about what you heard from relatives. At least one court has allowed reputation testimony from a person's workplace to be admitted under this exception. This is also used infrequently.

An example of evidence under this exception was testimony from an aunt that her nephew, who was allegedly an illegal alien, was not born in the United States.

Reputation Concerning Boundary or General History

There is an exception for land boundaries and general history. This exception is rarely used.

An example of its use was a statement regarding a boundary location.

> ## RULE 803(19) REPUTATION CONCERNING PERSONAL OR FAMILY HISTORY
>
> Reputation among members of a person's family by blood, adoption, or marriage, or among a person's associates, or in the community, concerning a person's birth, adoption, marriage, divorce, death, legitimacy, relationship by blood, adoption, or marriage, ancestry, or other similar fact of personal or family history.

> ### RULE 803(20) REPUTATION CONCERNING BOUNDARIES OR GENERAL HISTORY
>
> Reputation in a community, arising before the controversy, as to boundaries of or customs affecting lands in the community, and reputation as to events of general history important to the community or State or nation in which located.

Reputation as to Character

There is an exception for character evidence; however, such evidence may not be used to show that people acted consistent with their reputation. For example, a reputation as a heavy drinker could not be offered against a person charged with driving while intoxicated to prove that he or she had been drinking before the incident.

An example of its use was testimony that implied that a defendant in a drug case had previously delivered drugs, which was ruled admissible because it showed his good reputation in the drug community. Reputation evidence would be offered only in narrow circumstances for some purpose other than proving that a person acted according to his or her reputation, so this exception is not often used.

Prior Conviction Records

If a person pleads guilty or is convicted of a felony, that conviction may be entered into evidence. Civil judgments may not come into evidence through this exception. Evidence that an appeal is pending is admissible but does not preclude admission of the conviction.

> ### RULE 803(21) REPUTATION AS TO CHARACTER
>
> Reputation of a person's character among associates or in the community.

> ### RULE 803(22) JUDGMENT OF PREVIOUS CONVICTION
>
> Evidence of a final judgment, entered after a trial or upon a plea of guilty (but not upon a plea of nolo contendere), adjudging a person guilty of a crime punishable by death or imprisonment in excess of one year, to prove any fact essential to sustain the judgment, but not including, when offered by the Government in a criminal prosecution for purposes other than impeachment, judgments against persons other than the accused. The pendency of an appeal may be shown but does not affect admissibility.

> ### RULE 803(23) JUDGMENT AS TO PERSONAL, FAMILY OR GENERAL HISTORY, OR BOUNDARIES
>
> Judgments as proof of matters of personal, family or general history, or boundaries, essential to the judgment, if the same would be provable by evidence of reputation.

The exception for pleas of nolo contendre, which means "no contest," was rendered meaningless in one case due to the public records exception (exception 8), since a certified copy of a conviction obtained after a no contest plea was admissible under that exception.

Judgment as to Personal, Family, or General History or Boundaries

Civil judgments may be admitted under this exception if they prove matters of personal, family, or general history, or boundaries that were essential to the judgment and if the same assertion could be proven through reputation evidence.

An example of evidence admitted under this exception was land boundaries, established in a judgment from an earlier lawsuit.

Residual Exception

There is a catch-all exception, which is now Rule 807, but it used to be Rule 803(24). It is discussed below in the last section of this chapter.

WHEN DECLARANT IS UNAVAILABLE

There are additional exceptions to the hearsay rule that apply only if the declarant is unavailable to testify. Before examining these exceptions, we must consider what "unavailable" means. An **unavailable** declarant is one who

- has a legal privilege not to testify, such as doctor-patient or attorney-client privilege.
- refuses to testify or says he or she cannot remember the subject matter of his or her statement.
- is dead or physically or mentally unable to testify.
- disappears and cannot be found by the party trying to introduce his or her statement after a good-faith effort.

■ **UNAVAILABLE**
For purposes of hearsay, a witness is unavailable when the witness cannot testify due to privilege, physical inability, death, or the witness cannot be produced despite a good faith effort.

> ### RULE 804 HEARSAY EXCEPTIONS;
> ### DECLARANT UNAVAILABLE
>
> (a) Definition of unavailability. "Unavailability as a witness" includes situations in which the declarant—
>
> (1) is exempted by ruling of the court on the ground of privilege from testifying concerning the subject matter of the declarant's statement; or
>
> (2) persists in refusing to testify concerning the subject matter of the declarant's statement despite an order of the court to do so; or
>
> (3) testifies to a lack of memory of the subject matter of the declarant's statement; or
>
> (4) is unable to be present or to testify at the hearing because of death or then existing physical or mental illness or infirmity; or
>
> (5) is absent from the hearing and the proponent of a statement has been unable to procure the declarant's attendance (or in the case of a hearsay exception under subdivision (b)(2), (3), or
>
> (4), the declarant's attendance or testimony) by process or other reasonable means.
>
> A declarant is not unavailable as a witness if exemption, refusal, claim of lack of memory, inability, or absence is due to the procurement or wrongdoing of the proponent of a statement for the purpose of preventing the witness from attending or testifying.

A court may recognize that the declarant has a legal privilege against testifying such as the doctor-patient or attorney-client privilege. If the declarant is unable to testify due to a privilege, the declarant is unavailable. If the declarant refuses to testify, perhaps because the court declines to recognize the asserted privilege or maybe the declarant is scared of the criminal defendant or his associates, the court may issue an order forcing the declarant to testify, and if the declarant still refuses, he or she is unavailable.

For the declarant to be deemed unavailable due to a loss of memory, merely saying "I don't remember" is not sufficient. The party who is trying to have the witness declared unavailable must make a good-faith effort to get the witness to remember through refreshing the witness's recollection. It is not sufficient to have the witness declared unavailable if he or she only remembers bits and pieces of the subject matter of the statement. It does not matter if the witness does not remember giving a statement.

If a declarant is dead or has some sort of permanent injury that will prevent testimony indefinitely, for example being in a persistent vegetative state, the declarant is obviously unavailable. If the injury is temporary, a court will consider a number of factors such as how long it will take for the witness to become available, whether the trial could be delayed to allow the witness to recover, the importance of the testimony to the case, and the potential damage to the witness from testifying.

A party who wishes to have a witness declared unavailable due to inability to get the witness to court must show that an attempt was made to subpoena the witness or that the witness was outside the geographic jurisdiction of the court. For federal courts in civil cases, that generally means the witness was more than 100 miles from the location of the trial. For federal criminal cases, the jurisdiction is the entire country. For state courts, it varies but probably means anywhere within the state. The party must also be able to show that the witness cannot be induced to appear, and that an attempt was made to take the witness's deposition (unless the witness has already given a sworn statement or testified). However, these steps are also evaluated in terms of whether they are reasonable or not. Therefore, a party need not attempt to serve the witness if it can be shown that the witness cannot be found.

In criminal cases, hearsay exceptions based upon unavailability of witnesses can create constitutional issues due to the defendant's right to confront the witnesses against him or her. In order to get a statement into a criminal case under an unavailable witness exception, the statement must be backed up through some other evidence.

In the following case, the court considers whether a declarant who has been placed in a witness protection program is unavailable.

CASE
CONSOLIDATED RAIL CORP. V. DELAWARE RIVER PORT AUTHORITY, 880 A.2D 628 (PA. SUPER. CT., 2005.)

Conrail brought an action for breach of contract . . . Conrail offered, and the trial court accepted, a transcript of testimony of Mr. Angelucci to establish the contents of the containers in question. Mr. Angelucci had testified to the contents of these containers in a criminal trial concerning their theft. In exchange for testifying for the prosecution, Mr. Angelucci was placed in a witness protection program . . .

Thus, in *Lebo,* we found that proof of the efforts expended by the proponent to secure the declarant's presence was necessary to the qualification as "unavailable." We find the situation before us analogous, and so we reach a similar conclusion: a declarant is not unavailable per Rule 804 solely by virtue of participation in a witness protection program; the proponent of the statement must establish the reasonable measures taken to procure the declarant's attendance. In so holding, we again refuse to read the phrase, "the proponent of a statement has been unable to procure the declarant's attendance . . . by process or other reasonable means" out of the Rule. We do not speculate as to what efforts would satisfy this requirement. We simply hold that the mere assertion of such participation is not sufficient to establish a declarant's unavailability.

In reaching this conclusion, we are cognizant of the fact that *Lebo* involved a boot camp program; however, other courts have addressed the unavailability requirement in the context of witness protection programs.

(continues)

CASE

CONSOLIDATED RAIL CORP. V. DELAWARE RIVER PORT AUTHORITY,

880 A.2D 628 (PA. SUPER. CT., 2005.) *(continued)*

The record before us contains no evidence to prove that Conrail took any steps to procure the witness's appearance; rather, it appears that Conrail relied solely on Mr. Angelucci's membership in a witness protection program as proof of unavailability. As such, in the absence of evidence of measures taken to reach this witness, the trial court erred in finding Mr. Angelucci unavailable per Rule 804, and therefore erred in admitting the testimony.

The court found that merely being enrolled in a witness protection program is not enough to make a witness unavailable. The court declined to specify what steps could have been taken, but what Conrail could have done is questionable, since the whole point of a witness protection program is to allow the witnesses to change their identity, location, and occupation in order to avoid danger.

Four exceptions depend upon the witness being unavailable. Like the exceptions that do not depend upon unavailability, the rule that lists the exceptions indicates that the following are not excludable as hearsay and then lists exceptions. So when you read the rules in this section, remember that each one is part of a list that begins after the opening sentence of Rule 804; otherwise the exceptions sound like sentence fragments.

Former Testimony

When an unavailable witness has previously testified under oath, the former testimony may be admissible under this exception if the witness was then subjected to examination by the party against whom the testimony is offered or, in civil cases only, a person who had similar interests in terms of the issues needed to win the case.

Therefore, testimony taken in a deposition, trial, hearing, or other proceeding might be admitted into evidence if the witness is unavailable.

> ### RULE 804(B)(1)
> ### FORMER TESTIMONY
>
> Testimony given as a witness at another hearing of the same or a different proceeding, or in a deposition taken in compliance with law in the course of the same or another proceeding, if the party against whom the testimony is now offered, or, in a civil action or proceeding, a predecessor in interest, had an opportunity and similar motive to develop the testimony by direct, cross, or redirect examination.

Dying Declaration

There is a very narrow exception for time of near-death statements. The declarant must believe that he or she is about to die when making the statement, and the statement can be about only the circumstances or cause of the declarant's predicament. Such **dying declarations** are admissible in any civil case, but the only criminal case in which they can come into evidence is homicide.

In the following case, the court considers the statement of a shooting victim that implicated the defendants in her shooting.

> ### CASE
> ### UNITED STATES V. TAYLOR, 59 FED.APPX. 960 (9TH CIR. 2003).
>
> Taylor challenges the district court's decision to admit Alzinnia Keyes's statements to a fire department paramedic, Diane Benson, as a dying declaration. On the way to the hospital, Keyes grabbed Benson's arm and said "you need to get a hold of a DEA agent" and "tell him that Terile's people did this." Taylor challenges the admission of Keyes's statements to Benson as inadmissible hearsay. We affirm the district court's decision to admit Keyes's statements to Benson.
>
> In order for a statement to fall under the dying declaration exception, the declarant must have spoken without hope of recovery and in the shadow of impending death····
> Fear or even belief that illness will end in death will not avail itself to a make a dying
>
> *(continues)*

■ **DYING DECLARATION**

A hearsay exception that allows statements into evidence; that statement of a declarant who thinks he or she is about to die regarding the circumstances of incident.

CASE
UNITED STATES V. TAYLOR, 59 FED. APPX. 960 (9TH CIR. 2003).(continued)

declaration. There must be "a settled hopeless expectation" that death is near at hand, and what is said must have been spoken in the hush of its impending presence···· What is decisive is the state of mind. Even so, the state of mind must be exhibited in the evidence, and not left to conjecture. The patient must have spoken with the consciousness of a swift and certain doom.

Taylor argues that Keyes never stated that she believed she was going to die. A victim is not required, however, to make an explicit statement that he or she believes death is imminent. Rather, a victim's sense of impending death "may be made to appear from the nature and extent of the wounds inflicted being obviously such that he must have felt or known he could not survive." Here, the evidence shows that Keyes was bleeding profusely, in shock and in obvious pain after being shot. Paramedic Benson testified that Keyes appeared pale, cold, sweaty and that Keyes had an "impending doom look." In asking Benson to contact Agent Genualdi and tell him that "Terile's people did this," Keyes acted agitated and anxious; Keyes was grabbing at Benson's arm when Keyes made her request.

Furthermore, Dr. Johnson testified that Keyes arrived at the hospital emergency room "in extremis," meaning Keyes was in peril of dying. Dr. Johnson testified that people in Keyes's condition have a "feeling of potential impending doom" and "in particular this patient she felt like she was going to die."

It is permissible to infer from the evidence that Keyes believed she was dying. Such an inference would not be "conjecture," but a rational conclusion drawn from the obvious "nature and extent of the wounds inflicted." The content of Keyes's statements is also an indication that Keyes thought death was imminent. Keyes's statements were an attempt to identify her killers. In asking Benson to tell Agent Genualdi that "Terile's people did this," it is reasonable to believe that Keyes did not think that she would survive to tell Agent Genualdi herself. The district court did not err in admitting Keyes's statements under the dying declaration exception to the hearsay rule.

The court concluded that, because the circumstances indicated that she thought she was dying, her statement was a dying declaration admissible under this rule.

RULE 804(B)(2) STATEMENT UNDER
BELIEF OF IMPENDING DEATH

In a prosecution for homicide or in a civil action or proceeding, a statement made by a declarant while believing that the declarant's death was imminent, concerning the cause or circumstances of what the declarant believed to be impending death.

EXHIBIT 8–2   Dying Declaration, or Not

WHO SAID IT?	WHO WHERE THEY?	WHAT WERE THEIR LAST WORDS?	NOTES
Boromir	Character from *Lord of the Rings*	"Farewell, Aragorn. Go to Minas Tirith and save my people! I have failed."	He tried to take the evil magic ring.
Lady Nancy Witcher Langhorne Astor	British politician and aristocrat	"Am I dying or is this my birthday?"	She spoke those words on her death bed when she momentarily awoke with her family surrounding her.
John Wilkes Booth	The man who killed Lincoln	"Tell mother, tell mother, I died for my country.... useless... useless..."	He was mumbling after being shot.
Jane Dornacker	Traffic reporter (also a comedian and an actress who played a nurse in the movie *The Right Stuff*)	"Heading to New Jersey, the outbound Lincoln Tunnel looks a lot better for you, in New Jersey..." (Gasp) "Hit the water! Hit the water! Hit the water!"	The helicopter she was doing a radio traffic report from struck the sidewalk and a chain-link fence before falling into the Hudson River, where she drowned.
Dominique Bouhours	French grammarian	"I am about to—or I am going to—die; either expression is used."	Are not grammarians annoying? Wait, was that grammatical?
Princess Diana	Princess of Wales	"My God. What's happened?"	Her last words were recorded by the police.
Richard Loeb	Rich, convicted kidnapper and murderer	"I think I'm going to make it."	Killed in a prison shower fight.
Huey Long	Governor of Louisiana and senator	"I wonder why he shot me?"	He was killed by the relative of a previous opponent.
Franklin Delano Roosevelt	U.S. president	"I have a terrific headache."	He then died of a cerebral hemorrhage.
Hal 9000	Super-computer in *2001: A Space Odyssey*	"Dave, stop. Stop will you? Stop, Dave. Will you stop, Dave? Stop, Dave. I'm afraid. I'm afraid, Dave. Dave, my mind is going. I can feel it. I can feel it. My mind is...Good afternoon, I am a HAL 9000 computer..."	He then sings "Daisy" as he is turned off.
Thelma and Louise	Title characters of the movie *Thelma & Louise*	Louise: What are you talking about? Thelma: Go. (*indicating the Grand Canyon*) Louise: Go? Thelma: Go. Thelma: You're a good friend. Louise: You, too, sweetie, the best. Are you sure? Thelma: Hit it.	They crash their car into the Grand Canyon.

Statement Against Interest

If a declarant says something that goes so far against his or her interests that no reasonable person would make such a statement unless it were true, then it may be admissible under this hearsay exception. Statements might go against the declarant's financial interests or subject the declarant to jail time. The declarant must know that the statement is against his or her interest. However, statements that would merely subject the declarant to social problems such as being ridiculed are not covered by this exception. Statements against penal interest must be corroborated. This exception differs from the admission of a party opponent qualification of the hearsay definition in the previous chapter, because that qualification only applied when it was offered against the party.

Examples of statements against interest that were admitted under this exception include:

- a statement from a co-defendant in a criminal case that declarant had accompanied the defendant on several other drug deals.
- "Mr. Joyce informed me that he was told by [DSI owner] Danny Jackson to steal on approximately 75% of the deliveries and he was supposed to steal for between three and five minutes."
- a married woman admitting having sex outside the marriage.

Statement of Personal or Family History

There is an exception for a declarant to state information about the declarant's birth, adoption, marriage, divorce, "or other similar fact" of personal or family history. The exception is not frequently used.

RULE 804(B)(3) STATEMENT AGAINST INTEREST

A statement which was, at the time of its making, so far contrary to the declarant's pecuniary or proprietary interest, or so far tended to subject the declarant to civil or criminal liability, or to render invalid a claim by the declarant against another, that a reasonable person in the declarant's position would not have made the statement unless believing it to be true. A statement tending to expose the declarant to criminal liability and offered to exculpate the accused is not admissible unless corroborating circumstances clearly indicate the trustworthiness of the statement.

> **RULE 804(B)(4) STATEMENT OF PERSONAL OR FAMILY HISTORY**
>
> (A) A statement concerning the declarant's own birth, adoption, marriage, divorce, legitimacy, relationship by blood, adoption, or marriage, ancestry, or other similar fact of personal or family history, even though declarant had no means of acquiring personal knowledge of the matter stated; or (B) a statement concerning the foregoing matters, and death also, of another person, if the declarant was related to the other by blood, adoption, or marriage or was so intimately associated with the other's family as to be likely to have accurate information concerning the matter declared.

An example of a statement admitted under this section was a declarant's statement regarding the declarant's national origin and citizenship in an illegal alien smuggling case.

Catch-All Exception

Rule 803(5) was transferred to Rule 807, described below in the section titled "Catch-All Exception."

Forfeiture by Wrongdoing

If a declarant is unavailable due to a party's wrongdoing, then the declarant's statement will be admitted under this exception. Most courts have held that the party offering the statement must prove by a preponderance of the evidence that it was the actions of the party against whom the statement would be offered that rendered the declarant unavailable.

For example, if a criminal defendant kills an eyewitness to a murder after the eyewitness has given a statement to the police, the eyewitness's testimony will still be presented under this exception. This exception is not used frequently.

> **RULE 804(B)(6) FORFEITURE BY WRONGDOING**
>
> A statement offered against a party that has engaged or acquiesced in wrongdoing that was intended to, and did, procure the unavailability of the declarant as a witness.

CATCH-ALL EXCEPTION

In addition to all the exceptions already discussed, there is one that basically says if a statement does not fit one of the specifically listed exceptions, but it is just as trustworthy as something that does, it is admissible. It is called the residual exception or the **catch-all** exception. However, in order to come into evidence under this exception, the circumstances must be extraordinary. After all, what would be the point of the rule and all these detailed exceptions if the residual exception were an open door? Therefore, a statement admitted under the residual exception must be particularly trustworthy and relevant, it must be the most probative evidence available on the topic at hand, and admission of the statement must further the purposes of the rules of evidence and the interests of justice. Due to all these requirements, the rule is rarely used successfully, and that was the intent of the rule's drafters. Furthermore, if a party intends to offer evidence under this exception, it must give the other party notice that it intends to do so.

An example of a statement admitted under this section involved a police officer dictating a report with his informant standing next to him. The informant could have corrected him about something they had both witnessed. Most other attempts to get evidence admitted under this exception have failed.

RULE 807
RESIDUAL EXCEPTION

A statement not specifically covered by Rule 803 or 804, but having equivalent circumstantial guarantees of trustworthiness, is not excluded by the hearsay rule, if the court determines that (A) the statement is offered as evidence of a material fact; (B) the statement is more probative on the point for which it is offered than any other evidence which the proponent can procure through reasonable efforts; and (C) the general purposes of these rules and the interests of justice will best be served by admission of the statement into evidence. However, a statement may not be admitted under this exception unless the proponent of it makes known to the adverse party sufficiently in advance of the trial or hearing to provide the adverse party with a fair opportunity to prepare to meet it, the proponent's intention to offer the statement and the particulars of it including the name and address of the declarant.

SUMMARY

There are many exceptions to hearsay that arguably consume the rule. However, hearsay statements that do not meet all the criteria for an exception will be excluded. Therefore, despite all the qualifications and exceptions, some hearsay will not be admissible. There are many exceptions to consider; however, some are technical and not frequently used.

■ KEY TERMS

catch-all	learned treatise	res gestae
dying declaration	present sense impression	state of mind
excited utterance	recorded recollection	unavailable

■ REVIEW AND DISCUSSION QUESTIONS

1. To what extent do the exceptions and qualifications consume the rule?
2. What are the most important exceptions?
3. What do the exceptions have in common?
4. What steps can a party take to try to get witnesses declared unavailable on the grounds that the party cannot find them?
5. Think of or find an excited utterance or present sense impression from a book, movie, play, or TV show.
6. Think of a res gestae exception from your own life.

■ LEGAL RESEARCH PROJECTS

1. Get a copy of one of the cases excerpted in this chapter and read all of it. Brief the case by providing a summary of the facts, the legal issue, the holding, and the court's reasoning.
2. Does your state reject any federal hearsay exceptions? Which one(s)? Analyze whether the exceptions in your state really do swallow the rule that hearsay is inadmissible.
3. Find a statement in your life or in the print media, movies, television, or radio that would arguably be considered a hearsay statement that would meet the criteria for a res gestae exception. Explain why it would be hearsay and why it might or might not come under the res gestae exception.

For additional resources, visit our Web site at www.westlegalstudies.com

CHAPTER 9

Opinion

■ OBJECTIVES

❑ Classify opinion evidence as lay or expert
❑ Examine Rules 701–706
❑ Deduce the likelihood of opinion testimony being admissible
❑ Relate the process for obtaining expert testimony
❑ Contrast the different standards for admitting expert testimony such as *Frye* and *Daubert*

WHY LET OPINION EVIDENCE IN?

It is difficult to draw a hard-and-fast rule between fact and opinion. If a witness testifies that the light at the intersection was yellow for Driver A and red for Driver B in the moment before the accident, that statement is clearly factual. If the witness testifies that it was not safe for Driver A to proceed through the intersection, that is opinion. But what about a statement that the yellow light was not yellow for very long? Is that fact or opinion? There used to be a blanket rule that opinion evidence was not admissible. This rule proved to be unworkable. Yet making a distinction between fact and opinion has some utility in determining what evidence should be admitted. Therefore, witness statements that reach conclusions, draw inferences, or make evaluations are generally admissible.

There are two types of opinion evidence, lay testimony and expert testimony. **Lay opinion** testimony is from a non-expert that goes beyond stating facts and includes inferences, estimates, or conclusions. A person may not know how to design, fix, or fly an airplane, but his or her opinion of the altitude of an airplane would be admissible. Without some experience or education, however, that person would not be allowed to testify regarding the mechanical cause of a plane crash, or the proper procedure to land in a crosswind. Those things would require expert testimony. **Expert opinion** testimony is from a witness whose education, experience, or both will help the jury understand a medical, technical, professional, or scientific aspect of a case.

LAY OPINION TESTIMONY

It can be difficult to distinguish between fact and lay opinion evidence. Lay opinion evidence can involve allowing the witness to state the conclusion that was apparent from the obvious facts. Have you ever read a police report? Officers try to be very dry and state "just the facts." But this is not how people talk, nor is it compelling, persuasive, or interesting to listen to, and it is much less time consuming to give an opinion than to simply give the facts underlying the opinion. Testimony that is like a police report in that it simply states the facts might sound like this:

WITNESS: I noticed as soon as the defendant rolled down his car window a strong odor of alcohol. His eyes were red and watery. He could not stop laughing. He slurred his speech. His breath had a strong odor of alcohol. When he tried to get his wallet out he reached in three pockets before finding it. He then dropped the wallet on the floor.

How boring was that to read? Did you find it persuasive? Now consider the same testimony where the witness is allowed to state his opinion:

WITNESS: I thought he was one of the drunkest drivers I've seen in my twenty years as a cop.

Note how much shorter and yet more persuasive that testimony was.

A lay witness need not have any specialized knowledge through education, training, or experience in order to give testimony that does not require any special

> ■ **LAY OPINION**
> Opinion testimony from a non-expert that is admissible when it is about a subject that does not require training or experience in order for the witness to provide helpful insight to the fact finder.
>
> ■ **EXPERT OPINION**
> Opinion testimony from a witness with training, education, or experience that qualifies the witness to testify about a topic generally beyond the understanding of an average person, and is admissible when it would be helpful to the fact finder.

RULE 701. OPINION TESTIMONY BY LAY WITNESSES

If the witness is not testifying as an expert, the witness' testimony in the form of opinions or inferences is limited to those opinions or inferences which are (a) rationally based on the perception of the witness and (b) helpful to a clear understanding of the witness' testimony or the determination of a fact in issue.

background in order to have a valid opinion. A lay witness can testify about the apparent speed of a car, whether a person looks like the perpetrator of a crime, the color of an object, or the temperature of food. Exhibit 9–1 shows some related things that some courts have found to be admissible and inadmissible lay opinion.

A corollary to this rule is known as the **collective facts rule**, which allows a lay witness to testify to a conclusion or opinion. Under this rule, observations about how much another person suffered or another person's mental state would be admissible.

■ **COLLECTIVE FACTS RULE**

An opinion that is admissible when there is no other way to describe an observation because the phenomenon is too complex or subtle.

EXPERT OPINION TESTIMONY

The rules regarding expert opinion evidence vary from the rules for lay experts.

Qualifications of an Expert Witness

An expert needs to have either knowledge, skill, experience, training, or education that would qualify an individual to help the jury understand the evidence. The expert need not have testified as an expert before, nor have expertise in the exact topic at hand, or a specialized degree. As long as the expert has the background to support the expert testimony, the expert's testimony will be admissible. Courts are flexible when it comes to allowing experts to testify. This is because the courts assume that juries can weigh the persuasiveness of the testimony based upon the expert's qualifications. For example, if a witness is not a specialist within the profession, yet is testifying within a specialty, the court will generally allow such testimony. The lack of qualification will go to the weight of the evidence. Experts who lacked proper licenses in the state that they were testifying or held the minimum level of education needed to do their jobs, and a professor

---

EXHIBIT 9–1

ADMISSABLE OPINION	INADMISSABLE OPINION
Room smelled like marijuana	Street value of marijuana
Handwriting of someone witness knows	Signature on paper matched that of someone witness did not know
Value of witness' own house	Value of another person's house
Weather at time of accident	Accident was cause of miscarriage
Physical appearance of crack cocaine	Chemical composition of crack cocaine
Person was intoxicated	Effects on person who inhaled benzaldehyde
Paint color on tools matched paint color on burgled building	Effect of anti-graffiti ordinance on paint sales

EXHIBIT 9–1   Lay Opinion—Admissible or Not?

> ### RULE 702.
> ### TESTIMONY BY EXPERTS
>
> If scientific, technical, or other specialized knowledge will assist the trier of fact to understand the evidence or to determine a fact in issue, a witness qualified as an expert by knowledge, skill, experience, training, or education may testify thereto in the form of an opinion or otherwise.

who had not published on the topic of her testimony, were all allowed to testify as experts. On the other hand, when a plumber who was a union steward tried to testify about public finance, the court ruled that the expert's testimony was inadmissible.

Expert Testimony Must Assist the Trier of Fact

Expert testimony must assist the judge or jury in understanding something that is generally beyond the knowledge of the average citizen. Expert testimony will not be helpful to the trier of fact if it is conclusory or argumentative.

BENCH BRIEF ENTERTAINMENT NOTE

In the following scene from the screenplay for *My Cousin Vinny*, Mona Lisa Vito is an unemployed hairdresser, yet she is qualified as an expert on auto repair.

D.A. JIM TROTTER: Ms. Vito, what is your current profession?

LISA: I'm an out-of-work hairdresser.

D.A. JIM TROTTER: An out-of-work hairdresser. In what way does that qualify you as an expert in automobiles?

LISA: It doesn't.

[she indicates that her training is from working on cars her whole life]

D.A. JIM TROTTER: Now, Ms. Vito, being an expert on general automotive knowledge, can you tell me . . . what would the correct ignition timing be on a 1955 Bel Air Chevrolet, with a 327 cubic-inch engine and a four-barrel carburetor?

MONA LISA VITO: No, it is a trick question!

JUDGE CHAMBERLAIN HALLER: Why is it a trick question?

MONA LISA VITO: 'Cause Chevy didn't make a 327 in '55, the 327 didn't come out till '63. And it wasn't offered in the Bel Air with a four-barrel carb till '64. However, in 1964, the correct ignition timing would be four degrees before top-dead-center.

D.A. JIM TROTTER: Well . . . uh . . . she's acceptable, Your Honor.

In the following case, the court considers whether an expert's test of a refrigerator door to see if it would crush a carrot is useful to the trier of fact.

Here the trial court found that the testimony would not be helpful because no external force was alleged to have crushed the plaintiff's finger and because the expert's methodology was so lacking.

Standards for Admitting Expert Testimony

There are two standards that are used when determining the admissibility of expert testimony, the *Frye* and *Daubert* standards. When a party seeks to admit expert testimony, the area of expertise about which the expert would testify must meet whichever standard applies. If the topic about which the expert would testify does not meet the standard, then usually the expert will not be allowed to testify at all, unless he or she has some other relevant testimony to offer. Therefore, this textbook refers to experts and expert testimony interchangeably.

Frye Standard

■ **FRYE**

A standard for the admission of scientific expert testimony is based upon the acceptance of the topic by the scientific community.

Prior to the enactment of the Federal Rules of Evidence, admission of expert testimony was evaluated for admissibility using the **Frye** standard. In *Frye*, a federal district court considered whether expert testimony based upon a rough predecessor

CASE
BELOFSKY V. GENERAL ELEC. CO., 980 F. SUPP. 818 (D.V.I. OCT. 20, 1997)

Plaintiff claimed that she was injured by a General Electric . . . refrigerator when . . . [it] . . . closed by itself with enough force to crush her left thumb . . .

[P]laintiff sent Mr. Ervin Leshner a letter requesting his opinion as an expert witness. A mere ten days later, and without examining the refrigerator, talking to plaintiff, or doing any independent investigation, Leshner issued a report based solely on the representations of plaintiff and plaintiff's counsel contained in the letter. His report regurgitated the facts of plaintiff's letter and concluded with an opinion that plaintiff's injuries were caused by a dangerous pinch point and defective cam in the refrigerator door . . . .

In addition to the lack of reliable procedure or methodology used by Leshner in coming to his conclusions about the door's ability to close by itself, his test and opinion based on that test have nothing to do with plaintiff's claim that the door closed by itself on her thumb. Other than assuming the truth of representations made in the initial letter from plaintiff's counsel, the only procedure used by Leshner in testing was to see if the door would crush a carrot when force was used to push it shut. There is no fit between his technique and the facts of this case . . . . Therefore, the one "test" Leshner did perform is not helpful to the jury under Rule 702. Accordingly, Leshner's testimony about crushing the carrot must be excluded.

of the polygraph should be allowed into evidence. *Frye v. United States*, 293 F. 1013 (D.C. Cir. 1923). The *Frye* court based its decision not to admit the evidence on the fact that the test was not yet generally accepted by the scientific community. The *Frye* standard was pervasive, adopted by many states, and it had been the standard under which the scientific basis of proffered expert testimony was evaluated for more than 50 years. In 1993 the U.S. Supreme Court considered whether Rule 702 superseded *Frye* in **Daubert** *v. Merrell Dow Pharmaceuticals, Inc.*, 509 U.S. 579 (1993).

Daubert Overrules *Frye*

Daubert held that the *Frye* standard was incompatible with both Rule 702 and the intention of the drafters of the rules to remove obstacles to expert witness testimony. It said that courts should act as gatekeepers to make sure that expert testimony is admissible. A hearing is typically held outside the presence of the jury if a question is raised about the admissibility of expert testimony. The party offering the testimony must show that it is admissible by a preponderance of the evidence. A later case extended Daubert to all expert testimony, not just scientific experts. *Kumho Tire Co., Ltd. v. Carmichael*, 526 U.S. 137 (1999).

Daubert listed the following factors courts could use to consider the admissibility of expert testimony:

- Is the scientific theory testable and has it been tested?
- Has it been subject to the academic process of publication and peer review?
- What is the error rate?
- Are there standards controlling the technique?
- Is the technique generally accepted by scientists or those working in the alleged field of expertise?

The *Daubert* factors were not exclusive. Other courts have also considered:

- Was the expert's research conducted outside of litigation or did the expert develop the opinion for the sole purpose of giving expert testimony?
- How tenuous is the link between the expert's premise and the expert's conclusion?
- Did the expert consider alternative explanations?
- Is the expert using the same care in testifying that the expert uses in his or her profession?
- Is the field in which the expert is offering testimony known for reaching reliable results on the topic?

Judges are free to consider additional factors as well.

In response to *Daubert* and cases that applied it, Rule 702 was amended to make it clear that judges are to determine the admissibility of expert testimony. This is referred to as giving judges a **gatekeeper** role. The rule applies to all expert testimony, not just scientific testimony, and the party seeking to admit expert testimony has the burden to show that it is admissible.

■ DAUBERT
A standard for the admission of scientific testimony based upon a multi-factor test.

■ GATEKEEPER
The judge's role, under *Daubert*, to make sure that expert testimony will be helpful to the jury.

BENCH BRIEF

NOTE

As with rules, most attorneys do not have case names memorized or know what a case is about just from the name. *Daubert* and *Frye* are exceptions.

Some states have rejected *Frye* by adopting *Daubert* (or a similar test), while others have rejected *Daubert* by sticking with the *Frye* standard. Some states have not completely rejected *Frye* but use some *Daubert* factors, and a few states use their own tests. (See Exhibit 9–2.) Some states vary which test applies based upon the nature of the expert testimony being offered or the type of case. For example, West Virginia

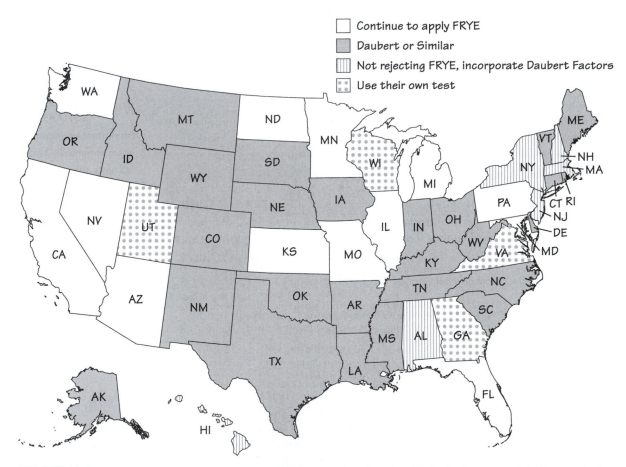

EXHIBIT 9–2   This map shows which states have rejected Frye and adopted Daubert; those that have retained the Frye standard, yet use some of the Daubert factors without rejecting Frye; and those that made up their own test.

PASSIM CASE **FIELDS VS. PRAIRIE BANK**

Prairie Bank routinely fingerprints all of its employees. Peter Fields agreed to have his fingerprints taken during the course of the investigation. On the Fields file a partial fingerprint was found that belonged neither to anyone at the bank nor to Fields (see Exhibit 9–3). Let us consider whether expert testimony regarding fingerprints would be admissible under *Frye* or *Daubert*.

EXHIBIT 9–3   Fingerprint.

Under *Frye*, the test for whether fingerprint comparison evidence is admissible is whether or not it is generally accepted by practitioners of the relevant field. For fingerprints, the relevant field would be forensic science. Fingerprints are some of the oldest biometric material admitted into evidence. They have been ruled admissible in court since at least 1911. Under *Daubert*, the question is whether fingerprint comparison evidence would be helpful to the jury.

does not apply *Daubert* to polygraph tests. Texas uses a test similar to *Daubert*, but not for ballistics experts.

Although the Supreme Court in *Daubert* indicated that a basis for its ruling was the intention of the drafters of the Rules of Evidence to make it easier to get expert testimony into evidence, the net effect may be to make it more difficult. Under *Frye*, if the topic on which the expert testimony is offered has general acceptance in the appropriate field, it is admissible. Under *Daubert*, the *Frye* test is incorporated along with many other factors.

CASE
UNITED STATES V. CRISP, 324 F.3D 261 (4TH CIR. 2003)

We turn first to whether the fingerprint evidence was properly admitted against Crisp. Crisp['s primary] . . . challenge [to] the admission of this evidence . . . is that the premises underlying fingerprinting evidence have not been adequately tested. Crisp also maintains that there is no known rate of error for latent fingerprint identifications, that fingerprint

(continues)

CASE
UNITED STATES V. CRISP, 324 F.3D 261 (4TH CIR. 2003) *(continued)*

examiners operate without a uniform threshold of certainty required for a positive iden-tification, and that fingerprint evidence has not achieved general acceptance in the rele-vant scientific community.

Crisp begins with the contention that the basic premises underlying fingerprint iden-tification have not been subjected to adequate testing. The two premises that he singles out as requiring more searching scrutiny are: (1) that no two persons share the same fingerprint; and (2) that fingerprint examiners are able to make reliable identifications on the basis of small, distorted latent fingerprint fragments. In support of his assertions, Crisp notes that the expert in this case, Brannan, was unable to reference any study establishing that no two persons share the same fingerprint; she was able only to testify that no study had ever proven this premise false.

Crisp next maintains that, because the basic premises behind fingerprint analysis have not been properly tested, there can be no established error rates. He also asserts that fingerprint examiners operate without uniform, objective standards, noting that Brannan herself testified that there is no generally accepted standard regarding the number of points of identification necessary to make a positive identification. Finally, Crisp contends that, while fingerprint analysis has gained general acceptance among fingerprint examiners themselves, this factor should be discounted because, according to Crisp, the relevant community "is devoid of financially disinterested parties such as academics."

Fingerprint identification has been admissible as reliable evidence in criminal trials in this country since at least 1911. While we have not definitively assessed the admissi-bility of expert fingerprint identifications in the post-*Daubert* era, every Circuit that has done so has found such evidence admissible. While the principles underlying fingerprint identification have not attained the status of scientific law, they nonetheless bear the imprimatur of a strong general acceptance, not only in the expert community, but in the courts as well.

As here, the defendant [in a seventh circuit case] . . . contended that "fingerprint comparisons are not reliable because the government admits that the basic premise that all fingerprints are unique remains unproven, and because there are no objective stan-dards for defining how much of a latent fingerprint is necessary to conduct a compari-son or for evaluating an individual examiner's comparison." Emphasizing that general acceptance remains an important consideration under *Daubert,* the Seventh Circuit con-cluded that the district court properly recognized that "establishing the reliability of fingerprint analysis was made easier by its 100 years of successful use in criminal trials, and appropriately noted that nothing presented at the hearing undermined [the expert's] testimony."

Since this was a federal case, the court had to use the *Daubert* test. However, the court focused on the single *Daubert* factor that stems from *Frye*—general acceptance. It found that fingerprint evidence had been admitted into court for 100 years and used that as the primary basis for deciding that the *Daubert* factors were met.

Factual Basis of Expert Testimony

What evidence can an expert rely upon when rendering an opinion? An expert does not need personal knowledge about the facts in a case. An expert may rely upon unsworn statements from other experts even if not admitted into evidence, hearsay such as medical records (as long as it is of a type upon which experts in the field rely), a party's statements, data the expert did not personally collect, summaries of data, and things that are inadmissible (however, experts may not generally disclose inadmissible evidence).

However, expert testimony should be excluded when the opinion is speculative, when it is based upon facts not in the record, assumed facts, or when it merely repeats what another expert said without evaluating it.

Ultimate Issue

There used to be a rule that experts could not testify on the **ultimate issue**. This meant that the expert was not supposed to testify to the jury about how to decide the case. The difference between providing a useful opinion and not saying how to decide the case was a thin one. Awkward questions and answers that pushed the border of speaking on the topic resulted. For example, an expert might not have been allowed to say "Plaintiff was negligent" but might have been allowed to say what the plaintiff's duty was, what the standards of the industry called for, how plaintiff

■ **ULTIMATE ISSUE**
A question the fact finder will be required to answer in order to return a verdict.

RULE 703. BASES OF OPINION TESTIMONY BY EXPERTS

The facts or data in the particular case upon which an expert bases an opinion or inference may be those perceived by or made known to the expert at or before the hearing. If of a type reasonably relied upon by experts in the particular field in forming opinions or inferences upon the subject, the facts or data need not be admissible in evidence in order for the opinion or inference to be admitted. Facts or data that are otherwise inadmissible shall not be disclosed to the jury by the proponent of the opinion or inference unless the court determines that their probative value in assisting the jury to evaluate the expert's opinion substantially outweighs their prejudicial effect.

> ### RULE 704 OPINION ON ULTIMATE ISSUE
>
> (a) Except as provided in subdivision (b), testimony in the form of an opinion or inference otherwise admissible is not objectionable because it embraces an ultimate issue to be decided by the trier of fact.
>
> (b) No expert witness testifying with respect to the mental state or condition of a defendant in a criminal case may state an opinion or inference as to whether the defendant did or did not have the mental state or condition constituting an element of the crime charged or of a defense thereto. Such ultimate issues are matters for the trier of fact alone.

breached the duty, and that the breach caused damages—all the elements of a negligence claim without explicitly stating that plaintiff was negligent. As a result, the ultimate issue rule allows experts to testify on the overarching questions that the jurors will answer in the jury room when they fill out their verdict form.

The exception comes in criminal cases where an expert may not testify about the defendant's state of mind, such as whether the defendant acted intentionally, knowingly, or with whatever *mens rea*, or state of mind, the crime requires. In the following case, the court considers whether an expert testified on the ultimate issue of whether the defendant possessed drugs with intent to distribute.

> ### CASE
> ### UNITED STATES V. WATSON, 260 F.3D 301 (3RD CIR. 2001)
>
> It is well established that experts may describe, in general and factual terms, the common practices of drug dealers. Expert testimony is admissible if it merely "support [s] an inference or conclusion that the defendant did or did not have the requisite mens rea, so long as the expert does not draw the ultimate inference or conclusion for the jury and the ultimate inference or conclusion does not necessarily follow from the testimony." "It is only as to the last step in the inferential process—a conclusion as to the defendant's mental state—that Rule 704(b) commands the expert to be silent." United States v. Dunn, 846 F.2d 761, 762 (D.C.Cir.1988).
>
> Rule 704(b) may be violated when the prosecutor's question is plainly designed to elicit the expert's testimony about the mental state of the defendant, or when the expert triggers the application of Rule 704(b) by directly referring to the defendant's intent, mental state, or mens rea, . . .
>
> *(continues)*

CASE
UNITED STATES V. WATSON, 260 F.3D 301 (3RD CIR. 2001) *(continued)*

Watson argues that the Government violated <u>Rule 704(b)</u> because its three witnesses testified as to Watson's mental state. First, Watson argues that Officer Schwartz's testimony concerning the purpose for the 100 plastic bags found on his person violated <u>Rule 704(b)</u>. We agree . . . Mr. Rocktashel's question to Officer Schwartz was plainly designed to elicit the expert's testimony about Watson's intent. Mr. Rocktashel's repeated references to Watson's intent elicited the offending response from Officer Schwartz when he testified that, in his opinion, Watson "possess[ed] with the intent to distribute to someone else."

Second, Watson argues that the colloquy between Mr. Rocktashel and Officer Mincer elicited testimony that violated <u>Rule 704(b)</u>. Prosecutors may not circumvent <u>Rule 704(b)</u> by repeatedly referring to a defendant's intent in a question to an expert. Mr. Rocktashel's repeated invocation of the word "intent," framed Mincer's "Yes sir," response in such a way that the necessary inference to be drawn from Mincer's response was that Watson possessed crack with the intent to distribute it. Therefore, Mincer's "Yes sir" response violated <u>Rule 704(b)</u>.

Third, Watson argues that Agent Paret's rebuttal testimony concerning the nature of Watson's bus travel itinerary violated Rule 704(b) . . . Mr. Rocktashel's question to Paret . . . was designed to elicit testimony about Watson's intent. Rocktashel asked whether Watson's particular "trip . . . [was] for the purpose of distribution, transfer and delivery of drugs, as opposed to procurement of drugs for personal use?" Although Agent Paret did not specifically refer to Watson in his response, and used the collective "they" when indicating "they'd gone into the city to purchase drugs to, ultimately, take back and resell at their starting point," Paret's opinion necessarily implies that the purpose of Walker's short bus trip was to distribute drugs rather than to obtain drugs for personal use. The unmistakable import of Agent Paret's opinion was that Watson intended to buy drugs to distribute them.

. . . the Government violated Rule 704(b) by repeatedly eliciting from its experts testimony as to Watson's mental state and the purpose of his actions . . . narcotics experts may testify about drug dealing, but they are in no way qualified to testify about a defendant's mental condition. Therefore, the District Court erred when it admitted the Government's expert testimony concerning Watson's mental state. That evidence went to the heart of the Government's case and plainly prejudiced defendant.

For the foregoing reasons, we will REVERSE the Judgment and Commitment Order and REMAND the case to the District Court for further proceedings.

The court found that the ultimate issue rule was broken in several different ways, and that the error was so prejudicial to the defendant that it needed to reverse the conviction.

Miscellaneous Expert Opinion Points

- Rule 705 allows experts to testify without first having to identify the factual basis for their opinion. This minimizes the need for hypothetical questions and puts the onus on the attorney cross-examining the witness to attack the basis of the opinion.
- Rule 706 allows courts to appoint their own experts. In civil cases, the court can require the parties to pay for it. In criminal cases the expert may be paid with public funds. The court may choose to inform the jury that it appointed the expert.
- Experts may not testify about the law.

SUMMARY

Opinion evidence is admissible. If it is from a lay person, no special training or experience is needed to form such an opinion. If it is from an expert, the expert must be qualified to testify on the topic, and the topic must be either well accepted by the relevant community (in *Frye* states) or scientifically verified or verifiable (in *Daubert* states and federal jurisdictions). Experts may rely on a wide variety of information in forming their opinion, including inadmissible evidence. They may testify regarding the ultimate question for the jury to decide, as long as the topic is not the state of mind of a criminal defendant.

■ KEY TERMS _____

collective facts rule	Frye	ultimate issue
Daubert	gatekeeper	
expert opinion	lay opinion	

■ REVIEW AND DISCUSSION QUESTIONS _____

1. Would lay opinion be admissible on the following?
   - the amount of pain another person experienced
   - the color of a car
   - the quality of a person's physical fitness
   - whether a person is careful or not
   - what constitutes a prudent practice in the operation of a tower crane
   - whether a person should have been fired
   - whether another witness is telling the truth

- the intentions of a party in a civil case
- how long candy appeared to be on the floor

2. Consider whether the following expert testimony would be admissible under *Frye* or *Daubert* (or your state's test):

- brain mapping (PET, SPECT, MRI, EEG, MEG, optical imaging, and neuroanatomical tools for evaluating the brain and motor systems, vision, attention, memory, and language)
- graphotheraphy (using handwriting as therapy to modify personality)
- phrenology (study of the shape and unevenness of the head to show intellectual aptitude and character traits)
- bullet identification
- astrology
- dating of photographs
- footprint or shoeprint identification
- forensic linguistic analysis ("Study, analysis and measurement of language in the context of crime, judicial procedure, or disputes in law.")
- handwriting
- microscopic comparison of bullets
- forensic serology
- blood stain pattern analysis
- numerology (the study of the occult meanings of numbers and their supposed influence on human life)
- tagging of explosives
- tool mark identification
- psychometry (the ability to read information about a person or place by touching a physical object)

■ LEGAL RESEARCH PROJECTS

1. Get a copy of one of the cases excerpted in this chapter and read all of it. Brief the case by providing a summary of the facts, the legal issue, the holding, and the court's reasoning.
2. Find and summarize a law review or law journal article about *Daubert* and its aftermath.
3. What standard for expert testimony does your state follow? *Frye*, *Daubert*, or something else?

For additional resources, visit our Web site at www.westlegalstudies.com

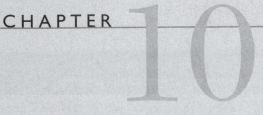
Getting Ready for Trial

Courtesy of CartoonStock.com.
www.CartoonStock.com

■ OBJECTIVES

❏ Relate the importance of having a paralegal organize a file
❏ Describe how to keep a file organized during its progression
❏ Construct a trial notebook
❏ Illustrate the steps taken to subpoena a witness for a deposition or trial
❏ Comprehend motions in limine
❏ Distinguish among the various alternative dispute resolution systems

WHY HAVING A PARALEGAL ORGANIZE A FILE IS IMPORTANT

File organization is one area where a paralegal can demonstrate tremendous value to an attorney and client. Attorneys left to their own devices may jam everything into a single file folder because they are either too busy, too disorganized, too much of an absent-minded professor type, or all three, to do a thorough job organizing a file. Most cases settle before trial anyway, they may figure, so why bother having everything ready for trial when there probably will not be one? Because that is how things get lost, an attorney can look bad in court, and perhaps even lose a case, and it can hinder the ability to settle the case in advance. Of course, such a lawyer intends to organize everything when the trial becomes imminent, but in the practice of law, Murphy's Law predominates. (Murphy's Law says, "If anything can go wrong, it will go wrong."). Back-to-back-to-back trials will be scheduled, starting the week after the lawyer returns from a long-delayed, often-promised vacation with the lawyer's spouse to celebrate their 20th anniversary. Or the lawyer will get sick, or be double booked. O'Toole's Corollary, also called Sod's Law or McGillicuddy's Law, says that Murphy was an optimist. It is much easier on staff, lawyers, and clients if the lawyer is not stuck at the office until all hours of the night or early morning organizing a file for trial.

HOW TO ORGANIZE A FILE

The best way to organize the data you collect through your investigation and the discovery process is to conduct the investigation and discovery in an organized way. There should be an orderly system that dictates what happens to documents as they arrive, whether by mail or by courier. Material needs to be logged as it comes in so that it does not get lost. Then the attorney can see the item before it is filed and give instructions regarding what to do about it, so that it ends up in the file in a logical place that will be the first place you, or the lawyer, will think to look for the item.

For example, perhaps the opposing attorneys send their Interrogatories and Requests for Production of Documents. What happens to the document? First, you should have a log of what comes in the mail or by delivery service. It should be logged there (see Exhibit 10–1). Second, a note in the **tickler system** should be made so that the deadline for answering it is noted, as well as reminders at 14 days, 7 days, and 3 days before, and including the day it is due (see Exhibit 10–2). Next, it should be

■ **TICKLER SYSTEM**
A computer or card index system designed to provide advance notice of important deadlines.

EXHIBIT 10-1		INCOMING MATERIAL LOG			
DATE	**DOCUMENT/ITEM**	**FROM**	**WHERE TO?**	**BY WHOM**	**FILE**
1/8/05	Memorandum of Law	Smith Vardon via mail	Barry's office	Martine	04-1213
1/8/05	Notice of Motion and Motion	Smith Vardon via mail	Filed and calendered	Martine	04-1213
1/8/05	Affidavit of Respondent regarding Child Support	Smith Vardon via mail	Barry's office	Martine	04-1213
1/8/05	letter dated 1/07 regarding custody proposal	Kelly Smith via mail	Danielle's office	Martine	04-100

(continues)

EXHIBIT 10–1   INCOMING MATERIAL LOG *(continued)*

DATE	DOCUMENT/ITEM	FROM	WHERE TO?	BY WHOM	FILE
1/8/05	Summons and Petition for Dissolution	New client Emma Jones	Constance's desk	Martine	05-109
1/9/05	Answers to Interrogatories	Q & Z Couriers	Jennifer's Office	Carolyn	04-574
1/12/05	Entire File— new file— Spencer, Inc	B,V. Legal Courier	Barry's office	Carolyn	Carolyn to open new file
1/12/05	Payment	City of Beaver Falls	Bank; entered into billing system	Barry	04-2020; invoice 678
1/12/05	Answer to Complaint	Mail	Barry's office	Carolyn	04-999
1/13/05	Interrogatories and Requests for production	Mail	Barry's Office and deadline tickled	Carolyn	04-403

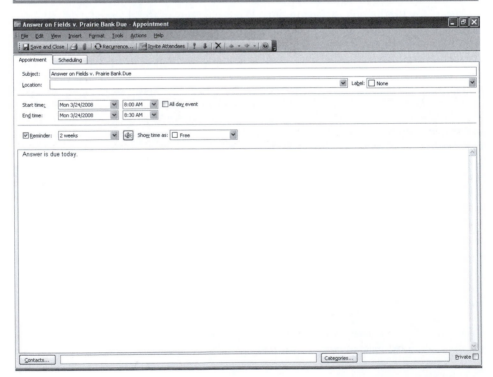

EXHIBIT 10–2   Tickler System Entry

routed to the attorney for review. The attorney will want it copied and sent to the client with instructions regarding setting up a meeting to discuss how to reply. Then it should be filed in the case file. The letter to the client should also go in the file, as should the letter from the opposing attorney that enclosed the document.

Filing systems will vary by firm size, practice area, how large the file is for a particular matter, and degree of automation. Smaller firms will have a decentralized filing system with each attorney having his or her files nearby the attorney's office. Centralized filing systems are more often found in large firms. Automation had been the province of large firms but may be seen increasingly often in medium and small firms.

An index should be maintained of anything that goes into a file, whether it is created by the attorney or received from someone else (see Exhibit 10–3). In this

EXHIBIT 10–3   FILE INDEX

Case: Fields v. Prairie Bank
Our File: 06-5831
Court File: 06-CV-1925

DATE	ITEM	LOCATION
2//2/06	Memorandum regarding initial client meeting	Memos
2/10/06	Legal research memorandum regarding i.d. theft claims from law clerk	Memos
2/17/06	Summons and Complaint	Pleadings
3/1/06	Answer from Bank	Pleadings
3/1/06	Notice of Court File number and Judge	Court Orders and Notices
3/1/06	Our Interrogatories and Requests for Prod.	Discovery
3/1/06	Their Interrogatories and Requests for Prod.	Discovery
3/1/06	Our request for admissions	Pleadings
3/4/06	Deposition notice to Peter Fields	Discovery
3/4/06	Letter from their attorney regard. settl.	Correspondence In
3/6/06	Letter to their attorney regard. settl.	Correspondence Out
3/6/06	Notice of Deposition of Teller	Discovery
3/8/06	Subpoena Duces Tecum to Bank	Discovery

(continues)

EXHIBIT 10–3   FILE INDEX *(continued)*

DATE	ITEM	LOCATION
3/8/06	Court order regarding A.D.R.	Court Orders and Notices
3/10/06	Letter to Mediator	Correspondence Out
3/17/06	Notice of Motion and Motion to Amend Complaint	Motions
3/17/06	First Amended Complaint	Pleadings

manner, a record is maintained of what should be in the file if it is complete, so that if something is removed from the file and not replaced, its absence will be noted. It also helps in locating documents, especially as files become voluminous as the case progresses. A file may start out as a pre-client file with just a few notes about the potential client, and blossom all the way into a room full of boxes.

HOW TO MAKE A TRIAL NOTEBOOK

The purpose of having a trial notebook is to make sure that key material is at the attorney's fingertips so that he or she is not fumbling for papers as the judge and client fume, the jury grows bored, and the opposing attorney smirks. A well-organized and stocked trial notebook can make an attorney appear well prepared, organized, and able to think and react quickly. With key documents, notes, questions, exhibits, and cases at the fingertip, the attorney can feel self-assured and act confidently.

A trial notebook is typically one or more three-ring notebooks with the essentials that a lawyer needs to try a case, such as notes for opening statements and closing arguments, anticipated objections, direct and cross-examinations, and final argument. It will also have pleadings such as complaints, answers, and counterclaims (and if those documents are lengthy they might be summarized). Other items may be jury selection questions, documents to be entered as exhibits (or if they will not fit in a notebook, a reminder to enter them into evidence), deposition summaries or excerpts, witness lists, legal memoranda, exhibit lists, jury instructions, and the verdict form. Some people call it a trial file. It is distinguishable from a case file because a case file would contain all

PASSIM CASE   **FIELDS V. PRAIRIE BANK**

Suppose your attorney made a motion before trial to have evidence about Peter Fields's driving while intoxicated conviction excluded and the judge granted the motion. Now in the middle of the trial, the opposing attorney starts to head down a path of questions toward the forbidden topic. With an organized file, the attorney can quickly find the order granting the motion to exclude the conviction, raise an objection, and remind the judge of the previous order.

the papers from the case, while the trial notebook would have only that material that is likely to be useful at trial. The exact formatting will differ from attorney to attorney.

The American Association for Justice sells a trial and deposition notebook system where all case files are maintained as three-ring notebooks. The Trial Notebook contains seven color-coded sections: 1. Pretrial Management, 2. Preparation, 3. Legal Research, 4. Trial, 5. Ideas, 6. Discovery, and 7. Post-trial Proceedings (see Exhibit 10–4). Software is available to produce electronic trial notebooks. Examples include TrialDirector® and Visync™ (see Exhibit 10–5). This commercial software allows attorneys to have their trial presentations, including speeches and witness examinations, supplemented with visual depictions of exhibits and testimony. An attorney can play back a portion of a videotaped deposition or display two versions of a document side by side. It is also possible to make an electronic trial notebook using standard office software such as a word processor, presentation software, and a scanner.

ATLA TRIAL NOTEBOOK 5th—
TABLE OF CONTENTS
BINDER 1
I. MANAGEMENT
  1. Contents
  2. File Index
  3. Tracking
  4. Investigation
  5. Experts
  6. A/V Aids
  7. Costs
  8. Settlement
II. PREPARATION
  1. To Do
  2. Trial Calendar
  3. Telephone Contacts
  4. Witness List
  5. Subpoenas
  6. Proo_ers/Stipulations
  7. Deposition Deliveries
  8. Judicial/Evid. Notice
  9. Jury Instructns/Interrogs.
  10. Premarked Exhibits
  11. Trial Brief
  12. Motions in Limine
  13. Voir Dire Questions
  14. Gen'l Jury Panel List
  15. Ideal Juror/Jury Survey
  16. Jury
III. LAW
  1. Research
  2. Evidence
  I
  3. Memoranda
  4. Trial Motions

  5. Pl's Requests for Charge
  6. Def's Requests for Charge
  7. Trial Court Instructions
  8. Verdict Form
IV(A). THRESHOLD
IV(B). TRIAL
  1. Pl's Pro_les/Chronology
  2. Themes
  3. Proof Matrix
  4. Opening/Summation
  5. In Camera/Sidebar
  6. Motions
  7. Errors
  8. Verdict
  9. Pl's Lay Witnesses
  10. Pl's Experts
  11. Def's Lay Witnesses
  12. Def's Experts
IV(C). EVIDENCE
V. TRIAL IDEAS/NOTES
VI. DISCOVERY
  1. Marked Pleadings
  2. Orders/Memoranda
  3. Pl's Interrog. Answers
  4. Def's Interrog. Answers
  5. Admissions/Stipulations
  6. Motions/Orders
  7. Dep. Digests/Dep. Exhibits
  8. Produced Documents
VII. POST-TRIAL
  APPENDIX
  FEDERAL RULES OF CIVIL
  PROCEDURE
  COURTROOM HANDBOOK ON
  FEDERAL EVIDENCE

EXHIBIT 10–4   Trial Notebook available from Thomson West and the American Association for Justice.

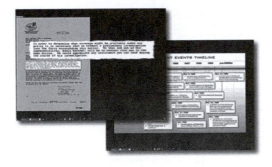

2
BINDER 2
VIII. FOCUS GROUPS/MOCK JURIES
1. FOCUS PLAN
2. CONFIDENTIALITY FORMS
3. JUROR'S BACKGROUNDDATA
4. JURY QUESTIONS
5. MINUTES/NOTES
6. LESSONS LEARNED
7. VISUAL STRATEGY
8. TRIAL PREP/TO DO
IX(A). SETTLEMENT OVERVIEW
1. STRATEGY
2. CASE EVALUATION
3. JURY VERDICT RESEARCH
4. SETTLEMENT HISTORY
5. FEE SHIFTING
6. ADR/CDR
7. LIENS
8. RECOVERY MANAGEMENT
IX(B). SETTLEMENT DATA
1. PLAINTIFF BACKGROUND
2. LIABILITY
3. INJURIES
4. ECONOMIC LOSS
5. "HUMAN LOSS"
6. $64 QUESTION
7. CONSORTIUM
8. PUNITIVE/BAD FAITH/FEE SHIFT
IX(C). SETTLEMENT BRIEFS
& PRESENTATIONS

EXHIBIT 10–4 *continued* *Trial Notebook.*

EXHIBIT 10–5 TrialDirector screen shot.

SUBPOENAING WITNESSES

SUBPOENA
A court order to appear at a proceeding.

SUBPOENA DUCES TECUM
An order to appear and bring documents or other specified items.

A **subpoena** is a court order to appear at a hearing, trial, or deposition. If a subpoenaed witness fails to appear, law enforcement can go get the witness and bring him or her to court. If the witness refuses to testify, the judge may hold the witness in contempt of court. If you want the witness to bring documents, or other items, obtain a **subpoena duces tecum** (see Exhibit 10–6 for an example).

The first step is to consider whether or not subpoenaing a witness is necessary. Some witnesses are bound to appear without a subpoena, and issuing one will be a waste of time and money and may anger the witness. For example, a prosecutor will almost never need to subpoena a police officer. A theft or burglary victim who has been pushing to have his or her own employee prosecuted for taking money from the till probably does not need a subpoena. A domestic violence victim needs a subpoena whether the victim promises to appear or not. Experts are not subpoenaed, especially not doctors. Witnesses who are neutral or hostile to your case should be subpoenaed.

United States District Court
Eastern District of Michigan

Subpoena to Testify Before A Grand Jury

TO:

CafePress.com
Abdul Popla
1515 Aurora Drive
San Leandro, CA 94577

G.J. # 04-1-167-1

SUBPOENA FOR
☐ ATTENDANCE
☐ DOCUMENT(S) OR OBJECT(S)

YOU ARE HEREBY COMMANDED to appear and testify before the Grand Jury of the United States District Court at the place, date and time specified below:

PLACE:	COURTROOM:
Theodore Levin U.S. Courthouse 231 W. Lafayette Detroit, MI 48226	Room 1056
	DATE AND TIME: June 24, 2004 9:00 a.m.

YOU ARE ALSO COMMANDED to bring with you the following document(s) or objects(s):

Provide a list of customers and their addresses who purchased product #8632701
from October 2003 through February 2004.

☐   *Please see additional information on reverse*

This subpoena shall remain in effect until you are granted leave to depart by the Court or by an officer acting on behalf of the court.

DATE: May 24, 2004	THIS SUBPOENA IS ISSUED ON APPLICATION OF THE UNITED STATES OF AMERICA
UNITED STATES DISTRICT COURT	NAME, ADDRESSS AND TELEPHONE NUMBER OF ASSISTANT UNITED STATES ATTORNEY:
DAVID J. WEAVER, CLERK OF COURT	Sheldon N. Light, AUSA 211 W. Fort Street Suite 2001 Detroit, MI 48226 (313) 226-9732

EXHIBIT 10–6   Subpoena Duces Tecum from thesmokinggun.com

When in doubt, issue a subpoena. An additional consideration is that if the witness is subpoenaed, your firm will pay them a small witness fee and a mileage fee (in most jurisdictions). The judge will be much more sympathetic to a party whose witness is missing if the witness was subpoenaed in a timely manner.

■ **CONTINUANCE**

A delay of a court date, usually of a trial or hearing, as in "The case is continued for two weeks."

■ **DATE CERTAIN**

A date for trial that is fixed and definite, barring only the most dire emergency.

■ **MOTION IN LIMINE (PRONOUNCED LIM'-IN-EE)**

A request made in advance of trial for the court to rule on the admissibility of evidence; generally, such motions are to exclude evidence and to preclude mentioning the inadmissible evidence in front of the jury.

■ **OBJECTION**

A request that the court rule that a question is improper or that evidence should not be admissible.

Subpoenas should be issued as far in advance of the trial as is possible, but only after it appears that the case will actually be tried. For example, suppose there is a pretrial conference four weeks before the trial date. It is possible that the case will settle there, so it would be too early to have the subpoenas served before then. Sometimes a case does not settle there, but negotiations are ongoing. In that case, it is better to assume that the case will be tried and to serve the subpoena. A subpoena must be served with enough advance warning for the witness to appear. A judge may not compel a witness to attend if he or she was served too close to a trial date. Local court rules may designate the number of days notice a witness must be given.

The "trial date" may not be the date the case is actually tried. Jurisdictions, even within states, differ on how trial calendars are managed. In some places numerous cases are called to trial for the same day, the court assuming and hoping that most of them will settle. However, if more cases are to be tried than there are judges available, those additional cases will be **continued**. Other jurisdictions provide a **date certain** to the parties and that is the trial date, period. No continuance will be granted barring the death or involuntary hospitalization of an attorney or party.

To obtain subpoenas, contact the deputy clerk of court and order the number of subpoenas that are needed. There will be a fee and the clerk will need the title and file number of the case for which the subpoena is needed. Once the subpoenas are obtained, the witness must be served with the subpoena. Typically, any adult not a party to the case can serve a subpoena (or other process). However, usually law firms either retain a professional process server or pay the sheriff's office to serve subpoenas. Make sure that, if a fee is required for the witness to appear, it is delivered with the subpoena.

ANTICIPATING EVIDENCE PROBLEMS

If it is apparent that an opposing party might attempt to present inadmissible evidence that would be damaging, it is possible to get it excluded in advance of the trial through a **motion in limine**. If the motion is not granted, or if you and your attorney fail to anticipate the evidence, your attorney can raise **objections**. Additionally, if your side intends to present evidence and anticipates an objection from an opponent, it is wise to plan a response to such objections.

Motions in Limine

Motions in limine are great methods to try to keep even the hint of inadmissible evidence away from a jury (see Exhibit 10–7). *Limine* means from the beginning. If a motion in limine is granted, it means that no reference may be made to the excluded item. A court may grant the motion in limine either absolutely or preliminarily. If it is granted

---

_____,
     Plaintiff   Motion in Limine

vs.

_____,
     Defendant

Plaintiff, [name of plaintiff], in the above cause and before trial and the selection of the jury, moves the court in limine to instruct the defendant and all defendant's counsel that defendant be prohibited from bringing to the jury's attention that plaintiff has remarried since the time of death of [plaintiff's former spouse], and that defendant be precluded from using any pleading, testimony remarks, questions, or arguments that might inform the jury of such fact.

If the above fact were to be made known to the jury, it would be highly improper and prejudicial to plaintiff, even though the court were to sustain an objection and instruct the jury not to consider such fact for any purpose.

This motion should also be granted because there is no other procedure by which the problem can be properly handled at the trial of this cause, and in all probability any such attempt would result in a mistrial. This motion is based on the attached memorandum of points and authorities, oral and documentary evidence that may be presented at the hearing of the motion, and the attached affidavit of [name of affiant]. WHEREFORE, plaintiff respectfully requests the court to instruct defendant and defendant's counsel not to mention, refer to, interrogate concerning, or attempt to convey to the jury in any manner, either directly or indirectly, the fact that plaintiff has remarried since the time of death of [plaintiff's former spouse], without first obtaining permission of the court outside the presence and hearing of the jury, and to further instruct defendant and defendant's counsel to make no reference to the fact that this motion has been filed and granted; and to warn and caution each and every one of their witnesses to strictly follow the same instructions.

Dated: [date].

[Signature and address]

EXHIBIT 10–7   Motion in Limine

■ **MOTION TO SUPPRESS**

A request for the court to exclude evidence from a criminal trial based upon the defendant's constitutional or statutory rights, such as the Fourth Amendment right against unlawful search and seizure.

absolutely, the evidence is permanently excluded from the case. If it is granted preliminarily, the party offering the evidence may offer it only after seeking a bench or chambers conference and getting advance approval to broach the subject. Less commonly, a party may use a motion in limine to move to have evidence ruled admissible in advance of trial.

Motions in limine should not be confused with **motions to suppress** in criminal court, which are made on the basis of constitutional or statutory arguments (see Exhibit 10–8). In contrast, motions in limine ask the court to use its judicial discretion and inherent power to exclude the evidence.

The purpose of such a motion is to avoid any reference to the prohibited topic. If there is a bright orange rhinoceros in a courtroom and the judge says, "ladies and gentlemen of the jury, please ignore the bright orange rhinoceros in the courtroom. It is not relevant and you are not to consider it," all the jurors are bound to notice it, and perhaps consider it, at least subconsciously. If there is a prejudicial orange rhinoceros in your case, it is better for the rhinoceros not to be mentioned than to have it there and to warn the jury to ignore it.

Suppose we have an employment law case where a woman is alleging sexual harassment by a supervisor. In the meantime, the Securities and Exchange Commission is publicly conducting an investigation into the company's accounting practices. This is wholly irrelevant to the case and the jurors might be prejudiced if they knew about the investigation. A motion in limine could exclude any reference or question about the securities investigation. Absent such a motion, the plaintiff's attorney could ask, "Your company is being investigated for stock fraud, isn't it?" The defense attorney could object and the judge could sustain the objection and order the jury to disregard the question, but that is like telling it to ignore the bright orange rhinoceros. With the motion in limine granted, the opposing attorney who asks a question on the banned topic is playing with fire.

BENCH BRIEF

DEFENDANT'S INSURANCE

Suppose there is a personal injury case and the defendants had insurance. Typically, the insurance company pays for the defense. Sometimes it even has its own in-house counsel providing the defense. However, the fact that there is insurance coverage available for the injuries is inadmissible. If the jurors knew that the defendants had insurance, they might be tempted to say, "well, it wasn't really the defendants' fault, but they have insurance and that poor plaintiff ought to get some money for her injuries." Or they might award more money to the plaintiff if they perceive the presence of an insurance policy. So it would be appropriate to make a motion in limine to exclude any reference to the defendants having insurance. This avoids having the jury infer from a question regarding insurance that there is an insurance policy to cover any award to the plaintiff.

State of _____

      Plaintiff,

vs.   Motion to Supress

_____,

      Defendant.

To: _____*[Specify appropriate prosecuting attorney]*

Please take notice that on _____*[date]*, at _____*[time]*, or as soon thereafter as counsel can be heard, at _____*[designate term or department or division]* of the above court located at _____*[street address]*, _____*[city]*, _____ County, _____*[state]*, defendant, _____*[name]*, pursuant to _____*[cite statute]*, will move the court for an order suppressing as evidence in any criminal proceeding against defendant all property illegally seized by police officers of the City of _____, _____*[state]*, whose names are unknown to defendant, from _____*[defendant's person or defendant's premises located at _____(specify exact location)]* on _____*[date]*, in violation of defendant's rights under the Fourth Amendment of the United States Constitution (U.S. Const. Amend. IV), _____*[if appropriate, add: suppressing as evidence any conversations or statements made by defendant in connection with the illegal seizure]*, _____*[if appropriate add: directing the return to defendant of all of the property illegally seized]*, and granting defendant such other and further relief as the court deems just and proper.
_____*[Specify ground or grounds for the motion, such as: The motion is based on the ground that _____(the search and seizure were made without a warrant, without lawful authority, and without defendant's consent or the search and seizure were unreasonable and not incident to a lawful arrest).]*
The motion will be based on this notice of motion, the attached affidavit of _____*[defendant or defendant's attorney]*, sworn to on _____*[date]*, the attached _____*[memorandum of law or points and authorities]*, and all papers and records filed in this action.
Dated: _____.
[Signature and address]

[Attach items mentioned in notice and proof of service, if required]

EXHIBIT 10–8 Motion to Suppress

In addition to excluding irrelevant evidence, motions in limine can be used to preclude witnesses from testifying if their mere appearance would be prejudicial and they will have nothing relevant to say. Privileged matters can be excluded. The use of highly inflammatory words can be also prohibited.

Objections That Can Be Anticipated

Parties should try to anticipate objections, both to evidence they intend to offer and to evidence that they expect to be offered. When a court **sustains** an objection to a question, it finds the objection valid and the witness cannot answer the question. If the objection is to the answer, the answer will be stricken from the record and the jury will be instructed to ignore it. When a court **overrules** an objection, it finds the question or answer acceptable; the witness must then answer the question, and if the answer has been given it will not be stricken. Rules of evidence supply the basis for the following objections (additional objections that cannot be anticipated are covered in Chapter 11).

Best Evidence Rule

An objection based upon the best evidence rule indicates that the proffered document is not the original document and argues that the original document is needed. The relevant rules are found in the Federal Rules of Evidence between 1001 and 1008. If you think that the opposing party may try to offer a copy of the document and that an original document is needed, or if you do not have the original and want to introduce a copy, you can anticipate the argument that needs to be made and help the attorney prepare for it. In the following excerpt, from the case where the state of Minnesota and an insurance company sued many tobacco companies, an attorney made an objection under the best evidence rule.

> **BENCH BRIEF** TRANSCRIPT
>
> State of Minnesota and Blue Cross and Blue Shield of Minnesota, Plaintiffs, vs. Philip Morris, Inc. Transcript, Ramsey County District Court, February 18, 1998.
>
> Q Doctor, looking at tab number 19, Exhibit [25], that is from The Star and Tribune, page E3, Health & Fitness, and does that contain the newspaper story which refers to you in it?
>
> A Yes, sir.
>
> Q And it refers to your discussion about homocysteine.
>
> A Yeah. It's a very brief, little clip.
>
> MR. MARTIN: We'll offer [25].
>
> MS. NELSON: Objection, Your Honor, this is not the best evidence. The witness has already testified to the topic. It's an improper use of the exhibit.
>
> THE COURT: The court will receive [25].

The court overruled the objection and received the exhibit into evidence because this was not a valid objection under the best evidence rule. No original document was required.

Irrelevance

Relevance objections can bar the admission of evidence that is not material to the case. Through the other party's discovery questions in interrogatories and depositions, it may be apparent that it valued, and may try to offer, such immaterial evidence.

In the following excerpt from the O.J. Simpson criminal trial, one of his defense attorneys has to rephrase his question twice until he is asking a question that is seeking relevant evidence.

BENCH BRIEF   TRANSCRIPT

People vs. Orenthal James Simpson Transcript, Superior Court Los Angeles County, July 25, 1995.

Q [by MR. BLASIER]: Weren't you expecting that you would be called as a prosecution witness up until the day they rested?

MS. CLARK: objection, that is irrelevant, your honor.

THE COURT: Sustained.

Q by MR. BLASIER: Wasn't your state of mind such that you knew or you anticipated that you would be called to testify by the prosecution in this case?

MS. CLARK: Objection, irrelevant.

THE COURT: Sustained.

Q by MR. BLASIER: Did you know when the data was destroyed that this trial was still going on?

MS. CLARK: Objection, irrelevant.

THE COURT: Overruled.

THE WITNESS: Yes.

Whether a witness expected to be called as a witness was not relevant, or at least that is what this judge ruled, twice. However, what the attorney was really trying to get at was that the witness destroyed his underlying data after he wrote his report. The court found this relevant.

Included within general relevance objections that can be anticipated would be objections related to rape shield laws, subsequent remedial measures, character evidence, negotiations, plea bargaining, and prejudice.

Can you imagine the prejudicial effect of marijuana on a rural jury? When something is lurking in a case and you hope the jurors do not hear about it because they may ignore the evidence that is important to your client, it is important to anticipate this and try to exclude it. Conversely, if such evidence will help your case, it is prudent to find a way to get it admitted.

The North Dakota Supreme Court heard a case about a car accident that occurred near the geographic center of North America, which is located in Rugby. The trial court ruled on the admissibility of evidence that a plaintiff passenger had marijuana in her possession, finding it relevant, but indicating that it would limit the use of the evidence. As noted in the opinion that is excerpted below, there were more than 130 references made to marijuana during the trial.

CASE
SLAUBAUGH V. SLAUBAUGH, 466 N.W.2D 573 (N.D. 1991)

In the early morning hours of April 13, 1986, Wilmer and Karen [Slaubaugh] were returning home from a wedding dance held at the Columbus Club, owned by the Knights of Columbus, in Rugby. Wilmer was driving, Karen was in the front passenger seat, and Wilmer's stepbrother, Johnny Slaubaugh, was in the back seat. Wilmer and Karen had been drinking, and they were arguing as they proceeded out of Rugby through the area of construction.

Traveling at a rate in excess of the speed limit, Wilmer drove through an unmarked "T" intersection. The vehicle sped through the intersection, became airborne, and hit a railroad embankment that ran parallel to the crossroad. Karen suffered severe and permanent injuries.

Wilmer's blood alcohol level was .21 at the time of the accident. Karen admitted that she was also intoxicated. In addition, police found marijuana in Wilmer's pants pocket and found marijuana and related paraphernalia in Karen's purse. Blood and urine samples from Wilmer tested negative for use of marijuana. No drug tests were performed on Karen . . .

The evidence established that Karen sustained devastating and permanent injuries. She suffered two crushed vertebrae and spinal cord injuries with a complete and permanent loss of bladder and bowel function, and loss of all sensation in her sexual organs. She has had extensive orthopedic surgery, including placement of steel rods and wires in her back. She also suffered a broken leg and damage to her right shoulder socket. Karen was twenty-three years old at the time of her injuries, but she will never regain bladder control, bowel control, or sexual sensation. Despite the obvious pain and mental anguish of her injuries, the jury awarded her no damages for pain, discomfort, or mental anguish . . .

Karen argues that her drug possession was greatly overemphasized by the defendants during trial, resulting in a trial of her character rather than a trial of the merits. We agree. Although the trial court stated that it would allow only limited use of this evidence and would not permit it to "confuse the issues," counsel for Karen has documented over 130 references to drug use or possession during trial. Thus, Karen's possession of the

(continues)

CASE
SLAUBAUGH V. SLAUBAUGH, 466 N.W.2D 573 (N.D. 1991) *(continued)*

marijuana and paraphernalia, which had limited circumstantial relevance, became a domi-
nant theme of the trial. Although the trial court has broad discretion over the presentation of the evidence and the conduct of the trial, it must exercise this discretion in a
manner that best comports with substantial justice. We caution that if this evidence is
admitted on retrial, the trial court must recognize its responsibility to control its use to
prevent it from predominating the trial.

The court ordered a new trial, partially because so much emphasis was placed on
marijuana as well as for the lack of pain and suffering damages awarded to the plaintiff.

Hearsay

The many exceptions and definitional loopholes are the key to whether or not
a hearsay objection is going to be sustained or overruled. If you can recognize that
a document might be considered hearsay, it is wise to consider what exception the
attorney can raise at trial to get the evidence admitted. In the following example,
the attorney apparently anticipated a hearsay objection and was prepared with an
exception.

BENCH BRIEF Tʀᴀɴꜱᴄʀɪᴘᴛ

State of Minnesota and Blue Cross and Blue Shield of Minnesota, Plaintiffs, vs. Philip
Morris, Inc. Transcript, Ramsey County District Court, morning session April 27, 1998
BY MR. BLEAKLEY:
Q And is this a document . . . dealing with tar and nicotine-content advertising in cigarettes?
A Yes.
MR. BLEAKLEY: Your Honor, we move the admission of Exhibit [18].
MR. GILL: . . . Object on the basis that it's hearsay, no applicable exception.
THE COURT: Okay. The objection is sustained.
MR. BLEAKLEY: This document is more than—it's dated 1966, it is 32 years old, it is
  an ancient document, it is therefore not precluded by the hearsay rule, Your Honor.
MR. GILL: Same objection, Your Honor. This is not the type of document to which that
  particular exception is applicable.
THE COURT: All right. I'll let it in on that basis.

With all the hearsay exceptions, it may be difficult to think of the right one in the heat of courtroom battle. However, the attorney here either thought on his feet or, more likely, he or his paralegal did their homework.

Opinion

Nonexpert opinion testimony can be anticipated if it appears from the opposing party's discovery responses, motions, and filings that it intends to offer such testimony.

In the trial of Erik and Lyle Menendez, the two California boys who killed their parents, the defense wanted to show that they were abused by their parents. The court ruled that evidence of physical abuse was admissible, but not emotional or verbal abuse. During the following examination of the father's sister, Marta Menendez Cano, the defense attorney tried to elicit her opinion about how her brother disciplined Erik and Lyle. In this transcript excerpt, opinion and other objections are made and the attorneys approached the bench for a **side bar** to discuss the objections with the judge.

■ **SIDE BAR**

A conference at the bench among the attorneys and the judge conducted so that the jurors cannot hear the discussion. Also called bench conference.

BENCH BRIEF   TRANSCRIPT

People Vs. Erik Galen Menendez and Joseph Lyle Menendez Transcript, Superior Court, Los Angeles County January 30, 1996, 9:30 AM session.

Q by MS. ABRAMSON: Did you believe that your brother treated his children abusively?

MR. CONN: Objection. Irrelevant. Improper opinion.

THE COURT: Sustained.

MS. ABRAMSON: Your honor, I think it's appropriate, given the questioning on cross.

THE COURT: I don't see how that's relevant.

Q by MS. ABRAMSON: Was your brother's main method of disciplining his children to hit them?

MR. CONN: Objection. Irrelevant and improper opinion. Calls for speculation.

THE COURT: Sustained.

Q by MS. ABRAMSON: Based on what you observed, was his main method of disciplining his children, or displaying his feelings towards them, to hit them?

MR. CONN: Objection. Irrelevant.

THE COURT: Sustained.

[After repeated requests, the judge finally allows the attorneys to approach]

MR. CONN: I think what we see is a pattern here, which is that every time following cross-examination counsel thinks: well, because the prosecution made a couple of points on cross-examination, now all the judge's rulings go out the window, and now I can get close to the fire and get back into the emotional and psychological abuse.

(continues)

BENCH BRIEF   TRANSCRIPT *(continued)*

She does it question after question after question, knowing what the court's rulings are. I think, if counsel feels that the court's ruling has been now vitiated by cross-examination, it would seem to me that would be something that would most appropriately be discussed with the court before counsel resumes her redirect, so we don't have to go into this. She never would have asked these questions on direct. If she thinks it's a new ball game now, I think she should bring it to the attention of the court so we don't have to have this type of display in front of the jury.

THE COURT: Okay. And now what is it that you wanted to bring up?

MS. ABRAMSON: Because of the way that the witness was cross-examined with respect to her specific memory of physical assaults, and the accusation that she is a liar, either because she got a car from my client, or because she's his godmother, I think I should be permitted to show that, for her, both at the time of the last trial and from the very beginning, her observations of her brother and sister-in-law's treatment of their children, through to the present—that the chief component of maltreatment that she was conscious of, that she was focused on, that she has the most extensive memories on, are the intimidating and hostile behavior of both—now I'm not getting into neglect and I'm not getting into dirt. I'm not getting into any of those things. But the intimidating and hostile behavior of both parents towards Erik Menendez. And the physical striking is a minor part of that, and that is why it was not that important to her, or doesn't spring into her memory, because what she saw on a regular basis was intimidating and hostility, and didn't see as much physical abuse. And that's all I'm trying to bring out. But that's the chief component of her memory.

THE COURT: The cross-examination clearly doesn't open up this area.

MS. ABRAMSON: Well, I mean, he's making a big deal that she doesn't remember the particular strikings, because in the big picture, they were a minor component.

THE COURT: Listen, if you take that theory, any time a witness gives an answer and you want to explain it, you can get in any opinion, any otherwise-objectionable testimony from a witness, just because the witness says: well, my mind was focused on something else, and let me tell you what's on my mind. I'll let the jurors hear everything I have to say.

The court apparently did not allow the attorneys to approach initially because the judge knew what the topic of the bench conference was going to be about and knew the ruling in advance. However, when both parties wanted to approach, the judge let them. The judge found that the attorney was asking for improper opinion testimony and sustained the objection.

Parol Evidence

In a case with a written contract, one party may attempt to offer evidence that shows the contract was orally modified or introduce a document that predates the contract. This is called **parol evidence**. It should be apparent well before trial that this attempt will be made. Legal research should be conducted regarding the admissibility of parol evidence, as it varies by jurisdiction. Typically, parol evidence is negotiations. For example, Seller proposes in writing to sell 100 widgets for $1 each to Buyer. Buyer replies, also in writing, "We'll buy 1,000 widgets if you give us a 20 percent discount." Then oral discussions are held about the details and a contract is written to memorialize the agreement. Here, the proposal and counterproposal as well as oral discussions would be parol evidence.

Privilege

There are a number of privileges that protect certain people from having to testify about certain things. For example, the attorney-client privilege, clergy-parishioner privilege, therapist-patient privilege, and doctor-patient privilege preclude these professionals from revealing information learned through relationships with clients. If one of these professionals is called as a witness, objections can be anticipated if the examination strays into an area covered by the privilege.

In the New Hampshire case included, the court considers who may assert the therapist-patient privilege.

■ **PAROL EVIDENCE**
Evidence that a written contract was modified by something outside the four corners of the contract such as a verbal modification, or that a writing prior to the contract should be considered a part of it.

CASE
IN RE BERG, 886 A.2D 980 (N.H. 2005)

The father argues that minor children are not protected by the therapist-client privilege, as codified in RSA 330-A:32 (2004), because the statute does not expressly confer the privilege upon them. "In matters of statutory interpretation, we are the final arbiter of legislative intent as expressed in the words of the statute considered as a whole." We construe the statute's language according to its plain and ordinary meaning. RSA 330-A:32 provides, in pertinent part: "The confidential relations and communications between any [licensed mental health practitioner] and such licensee's client are placed on the same basis as those provided by law between attorney and client . . . ."

"Client" is defined as "a person who seeks or obtains psychotherapy." RSA 330-A:2, III (2004). The statute does not define the term "person." See RSA 330-A:2. However, the plain meaning of "person" does not exclude minors. We also note that the statute does not use the word "adult." See RSA 330-A:2,:32. "Adult" is defined in RSA 21:44 (2000) as "those persons who have attained the age of 18 years." We therefore reject the father's argument that, on its face, the statute excludes minors from its protection.

The father next argues that, absent language expressly conferring the therapist-client privilege upon minor children, we must conclude that the privilege is conferred exclusively upon the minor child's parents based upon their status as natural guardians, and thus only a

(continues)

CASE

IN RE BERG, 886 A.2D 980 (N.H. 2005) *continued*

parent may assert or waive the privilege on the child's behalf. The statute does not identify who may claim the privilege on behalf of the client. However, the statute places the therapist-client privilege upon the same basis as the lawyer-client privilege. New Hampshire Rule of Evidence 502, which governs the lawyer-client privilege, specifically identifies who may claim the privilege. Rule 502(c) states that the lawyer-client privilege may be claimed on behalf of the client by, among others, the client himself, the client's guardian or conservator, or the client's lawyer. Similarly, we conclude that the therapist-client privilege may be claimed by, among others, the client, the client's guardian or the client's therapist.

The court concluded that juvenile patients may assert the therapist-patient privilege.

ALTERNATIVE DISPUTE RESOLUTION AND NEGOTIATIONS

Overburdened courts are increasingly sending parties to have their disputes resolved outside of the courtroom. Such proceedings are called **alternative dispute resolution (ADR)**. Attorneys and judges often encourage parties to settle their cases. Some states require parties to go through some sort of alternative dispute resolution before going to trial, or to explain why it is not appropriate. The rules of evidence do not generally apply in alternative dispute resolution proceedings; however, they do have an impact since material that would be inadmissible at trial is not going to impact negotiation. If a company redesigned a toy to make it safer, and this fact would be inadmissible due to the subsequent remedial measures rule, the parties could bring it up in an ADR session, but not at trial.

Trials are unpredictable, which means there are tremendous risks to both sides. A defendant may end up paying significantly more than he or she ever imagined as a result of a verdict, or a plaintiff might not get a dime. Trials are expensive. Imagine paying an attorney and the attorney's staff to get ready for a trial, and then sitting in trial for eight hours a day for a week at several hundred dollars per hour. Even in contingency fee cases, attorneys often receive a bigger share of the award if the case is tried than if it is settled. If some number can be found that neither party likes but both are willing to accept, negotiations can be successful.

Plea Bargaining

When the defense in a criminal case negotiates with a prosecutor, it is called **plea bargaining**. The defendant may be looking at years or life in prison and the state has to consider the risk that the defendant will be acquitted. Negotiated settlements can include having the case continued for dismissal so that if the defendant does not reoffend within a year, the case is dismissed; having the defendant plead guilty to a lesser charge; setting the amount of jail or prison time the defendant will serve; or dropping some charges in exchange for guilty pleas to others.

■ **ALTERNATIVE DISPUTE RESOLUTION (ADR)**
Processes other than court and jury trials utilized to resolve disputes.

■ **PLEA BARGAINING**
A discussion between the prosecutor and the defense regarding whether the defendant will plead guilty in exchange for a reduction in charges, prison time or other considerations.

Arbitration

In civil cases there are a number of alternative dispute resolution techniques. In arbitration the parties present evidence to an arbitrator in a shortened proceeding and the arbitrator makes a decision. Arbitration can be **binding** or **nonbinding**. Binding arbitration has the advantage of being quicker and less expensive than a trial. Its main disadvantage is that a party disappointed in the arbitrator's ruling is not likely to get very far in the court system trying to overturn the arbitrator's decision. Nonbinding arbitration is also less expensive than a trial, but its primary disadvantage is that the arbitrator's ruling only provides guidance to the parties. They are free to ignore the arbitrator's decision and plow on ahead to court.

Mediation

Mediation involves both parties and their attorneys meeting with a mediator to try to resolve the dispute. The mediator typically meets first with everyone to discuss the ground rules for the mediation. Then the mediator practices shuttle diplomacy by going back and forth between the two rooms the parties are in to find out how their interests can be combined into an acceptable settlement. The advantages of mediation are a lower cost compared to litigation, a better chance that the parties will be able to get along in the future, and be more creative in crafting a settlement. The disadvantage is that the mediator has no power to force the parties to reach an agreement and if no agreement is reached, the whole process is arguably a waste of time and money and makes the overall case more expensive.

■ **BINDING ARBITRATION**

A proceeding where a nonjudge hears evidence in a shortened proceeding and makes a ruling that is binding to all parties.

■ **NONBINDING ARBITRATION**

A proceeding where a nonjudge hears evidence.

■ **MEDIATION**

A method of resolving a dispute through informal negotiations with a third-party neutral facilitating the discussions.

BENCH BRIEF

HI-LOW ARBITRATION

Major League Baseball utilizes hi-low arbitration. When a player is eligible to file for arbitration, he and the ball club submit "final" offers to the arbitrator. The team presumably submits a number slightly higher than the highest number it is willing to take out of fear that the arbitrator will adopt the player's higher number. The player then submits a number slightly lower than the lowest number he is willing to accept out of the opposite fear. After these numbers are submitted, the parties often settle for a number between the two submitted. However, if not, an arbitrator must pick either the player's number or the team's number. Therefore, the player and team each feel pressure to move their number toward the middle.

Medarb

Medarb combines mediation with arbitration. The third-party neutral serves first as mediator, trying to get the parties to agree to a negotiated settlement, and failing that, he or she makes a decision as an arbitrator. The advantage is that it combines the advantages of mediation and arbitration. Absent the combination, if the parties wanted to try arbitration after mediation, they would need to start over with an arbitrator. However, the disadvantage is that the neutral may have difficulty remaining neutral after meeting with both parties. The parties cannot go back in time and take back things that they would not have presented to an arbitrator, or get the neutral to forget about material for which they have valid objections. Further, the parties may hold back from a mediator who they know might end up serving as an arbitrator.

■ **MEDARB**
An alternative dispute resolution process that combines mediation and arbitration.

Mini-trial

Another form of alternative dispute resolution is a **mini-trial**, also called a summary jury trial. The parties get together with some people paid to sit through a short version of the case as mock jurors and render an advisory opinion. Each side may be given an opportunity to make an opening statement, present a few hours of testimony, and make a closing argument. Then they watch and listen to the "jurors" deliberate about the case and reach a nonbinding "verdict." This has the advantage of being less expensive than an actual trial, and the parties can see what types of things a jury might focus upon. Disadvantages include that it is more expensive than most other alternative dispute resolution techniques, it may give away trial strategy, and it requires boiling down a case into a very small version of what it will actually contain.

■ **MINI-TRIAL**
An abbreviated trial conducted before paid jurors who render an advisory verdict. Also called summary jury trial.

PASSIM CASE 　 **FIELDS VS. PRAIRIE BANK**

If our case went to medarb, Peter Fields might tell the neutral, "I would be willing to accept an apology, $10,000 and a free credit report run for the next ten years." The bank may tell the neutral, "We don't want to pay him a dime, but the nuisance value to us in trying this case is $5,000. We'll give him $2,500, but we're not apologizing because we didn't do anything wrong." The neutral, while serving as mediator will try to get the bank to apologize that Peter's identity was stolen without admitting responsibility, and try to get Peter to take less than $10,000 and the bank to give more than $2,500. The neutral meets with each side and points out failings in their case, discusses how the situation makes them feel, and serves as a sounding board. Failing that, the case now goes to arbitration and suddenly the friendly mediator who has been hearing about how much it stunk to have Peter's identity stolen, and from the bank about how it is rotten that they are getting blamed for something they did not do, is now suddenly supposed to evaluate the case and effectively say who wins.

Other Forms of ADR

Other forms of alternative dispute resolution include appointing by consent a special magistrate who issues a binding opinion that is appealable to an appellate court; early neutral evaluation in which the parties and their attorneys meet before discovery with a neutral to hear the strengths and weaknesses of their respective cases; and neutral fact finding in which a neutral makes a nonbinding determination of facts.

PRETRIAL HEARINGS

A pretrial hearing is the court's last opportunity to get the parties to settle the case. Many times cases settle at the pretrial hearing. However, barring that, it is the court's opportunity to rule on any remaining pretrial motions and to address any other issues that are related to the trial. Motions in limine may be presented, and jury instructions and jury selection may be discussed, as well as the anticipated length of the trial and any other last-minute trial issues.

SUMMARY

Having an organized file is important and it is something that a paralegal can do well. There are various ways to organize a file. The best way is to have it organized for trial from its inception. A trial notebook is an important tool for an attorney in a trial. It contains pleadings, jury selection questions, outlines of witness examinations, opening statements, and closing arguments. A subpoena is a court order that compels a witness to appear at a proceeding such as a deposition, trial, or hearing. Parties obtain subpoenas and have them served on witnesses by a process server. Motions in limine can be used to exclude evidence. Some objections and responses to objections can be anticipated. There are a variety of alternative dispute resolution techniques available to try to end a case short of trial.

■ KEY TERMS

alternative dispute resolution (ADR)
binding arbitration
continuance
date certain
medarb
mediation
mini-trial
motion in limine
motion to suppress
nonbinding arbitration
objection
overrule
parol evidence
plea bargaining
side bar
subpoena
subpoena duces tecum
sustain
tickler system

■ HELPFUL WEB SITES

http://www.adr.org
http://www.nmb.gov
http://www.voma.org
http://www.bindertek.com
http://www.atla.org
http://www.indatacorp.com
http://www.visync.com

■ REVIEW AND DISCUSSION QUESTIONS

1. Why is it important for a paralegal to organize a file?
2. What is a tickler system?
3. What goes in a trial notebook?
4. What can trial software do?
5. Under what circumstances should a witness be subpoenaed?
6. What are the advantages and disadvantages of subpoenaing a witness?
7. What objections can you anticipate?
8. What is parol evidence?
9. What is arbitration and how does it differ from mediation?
10. What alternative dispute resolution technique would be best for our Passim case? Why?

■ LEGAL RESEARCH PROJECTS

1. Find a form for a motion in limine or a motion to suppress in your state.
2. What evidentiary privileges are available in your state? Are they established by statute or case law?
3. Does your state require or encourage parties to engage in alternative dispute resolution? How does it do so?
4. Draft a motion in limine and supporting argument to exclude evidence from the trial of our Passim case.

For additional resources, visit our Web site at www.westlegalstudies.com

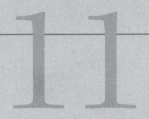

Courtesy CartoonStock.com.
www.CartoonStock.com

Trials and Appeals

■ OBJECTIVES _____

❑ Relate the steps in a trial

❑ Relate how a paralegal can help during trial

❑ List the goals of jury selection

❑ Discuss the difference between an opening statement and a closing argument

❑ Distinguish between direct and cross-examination

❑ Relate objections that cannot be anticipated prior to trial

TRIAL

This section will discuss all the parts of a jury trial: jury selection, preliminary instructions, opening statements, presentation of evidence through direct and cross-examination, rebuttal, closing argument, final jury instructions, and appeal. Some parts of this process will be missing from certain proceedings such as court trials (case tried by a judge without a jury) and administrative hearings. Court trials will lack jury selection and usually will not have opening and closing arguments. Instead, the court will usually have the attorneys submit written arguments and proposed orders. Administrative hearings will also lack jury instructions and they will usually be held in settings less formal than a courtroom.

Trials take place in courtrooms. In the typical arrangement, the judge sits on an elevated bench, usually in the front and center of the room. The jury sits in a jury box on one side. The court reporter sits next to the judge, down a bit lower, and the witness box is next to the court reporter. There is also a spot for a deputy clerk of court. The attorneys and their clients sit at tables located in front of the bench and to the side of the jury box. There is often room for an audience, although most of the time very few people are watching.

Jury Selection

Would you be interested in going with a friend to see *Sesame Street Live*? Probably only if you have kids. Would you listen to a polka band? Probably only if you have German heritage. How well do you think a speech by the president of NARAL Pro-Choice America would be received at the National Right to Life convention? See how important the audience is? The jury is the voting audience for a trial; therefore, jury selection is picking the voters for the verdict. However, the attorneys are not able to recruit and choose jurors, so it would be more appropriate to call it jury deselection, as attorneys are given the opportunity to remove jurors who are not likely to favor their case. Jury selection is also referred to as **voir dire**.

■ **VOIR DIRE**
(pronounced v-'wah deer)
The process of choosing a jury.

BENCH BRIEF

DIARY OF A MAD BLACK WOMAN

Compare how two people of different backgrounds reacted to the same movie.

When Roger Ebert, a white male in his 60s, reviewed the movie *Diary of a Mad Black Woman*, he said, "[It] begins as the drama of a wife of 18 years, dumped by her cruel husband and forced to begin a new life. Then this touching story is invaded by the Grandma from Hell, who takes a chainsaw to the plot, the mood, everything. A real chainsaw, not a metaphorical one. The Grandma is not merely wrong for the movie, but fatal to it—a writing and casting disaster. And since the screenplay is by the man who plays Grandma in drag, all blame returns to Tyler Perry. What was he *thinking?*" (emphasis in original)

Reader Dedra Brown replied to his review in this way: "Before your critics review Black Films, make sure they do their research. How can they say something is not true, just because it doesn't fit into their White world. We, as African Americans, do have a culture in this country (The Good, The Bad, and The Ugly, but a culture all the same), and 'Diary of a Mad Black Woman' captures very real issues in our community. Everyone at the theatre that I went to knew exactly what was going on and could relate. I can't relate to many White movies I see. I feel that they are 'White people being White,' but, at the same time, I am not trying to critique their actions."

See how the audience affects how the movie is perceived?

■ **VENIRE**

The group of potential
jurors from which the
jury is selected.

Through a random process, the clerk of court summons individuals who are eligible to serve as jurors to the courthouse. Potential jurors are often selected from driver's license, voter registration, mailing, utility company, and state identification card lists and from telephone directories. Jurors must typically be 18, citizens of the United States, and residents of the jurisdiction where the trial is taking place. From the pool of potential jurors a **venire** is summoned to the courtroom. The judge welcomes them and they take an oath. The judge begins with preliminary questions to make sure everyone is qualified to serve, such as age and residency requirements, whether they are available to serve the length of the trial, and whether they know or are related to the parties, attorneys, or witnesses. The judge will also ask if they know anything about the case that would prevent them from keeping an open mind, and whether they have served on a similar case previously.

BENCH BRIEF

JURY SURVEYS

Sometimes, in advance of trial, especially in cases where it will be difficult to get a good pool of jurors, a survey is filled out in advance. For example, in a case that has a lot of pretrial publicity it may be difficult to find people who will say that they are not going to be influenced by what they read about the case in the paper, saw on the TV, or heard on the radio. A questionnaire can save time for the potential jurors, the attorneys, and the judge. For example, a court might utilize a survey in a criminal sexual conduct case that asks if the potential juror has been the victim of sexual assault or knew someone who had been such a victim, and whether the juror had been so accused or knew someone who had. In contrast, questionnaires in large, lengthy cases can be hundreds of questions long. In the O. J. Simpson criminal trial, for example, potential jurors first filled out a hardship questionnaire, and those remaining after being excused for hardship filled out a survey of approximately 50 pages.

In some courts, attorneys are allowed to ask follow-up questions only after the judge has asked more extensive jury selection questions. In others, the attorneys are given an extensive opportunity to ask questions. Attorneys want to know which jurors have backgrounds and demeanor that make them more likely to side with their client and who is more likely to be sympathetic to the opposition.

BENCH BRIEF

JURY CONSULTANTS

Jury consultants are paid to use social science and body language interpretation to assist attorneys in picking juries. They are generally used only in high profile or high value cases due to their cost. Their success rate is subject to debate. In the O. J. Simpson criminal case, the prosecution is said to have ignored its consultant's advice, while the defense fol-

(continues)

BENCH BRIEF *(continued)*

lowed its quite closely. On the other hand, absent the jury consultants, would the result have been any different? The only way to find that out for sure is to go back in time and retry the case without jury consultants.

A jury consultant can help an attorney determine what to look for in a juror by analyzing demographic factors, such as race, gender, socioeconomic status, type of employment, and the like. Jury consultants can also help an attorney develop the **theme of the case**. The jury consultant will conduct case-specific research such as recruiting mock jurors from the jurisdiction where the case will be tried, or if that is not possible, from a similar location. A sort of mini-trial will be held, with attorneys presenting witnesses and arguments from both sides and then having the jurors deliberate. In this manner, arguments, exhibits, and testimony can be evaluated and later adapted for the trial. Another technique is to take a telephone survey of jurors in the jurisdiction regarding the case, being careful not to call actual jurors.

Jury consultants are very expensive and should be used only in cases where the stakes are high enough to justify the cost.

A poor man's jury consultant is now available through software. MRI's SmartJury™ is software that allows users to enter basic jury pool information provided by the court and information about the case. The program compares it against extensive demographic profiling to recommend which jurors to select or strike.

■ **THEME OF THE CASE**
A party's position regarding the facts and the theory of why that party should win the case.

Attorneys should have in mind the type of person that they want on a jury and who they do not want. For example, attorneys may decide that they want married jurors with a college education and young children who are comfortable financially but not well off. Sometimes these determinations are made using social science, other times with stereotypes or educated guesses. Stereotypes might be based upon gender, socioeconomic status, race, occupation, or background. For example, attorneys may not want someone with a rural farmer background on a soft tissue personal injury case, on the theory that farmers are self-reliant, tough people who will not think well of a plaintiff who is complaining about an injury that did not result in a hospital stay or a broken bone.

Attorneys may also consider potential jurors' body language. Such body language may create a feeling, intuition, or instinct that a juror does not like the attorney. Attorneys should trust their judgment on this, as these considerations usually show that the brain is accurately reading nonverbal cues. Attorneys may try to determine which jurors are likely to be the leaders of the jury. They may want a strong leader type and a bunch of followers, or they may want several leaders.

Jury selection can also be utilized by attorneys to educate the jury about their case. For example, in a criminal case, the defense attorney may ask, "Do you think my client is innocent or guilty?" If the juror says "I don't know," then the attorney gets the opportunity to educate the jury panel about the presumption of innocence such as by saying, "Well, in our system the defendant is presumed innocent until proven guilty so right now as far as you are concerned you should think of him as not guilty." Courts give differing amounts of leeway to attorneys in jury selection. Some will allow this type of questioning, developing their case at this early stage, and others will not allow it.

PASSIM CASE ⚖ FIELDS VS. PRAIRIE BANK

Potential Jury Selection Questions

QUESTION	FIELDS'S CONCERN	BANK'S CONCERN
Have you or anyone close to you ever been a victim of theft?	Did they think the person made too big a deal out of it?	Maybe too sympathetic to plaintiff.
How careful are you with your personal data?	Careful person may make a good juror.	Probably prefers person who is not very careful.
Are you worried at all about identity theft?	Probably likes a worried juror.	Probably would prefer not to have a worried juror.
Do you use a credit card?	Person without credit cards may have some bias against borrowing.	Probably no impact.
Do you own a personal shredder? (If yes: What do you shred? / Why did you buy it?)	Probably likes people with shredders.	Probably does not want people with shredders.
Have you ever done business with Prairie Bank?	Probably does not like other Prairie Bank customers.	Probably happy to have happy Prairie Bank customers.
Have you seen any of their advertisements?	Probably likes people who saw ads and thought it was a safe bank.	Probably does not care.
Have you ever had any trouble with bureaucracy?	Maybe they will think Bank was bureaucratic with Fields?	Probably does not care.
What do you think about banks in general?	Jurors who hate banks are good.	Jurors who love banks are good.

A good way for a paralegal to contribute to jury selection is to help the attorney study the jury. Paralegals may accompany attorneys to trial to assist with a case. Two sets of eyes are better than one. It can be difficult for an attorney to ask questions, observe the jurors, take notes, and notice potential juror reactions and body language. A paralegal can be of great assistance in making this an easier task.

The jury selection process is also an opportunity for the attorney to adapt the presentation of the case to the audience. The attorney could change the focus of the opening statement, adjust which witnesses to call, or modify word choices based upon who ends up on the panel. Suppose, for example, that somehow the jury panel members are all highly educated with at least college degrees, and many have additional education. They are all avid readers who rarely watch TV. Their hobbies are somewhat nerdy and cerebral, such as playing chess and solving Sudoku puzzles. The vocabulary that the attorney can use might be wider and include more complex, multisyllable words such as *syllogism* and *supposition*. In contrast, if only one of the jurors even went to college, their favorite TV shows are *Jerry Springer* and *Fear Factor*, and they read one book a year that is a Harlequin romance, the attorney may want to use *logic* and *assumption* instead.

There are two ways to get potential jurors off the jury. The first is to have them **removed for cause**. Panel members may be excused for cause if they are unable to be impartial. For example, suppose in a bank robbery case where the victim was robbed at gunpoint, a panel member's wife is a teller who frequently speaks of her fear of being at the bank when it is robbed, and the panel member says that he will have difficulty being objective. That juror may be excused for cause. A potential juror with a felony conviction whose rights have not been restored will also be excused, as will a person with mental or physical defects that render the person incapable of performing the duties of a juror. For example, a mentally ill potential juror who is hearing voices would be excused for cause. Jurors may not be related to the attorneys or parties nor may they have a guardian-ward, attorney-client, employer-employee, or landlord-tenant relationship with the attorneys or parties, or the victim in a criminal case. If panel members have sued or been sued by a party, they will be excused for cause. In a criminal case, if the panel member was on the grand jury that indicted the defendant, or served on a case that tried a person for the same or a similar offense, or was on a jury that tried the same defendant, the potential juror will be excused for cause.

The other way attorneys can get jurors excused is with **peremptory challenges**. The number of challenges varies by court, by case type, and by which party has the burden of proof. For example, in a federal civil case, attorneys for each side are given three peremptory strikes. If there are several plaintiffs or several defendants, the court may allow each party three strikes or allow only three challenges to be shared by all parties of each type. In a federal criminal case involving the death penalty each side gets 20 peremptory challenges. In non-death penalty felony cases, the prosecutor receives six strikes and the defendant receives ten. In misdemeanor cases each side receives three challenges. In federal civil cases, the court may grant the attorneys additional strikes. In criminal cases, only the defense may be given additional challenges.

An attorney can use a peremptory strike to get rid of a juror for any reason at all, except for race (see Batson Challenges Bench Brief). How can a court determine if a strike is being made for racial reasons? Usually, the issue comes up when there is a difference between the race of the party and the race of the potential juror and there is no obvious, nonracial reason for the potential juror to be struck. An attorney may have a superstition about jurors wearing purple and have them removed; or may disfavor overtly religious people with large religious necklaces; or may not want any motorcyclists. The most common reason to use a peremptory strike, however, is that the court will not remove the potential juror for cause, yet the attorney is concerned that something in the person's background, upbringing, social class, occupation, attitude, or hobbies will cause him to favor the other side.

■ **REMOVAL FOR CAUSE**
The court's removal of a potential juror from the panel because he is not qualified to serve on the case.

■ **PEREMPTORY CHALLENGE**
An attorney's request, at his discretion, for the court to remove a potential juror. Also called **peremptory strike**.

> **BENCH BRIEF**
>
> ### *BATSON* CHALLENGES
>
> In the U.S. Supreme Court case *Batson v. Kentucky*, 476 U.S. 79 (1986), the Court held that the Fourteenth Amendment's Equal Protection Clause prohibits attorneys from using peremptory challenges strictly on the basis of race. In *Batson*, the prosecutor excluded people of Batson's race. The defendant objected to the use of the peremptory strikes but the trial court overruled the objection. The Supreme Court laid out a test to determine if peremptory challenges were being improperly used based upon race. First, the defendant must be a member of a cognizable race, and the prosecutor must have excluded members of that race. (Subsequently, this prong of the test was modified so that the prosecutor only needs to use strikes to exclude members of a particular race, regardless of whether the defendant is a member of that race or not.) Second, the burden shifts to the state to show a nondiscriminatory intent, a race-neutral reason to exercise the strike. Subsequently, a third step developed where the objecting party receives an opportunity to explain why the given reason is still a fake reason and the real motivation was racial.

■ **ALTERNATE JUROR**
A person who listens to a case as a member of the jury but who generally does not deliberate or vote unless one of the nonalternate jurors becomes unable to serve.

A court may impanel **alternate jurors** as well, and those people may not know that they are the alternates for fear that they will not pay as much attention if they know in advance that they will be excused without deliberating unless one of the actual jurors becomes unable to serve. In the event that one of the regular jurors is excused, an alternate will become party of the actual voting jury panel. Additional strikes may be given if alternates are utilized..

Sometimes jury selection is handled one potential juror at a time, and other times the whole panel is examined at once. If only one juror is examined at a time, it is more difficult to decide how to use peremptory challenges. There is always the question of whether the attorney will regret using a strike when the next juror is even worse for the case. It is tempting to never use the last strike. When the whole panel is examined at the same time, the attorneys "pass the panel for cause." The attorneys are then given a list of the jurors and they take turns striking one juror at a time from the panel until the strikes are consumed. Once the strikes are utilized, the jurors and alternates are sworn. In criminal cases, jeopardy for the purposes of **double jeopardy** attaches when the jury is sworn.

■ **DOUBLE JEOPARDY**
Being placed at risk of life or liberty more than once for the same crime. The Fifth Amendment to the U.S. Constitution prohibits double jeopardy.

Preliminary Jury Instructions

After the jury is impaneled, the court will provide preliminary instructions that are designed to give a framework of the facts and major contentions, describe the structure of the trial from opening statements through closing arguments, advise the jurors of the likely daily schedule, and direct them not to discuss the case or communicate with the attorneys, parties, or witnesses, or with one another, and to avoid publicity about the case.

Opening Statement

The party with the burden of proof is given the advantage of speaking first. That means the plaintiff's attorney in a civil case and the prosecutor in a criminal case speak first. An opening statement is not supposed to be argumentative. The attorney is allowed to state only what the evidence will show. However, the opening statement will still be from the client's perspective, and it is possible that some argument will slip into the opening statement. It is generally a bad idea for an attorney to object during an opening statement, and knowing that, an attorney might slip in some argument, possibly by saying, "The evidence will show (insert argument here)." This magic phrase has the effect of making what otherwise would be an argument a preview of the evidence.

Even from the opening statement of a trial, jurors are beginning to make up their minds. Lawyers craft their opening statements with great care because they know that once a juror forms an opinion, it is difficult to change his or her mind. Therefore, early in the opening statement the attorney should develop the theme of the case. This is the overall thesis of what the facts are and why the attorney's client should win the case. It is useful if a catchy phrase can sum up the theme. For example, in a home construction case the plaintiff attorney's catch phrase might be that "they promised a dream house and delivered a nightmare: a leaking firetrap shack."

The opening statement may differ depending upon the amount of leeway the attorney was given during jury selection. Some of the topics that are discussed in this section may be addressed by the attorney during jury selection rather than in the opening statement, or perhaps during both. The attorney usually starts out with an introduction, often restating his name and who he represents. The purpose and limitations of the opening statement are given, such as by saying, "I'm not allowed to argue my case at this stage." The attorney indicates who the parties are and the nature of their relationship. If the case is about an incident that occurred in a particular place, the attorney may describe the scene with such information as the date, time, and weather. If an object was important in the case, such as a gun or a car, the attorney may describe it. The attorney may indicate the essence of what the case is about by stating what the issue is. For example, in a dog bite case, the attorney might state, "The issue is whether or not the defendant knew or should have known that Lucifer the Doberman was a dangerous animal." The attorney may give a theory about what happened and the basis for liability or nonliability, guilt or innocence. The plaintiff's attorney or the prosecutor may anticipate and refute defenses. In civil cases, damages may be addressed. Finally, the attorney may end with a brief conclusion.

The following are excerpts from the plaintiff's opening statement in a tobacco lawsuit. The attorney does an excellent job of establishing his theme, anticipating the defense and refuting it, and previewing his evidence. He also is able to sneak in quite a bit of argument by saying, "the evidence will show."

BENCH BRIEF   TRANSCRIPT

In Re NEW YORK CITY ASBESTOS LITIGATION vs. AC&S Inc. Transcript, Supreme Court, New York County, Trial Term Part 44, October 4, 2004, 2004 WL 2607798.

Opening Statement by Jerome Block:

May it please the Court, your Honor, counsel, and Ladies and Gentlemen of the jury. Good morning.

First of all, thank you so much for committing to serve as jurors in such an important case.

It's my honor to be here representing Frank and Jessie Gadaleta …

This case, ladies and gentlemen, is about the choices that Lorillard made, the choices that Lorillard made when faced with information that their product, cigarettes, were causing people to die in the 1950s and the 1960s, choices that Lorillard made that were wrong, choices that Lorillard made that were negligent, that were reckless, and that were fraudulent. This case is about what happens when a corporation finds out that it's selling a deadly product and, not only fails to warn people that the product could cause your death, that the product could cause lung cancer, but misleads people, misleads people so they'll continue to use the product, and continue to hurt themselves. This case is a story about tragic consequences resulting from corporate deceit and lack of corporate responsibility.

. . .

It was March of 1952. Lorillard Tobacco Company, which was then called P. Lorillard, launched a massive advertising campaign advertising their Kent cigarette with the Micronite filter, and what Lorillard said, in 1952 and in subsequent years, was that the Kent cigarette with the Micronite filter gave smokers health protection, that the Micronite filter would filter anything out of cigarettes that might be bad, and protect the health of the smoker, they called it "the greatest health protection in the history of smoking."

And we're going . . . to show you the advertisements that Lorillard was putting out there about the Kent cigarette with the Micronite filter, and you'll see the words "health protection," and you'll see the promises that Lorillard was making about the Kent cigarette with the Micronite filter, we'll show you the advertisements we observed.

(continues)

BENCH BRIEF Tʀᴀɴsᴄʀɪᴘᴛ *(continued)*

You'll hear evidence, ladies and gentlemen, that Mr. Gadaleta was so convinced that the Micronite filter was a safe cigarette and would give him health protection that when he met his wife in September of 1953—they met at work—he told her . . . if you're going to smoke cigarettes, smoke the Kent cigarette with the Micronite filter because this is a safe cigarette, the advertisements say this cigarette is safe, that it will give you health protection, . . .

In 1952, Mr. Gadaleta, believing in those promises made by Lorillard, became a brand-loyal smoker of the Kent cigarette with the Micronite filter, and he continued to smoke these cigarettes up through the 1980s. . . . And in Mr. Gadaleta's mind the micronite filter meant safe. The micronite filter meant health protection . . . . And Mr. Gadaleta's choice was based on the information that he received from Lorillard . . . .

The evidence will show, ladies and gentlemen, that Lorillard's representation that a cigarette, that any cigarette would provide health protection was outrageous. And the evidence will show that it was even more outrageous, because from March 1952 through May 1956, for over four years, okay, for 50 months there was up to 25 percent asbestos in the filter of Kent cigarettes.

The cigarettes that were supposed to be the greatest health protection in smoking history. The evidence will show is the most dangerous cigarette in smoking history.

Ladies and gentlemen, that's because in 1952 asbestos was known to cause a disease called asbestosis, a disabling disease of the lungs that could cause lung cancer . . . .

Dr. Barry Castleman will be testifying, probably this week. He will be here in that witness box and he'll tell you about the history of knowledge about asbestos and disease. And he's written a book in this topic and he published papers, he will explain, it was known as far back as the 1890s, that breathing asbestos could cause damage to the lungs and cause death. He will tell you that in the early 1900s the term asbestosis was coined as a disabling disease of the lungs caused only by the asbestos that could cause death.

He will tell you that in the 1940s it became known that asbestos was a cause of lung cancer. And the evidence will show, ladies and gentlemen, that Lorillard was on notice that as asbestos was a dangerous cancer-causing substance before they even put asbestos in the micronite filter and sold the first cigarette in March of 1952.

. . .

So understand this. The evidence is going to show, not only did Lorillard, in finding out about these studies, smoking and lung cancer, not warning, but they did the opposite. The evidence is going to show that they engaged in a campaign to reassure the public that smoking doesn't cause any disease and that the case against smoking had not been proven.

(continues)

BENCH BRIEF TRANSCRIPT *(continued)*

...This case is about choices, and Lorillard has to live with their choice. Their choices to market a cigarette that had asbestos in it that they said had health protection, to stick with that trade name, micronite filter, that was falsely advertised as having health protection, to join these [tobacco lobby] organizations and to permit these kinds of statements to falsely reassure the public, to make the public feel like they weren't hurting themselves when they smoked cigarettes, that they weren't causing themselves to die.

...

But in 1985 that was the first time there was a warning that said: Warning, smoking causes lung cancer. 1985.

Mr. Gadaleta will tell you that he didn't know that smoking caused lung cancer until he picked up the pack of Kent cigarettes in the mid-1980s and saw a warning that said for the first time "smoking causes lung cancer" on those packs of cigarettes.

And Mr. Gadaleta will tell you this was the first warning that really got his attention, because it said "cancer."

And Mr. Gadaleta, when he saw cancer, he knew what that meant. He knew it meant that he that if he continued to smoke it knew it would kill him.

There's not going to be any witness in this case that's going to refute Mr. Gadaleta's testimony that he didn't know that smoking caused lung cancer until he saw the warnings on the packs in the mid-80s that said lung cancer.

I expect you're going to hear a lot of evidence about information that was in news articles, that was on TV, you know, in all kinds of sources.

But you have to consider the information that Mr. Gadaleta relied upon for the Kent cigarette that he chose to smoke and the information that he believed, and the information that he relied upon.

And no witness in this case will refute Mr. Gadaleta's testimony that he didn't know that smoking caused lung cancer until the mid-80s when he saw the warning about lung cancer on the packs of his Kent cigarettes for the first time.

The issue of addiction. You heard about that in jury selection, you'll hear about that in this case .... And, as the plaintiffs in this case, we have to fight hard to put on evidence, and we're going to, on liability, but we believe the most important issue in this case is damages, and on the issue of damages, you are going to hear evidence from Mr. Gadaleta, you are going to hear evidence from Mrs. Gadaleta, you're going to hear evidence from Dr. Markowitz, who has reviewed the medical evidence, and he's going to talk to you about all the procedures that Mr. Gadaleta has been through, the countless numbers of chemotherapies and medical procedures, and

(continues)

BENCH BRIEF Transcript *(continued)*

you'll hear about Mr. Gadaleta's painful four-year struggle with stage IV lung cancer. You'll hear about the physical pain he's endured, you'll hear about the emotional suffering he's endured, and you'll hear about the loss of enjoyment of life.

. . .

At the end of the case we will ask you to award damages of the highest magnitude. Not because of sympathy, but because the evidence warrants it. Because this case is that serious. On the evidence of damages. At end of the case we will ask for substantial damages for Mrs. Gadaleta as well. We'll ask for separate damages for Mrs. Gadaleta as well. Who, because of her lung cancer, has had her life turned upside down and suffered terrible loss of her own.

And we'll also ask for damages for both Mr. & Mrs. Gadaleta that will continue into the future. Because Mr. Gadaleta is still with us, he still wants to be with us. But we are asking for damages that will go on into the future.

Ladies and gentlemen, this is the last time that I'm going to be addressing you directly until closing arguments in this case.

And I ask you to listen to the evidence, try to be patient. Some of the evidence is going to come in, in different forms and documents. It's not all going to be live witnesses. I wish we were able to call all live witnesses. Sometimes we're going to be putting in documents. It's kind of going to be like putting a puzzle together.

And what I tried to do is give you sort of the box cover. To show you what we believe the picture looks like. So that when the pieces of the puzzle come in you can think, oh, yeah that's where that piece fits. Some of the pieces are going to be more obvious than others.

At the end of the case I will have the opportunity to get up here and help you put all the pieces together. And by the end of the case, I believe, with my co-counsel, Ms. Markakis, on behalf of my clients, Mr. and Mrs. Gadaleta, that we will have met our responsibility of meeting our burden of proof so that you can render a decision in this case that you believe is just, that you believe is fair and that you believe is right.

Thank you very much for your patience this morning. And thank you again for your service as jurors.

A defense verdict was returned in the case. The jury concluded that the plaintiff did not smoke the defendant's cigarettes.

First Party's Case

Following the opening statements, the party with the burden of proof begins to present its case. It can call witnesses and introduce exhibits. When a witness is called

■ DIRECT EXAMINATION

Questioning of a witness by the party who called the witness to the stand.

to the stand, the party calling the witness conducts a **direct examination**. During a direct examination, the party who called the witness may ask about relevant and otherwise admissible topics. Leading questions are not allowed on direct examination.

A good direct examination will introduce the witness, giving background information such as occupation, where he lives, and connection to the case. Where it goes from there is highly dependent upon the case, but a good rule of thumb is to follow a chronological order. Sometimes it might be more effective to focus on the most dramatic testimony early in the examination when the jury is most attentive. The questions on direct should lead the witness along a narrative path. However, the attorney may not just ask a question that does not provide any direction, such as "So tell us what happened?" Rather, the attorney must ask about a specific topic, such as "What did you do upon arriving at the murder scene?" It is also a good idea to anticipate issues that may be addressed during cross-examination and provide a response that dims the impact of bringing it up during the opposing attorney's opportunity to question the witness.

■ CROSS-EXAMINATION

Questioning of a witness by the party who is adverse to the one who called the witness.

Following the conclusion of the direct examination, the other party or parties may conduct a **cross-examination**. Leading questions are allowed, and in fact should be almost exclusively utilized, during cross-examination. The attorney should have a plan of attack for the cross-examination in advance of hearing the direct testimony and should try to make a few basic points that favor his case. The attorney should know the answers before asking the questions. Asking an open-ended question on cross-examination is asking for trouble.

BENCH BRIEF

WHAT DOES A PARALEGAL DO DURING A TRIAL?

At some firms a paralegal may have the opportunity to attend a trial. It is good to just experience seeing a trial, especially of a case that the paralegal worked on, so that he or she can see all the hard work come to fruition. Also, as someone who knows the file inside and out, a paralegal can be invaluable to the attorney.

In some cases, a paralegal will help the attorney find documents, stay organized, figuratively hold the client's hand, watch the jury for reactions, take notes, and make sure that the attorney is not so wrapped up in the trial as to not realize that his zipper is down or her blouse is untucked. Other times, the paralegal would not attend, except as an observer.

PASSIM CASE **FIELDS VS. PRAIRIE BANK**

Here is an example of why asking an open-ended question during cross-examination is a bad idea. Suppose the president of Prairie Bank is testifying under cross-examination by Peter Fields's attorney.

ATTORNEY: Why can't you do a better job of protecting your customer's data?

PRESIDENT: Our customers' privacy is our highest concern. We have spared no resource in protecting our customers' data. We have layers upon layers of security, including password protection, shredding of documents, background

(continues)

PASSIM CASE **FIELDS VS. PRAIRIE BANK** *(continued)*

checks for our employees, data monitoring. We have someone with a Ph.D. in computer security that tries all day to hack into our system and fixes any vulnerabilities that he finds. We have hired security consultants, banking consultants and taken many, many additional data security precautions, some of which I am not at liberty to discuss here because those security measures would be compromised if they were disclosed.

Following is a brief excerpt of a good direct examination and cross-examination from the Rodney King case found on Professor Douglas O. Linder's excellent Web site on notable trials (http://www.law.umkc.edu).

BENCH BRIEF **TRANSCRIPT**

Direct examination of Melanie Singer by the Prosecutor:

Q. What happened next?

A. . . . Officer Powell came up to the right of him and in a matter of seconds, he took out his baton, he had it in a power swing, and he struck the driver across the top of his cheekbone, splitting the face from the top of his ear to his chin.

Q. Prior to Officer Powell hitting him with a baton, did anyone give the driver any type of commands after this second taser shot that you described?

A. No, sir.

Q. Was there any reason for the strike to the head by Officer Powell at the time he struck him?

A. In my opinion, no sir, there was no reason for it.

Cross-examination

Q. Well, you described in your earlier testimony, and you just reiterated, the skin was split from the ear to the chin, was that right?

A. Yes.

Q. Does that [referring to a picture of King's face] appear to be sutured in that photograph?

A. Pardon me sir? No, sir.

Q. Does that appear to be split in that photograph?

A. No, sir.

Q. Do you have any explanation for that?

A. I saw what I saw, sir.

In this case, the attorney was able to get away with not asking leading questions on cross-examination because the picture contradicted what the witness said on direct. There is no possible way she could explain herself out of that testimony on direct.

Following cross-examination, **redirect** is allowed. The redirect must be limited to the areas covered on cross-examination. **Recross** follows redirect and it must be limited to the areas covered under redirect. This could go on forever, so usually it stops here, but a court has discretion to allow additional examinations such as re-redirect and re-recross. Further, a witness who was called during the presentation of the **case in chief** can be called later as a rebuttal witness.

To get exhibits entered into evidence, foundation must be established (see chapter 5, "Foundation and Chain of Custody"). The requirements for foundation vary from item to item. Foundation is generally established during direct examination. Sometimes it is necessary to establish foundation with a series of witnesses before the exhibit is offered, as with establishing the chain of custody of a weapon from a crime scene through several witnesses. There is no prohibition against introducing evidence during cross-examination.

Motions at the Close of the First Party's Case

At the conclusion of the plaintiff's or prosecutor's case in chief, the defendant may, and in some cases must, make a motion for a directed verdict. If such a motion is required but is not made, that may limit the defendant's rights to ask for a new trial or judgment not withstanding the verdict or to appeal.

Second Party's Case

Following the prosecutor's or plaintiff's case in chief, the defense may follow the same procedure to present its case in chief. Witnesses are called, exhibits are entered into evidence. Direct, cross-, redirect and recross examinations are conducted. In criminal cases, the defendant does not have to submit any evidence.

Rebuttal and Surrebuttal

Following the conclusion of the defense case, the plaintiff or prosecution may present rebuttal evidence. This may not bring up new issues, but must refute some point made by the defense. Following rebuttal is surrebuttal, which is the defense's opportunity to rebut the plaintiff's or prosecution's rebuttal case. Again, new matter may not be brought up at this stage.

Objections That Cannot Be Anticipated

Certain objections are based upon the form of the question, hence, they may not be anticipated.

■ **REDIRECT**

An examination following cross-examination by the party originally calling the witness.

■ **RECROSS**

Questioning by an adverse party that follows redirect.

■ **CASE IN CHIEF**

The original opportunity a party has to present its case through witnesses and exhibits.

Argumentative

This is likely to come up during cross-examination. Wide latitude is permitted when cross-examining a witness, but it is improper to badger or argue with the witness. For example, in the following transcript from the damages phase of the O. J. Simpson civil case, an argumentative question is objected to and the objection is sustained.

BENCH BRIEF TRANSCRIPT

Sharon Rufo et al vs. Orenthal James Simpson Transcript, Superior Court, Los Angeles County, February 6, 1997, 1997 WL 47796

Q. (*by O.J.'s attorney Robert Baker*). There's the residence of Mr. Simpson's mother since 1969, correct?

A. (*an expert witness*) That's what the footnote says, yes, sir.

Q. And Mr. Simpson has indicated that he does not have a beneficial interest in that property, correct?

A. Other than the footnote, I don't know.

Q. Well, you were advised that, that's where his mother has lived for the last almost 30 years?

A. Yes, sir.

Q. And she has the beneficial interest in that house?

A. I'm not prepared to make that legal conclusion.

Q. I see. You're prepared to make the jump of 25 million, but you're not prepared to make a conclusion that Mrs. Simpson has the beneficial interest in a house that she's been living in for 28 years; is that the way you want to leave it with the jury?

MR. GELBLUM: Objection, argumentative.

THE COURT: Sustained.

Q. (*by Mr. Baker*) Now, you say a reasonable person would pay $25 million to Mr. Simpson for his name and likeness for the next 25 years, right?

A. That's correct.

Q. And did you try to contact any reasonable person to see if there is a reasonable person alive who would pay $25 million to have sole exclusive rights of Mr. Simpson's name and likeness?

A. That's not the basis of my testimony.

Q. Can you answer my question. Did you contact one person to see if they would pay anything for the name and likeness of Mr. Simpson, much less $25 million?

A. No, sir. That's not the basis of my testimony.

(continues)

Q. Do you know any banker who would loan $5 million on this purported $25 million value of Mr. Simpson's name and likeness? If so, name one; we'll call him and get him on the witness stand.

MR. GELBLUM: Objection, relevance, whether he knows anybody.

THE COURT: Sustained . . . as argumentative.

It is apparent from the transcript where the line is between a good, tough question on cross and a question that is argumentative, at least in that judge's courtroom, on that day.

Asked and Answered

Sometimes attorneys do not like a witness's answer, or they want to be aggressive, or they are disorganized, or maybe they want to waste time and put the jury to sleep. Any of these things may cause an attorney to ask the same witness in the same proceeding essentially the same question more than once. This is not allowed. Rule 403, in addition to prohibiting prejudical information, also prevents offering redundant evidence. The court also has authority under Rule 611 to control the questioning.

Usually the attorney will not literally ask the same question word for word; rather, the lawyer will rephrase the question but still have it ask for the same information.

RULE 611. MODE AND ORDER OF INTERROGATION AND PRESENTATION

(a) Control by court. The court shall exercise reasonable control over the mode and order of interrogating witnesses and presenting evidence so as to (1) make the interrogation and presentation effective for the ascertainment of the truth, (2) avoid needless consumption of time, and (3) protect witnesses from harassment or undue embarrassment.

(b) Scope of cross-examination. Cross-examination should be limited to the subject matter of the direct examination and matters affecting the credibility of the witness. The court may, in the exercise of discretion, permit inquiry into additional matters as if on direct examination.

(c) Leading questions. Leading questions should not be used on the direct examination of a witness except as may be necessary to develop the witness' testimony. Ordinarily leading questions should be permitted on cross-examination. When a party calls a hostile witness, an adverse party, or a witness identified with an adverse party, interrogation may be by leading questions.

Assumes Facts Not in Evidence

Rule 611(a) also allows an objection to a question that assumes facts not in evidence. Another basis is that attorneys are not allowed to testify in cases when they are serving as an attorney, and that evidence must have a foundation. One of the reasons the question "Have you stopped beating your wife yet?" is objectionable is that it assumes facts not in evidence. In order to ask a nonpreliminary question, the attorney must first establish a basis for asking it. If an attorney wanted to ask "Have you stopped beating your wife yet?" the attorney would have to establish that the witness is married, and has beaten his wife previously, and, arguably, on more than one occasion.

BENCH BRIEF TRANSCRIPT

State of Minnesota v. Phillip Morris, Transcript, Minnesota District Court, Second Judicial District, Ramsey County, April 3, 1998 1998 WL 152604.

Q. Having made the finding of compensation in the 1981 report, what did the Surgeon General do with the policy of general reduction? Was it abandoned, was it maintained, was it qualified in 1981?

MR. GILL: Your Honor, assumes facts not in evidence. No—no indication in the record that that was the policy of the Surgeon General.

THE COURT: Okay. The objection is sustained.

Calls for a Conclusion

When a question calls for a legal conclusion or for the witness to do the jury's job and reach a factual conclusion, that question is objectionable. However, experts in some jurisdictions may testify on the **ultimate question of fact**; for example, in a will contest, whether or not the **testator** was competent. Experts may not testify regarding legal conclusions.

In the following case, the court considers an objection to a question asked of an FBI agent by a **pro se** defendant.

BENCH BRIEF TRANSCRIPT

Barker v. State, 2001 WL 83564, at *4 (Tex. App. Feb. 1, 2001)

Q. All right. Just to refresh everybody's memory you said armed and possible dangerous suspect, the officers, the resident possibly, if there was one, neighbors might have been vulnerable, possible destruction of evidence, you were losing the signal because of the weakening battery. I'm asking you that without those things, with just the other three things, the robbery, tracking devices and locating the house, would that have been enough for you to enter the house?

PROSECUTOR: Objection, Your Honor, calls for a legal conclusion.

COURT: That will be sustained.

- **ULTIMATE QUESTION OF FACT**
A key determination in a case regarding what happened.

- **TESTATOR**
The person who signed his last will and testament.

- **PRO SE**
Representing himself in litigation.

BENCH BRIEF

When your opponent is successful in getting the judge to exclude evidence, it is important to make an offer of proof. This involves taking testimony outside the presence of the jury so that an appeals court can see what testimony was missing. Absent an offer of proof, the appeals court does not know what the evidence was and cannot assess its potential impact. Therefore, in order to protect the record so that the issue can be preserved for appeal, it is best to make an offer of proof. The party whose evidence was excluded requests an opportunity to make an offer of proof. The jury is excused and the party makes a record of what it would have presented to the jury had it been allowed to do so.

Confusing

When a question is confusing, there is a possibility that the jury or witness will not understand the question. If the witness does not understand the question, the witness's answer may not really be the answer to the question that is being asked. Objections of this type also have their basis in Rule 611.

Conjecture or Speculation

Witnesses must testify regarding what they hear, see, smell, taste, feel, or otherwise know. Witnesses may not speculate. To the extent that speculation or conjecture are needed to reach a conclusion, it is for the jury to make those leaps. For example, the infamous gangster Al Capone was convicted of tax evasion. The prosecutor called witness after witness who testified about how much money the defendant spent with the witness. All the money spent exceeded the income that he reported to the Internal Revenue Service. However, it was the jury's task to add up all the money spent, consider evidence of what was earned, and conclude that he underreported his income.

In the following transcript from the O. J. Simpson criminal trial, the state's serologist is being examined by prosecutor Hank Goldberg.

BENCH BRIEF TRANSCRIPT

People V. O.J. Simpson Transcript, Superior Court, Los Angeles County, Department No. 103, May 15, 1995, 1995 WL 264351

Q. (by Mr. Goldberg:) Now, with respect to the next date, June the 20th, did you place a sticker on when the defense was questioning you for .70, to your recollection?

A. Yes, I believe we did.

Q. Do you know where that number comes from?

A. It was reflective of what toxicology did. I am not aware of the exact number.

(continues)

BENCH BRIEF Tʀᴀɴsᴄʀɪᴘᴛ *(continued)*

Q. But did—did you find an actual record that contained that .70?

A. I don't believe so, no.

Q. And do you have any personal knowledge of exactly how that .70 was arrived at?

A. No, I do not.

Q. Okay. Are any of your measures that you do in the laboratory accurate to within .1 milliliters, generally?

A. Any measurement?

Q. Well, measurements of blood from a vial in connection with transactions such as the ones that they do in toxicology?

A. I don't believe so, no.

Q. Okay. So this .07, wherever it came from then, is not an exact figure; is that correct.

MR. BLASIER: Objection, argumentative.

THE COURT: Speculative, sustained.

Q. *(by Mr. Goldberg:)* sir, based upon your understanding of the practices in toxicology, is that an exact figure as in .70000?

MR. BLASIER: Objection, calls for speculation.

THE COURT: Sustained.

Note that the court sustained the objection under different grounds than those offered by the attorney, and the attorney then took the hint and made his next objection on the grounds stated by the court.

Cumulative

A cumulative objection is analogous to asked and answered. When evidence is admissible but the same information has already been presented, it is cumulative. To take an extreme example, if a fan ran out on the field at the Super Bowl, and he was charged with trespassing and disorderly conduct, testimony could be taken from all 60,000 fans in the stands, and all 1 billion people who watched the game on television. However, after testimony from a few of them, the remainder would be cumulative. Cumulative objections are also governed by the portion of Rule 403 that prohibits unnecessary repetition, and by Rule 611.

Narrative

An attorney cannot put a witness on the stand and ask a question that is so open ended as to just let the witness ramble on and on. The reason is that doing so prevents the opposition from being able to object until objectionable testimony has already been presented. This is another objection that is governed by Rule 611. The attorney must take the witness through the story with questions.

In the following transcript, the witness starts to tell a story, which is objected to as being narrative.

BENCH BRIEF TRANSCRIPT

Erik Menendez's testimony, People v. Erik Galen Menendez And Joseph Lyle Menendez, Defendants, Transcript, Superior Court, Los Angeles county, December 1, 1995. 1995 WL 730929.

Q. Was Lyle Menendez a bed-wetter?

A. Yes.

Q. How did you know that?

A. Because I remember my mother putting the sheets in the middle of the dinner table so that when my dad got home she (sic) would see Lyle wet his bed. She would rub the sheets in my brother's face and say, you know, you're wetting your bed. You're not supposed to wet your bed. You're just a sissy. And my dad would explode at him and say, you're just being like Erik; although I didn't wet my bed, Lyle did. She used to talk about it in terms of if anyone found out, how embarrassing it would be and how shameful it would be that Lyle wet his bed.

I remember one time—

MR. CONN: Objection. Calls for a narrative. No question pending.

THE COURT: Yes, it does. Objection sustained.

BENCH BRIEF

It used to be that attorneys needed to note an exception when their objection was overruled in order to protect their right to appeal. This is no longer the case. However, an attorney may still note an exception for the record although it has no practical effect. The exchange goes like this:

ATTORNEY: Objection, Your honor, (a reason is given).

JUDGE: Overruled.

ATTORNEY: Exception.

JUDGE: Noted.

Closing Argument

At the end of the case, each side has an opportunity to argue its side. Note the difference: the ending presentation is referred to as an "argument" while the opening presentation was called a "statement." That represents the fact that the attorney is given very wide latitude to argue the case.

A typical closing argument will start out covering some of the material that was covered during the opening statement. The attorney will thank the jurors for their service and introduce the purpose of the closing argument. The attorney will talk about the parties, witnesses, and the scene or instrumentality if there was one. At this stage of the trial, the attorney will know what instructions the judge will be giving the jury, and those can be incorporated throughout the argument. The attorney can interweave instructions and facts, explaining why his client should win the case. He can go back through witness testimony and explain why the attorney's witnesses were more credible than the opposition's, refute the other side's case, argue the client's case, and discuss an appropriate amount for damages. Finally, the attorney should end with a powerful conclusion that sums up why the jury should find in favor of the attorney's client.

BENCH BRIEF

O. J.'S THEME

Johnnie Cochran did a fine job creating a theme of his case for O. J. Simpson's criminal trial, and modifying it with events that occurred during the trial during his closing argument. The prosecutor made a well-known mistake of having the defendant put on one of the gloves associated with the crime. Either the glove did not fit, or it did not fit over the latex glove Simpson had on under it, or Simpson made it look like it did not fit. This allowed Cochran to use a catch phrase to highlight his theme of the case: that the Los Angeles Police Department, in a rush to judgment motivated by concerns about publicity, performed a lousy investigation that was tainted by a racist cop, assumed right away that O. J. was the killer, and sought to prove it rather than conduct a thorough investigation to find "the real killer."

He said, "If it doesn't fit, you must acquit," and he repeated that phrase several times during his closing argument. For example, "If he went in that house with bloody shoes, with bloody clothes, with his bloody hands as they say, where's the blood on the doorknob, where's the blood on the light switch, where's the blood on the banister, where's the blood on the carpet? That's like almost white carpet going up those stairs. Where is all that blood trail they've been banting about in this mountain of evidence? You will see

(continues)

BENCH BRIEF *(continued)*

it's little more than a river or a stream. They don't have any mountain or ocean of evidence. It's not so because they say so. That's just rhetoric. We this afternoon are talking about the facts. And so it doesn't make any sense. It just doesn't fit. If it doesn't fit, you must acquit."

In another example, looking a bit silly while wearing a knit cap, he said, "O. J. Simpson in a knit cap from two blocks away is still O. J. Simpson. It's no disguise. It's no disguise. It makes no sense. It doesn't fit. If it doesn't fit, you must acquit." Finally, he said, "If he took a shower, there's so much blood, he's covered with blood, why didn't they bring the towels in here? Something is wrong in this case. It just doesn't fit. When it doesn't fit, you must acquit."

The order of closing arguments varies from state to state and depends upon whether it is a civil or criminal case. In some states, the party who speaks first may also have a rebuttal.

Below are excerpts from two closing arguments, one for the plaintiff in a personal injury case, and the other from the prosecutor in a criminal case. In the first closing argument, the plaintiff is suing a health care cooperative because its ambulance arrived late when a woman was having difficulty breathing, causing her brain damage. The defense had already given its closing argument.

BENCH BRIEF   TRANSCRIPT

Blatz v. Allina Health Systems, Transcript, District Court, Ramsey County Minnesota, Court file 1997-11134, page 814

Closing argument by Chris Messerly:

May it please the court, counsel, Pat and family:

> . . . This is a case about a corporation's failure, its unwillingness to accept responsibility for forever changing the life of Mary and Pat as they once knew it. In a case in which every second counts, minutes were lost. Allina was negligent. Its negligence was the direct cause of Mary's injuries and Pat's damages. And the damages are substantial.

The first thing you are going to consider on the special verdict form is the negligence question, number one . . . Was Allina negligent? I want to talk about why they were. And the most important reason for that is because Allina's employees had admitted

(continues)

BENCH BRIEF   TRANSCRIPT *(continued)*

they are negligent. They admitted they broke the rules . . . The employee who was on the stand admitted that there was a standard, a criteria . . . to get to this home within 15 minutes . . . this is an Allina document. They note Exception: 17 minutes this call. It took them too long. They broke their own rules. By their own admission, they are negligent. The defendants—the employees admit that every second counts. All three of the employees who testified, both of the ambulance personnel testified that every second counts . . .

What did they do? Having gone some 12 miles, going directly right to Halifax, they go all the way down Halifax and between these last two driveways before Pat and Mary's . . . they decide [to turn around] right in the middle of the road…not in the turnaround. What's a turnaround for? They decide in the middle of the road to make a four-point turn. What is that? Keep in mind they have got a one-ton vehicle they are driving . . . Remember he said the visibility out the back was very poor . . . They put on the brakes; shift in reverse; back up; put on the brakes; shift into forward; go forward; put on the brakes; shift into reverse; back up; put on the brakes; shift into forward; go forward. They turned around in the middle of the street instead of turning around in the turnaround.

The law doesn't require perfection, but what it does require is reasonable care . . . Would a reasonable person after all this turn around, four-point turn, three-point turn in the middle of the road with a clearly visible right in front of them turnaround a second or two or three in front of them so they wouldn't have to back up? Just turn around and go the other way. Had they gone there, they would have seen it. They did the second time.

Wondra [a Sheriff's deputy who also responded to the call] found it…Wondra found it with no problem. He just goes down there and finds it. He had never been down there.

Deputy Wondra when he gets there said, When I got there right at that time, she did not have a heartbeat; she was not breathing. This is the arrest . . . They get there at 9:08. It's undisputed. What's this window? It's a five minute window. The dispatch for Wondra…and for HealthSpan was at 8:51…Wondra's arrival at the home, 9:03. ..If they were there four minutes earlier, clearly they are within the window.

Take the shortest time Mary is lying on the floor. The paramedics should have been there.

[pause for 90 seconds]

That's uncomfortable to sit for just a minute and a half. I don't do it to waste your time because your time is important, too, but if that's the shortest delay, that long when someone is lying on the floor and every second counts in preventing brain damage, they would have gotten there…Dr. Condo…said…the sooner you revive someone,

(continues)

BENCH BRIEF TRANSCRIPT *(continued)*

the faster they are revived. If it would have been caught up closer to 9:03, boom, you wait until 9:08, longer, minute, two minutes, three minutes? How long was it before they revived her?

Now I want to talk a little bit more about the other experts…They are on the Allina staff. Remember that? United Hospital is an Allina facility…It is a financial relationship that they have with this defendant corporation. Don't you think that the biggest health care cooperative in the state of Minnesota owning oxygen companies and other things could have any expert they want anywhere?…What's their experience? They didn't have any experience like Dr. Condo had. One is a neurologist, deals with nerves. One was a pulmonologist, deals with lungs…

Were they frank and direct? …They refused to admit that every second counts…You know what's a little bit funny?…I don't think Allina believes their own argument…If they say the delay doesn't make any difference…why did they even contest whether it's one or three or five minutes? If they are saying it doesn't matter, who cares from their perspective? …I think because they know what their employees know. Time is of the essence. Every second counts …

You are then left with the damages questions …"What amount of money will fairly and adequately compensate the plaintiffs for damages from June 18th to the time of trial? It's in the records—there is an exhibit—but that's $468,961…How about loss of earnings…they have no evidence of any kind…to refute what…the economist from Macalester said…$161,000. Next I'm going to talk about …"What amount of money will fairly and adequately compensate plaintiff for damages from the time of this trial into the future?…If you take the group home, if they could find one, if they meet the criteria, it's about $1.9 million. That's in today's costs…

The defense makes a good point. You have to deduct the cost of her typical living had she not—had Allina not been late. Had they not been negligent, had they not been the direct cause of this, she would have incurred expenses anyway. She would have had to buy gardening tools for her garden and you ought to deduct those. She would have to buy paint and paintbrushes for the gifts she made to give to people at Christmas. You ought to deduct those costs because she doesn't do it now, but she would have…and maybe a beautiful dress she needs going out with her husband on the town because she doesn't need those anymore…And future loss of earning capacity…$667,000, and that's in [the economist's] report.

I'm now going to talk to you about things that are harder to deal with. There is a question about this pain, disability, disfigurement, and embarrassment for both past and future for Mary…This is a woman who…was a proud woman and an independent woman. She

(continues)

took tremendous pride in her job…Just think of the simple things. Driving. Her ability, like our ability, to get in a car and say, "I'm just going to go here" and do it. Mary sits and waits now. Does that cause distress? She sits at [the nursing home]. They are good providers, but she is in a home with people substantially older than she is, and she waits for someone to come and take her somewhere. Is it embarrassing? Mary—is it embarrassing to have to have someone change your diapers, including her husband?…She was proud of her cooking, holiday dinners, the pride she took in that. . . . She took pride in her menagerie of animals. She took pride in her garden. She took pride in decorating her home….Her appearance is different. She has to have people cook for her. She can't do art. She can't ever work again. She can't care for animals and she can never garden again and she can't decorate her home and can't socialize at least in the way she did before….She identified herself as someone with hope and that's gone.

How about now? I mean Mary is still with us. She survived and she has still got some things going on, despite the serious brain damage. She can sing Amazing Grace on the K-Mart karaoke machine with vigor. She can walk around or shuffle from place to place. She can move around. She can talk. She can respond to people. And she has memories. She remembers things that happened before this. And maybe that's the worst things about her distress. It might be better—please excuse how I use that—if she had such brain damage, she couldn't remember who she was or what life was like.

…Defense counsel suggests to you that the value of all these things is worth less than what she earns. I submit that we are not created as having value of only what we earn. I submit that someone who spends their time at home with their children, raising them in a proper way, who may not work at all may have a value far greater than someone who makes more money than anyone in the world…the rule of threes is that because inherently human beings are so much more than what they earn that the value of those intangible damages when they are so severe and catastrophic is three times those firm or hard numbers that the economists could figure out…

And if you just look at the past damages for Mary and if you add those up to ones I've shown you, and if you just take the rule of threes—and you may decide it's times four; you may decide it's only times two—it's just a guidepost that's been used for an eternity. Her past distress, the loss of the life that she once knew… $1.8 million. It's a lot of money. But it's justice and it's fair…

The future is a lot bigger. She is going to live to 81 years old, all these years, with the same memories that every time she looks at a garden, she is going to know it's not hers. She can't go out and do anything with it. If you follow the rule of threes, it's over $7 million . . .

(continues)

BENCH BRIEF TRANSCRIPT *(continued)*

. . .This is their only chance for justice. When I sit down, neither Pat nor Marry nor anyone else like me will have an opportunity to speak for them and ask you to do the right thing.

We are very grateful for your patience and the extremely close attention you have paid on a very long trial. We are confident that after you conclude your deliberations, complete justice and full justice will be served and that you will find Allina was negligent, that its negligence was the direct cause of Mary's injuries and that her injuries and Pat's are substantial. Thank you.

The plaintiff was awarded $11 million.

The criminal closing argument is from the Oklahoma City bombing case.

BENCH BRIEF TRANSCRIPT

United States v. McVeigh Transcript, U.S. District Court for the District of Colorado, May 29, 1997, 1997 WL 280943

Closing Argument by Larry Mackey:

Mr. Jones, Counsel, Mr. Hartzler, my colleagues, ladies and gentlemen of the jury, good morning. The events that were set in motion two years ago are drawing to a close. On April 19, 1995, a crime of ghastly proportions was committed. On that day a truck packed with explosives parked in downtown Oklahoma City filled with explosives. Only a wall of windows separated the unsuspecting children and women and men inside that building from the truck and the explosives that set outside. The truck bomb exploded, the building gave way, and suddenly many lives were ended and many, many more were changed forever.

America stood in shock. Who could do such a thing? Who could do such a thing? It's a question that began to ripple across this country coast to coast. And finally it's come to rest right here in this courtroom. It's fallen to you as members of this jury to answer that question.

Based on the evidence, based on what you've heard, the answer is clear. Tim McVeigh did it. Tim McVeigh and Terry Nichols in concert with each other planned and executed the violent attack on the Murrah Building and are responsible for the murders of those persons who died . . .

(continues)

BENCH BRIEF TRANSCRIPT *(continued)*

When Mr. Hartzler first spoke to you in the opening and told you what the Government intended to do, to fairly present the evidence against Mr. McVeigh, he told you that the evidence would make your job easier, that it would amount to overwhelming evidence of guilt, that it would build brick by brick, witness by witness, a wall, a wall that added up to the guilt of Tim McVeigh. After a month of trial and hammered away at by a very experienced, very skilled team of defense lawyers and experts, that wall still stands, stands tall and strong, and it adds up to the guilt of Tim McVeigh.

When you retire to the jury room, evaluate what promises were made by Joe Hartzler against the evidence and see if we haven't kept our word. We promised and we've proven, in more ways than one, a number of important factual propositions.

No. 1, Timothy McVeigh, motivated by hatred of the Government, in a rage over the events at Waco, deliberately and with premeditation planned the bombing of the Murrah Building;

No. 2, that he educated himself on how to build bombs;

No. 3, that he enlisted at least one coconspirator and attempted to recruit yet another, Michael Fortier, to help him in that criminal act and that he and Terry Nichols acquired and attempted to acquire all of the necessary components to build a massive bomb; that Timothy McVeigh carefully, very deliberately selected his target, the Murrah Building, he surveyed it, and that in April of 1995, he rented the truck, built the bomb, and detonated it against the Murrah Building. That's the Government's case. Promises made, promises kept.

. . . And later when Michael Fortier asked him, Well, what exactly do you have in mind when you talk about taking offensive action against the Government, he said: I mean to bomb a federal building.

. . . Rejected by Michael Fortier in September of 1994, Tim McVeigh…headed back to Kansas, back to someone who did agree with him, back to Terry Nichols. And in the fall of 1994, as you heard, they began using all their energy, all of their limited funds, all their efforts to acquire ingredients that would one day, if put together, would bring down a nine-story office building.

. . .First of all, the question is did the evidence prove that Tim McVeigh knew how to build a bomb . . . .There are two witnesses…who said [i]t's easy to build your own improvised explosive device. All you need are ingredients to make a main charge and then something to set that main charge off. And both of them agreed that if you've got ammonium nitrate, nitromethane, Tovex sausages, Primadet blasting caps, TNT, and det cord, that's all you need; you can make a bomb.

(continues)

BENCH BRIEF TRANSCRIPT *(continued)*

Well, how do you know that Tim McVeigh knew what to do with those ingredients? In this free society, any of us can write away for a book on how to build a bomb. And you heard from Dana Rogers, the account representative from Paladin Press,...Tim McVeigh ordered twice from their company, both times how to build bombs. In May 1993, he ordered the book, Homemade C-4 . . .

...Tim McVeigh emptied her kitchen cabinet, took out the soup cans, and using those soup cans to simulate barrels full of explosive material demonstrated for her how he intended to configure his bomb . . .

And as you test that testimony, think about why Tim McVeigh was doing what he was doing. He was trying to demonstrate to this woman what he knew about bomb-building in a special way...whoever built that bomb, took a lot of time, educated themselves to the end, made sure that they got the right ingredients, made sure they configured it in a way that would produce the results they intended. Somebody like—somebody like a man who would sprawl out on a kitchen floor and use soup cans months and months before the bombing to say, This is what I'm going to do and this is why I'm going to do it.

Finally, let me return to the Bridges [phone] card. If you want other proof that they had what they were looking for by that date, go back to the Bridges card; and when you scroll through the activity there, you'll find that after October 21, after the date of the receipt, all of the phone calls...they end. No more phone calls after that date. They didn't have to call anymore. They had what they needed...

Greg Pfaff, one of the early witnesses:...He remembers this unexpected phone call in the fall of 1994 from Tim McVeigh, this person he knew; and Tim McVeigh says, Can you get me det cord? Can you get me det cord? Now, you judge Mr. Pfaff and judge whether that might be a conversation he would recall. He recalled it; and recall, too, that Mr. McVeigh said, If you can get it, I'm prepared to drive across the country to get it, to get it from you. Don't send it by mail. I'll come get it.

That's not where Tim McVeigh got the det cord, but that's evidence you can consider as to whether Tim McVeigh was intent to getting det cord.

He obviously got it from somewhere. Tim McVeigh got det cord from somewhere, because, as you remember, det cord is this hollow tube. And running down the center of this hollow tube is something called PETN. PETN. It's the same substance that Mr. Burmeister—Agent Burmeister said he found on Tim McVeigh's clothes, in his pockets, and on the earplugs. That's where PETN rests until you cut it, until you handle it, until you do so in a manner that can leave residue...

The defense has suggested that you should ignore—more than ignore—maybe condemn the PETN finding testimony of Agent Burmeister. You shouldn't do that...because if

(continues)

you reject it, you will have had to imagine…a little fairy that would sprinkle PETN in the clothes of Tim McVeigh, knowing you ought to put more PETN the right pocket for a right-handed man than in the left…

The fact of the matter is that 75 minutes after the bombing and 78 miles from the bombing, Tim McVeigh was pulled over at that precise moment he was wearing clothes with PETN and other explosives residues consistent with all the other evidence in this case.

…And during that trip, McVeigh drove Fortier up an alley and he said, this is going to be my escape route…In that alley, in the very same alley, the FBI later found the key to the bomb truck.

You might not be surprised that a bomber, any bomber, once he left the truck would get rid of the key. Any bomber would want to get rid of incriminating evidence, and what could be more incriminating than the key to the bomb truck?

It was found in the alley, the very same alley, that Michael Fortier had described to you as being the alley designated by Tim McVeigh as his escape route…

And what you learned from this evidence is either that Tim McVeigh bombed the Murrah Building and killed the people inside, or that he was the unluckiest man in the world:

Tim McVeigh just happened to be at a motel in Arizona when someone using the Bridges card called a Ryder dealership. Tim McVeigh just happened to buy a car at a Firestone store in Junction City on the same morning that someone using the Bridges card called a Ryder dealership in Junction City, someone using the name Bob Kling. Tim McVeigh just happened to check into the Dreamland Motel in Junction City on that same day. Tim McVeigh just happened to be the only registered guest at the Dreamland Motel when someone using the last name "Kling" ordered Chinese. The Dreamland Motel just happened to be walking distance from the Plaza Stop pay phone where a cab picked up a rider for McDonald's. And Tim McVeigh just happened to be captured on the security camera at that same McDonald's as he leaves the restaurant 20 minutes before someone, it just so happens, named Kling arrived at the Elliott dealership down the street, which just happens to be located within 20 minutes' walking distance. Tim McVeigh just happened to check out of the Dreamland Motel the day before the bombing. And a key that would operate this Ryder truck, the bomb truck, just happened to be found in the same alley that Michael Fortier told you was his escape route. Tim McVeigh just happened to be 75 minutes and 78 miles away from the bomb scene on the day of the bombing. And when arrested, Tim McVeigh just happened to be carrying literature—literature that declared his intent. And when arrested, Tim McVeigh just happened to have traces of high explosives residue on his clothing, in his pockets, and on his earplugs.

(continues)

The defendant was convicted, sentenced to death, and executed.

Final Jury Instructions and Deliberations

After the attorneys have concluded their closing arguments, the judge reads the final jury instructions aloud. The jurors may also bring written copies of the jury instructions with them to the jury room; this is required in some states, prohibited in others, and permitted in most. Sometimes it depends upon whether the case is civil or criminal. For example, Louisiana requires the consent of both the defendant and the state in a criminal case in order for the jury to receive written copies of the instructions. These instructions contain general instructions on how to deliberate, as well as the law for the specific case.

Sometimes the jury instructions can be written in a bit of legalese. For example from Washington Pattern Jury Instructions—Civil 120.02.01: "An [owner] [occupier] of premises owes to a [licensee] [social guest] a duty of ordinary care in connection with dangerous conditions of the premises of which the [owner] [occupier] has knowledge or should have knowledge and of which the [licensee] [social guest] cannot be expected to have knowledge. This duty includes a duty to warn the [licensee] [social guest] of such dangerous conditions." The court would select the appropriate words in brackets, but it still sounds convoluted. To remedy this, California recently approved plain English versions of its civil and criminal jury instructions.

BENCH BRIEF

CALIFORNIA PLAIN LANGUAGE

The California Administrative Office of the Courts (AOC) recently published plain English jury instructions, which can be used instead of the jury instructions that have been developed and approved over time. The new plain language civil instructions, referred to as CACI, and the plain language criminal instructions, referred to as CALCRIM, are not required; rather, they serve as an alternative. Because these instructions are so new (the civil were approved only as of 1993 and the criminal as of 1996), there is a paucity of case law on their validity. It will be interesting to see if they catch on or if courts stick with the old version, called BAJI, since those have generally been approved by court decisions.

Compare these two instructions for **res ipsa loquitor**.

First the old, court-tested, and approved version:

BAJI 4.00. Res Ipsa Loquitur—Necessary Conditions For Application

On the issue of negligence, one of the questions for you to decide in this case is whether the [accident] [injury] involved occurred under the following conditions:

First, that it is the kind of [accident] [injury] which ordinarily does not happen unless someone is negligent;

Second, that it was caused by an agency or instrumentality [in the exclusive control of the defendant] [over which the defendant had the exclusive right of control] [originally, and which was not mishandled or its condition otherwise changed after defendant relinquished control]; and

[Third, that the [accident] [injury] was not due to any voluntary action or contribution on the part of the plaintiff which was the responsible cause of plaintiff's injury.]

Second, the plain English version:

CACI 417. Special Doctrines: Res Ipsa Loquitur

In this case, [*name of plaintiff*] may prove that [*name of defendant*]'s negligence caused [his/her] harm if [he/she] proves all of the following:

1. That [*name of plaintiff*]'s harm ordinarily would not have happened unless someone was negligent;

2. That the harm was caused by something that only [*name of defendant*] controlled; and

(continues)

■ **RES IPSA LOQUITOR**
Literally, the thing speaks for itself. A doctrine indicating that the occurrence of an injury by itself creates an implication that the defendant was negligent in the way he handled an item.

BENCH BRIEF *(continued)*

3. That [*name of plaintiff*]'s voluntary actions did not cause or contribute to the event[s] that harmed [him/her].

If you decide that [*name of plaintiff*] did not prove one or more of these three things, then [*insert one of the following*]

[your verdict must be for [*name of defendant*].]

[*or*]

[you must decide whether [*name of defendant*] was negligent in light of the other instructions I have read.]

If you decide that [*name of plaintiff*] proved all of these three things, you may, but are not required to, find that [*name of defendant*] was negligent or that [*name of defendant*]'s negligence was a substantial factor in causing [*name of plaintiff*]'s harm, or both.

You must carefully consider the evidence presented by both [*name of plaintiff*] and [*name of defendant*] before you make your decision. You should not decide in favor of [*name of plaintiff*] unless you believe, after weighing all of the evidence, that it is more probable than not that [*name of defendant*] was negligent and that [his/her] negligence was a substantial factor in causing [*name of plaintiff*]'s harm.

Here is an instruction for criminal identity theft in the first degree from New York.

NEW YORK MODEL JURY INSTRUCTION
41A:2. IDENTITY THEFT IN THE FIRST DEGREE

A person is guilty of identity theft in the first degree when he or she knowingly and with intent to defraud assumes the identity of another person by presenting himself or herself as that other person, or by acting as that other person or by using personal identifying information of that other person, and thereby:

(1) obtains goods, money, property or services or uses credit in the name of such other person in an aggregate amount that exceeds two thousand dollars;

(2) causes financial loss to such person or to another person or persons in an aggregate amount that exceeds two thousand dollars;

(3) commits or attempts to commit a class D felony or higher level crime or acts as an accessory in the commission of a class D or higher level felony;

(4) commits the crime of identity theft in the second degree as defined in § 190.79 of this article and has been previously convicted within the last five years of:

• identity theft in the third degree as defined in § 190.78

(continues)

> **NEW YORK MODEL JURY INSTRUCTION**
> **41A:2. IDENTITY THEFT IN THE FIRST DEGREE** *(continued)*
>
> - identity theft in the second degree as defined in § 190.79
> - identity theft in the first degree as defined in this section
> - unlawful possession of personal identification information in the third degree as defined in § 190.81
> - unlawful possession of personal identification information in the second degree as defined in § 190.82
> - unlawful possession of personal identification information in the first degree as defined in § 190.83
> - grand larceny in the fourth degree as defined in § 155.30
> - grand larceny in the third degree as defined in § 155.35, grand larceny in the second degree as defined in § 155.40
> - grand larceny in the first degree as defined in § 155.42 of this chapter.

■ **SPECIAL VERDICT FORM**
A questionnaire that the jury fills out in order to make specific factual determinations so that the verdict encompasses the answers to a series of questions.

PASSIM CASE   FIELDS VS. PRAIRIE BANK

Model jury instructions are frequently available, especially for common types of cases such as car accidents, negligence, and crimes. When a case is novel or a crime is charged only infrequently, there may not be a model instruction and the court may have to draft one. In such cases, the court may request the attorneys to draft proposed instructions. At this point there is no readily available civil jury instruction for identity theft or for negligence by a bank or financial institution. However, there are several model criminal identity theft instructions and many negligence instructions. A good way to write proposed instructions is to start with existing instructions that are close and to then adapt them.

In a civil case, the jurors are usually also given a **special verdict form,** which requires them to answer yes-or-no questions and to fill in blanks (see Exhibit 11–1). For example, in a case involving **comparative negligence** the jury will be asked to fill in the percentage of fault for each party, and to indicate how much should be awarded in damages.

■ **COMPARATIVE NEGLIGENCE**
The situation where the plaintiff's recovery is reduced by the percentage of his fault.

APPEAL

During the trial, it is very important to protect the record for the appeal. Appellate courts do not accept evidence. They review the record that is before them; no testimony or exhibits are given. In fact, the most important part of an appeal is the legal writing on the briefs. Attorneys get an opportunity to present oral arguments to an appellate court, but the conventional wisdom is that the attorney can only lose the case by making a bad argument; the attorney cannot win the case with a stellar argument.

4:20 SPECIAL VERDICT FORM--COMPARATIVE NEGLIGENCE OR FAULT--NO
COUNTERCLAIM--SINGLE OR MULTIPLE DEFENDANTS--DESIGNATED NONPARTY OR
NONPARTIES (NEW INSTRUCTION)

IN THE _____ COURT IN AND FOR THE
COUNTY OF _____, STATE OF COLORADO

Civil Action No. _____

_____)
                    Plaintiff,)
)
               v.   ) SPECIAL VERDICT
)
_____)
                    Defendant.)

    You are instructed to answer the following questions. You must all agree on your answer to each
question and you must all sign the completed form on the signature lines.
    1. Do you find that the plaintiff, *(name)*, is entitled to recover damages from the defendant, *(name of
the first defendant)*, on (his) (her) claim of *(insert appropriate description, e.g., "negligence," "breach of
the warranty of ...," etc.)* under instruction No. *(insert the number assigned in the case to the instruction
that sets forth the basic elements of liability for the claim.)* ? (Yes or No)
    ANSWER: _____
    *(Insert additional separately numbered similar paragraphs so as to include all
claims being made against the first defendant.)*
    ANSWER: _____
    2. Do you find that the plaintiff, *(name)*, is entitled to recover damages from the defendant, *(name of
second defendant)*, on (his) (her) claim of *(insert appropriate description, e.g., "negligence," "breach of
the warranty of ...," etc.)* under instruction No. *(insert the number assigned in the case to the instruction
that sets forth the basic elements of liability for the claim)* ? (Yes or No)
    ANSWER: _____
    *(Insert additional separately numbered similar paragraphs so as to include all claims being made
against the second defendant.)*
    ANSWER: _____
    If you answered all of the above questions "No", then stop here and sign the special verdict form as
indicated below.
    If, on the other hand, you answered "Yes" to any or all of the above questions, then answer the
following questions.
    3. Do you find that the plaintiff was (negligent) (or) (at fault) in causing (his) (her) own (injuries)
(damages) (losses) as set forth in instruction No. *(insert the number assigned in the case to the instruction
that sets forth the basic elements of any form of comparative negligence or fault.)* ? (Yes or No)

    ANSWER: _____
    *(Insert, as above in question 3, but in separately numbered questions, any additional forms of
comparative negligence or fault.)*
    ANSWER: _____

EXHIBIT 11-1   Special Verdict Form.

4. Do you find that the designated nonparty, *(name of first designated nonparty)*, was (negligent) (or) (at fault) in causing plaintiff's (injuries) (damages) (losses) as set forth in instruction No. *(insert the number assigned in the case to the instruction which sets forth the basic elements of any form of comparative negligence or fault.)* ? (Yes or No)

ANSWER: _____

(Insert, as above in question 4, but in separately numbered questions, any additional forms of comparative negligence or fault.)

ANSWER: _____

5. Do you find that the designated nonparty, *(name of second designated nonparty)*, was (negligent) (or) (at fault) in causing plaintiff's (injuries) (damages) (losses) as set forth in instruction No. *(insert the number assigned in the case to the instruction that sets forth the basic elements of any form of comparative negligence or fault.)* ? (Yes or No)

ANSWER: _____

(Insert, as above in question 5, but in separately numbered questions, any additional forms of comparative negligence or fault.)

ANSWER: _____

6. Taking as 100 percent the combined (negligence) (or) (fault) that caused the plaintiff's (injuries) (damages) (losses), what percentage of the plaintiff's damages was caused by the (negligence) (or) (fault), if any, of:

a. the plaintiff; and

b. each of the defendants from whom you have found the plaintiff is entitled to recover;

c. (the designated nonparty) (any one or more of the designated nonparties).

You must enter the figure of zero, "0," for any party and designated nonparty you have found was not (negligent) (or) (at fault).

```
                                               ANSWER:
Percentage, if any, charged to plaintiff, (name):     _____%
Percentage, if any, charged to defendant,
(name of first defendant):                            _____
Percentage, if any, charged to defendant,
(name of second defendant):                           _____
Percentage, if any, charged to designated nonparty,
(name of first designated nonparty)                   _____
Percentage charged to designated nonparty,
(name of second designated nonparty)                  _____
                                      MUST TOTAL: 100%
```

7. State the total amount of plaintiff's damages under instruction No. *(insert the number assigned in the case to the instruction that sets forth the damages recoverable by the plaintiff. See, e.g., Instruction 6:1)*, caused by the combined (negligence) (or) (fault) of all the parties and (the) designated nonpart(y)(ies).

ANSWER: $_____

Please sign this special verdict form on the signature lines provided below.

_____ _____

_____ _____

_____ _____
              Foreperson

The record on appeal consists of the testimony, exhibits, pleadings, and material in the trial court file related to the case. If the appeal is from an administrative agency, the record consists of the material that was presented to the agency. The reason for limiting the review to the record is that appeals are not supposed to be a second opportunity for a party to retry the case. If that were true, then appeals courts would be even more overburdened than they already are, and litigation would go on and on even more than it already does.

It can be difficult to read a record if care is not taken to make sure that someone just reading a transcript can follow what is happening. For example, in a transcript, a verbal yes "uh-huh" might look the same as a verbal no "uh-huh." Court reporters are using shorthand to type in sounds rather than letters, so if care is not taken to get the witness to say "yes" or "no," the answer will be unclear. Court reporters cannot note tone of voice. Another example is where information is conveyed visually but the visual expression is not verbalized clearly. For example, "We were only standing about this far apart." When a witness does that, the attorney or judge should say, "For the record, the witness is indicating approximately two feet."

Appeals courts generally review decisions of law **de novo** but reverse factual findings only if they find a clear abuse of discretion such that no reasonable jury could have found the facts the way it found them. In criminal cases that are tried through to acquittal, the state may not appeal.

An appeal should raise at least one legal issue that is subject to review by the appellate court. A legal issue can be stated as a question such as "Is window peeping by a police officer standing on a public street a violation of the Fourth Amendment right against unreasonable search and seizure?" or "Did the trial court err by admitting inadmissible lay opinion regarding DNA evidence which requires expert testimony?" If the appeal is really about the facts not supporting the verdict, the chance of the appellant winning the case are about the same as being dealt a natural royal flush in a five-card poker game with no wild cards and no jokers. Appellate courts are reluctant to substitute their own judgment for that of the jury, since the judges were not the ones hearing the testimony and observing the witnesses.

A paralegal might do some or all of the legal research for an appellate brief, depending upon the attorney, firm, practice area, specific case, and amount of experience the paralegal has. A paralegal might also prepare some of the material that usually goes at the front of the brief, such as the front cover, table of authorities, statement of the case, statement of facts, and statement of the issues.

One useful tool for making a table of authorities is WestCiteLink, which is free software that attaches to a word processing program such as Microsoft Word or WordPerfect. It looks through a document for citations, gathers them up, and places them in a Table of Authorities, which is automatically created within the document at either the start of the document, the end of the document, or another designated location. It can also be utilized to make hyperlinks to cases cited within documents.

■ **DE NOVO**

A review by an appellate court that ignores what the trial court found.

SUMMARY

A trial starts with jury selection. It might be better to call it jury deselection, since the attorneys can only eliminate potential jurors, through either peremptory strikes or getting the judge to remove them for cause. Each side makes an opening statement to preview its case. Argument is not allowed at this stage. The party with the burden of proof starts by presenting its case. It conducts a direct examination of its witnesses, who are subject to cross-examination. Following cross-examination, the party calling the witness may examine on redirect, but that examination must be limited to the topics covered on cross-examination. Recross follows redirect, but it must also be limited to topics covered on redirect. Certain objections, usually relating to the form or repetitious nature of a question, cannot be anticipated before trial. Following the presentation of the case by the party with the burden of proof, the other party may present its evidence. Following that, the party with the burden of proof may present rebuttal witnesses, and the other party may follow that with surrebuttal. After all the evidence is in, the attorneys present closing arguments, which explain why the jury should vote in favor of their client. The judge instructs the jury on the law, and the jury renders a verdict. Following the verdict, the losing party may appeal. It is important to protect the record for appeal. The most important part of an appeal is writing the appellate brief.

■ KEY TERMS

alternate juror	peremptory challenge	special verdict form
case in chief	pro se	testator
comparative negligence	recross	theme of the case
cross-examination	redirect	ultimate question of fact
de novo	removal for cause	venire
direct examination	res ipsa loquitor	voir dire
double jeopardy		

■ HELPFUL WEB SITES

http://www.nita.org
http://www.mri-research.com
http://west.thomson.com/software/default.asp
http://courttv.com
http://www.law.umkc.edu

■ REVIEW AND DISCUSSION QUESTIONS

1. What are the characteristics of the ideal juror for our Passim case for the plaintiff? For the defense?
2. What types of people do the plaintiff and defense in our Passim case not want on the jury?
3. Why does it make sense to call jury selection "jury deselection" instead?
4. What are some reasons a juror can be stricken for cause?
5. What is the primary difference between an opening statement and a closing argument?
6. What is the difference between direct and cross-examination?
7. Who goes first with respect to presentations such as the opening statement, closing argument, and presentation of the case?
8. What type of objections cannot be anticipated?
9. What must an attorney do to protect the record for an appeal?
10. What is the paralegal's role at a trial?

■ LEGAL RESEARCH PROJECTS

1. Get a copy of one of the cases excerpted in this chapter and read all of it. Brief the case by providing a summary of the facts, the legal issue, the holding, and the court's reasoning.
2. What reasons in your state require a court to remove a potential juror from the panel?
3. Pretend you have lost the Passim case in your state and your attorney wants to know the deadline to file an appeal. Find the rule or statute that sets the deadline.

For additional resources, visit our Web site at www.westlegalstudies.com

12

Technology, Evidence, and the Future

"We decided to recall our new drug because a common side-effect is lawsuits."

Courtesy of CartoonStock.com.
www.CartoonStock.com

■ OBJECTIVES

❏ Consider upcoming changes in population, demographics, and technology

❏ Identify how changes in population, demographics, and technology have affected the legal profession and the rules of evidence

❏ Examine how traditional rules of evidence apply to new technologies

❏ Consider likely hot topics in litigation

LIKELY TRENDS

"The best of prophets of the future is the past," said Lord Byron. The recent past is the best predictor of the near future. The 20th century saw tremendous leaps in the development and improvement of technology. Technology affects the way lawyers get ready for trial, including conducting discovery, making a trial notebook, and presenting a case. Technology also opened up new potential cases and theories. The legal profession does not exist in a vacuum. As changes occur in society, they impact the practice of law. Changes in population, demographics, technology, and politics all impact the types of cases that will be brought and the nature of law practice.

According to the *U.S. Census Bureau Interim Projections 2004*, the population of the United States will grow from approximately 282 million in 2000 to 335 million by 2020, and the percentage of people 65 or older will increase from 12.4 in 2000 to 16.3 in 2020. The older population will be better educated and more racially and ethnically diverse.

Technology is making people more connected. Cities such as Austin, Texas; Baton Rouge, Louisiana; Orlando, Florida; Minneapolis, Minnesota; and San Francisco, California are on the forefront of having citywide public wireless high-speed Internet coverage. The number of cell phone users doubled between 2000 and 2006 to 215 million. According to *Supply House Times*, the number of personal digital assistant (PDA) users in the country will reach 20 million by 2008, or 7 percent of the population. In short, the population of the future will be older, even more connected, and more technologically advanced.

Digital convergence will see the merger of television, Internet, and home and wireless phones. 3G technology, which will allow high-speed Internet-style transmission of data and video to cellular phones, will be commonplace in the United States by 2010, according to a March 26, 2006 *U.S. News and World Report* article. Already, people can send and receive photos and video images through cell phones. At least one online poker site has a cell phone version of its games.

THE FUTURE OF EVIDENCE

The changes in population and technology will impact the law office in terms of both the types of cases and the practical aspects of running a law office.

With more older people, elder law and estate planning will be growing fields. As people age they become concerned about making sure that their assets go where they want them to go when they die. They may need a will, or if their estate will be substantial, they may need a trust or other more complicated estate planning tool. After death, their estates must be probated. Elder law also includes grandparental rights and rights related to nursing homes and other adult, long-term care facilities.

Another area that is expected to grow is animal law, which includes estate planning for companion animals and conflicts about liability and where an animal may be kept, among other things. The American Bar Association now has an animal law section.

At least one firm recently established a video game practice.

Courtroom and Law Office Technology

As the world becomes more connected, clients will expect to be able to contact their attorneys with greater ease, and will expect faster replies, potentially raising the stress level for attorneys and support staff such as paralegals. Technology will continue to develop at exponential rates. Computers will be faster, cheaper, and able to hold more data; old software will be improved and new software will be developed.

New technology will be adopted in law offices and, more slowly, in courtrooms. Trial presentation software such as TrialDirector®, Sanction®, and Visionary™ will be improved and more widely adopted.

New, specialized software will be developed for attorneys and paralegals that will aid in the acquisition, organization, and presentation of evidence. Electronic discovery will continue to grow in importance as more and more documents are created and stored solely on a computer. Its importance will spread to family law cases as computers become even more affordable and additional families buy them and put their family finances into programs such as Quicken®.

Courtrooms will increase their usage of technology in ways such as video conferencing feeds; projection of documents onto a TV, computer, or film screen; Internet access at counsel tables; and instant messaging among counsel, cocounsel, opposing counsel, the lawyers' offices, and the judge. Perhaps attorneys will be able to have a sidebar through instant messaging. This would improve the privacy of such sidebars, as it is difficult to whisper loudly enough for the judge and opposing counsel to hear but softly enough so that the jury does not; and it is a time-consuming interruption to dismiss the jurors every time the court and counsel need to discuss something outside of their presence. Courtroom Connect provides high-speed wireless Internet access in courtrooms at no charge to the court and then charges attorneys to access its network. This service is in courtrooms in California, Delaware, District of Columbia, Florida, Georgia, Maryland, Massachusetts, New York, Pennsylvania, Texas, and Virginia.

As technology becomes more and more accepted, foundation and authentication requirements will be relaxed. For example, videotapes used to require a lot of foundation about how the tape was made and whether it was accurate, but now they are considered similar to photographs.

New Technology and Improved Technology

Technology will create new types of cases and make existing cases easier to prove. New, unforeseen technologies will continue to develop. In the 21st century, breath test machines for driving while under the influence cases were developed and deployed. Drastic improvements were made over the earliest adjustable machines, which could be set so that different readings could result from the same breath sample depending upon the setting. New technology may create new types of cases or make it easier to prove other types of cases. For example, the invention of magnetic resonance imaging (MRI) made it easier to prove **shaken baby syndrome.**

Evolving Technology in Evidence

Law tends to evolve slowly, while technology and science have been evolving at a breakneck pace. The doctrine of **stare decisis** tends to slow down changes in

■ **SHAKEN BABY SYNDROME**
A litany of injuries such as blindness, brain damage, paralysis, and developmental disabilities caused by violently shaking an infant or small child.

■ **STARE DECISIS (STAR-EE' DE-SEYE'-SIS)**
A legal doctrine that requires a court to follow legal holdings and rules of law that were established in earlier cases.

case law. Changes are usually made in an incremental manner as cases that no longer make sense are criticized or distinguished rather than overturned. In stark contrast, consider Moore's Law, which says that computer speed and memory doubles every 18 months. As new tests and types of evidence come into play, courts need to determine how old evidentiary rules should apply. Science and technology also develop at a much brisker pace than the law. An example from the recent past is **DNA testing**.

Prior to DNA testing, scientists were able to use blood samples as genetic markers, but they did not acquire this ability until the early 1900s. (See Heidi C. Schmitt, "Post-conviction Remedies Involving the Use of DNA Evidence to Exonerate Wrongfully Convicted Prisoners: Various Approaches Under Federal and State Law," 70 *UMKC Law Review* 1001, 1002–06 (Summer 2002).) In 1925 the gene frequency of blood types was known. However, blood testing was not generally able to meet the evidentiary standard needed to win a criminal case.

According to Schmitt, DNA testing was first used in criminal trials in the United States in 1986. The first type of DNA test that was used was RFLP (restriction fragment length polymorphism). This requires a relatively large sample of 100,000 cells (a dime-sized blood stain, for example), and is time consuming. RFLP testing is somewhat analogous to comparing bar codes. Later, PCR (polymerase chain reaction) testing was developed, which needs only about 50 cells because it is comparing multiple locations in the genetic map that are unique to every individual. PCR testing is analogous to making blown-up genetic photocopies of a particular area on the DNA strand. (A third type of DNA testing, mitochondrial analysis, is used much less frequently.) Because scientists are comparing the genetic map at multiple locations, PCR is considered more accurate than RFLP. Scientists are continuing to improve the accuracy of DNA testing. The database of potential locations in the DNA map that are unique to every individual will continue to grow, and improvements in sample collection will be made. By 2010, it may be possible for crime scene investigators to conduct DNA testing at a crime scene.

Photography was developed in the 1800s, and it took a long time for the technology to develop. Various techniques were developed between 1826, when the first permanent photographic image was created, and 1871, when the dry plate process was invented. It took until 1907 for commercially available color photographs to be available. The first commercial electronic still camera was released in 1981. In 1990 Kodak released the photo CD system, and in the mid-1990s digital cameras became available to consumers.

Photographs were probably not admitted into evidence in American courtrooms until the late 1850s, and there was "grave concern about this novel form of proof. The doctrine that emerged from this marriage of enthusiasm and unease was a peculiar one, a precarious balancing act not wholly internally consistent. By linking photographs analogically to maps, models, and drawings, this new doctrine invented a pedigree for the new technology," according to Jennifer L. Mnookin ("The Image of Truth: Photographic Evidence and the Power of Analogy," 10 *Yale Journal of Law and the Humanities* 1, 8 (Winter 1998)). Now photographs are admissible, but the advances in technology continue to create evidentiary issues.

■ **DNA TESTING**
An identification test using genetic material such as blood to compare parts of the material in the nucleus of cells that serves as a genetic map of the body.

With digital photography and software programs such as Adobe® Photoshop®, it is possible to alter photographs. A skilled person can take one person's head and make it look as if it belongs on another person's body, or make a police car's lights appear to be flashing when they are actually off. Of course, the photographer can touch up, crop, and otherwise alter regular nondigital photographs, but it is much easier to manipulate a digital photo, and manipulations are more difficult to detect. So are digital images admissible?

Consider Rule 901.

RULE 901(A)

The requirement of authentication or identification as a condition precedent to admissibility is satisfied by evidence sufficient to support a finding that the matter in question is what its proponent claims.

The same standards for the authentication of film photography are utilized when considering digital images. In order for an image to be admissible, a witness must testify that the image accurately represents what it purports to show; for example, that the digital photo accurately shows the car accident scene.

In the following convenience-store robbery case, the court considers the admissibility of still photos taken from a surveillance camera.

CASE
OWENS V. STATE, 363 ARK. 413 (ARKANSAS 2005).

Owens next contends that the State did not lay a proper foundation for the admission of . . . still photographs that were taken from the videotape in the E-Z Mart surveillance camera. According to Owens, the State, as the proponent of the evidence, had the burden of proving that the photographs had not been altered and that there existed a proper chain of custody for this evidence. He claims that the prosecutor failed to meet this burden, because he did not admit the photographs through a witness who could inform the court whether the images had been enhanced or altered. Merely offering the evidence through the victim, Paul Aku, was, according to Owens, improper in this case because Aku did not take the photographs, and he had not viewed the videotape from which the photos were digitally derived. Thus, according to Owens, Aku had nothing to do with the preparation of the photographs and had no idea whether they had been enhanced or manipulated by a computer.

(continues)

CASE
OWENS V. STATE, 363 ARK. 413 (ARKANSAS 2005) *(continued)*

. . . Owens urges that the foundational deficiency was not cured by the admission of the videotape into evidence. He emphasizes that even though the jury was allowed to view the videotape made by the surveillance camera at E-Z Mart, the jury did so well after the photographs had been introduced into evidence. As a result, the jury did not have a full and fair opportunity to compare the videotape to the photographs, because the jury saw and heard about them before it saw the videotape and never had an opportunity to actually compare the photographs to the tape. Thus, Owens concludes that these circumstances should not relieve the State of its burden of laying the foundation for [the photos].

. . . In discussing our standard of review for evidentiary rulings, we have said that the trial courts have broad discretion and that a trial court's ruling on the admissibility of evidence will not be reversed absent an abuse of that discretion. As an initial matter, we disagree that it was essential for purposes of laying a proper foundation to have the person who actually took the still photographs from the videotape be in court to testify. Our Rules of Evidence provide that authentication or identification of evidence may be proven by: "Testimony of a witness with knowledge that a matter is what it is claimed to be." Ark. R. Evid. 901(b)(1) (2005). In the instant case, the State provided exactly that. Paul Aku testified that the still photographs taken from the surveillance camera's videotape depicted the scene at that convenience store accurately . . .

In sum, Paul Aku, the only eyewitness to the crime, testified that the photographs were an accurate depiction of the events that took place on the evening of November 15, 2003. He further testified about his knowledge of the surveillance cameras and the types of images he frequently had observed on the monitors at the E-Z Mart. We hold that the State met its burden of proof required for authenticating the photographs in this case, and, thus, laid a proper foundation for admission of the photographs. In addition, we do not agree that this court should impose a higher burden of proof for the admissibility of digital photographs merely because digital images are easier to manipulate. There was no abuse of discretion by the circuit court in this regard.

Moreover, we further disagree with Owens that expert testimony of no alteration was required when there was no indication that the still photographs had been enhanced from the videotape or altered in any way. This is unlike the situation in *Nooner* . . . where the still photographs had been enhanced and the State used witnesses to explain the enhancement process and to show the photographs had been enhanced, but not altered, from the images on the videotape.

The court affirmed the admission of the digital pictures taken from the surveillance camera through an analysis using Rule 901, and declined to establish a different standard for digital photos.

Hot Topics in Litigation

Legal newspapers indicate other upcoming hot topics such as copyright issues with digital media, Internet disputes, education finance litigation, securities fraud, **Ponzi schemes**, **toxic torts**, and product liability cases relating to prescription drugs and herbal supplements.

With the aging of the United States population, there is a large profit potential for prescription medications. The dynamics of the stock market, which has a strong appetite for hefty profits and the growth potential of new drugs, as well as strong consumer demand to get new drugs for sick people available as quickly as possible, has caused

---

BENCH BRIEF

GIGANTIC VERDICTS AND PENALTIES IN SECURITIES CASES

- **Worldcom: $11 billion** Accounting fraud at the company led to the largest bankruptcy in history and a 25-year prison sentence for the CEO.

- **Enron: $2 billion** The former CEO of the company faced 35 criminal counts including insider trading related to investment schemes designed to inflate the stock price.

- **McKesson: $1.2 billion** Class action settlements stemming from financial fraud related to an acquisition.

- **Time Warner: $2.4 billion** The company settled investor claims related to a failed merger with America Online, plus it had to reserve another $600 million. It inflated ad revenue and subscriber numbers.

- **Global Crossing: $325 million** Executives inflated revenue at the company.

- **Bristol-Myers Squibb: $300 million** The firm settled claims that it used false sales figures to artificially enhance its stock price.

- **Qwest: $250 million** The company settled with the Securities and Exchange Commission.

- **Charter Communications: $144 million** Class actions were settled for cash, stock, and the right to buy stock after accounting and other fraud allegations.

- **CVS Corp.: $110 million** A shareholder suit alleged that the company made misleading statements to artificially boost its stock price.

- **Symbol Technologies: $139 million** This was another shareholder suit alleging accounting fraud.

- **Raytheon: $90 million** Accounting and disclosure problems in a subsidiary resulted in two settlements, one for $51 million and one for $39 million; plus it was penalized another $12 million.

■ **PONZI SCHEME**

A fraudulent investment scenario in which returns of early investors are inflated by using later investors' capital contributions to create the false perception of profits for the early investors, thereby generating even larger investments.

■ **TOXIC TORT**

An injury claim based upon plaintiffs being exposed to a toxic substance such as asbestos.

some drugs to be released before their safety was thoroughly tested, or perhaps even with the drug companies knowing about potential safety problems. For example, Wyeth was sued after physicians prescribed Phentermine and Fenfluramine (Phen-Fen) and patients developed heart valve problems. It has set aside $21 billion to settle lawsuits over the diet drugs. Merck is expected to have to pay between $18 billion and $50 billion for problems related to Vioxx, a painkiller that also can cause heart problems.

Litigation involving the civil liberties aspects of DNA fingerprinting may address such issues as "(1) who should be included in forensic databases; (2) tissue collections as potential databases; (3) sample retention; (4) length of retention; (5) access to forensic DNA databanks; (6) 'partial matches' and effects on relatives; (7) racial identification using DNA hapotype analysis; (8) resource allocation; (9) federal versus state roles; (10) role of medical personnel; (11) the 'autonomy of science'; (12) uses of samples in medical research; (13) behavioral genetic research; (14) informed consent for research; (15) commercialization; (16) use for epidemiological purposes; (17) fiduciary issues versus the common good; (18) use of DNA collected for identification in mass disasters; and (19) national DNA identification cards." (Benjamin Moultin, "D.N.A. Fingerprinting and Civil Liberties," 34 *Journal of Law Medicine and Ethics* 147 (Summer 2006).)

Increased Use of Alternative Dispute Resolution

Courts are under pressure to keep costs down due to pressure from taxpayers to keep taxes low and government services efficient. Yet, at the same time, they are experiencing increasing caseloads as we continue to be a litigious society willing to sue over such things as tough summer homework assignments or becoming obese after eating repeatedly at a fast-food restaurant. To deal with these dynamics, courts will continue to refer parties to alternative dispute resolution so that the cases can be resolved outside of the court system.

Rules Will Be Less Uniform

Prior to the adoption of the Federal Rules of Evidence, states had a variety of evidentiary rules that were primarily based upon case law. After the Federal Rules of Evidence were adopted, many states adopted them as well and there was a trend toward uniformity in evidentiary rules. Subsequently, as states and the federal government amended their rules, and federal and state courts issued opinions interpreting their own rules of evidentiary, the uniformity began to devolve. This trend will continue, although the differences will be mostly technical.

SUMMARY

Changes in demographics and technology will impact the practice of law in terms of the types of cases that are brought, how law offices are run, how attorneys and clients communicate, and how evidence is presented in courtrooms. The law tends to develop at a slow pace while technology is developing very quickly. In recent years, DNA testing has been developed and improved, and there are many legal issues related to it that will need to be resolved.

The gathering, organization, and presentation of evidence will continue to be impacted by technology. Technology will also allow new types of cases to be brought. Economic pressure on courts and litigants will continue to drive the expansion of alternatives to litigation such as mediation, arbitration, and other forms of alternative dispute resolution.

■ KEY TERMS

DNA testing	shaken baby syndrome	toxic tort
Ponzi scheme	stare decisis	

■ HELPFUL WEB SITES

http://www.census.gov
http://www.shakenbaby.com
http://www.sbsdefense.com
http://www.courtroomconnect.com
http://www.trialdirector.com
http://www.verdictsystems.com

■ REVIEW AND DISCUSSION QUESTIONS

1. What are some demographic or technological changes that are expected?
2. How will upcoming changes in demographics or technology impact the law office?
3. How will upcoming changes in demographics or technology impact the types of cases that are brought?
4. What impact will technology have on clients' expectations regarding their attorney's availability?
5. What are some issues yet to be resolved with regard to DNA testing?

6. How can the historical courtroom treatment of the admissibility of photographs be analyzed in terms of the admissibility of new technology?

7. What are some hot topics in litigation?

8. What is likely to happen with regard to the usage of alternative dispute resolution?

■ LEGAL RESEARCH PROJECTS

1. Find an article in a legal newspaper about a type of case mentioned in this chapter.

2. Find a law review article that considers an Internet or high-technology issue.

3. Write a memo about the admissibility of a new technology item. You may consider one listed in this chapter or something else.

For additional resources, visit our Web site at www.westlegalstudies.com

Federal Rules of Evidence

Rule 101

These rules govern proceedings in the courts of the United States and before the United States bankruptcy judges and United States magistrate judges, to the extent and with the exceptions stated in rule 1101.

Rule 102

These rules shall be construed to secure fairness in administration, elimination of unjustifiable expense and delay, and promotion of growth and development of the law of evidence to the end that the truth may be ascertained and proceedings justly determined.

Rule 103

(a) **Effect of Erroneous Ruling.**—Error may not be predicated upon a ruling which admits or excludes evidence unless a substantial right of the party is affected, and

(1) **Objection.**—In case the ruling is one admitting evidence, a timely objection or motion to strike appears of record, stating the specific ground of objection, if the specific ground was not apparent from the context; or

(2) **Offer of Proof.**—In case the ruling is one excluding evidence, the substance of the evidence was made known to the court by offer or was apparent from the context within which questions were asked.

Once the court makes a definitive ruling on the record admitting or excluding evidence, either at or before trial, a party need not renew an objection or offer of proof to preserve a claim of error for appeal.

(b) **Record of Offer and Ruling.**—The court may add any other or further statement which shows the character of the evidence, the form in which it was offered, the objection made, and the ruling thereon. It may direct the making of an offer in question and answer form.

(c) **Hearing of Jury.**—In jury cases, proceedings shall be conducted, to the extent practicable, so as to prevent inadmissible evidence from being suggested to the jury by any means, such as making statements or offers of proof or asking questions in the hearing of the jury.

(d) **Plain Error.**—Nothing in this rule precludes taking notice of plain errors affecting substantial rights although they were not brought to the attention of the court.

Rule 104

(a) **Questions of admissibility generally.**—Preliminary questions concerning the qualification of a person to be a witness, the existence of a privilege, or the admissibility of evidence shall be determined by the court, subject to the provisions of subdivision (b). In making its determination it is not bound by the rules of evidence except those with respect to privileges.

(b) **Relevancy conditioned on fact.**—When the relevancy of evidence depends upon the fulfillment of a condition of fact, the court shall admit it upon, or subject to, the introduction of evidence sufficient to support a finding of the fulfillment of the condition.

(c) **Hearing of jury.**—Hearings on the admissibility of confessions shall in all cases be conducted out of the hearing of the jury. Hearings on other preliminary matters shall be so conducted when the interests of justice require, or when an accused is a witness and so requests.

(d) **Testimony by accused.**—The accused does not, by testifying upon a preliminary matter, become subject to cross-examination as to other issues in the case.

(e) **Weight and credibility.**—This rule does not limit the right of a party to introduce before the jury evidence relevant to weight or credibility.

Rule 105

When evidence which is admissible as to one party or for one purpose but not admissible as to another party or for another purpose is admitted, the court, upon request, shall restrict the evidence to its proper scope and instruct the jury accordingly.

Rule 106

When a writing or recorded statement or part thereof is introduced by a party, an adverse party may require the introduction at that time of any other part or any other writing or recorded statement which ought in fairness to be considered contemporaneously with it.

Rule 201

(a) **Scope of rule.**—This rule governs only judicial notice of adjudicative facts.

(b) **Kinds of facts.**—A judicially noticed fact must be one not subject to reasonable dispute in that it is either (1) generally known within the territorial jurisdiction of the trial court or (2) capable of accurate and ready determination by resort to sources whose accuracy cannot reasonably be questioned.

(c) **When discretionary.**—A court may take judicial notice, whether requested or not.

(d) **When mandatory.**—A court shall take judicial notice if requested by a party and supplied with the necessary information.

(e) **Opportunity to be heard.**—A party is entitled upon timely request to an opportunity to be heard as to the propriety of taking judicial notice and the tenor of the matter noticed. In the absence of prior notification, the request may be made after judicial notice has been taken.

(f) **Time of taking notice.**—Judicial notice may be taken at any stage of the proceeding.

(g) **Instructing jury.**—In a civil action or proceeding, the court shall instruct the jury to accept as conclusive any fact judicially noticed. In a criminal case, the court shall instruct the jury that it may, but is not required to, accept as conclusive any fact judicially noticed.

Rule 301

In all civil actions and proceedings not otherwise provided for by Act of Congress or by these rules, a presumption imposes on the party against whom it is directed the burden of going forward with evidence to rebut or meet the presumption, but does not shift to such party the burden of proof in the sense of the risk of nonpersuasion, which remains throughout the trial upon the party on whom it was originally cast.

Rule 302

In civil actions and proceedings, the effect of a presumption respecting a fact which is an element of a claim or defense as to which State law supplies the rule of decision is determined in accordance with State law.

Rule 401

"Relevant evidence" means evidence having any tendency to make the existence of any fact that is of consequence to the determination of the action more probable or less probable than it would be without the evidence.

Rule 402

All relevant evidence is admissible, except as otherwise provided by the Constitution of the United States, by Act of Congress, by these rules, or by other rules prescribed by the Supreme Court pursuant to statutory authority. Evidence which is not relevant is not admissible.

Rule 403

Although relevant, evidence may be excluded if its probative value is substantially outweighed by the danger of unfair prejudice, confusion of the issues, or misleading the jury, or by considerations of undue delay, waste of time, or needless presentation of cumulative evidence.

Rule 404

(a) **Character Evidence Generally.**—Evidence of a person's character or a trait of character is not admissible for the purpose of proving action in conformity therewith on a particular occasion, except:

(1) **Character of Accused.**—Evidence of a pertinent trait of character offered by an accused, or by the prosecution to rebut the same, or if evidence of a trait of character of the alleged victim of the crime is offered by an accused and admitted under Rule 404(a)(2), evidence of the same trait of character of the accused offered by the prosecution;

(2) **Character of Alleged Victim.**—Evidence of a pertinent trait of character of the alleged victim of the crime offered by an accused, or by the prosecution to rebut the same, or evidence of a character trait of peacefulness of the alleged victim offered by the prosecution in a homicide case to rebut evidence that the alleged victim was the first aggressor;

(3) **Character of Witness.**—Evidence of the character of a witness, as provided in Rules 607, 608, and 609.

(b) **Other Crimes, Wrongs, or Acts.**—Evidence of other crimes, wrongs, or acts is not admissible to prove the character of a person in order to show action in conformity therewith. It may, however, be admissible for other purposes, such as proof of motive, opportunity, intent, preparation, plan, knowledge, identity, or absence of mistake or accident, provided that upon request by the accused, the prosecution in a criminal case shall provide reasonable notice in advance of trial, or during trial if the court excuses pretrial notice on good cause shown, of the general nature of any such evidence it intends to introduce at trial.

Rule 405

(a) **Reputation or opinion.**—In all cases in which evidence of character or a trait of character of a person is admissible, proof may be made by testimony as to reputation or by testimony in the form of an opinion. On cross-examination, inquiry is allowable into relevant specific instances of conduct.

(b) **Specific instances of conduct.**—In cases in which character or a trait of character of a person is an essential element of a charge, claim, or defense, proof may also be made of specific instances of that person's conduct.

Rule 406

Evidence of the habit of a person or of the routine practice of an organization, whether corroborated or not and regardless of the presence of eyewitnesses, is relevant to prove that the conduct of the person or organization on a particular occasion was in conformity with the habit or routine practice.

Rule 407

When, after an injury or harm allegedly caused by an event, measures are taken that, if taken previously, would have made the injury or harm less likely to occur, evidence of the subsequent measures is not admissible to prove negligence, culpable conduct, a defect in a product, a defect in a product's design, or a need for a warning or instruction. This rule does not require the exclusion of evidence of subsequent measures when offered for another purpose, such as proving ownership, control, or feasibility of precautionary measures, if controverted, or impeachment.

Rule 408

Evidence of (1) furnishing or offering or promising to furnish, or (2) accepting or offering or promising to accept, a valuable consideration in compromising or attempting to compromise a claim which was disputed as to either validity or amount, is not admissible to prove liability for or invalidity of the claim or its amount. Evidence of conduct or statements made in compromise negotiations is likewise not admissible. This rule does not require the exclusion of any evidence otherwise discoverable merely because it is presented in the course of compromise negotiations. This rule also does not require exclusion when the evidence is offered for another purpose, such as proving bias or prejudice of a witness, negativing a contention of undue delay, or proving an effort to obstruct a criminal investigation or prosecution.

Rule 409

Evidence of furnishing or offering or promising to pay medical, hospital, or similar expenses occasioned by an injury is not admissible to prove liability for the injury.

Rule 410

Except as otherwise provided in this rule, evidence of the following is not, in any civil or criminal proceeding, admissible against the defendant who made the plea or was a participant in the plea discussions:

(1) a plea of guilty which was later withdrawn;

(2) a plea of nolo contendere;

(3) any statement made in the course of any proceedings under Rule 11 of the Federal Rules of Criminal Procedure or comparable state procedure regarding either of the foregoing pleas; or

(4) any statement made in the course of plea discussions with an attorney for the prosecuting authority which do not result in a plea of guilty or which result in a plea of guilty later withdrawn.

However, such a statement is admissible (i) in any proceeding wherein another statement made in the course of the same plea or plea discussions has been introduced and the statement ought in fairness be considered contemporaneously with it, or (ii) in a criminal proceeding for perjury or false statement if the statement was made by the defendant under oath, on the record and in the presence of counsel.

Rule 411

Evidence that a person was or was not insured against liability is not admissible upon the issue whether the person acted negligently or otherwise wrongfully. This rule does not require the exclusion of evidence of insurance against liability when offered for another purpose, such as proof of agency, ownership, or control, or bias or prejudice of a witness.

Rule 412

(a) **Evidence generally inadmissible.**—The following evidence is not admissible in any civil or criminal proceeding involving alleged sexual misconduct except as provided in subdivisions (b) and (c):

(1) Evidence offered to prove that any alleged victim engaged in other sexual behavior.

(2) Evidence offered to prove any alleged victim's sexual predisposition.

(b) Exceptions.—

(1) In a criminal case, the following evidence is admissible, if otherwise admissible under these rules:

(A) evidence of specific instances of sexual behavior by the alleged victim offered to prove that a person other than the accused was the source of semen, injury or other physical evidence;

(B) evidence of specific instances of sexual behavior by the alleged victim with respect to the person accused of the sexual misconduct offered by the accused to prove consent or by the prosecution; and

(C) evidence the exclusion of which would violate the constitutional rights of the defendant.

(2) In a civil case, evidence offered to prove the sexual behavior or sexual predisposition of any alleged victim is admissible if it is otherwise admis-

sible under these rules and its probative value substantially outweighs the danger of harm to any victim and of unfair prejudice to any party. Evidence of an alleged victim's reputation is admissible only if it has been placed in controversy by the alleged victim.

(c) Procedure to determine admissibility.

(1) A party intending to offer evidence under subdivision

(b) must—

(A) file a written motion at least 14 days before trial specifically describing the evidence and stating the purpose for which it is offered unless the court, for good cause requires a different time for filing or permits filing during trial; and

(B) serve the motion on all parties and notify the alleged victim or, when appropriate, the alleged victim's guardian or representative.

(2) Before admitting evidence under this rule the court must conduct a hearing in camera and afford the victim and parties a right to attend and be heard. The motion, related papers, and the record of the hearing must be sealed and remain under seal unless the court orders otherwise.

Rule 413

(a) In a criminal case in which the defendant is accused of an offense of sexual assault, evidence of the defendant's commission of another offense or offenses of sexual assault is admissible, and may be considered for its bearing on any matter to which it is relevant.

(b) In a case in which the Government intends to offer evidence under this rule, the attorney for the Government shall disclose the evidence to the defendant, including statements of witnesses or a summary of the substance of any testimony that is expected to be offered, at least 15 days before the scheduled date of trial or at such later time as the court may allow for good cause.

(c) This rule shall not be construed to limit the admission or consideration of evidence under any other rule.

(d) For purposes of this rule and Rule 415, "offense of sexual assault" means a crime under Federal law or the law of a State (as defined in section 513 of title 18, United States Code) that involved—

(1) any conduct proscribed by chapter 109A of title 18, United States Code;

(2) contact, without consent, between any part of the defendant's body or an object and the genitals or anus of another person;

(3) contact, without consent, between the genitals or anus of the defendant and any part of another person's body;

(4) deriving sexual pleasure or gratification from the infliction of death, bodily injury, or physical pain on another person; or

(5) an attempt or conspiracy to engage in conduct described in paragraphs (1)–(4).

Rule 414

(a) In a criminal case in which the defendant is accused of an offense of child molestation, evidence of the defendant's commission of another offense or offenses of child molestation is admissible, and may be considered for its bearing on any matter to which it is relevant.

(b) In a case in which the Government intends to offer evidence under this rule, the attorney for the Government shall disclose the evidence to the defendant, including statements of witnesses or a summary of the substance of any testimony that is expected to be offered, at least 15 days before the scheduled date of trial or at such later time as the court may allow for good cause.

(c) This rule shall not be construed to limit the admission or consideration of evidence under any other rule.

(d) For purposes of this rule and Rule 415, "child" means a person below the age of 14, and "offense of child molestation" means a crime under Federal law or the law of a State (as defined in section 513 of title 18, United States Code) that involved—

(1) any conduct proscribed by chapter 109A of title 18, United States Code, that was committed in relation to a child;

(2) any conduct proscribed by chapter 110 of title 18, United States Code;

(3) contact between any part of the defendant's body or an object and the genitals or anus of a child;

(4) contact between the genitals or anus of the defendant and any part of the body of a child;

(5) deriving sexual pleasure or gratification from the infliction of death, bodily injury, or physical pain on a child; or

(6) an attempt or conspiracy to engage in conduct described in paragraphs (1)–(5).

Rule 415

(a) In a civil case in which a claim for damages or other relief is predicated on a party's alleged commission of conduct constituting an offense of sexual assault or child molestation, evidence of that party's commission of another offense or offenses of sexual assault or child molestation is admissible and may be considered as provided in Rule 413 and Rule 414 of these rules.

(b) A party who intends to offer evidence under this Rule shall disclose the evidence to the party against whom it will be offered, including statements of witnesses or a summary of the substance of any testimony that is expected to be offered, at least 15 days before the scheduled date of trial or at such later time as the court may allow for good cause.

(c) This rule shall not be construed to limit the admission or consideration of evidence under any other rule.

Rule 501

Except as otherwise required by the Constitution of the United States or provided by Act of Congress or in rules prescribed by the Supreme Court pursuant to statutory authority, the privilege of a witness, person, government, State, or political subdivision thereof shall be governed by the principles of the common law as they may be interpreted by the courts of the United States in the light of reason and experience. However, in civil actions and proceedings, with respect to an element of a claim or defense as to which State law supplies the rule of decision, the privilege of a witness, person, government, State, or

political subdivision thereof shall be determined in accordance with State law.

Rule 601

Every person is competent to be a witness except as otherwise provided in these rules. However, in civil actions and proceedings, with respect to an element of a claim or defense as to which State law supplies the rule of decision, the competency of a witness shall be determined in accordance with State law.

Rule 602

A witness may not testify to a matter unless evidence is introduced sufficient to support a finding that the witness has personal knowledge of the matter. Evidence to prove personal knowledge may, but need not, consist of the witness' own testimony. This rule is subject to the provisions of Rule 703, relating to opinion testimony by expert witnesses.

Rule 603

Before testifying, every witness shall be required to declare that the witness will testify truthfully, by oath or affirmation administered in a form calculated to awaken the witness' conscience and impress the witness' mind with the duty to do so.

Rule 604

An interpreter is subject to the provisions of these rules relating to qualification as an expert and the administration of an oath or affirmation to make a true translation.

Rule 605

The judge presiding at the trial may not testify in that trial as a witness. No objection need be made in order to preserve the point.

Rule 606

(a) **At the trial.**—A member of the jury may not testify as a witness before that jury in the trial of the case in which the juror is sitting. If the juror is called so to testify, the opposing party shall be afforded an opportunity to object out of the presence of the jury.

(b) **Inquiry into validity of verdict or indictment.** —Upon an inquiry into the validity of a verdict or indictment, a juror may not testify as to any matter or statement occurring during the course of the jury's deliberations or to the effect of anything upon that or any other juror's mind or emotions as influencing the juror to assent to or dissent from the verdict or indictment or concerning the juror's mental processes in connection therewith, except that a juror may testify on the question whether extraneous prejudicial information was improperly brought to the jury's attention or whether any outside influence was improperly brought to bear upon any juror. Nor may a juror's affidavit or evidence of any statement by the juror concerning a matter about which the juror would be precluded from testifying be received for these purposes.

Rule 607

The credibility of a witness may be attacked by any party, including the party calling the witness.

Rule 608

(a) **Opinion and reputation evidence of character.**—The credibility of a witness may be attacked or supported by evidence in the form of opinion or reputation, but subject to these limitations: (1) the evidence may refer only to character for truthfulness or untruthfulness, and (2) evidence of truthful character is admissible only after the character of the witness for truthfulness has been attacked by opinion or reputation evidence or otherwise.

(b) **Specific instances of conduct.**—Specific instances of the conduct of a witness, for the purpose of attacking or supporting the witness' character for truthfulness, other than conviction of crime as provided in rule 609, may not be proved by extrinsic evidence. They may, however, in the discretion of the court, if probative of truthfulness or untruthfulness,

be inquired into on cross-examination of the witness (1) concerning the witness' character for truthfulness or untruthfulness, or (2) concerning the character for truthfulness or untruthfulness of another witness as to which character the witness being cross-examined has testified.

The giving of testimony, whether by an accused or by any other witness, does not operate as a waiver of the accused's or the witness' privilege against self-incrimination when examined with respect to matters that relate only to character for truthfulness.

Rule 609

(a) **General rule.**—For the purpose of attacking the credibility of a witness,

(1) evidence that a witness other than an accused has been convicted of a crime shall be admitted, subject to Rule 403, if the crime was punishable by death or imprisonment in excess of one year under the law under which the witness was convicted, and evidence that an accused has been convicted of such a crime shall be admitted if the court determines that the probative value of admitting this evidence outweighs its prejudicial effect to the accused; and

(2) evidence that any witness has been convicted of a crime shall be admitted if it involved dishonesty or false statement, regardless of the punishment.

(b) **Time limit.**—Evidence of a conviction under this rule is not admissible if a period of more than 10 years has elapsed since the date of the conviction or of the release of the witness from the confinement imposed for that conviction, whichever is the later date, unless the court determines, in the interests of justice, that the probative value of the conviction supported by specific facts and circumstances substantially outweighs its prejudicial effect. However, evidence of a conviction more than 10 years old as calculated herein, is not admissible unless the proponent gives to the adverse party sufficient advance written notice of intent to use such evidence to provide the adverse party with a fair opportunity to contest the use of such evidence.

(c) **Effect of pardon, annulment, or certificate of rehabilitation.**—Evidence of a conviction is not admissible under this rule if (1) the conviction has been the subject of a pardon, annulment, certificate of rehabilitation, or other equivalent procedure based on a finding of the rehabilitation of the person convicted, and that person has not been convicted of a subsequent crime which was punishable by death or imprisonment in excess of one year, or (2) the conviction has been the subject of a pardon, annulment, or other equivalent procedure based on a finding of innocence.

(d) **Juvenile adjudications**.—Evidence of juvenile adjudications is generally not admissible under this rule. The court may, however, in a criminal case allow evidence of a juvenile adjudication of a witness other than the accused if conviction of the offense would be admissible to attack the credibility of an adult and the court is satisfied that admission in evidence is necessary for a fair determination of the issue of guilt or innocence.

(e) **Pendency of appeal.**—The pendency of an appeal therefrom does not render evidence of a conviction inadmissible. Evidence of the pendency of an appeal is admissible.

Rule 610

Evidence of the beliefs or opinions of a witness on matters of religion is not admissible for the purpose of showing that by reason of their nature the witness' credibility is impaired or enhanced.

Rule 611

(a) **Control by court.**—The court shall exercise reasonable control over the mode and order of interrogating witnesses and presenting evidence so as to (1) make the interrogation and presentation effective for the ascertainment of the truth, (2) avoid needless consumption of time, and (3) protect witnesses from harassment or undue embarrassment.

(b) **Scope of cross-examination.**—Cross-examination should be limited to the subject matter of the direct examination and matters affecting the credibility of the witness. The court may, in the exercise of discretion, permit inquiry into additional matters as if on direct examination.

(c) **Leading questions.**—Leading questions should not be used on the direct examination of a witness except as may be necessary to develop the witness' testimony. Ordinarily leading questions should be permitted on cross-examination. When a party calls a hostile witness, an adverse party, or a witness identified with an adverse party, interrogation may be by leading questions.

Rule 612

Except as otherwise provided in criminal proceedings by section 3500 of title 18, United States Code, if a witness uses a writing to refresh memory for the purpose of testifying, either—

(1) while testifying, or

(2) before testifying, if the court in its discretion determines it is necessary in the interests of justice, an adverse party is entitled to have the writing produced at the hearing, to inspect it, to cross-examine the witness thereon, and to introduce in evidence those portions which relate to the testimony of the witness. If it is claimed that the writing contains matters not related to the subject matter of the testimony the court shall examine the writing in camera, excise any portions not so related, and order delivery of the remainder to the party entitled thereto. Any portion withheld over objections shall be preserved and made available to the appellate court in the event of an appeal. If a writing is not produced or delivered pursuant to order under this rule, the court shall make any order justice requires, except that in criminal cases when the prosecution elects not to comply, the order shall be one

striking the testimony or, if the court in its discretion determines that the interests of justice so require, declaring a mistrial.

Rule 613

(a) **Examining witness concerning prior statement.**—In examining a witness concerning a prior statement made by the witness, whether written or not, the statement need not be shown nor its contents disclosed to the witness at that time, but on request the same shall be shown or disclosed to opposing counsel.

(b) **Extrinsic evidence of prior inconsistent statement of witness.**—Extrinsic evidence of a prior inconsistent statement by a witness is not admissible unless the witness is afforded an opportunity to explain or deny the same and the opposite party is afforded an opportunity to interrogate the witness thereon, or the interests of justice otherwise require. This provision does not apply to admissions of a party-opponent as defined in rule 801(d)(2).

Rule 614

(a) **Calling by court.**—The court may, on its own motion or at the suggestion of a party, call witnesses, and all parties are entitled to cross-examine witnesses thus called.

(b) **Interrogation by court.**—The court may interrogate witnesses, whether called by itself or by a party.

(c) **Objections.**—Objections to the calling of witnesses by the court or to interrogation by it may be made at the time or at the next available opportunity when the jury is not present.

Rule 615

At the request of a party the court shall order witnesses excluded so that they cannot hear the testimony of other witnesses, and it may make the order of its own motion. This rule does not authorize exclusion of (1) a party who is a natural person, or (2) an officer or employee of a party which is not a natural person designated as its representative by its attorney, or (3) a person whose presence is shown by a party to be essential to the presentation of the party's cause, or (4) a person authorized by statute to be present.

Rule 701

If the witness is not testifying as an expert, the witness' testimony in the form of opinions or inferences is limited to those opinions or inferences which are (a) rationally based on the perception of the witness, (b) helpful to a clear understanding of the witness' testimony or the determination of a fact in issue, and (c) not based on scientific, technical, or other specialized knowledge within the scope of Rule 702.

Rule 702

If scientific, technical, or other specialized knowledge will assist the trier of fact to understand the evidence or to determine a fact in issue, a witness qualified as an expert by knowledge, skill, experience, training, or education, may testify thereto in the form of an opinion or otherwise, if (1) the testimony is based upon sufficient facts or data, (2) the testimony is the product of reliable principles and methods, and (3) the witness has applied the principles and methods reliably to the facts of the case.

Rule 703

The facts or data in the particular case upon which an expert bases an opinion or inference may be those perceived by or made known to the expert at or before the hearing. If of a type reasonably relied upon by experts in the particular field in forming opinions or inferences upon the subject, the facts or data need not be admissible in evidence in order for the opinion or inference to be admitted. Facts or data that are otherwise inadmissible shall not be disclosed to the jury by the proponent of the opinion or inference unless the court determines that their probative value in assisting the jury to evaluate the expert's opinion substantially outweighs their prejudicial effect.

Rule 704

(a) Except as provided in subdivision (b), testimony in the form of an opinion or inference otherwise admissible is not objectionable because it embraces an ultimate issue to be decided by the trier of fact.

(b) No expert witness testifying with respect to the mental state or condition of a defendant in a criminal case may state an opinion or inference as to whether the defendant did or did not have the mental state or condition constituting an element of the crime charged or of a defense thereto. Such ultimate issues are matters for the trier of fact alone.

Rule 705

The expert may testify in terms of opinion or inference and give reasons therefor without first testifying to the underlying facts or data, unless the court requires otherwise. The expert may in any event be required to disclose the underlying facts or data on cross-examination.

Rule 706

(a) **Appointment.**—The court may on its own motion or on the motion of any party enter an order to show cause why expert witnesses should not be appointed, and may request the parties to submit nominations. The court may appoint any expert witnesses agreed upon by the parties, and may appoint expert witnesses of its own selection. An expert witness shall not be appointed by the court unless the witness consents to act. A witness so appointed shall be informed of the witness' duties by the court in writing, a copy of which shall be filed with the clerk, or at a conference in which the parties shall have opportunity to participate. A witness so appointed shall advise the parties of the witness' findings, if any; the witness' deposition may be taken by any party; and the witness may be called to testify by the court or any party. The witness shall be subject to cross-examination by each party, including a party calling the witness.

(b) **Compensation.**—Expert witnesses so appointed are entitled to reasonable compensation in whatever sum the court may allow. The compensation thus fixed is payable from funds which may be provided by law in criminal cases and civil actions and proceedings involving just compensation under the Fifth Amendment. In other civil actions and proceedings the compensation shall be paid by the parties in such proportion and at such time as the court directs, and thereafter charged in like manner as other costs.

(c) **Disclosure of appointment.**—In the exercise of its discretion, the court may authorize disclosure to the jury of the fact that the court appointed the expert witness.

(d) **Parties' experts of own selection.**—Nothing in this rule limits the parties in calling expert witnesses of their own selection.

Rule 801

The following definitions apply under this article:

(a) **Statement.**—A "statement" is (1) an oral or written assertion or (2) nonverbal conduct of a person, if it is intended by the person as an assertion.

(b) **Declarant.**—A "declarant" is a person who makes a statement.

(c) **Hearsay.**—"Hearsay" is a statement, other than one made by the declarant while testifying at the trial or hearing, offered in evidence to prove the truth of the matter asserted.

(d) **Statements which are not hearsay**.—A statement is not hearsay if—

(1) *Prior statement by witness.* The declarant testifies at the trial or hearing and is subject to cross-examination concerning the statement, and the statement is (A) inconsistent with the declarant's testimony, and was given under oath subject to the penalty of perjury at a trial, hearing, or other proceeding, or in a deposition, or (B) consistent with the declarant's testimony and is offered to rebut an express or implied charge against the declarant of recent fabrication or improper influence or motive, or (C) one of identification of a person made after perceiving the person; or

(2) *Admission by party-opponent.* The statement is offered against a party and is (A) the party's own statement, in either an individual or a representative capacity or (B) a statement of which the party has manifested an adoption or belief in its truth, or (C) a statement by a person authorized by the party to make a statement concerning the subject, or (D) a statement by the party's agent or servant concerning a matter within the scope of the agency or employment, made during the existence of the relationship, or (E) a statement by a coconspirator of a party during the course and in furtherance of the conspiracy. The contents of the statement shall be considered but are not alone sufficient to establish the declarant's authority under subdivision (C), the agency or employment relationship and scope thereof under subdivision (D), or the existence of the conspiracy and the participation therein of the declarant and the party against whom the statement is offered under subdivision (E).

Rule 802

Hearsay is not admissible except as provided by these rules or by other rules prescribed by the Supreme Court pursuant to statutory authority or by Act of Congress.

Rule 803

The following are not excluded by the hearsay rule, even though the declarant is available as a witness:

(1) **Present sense impression.**—A statement describing or explaining an event or condition made while the declarant was perceiving the event or condition, or immediately thereafter.

(2) **Excited utterance.**—A statement relating to a startling event or condition made while the declarant was under the stress of excitement caused by the event or condition.

(3) **Then existing mental, emotional, or physical condition.**—A statement of the declarant's then existing state of mind, emotion, sensation, or physical condition (such as intent, plan, motive, design, mental feeling, pain, and bodily health), but not including a statement of memory or belief to prove the fact remembered or believed unless it relates to the execution, revocation, identification, or terms of declarant's will.

(4) **Statements for purposes of medical diagnosis or treatment.**—Statements made for purposes of medical diagnosis or treatment and describing medical history, or past or present symptoms, pain, or sensations, or the inception or general character of the cause or external source thereof insofar as reasonably pertinent to diagnosis or treatment.

(5) **Recorded recollection.**—A memorandum or record concerning a matter about which a witness once had knowledge but now has insufficient recollection to enable the witness to testify fully and accurately, shown to have been made or adopted by the witness when the matter was fresh in the witness' memory and to reflect that knowledge correctly. If admitted, the memorandum or record may be read into evidence but may not itself be received as an exhibit unless offered by an adverse party.

(6) **Records of Regularly Conducted Activity.**—A memorandum, report, record, or data compilation, in any form, of acts, events, conditions, opinions, or diagnoses, made at or near the time by, or from information transmitted by, a person with knowledge, if kept in the course of a regularly conducted business activity, and if it was the regular practice of that business activity to make the memorandum, report, record or data compilation, all as shown by the testimony of the custodian or other qualified witness, or by certification that complies with Rule 902(11), Rule 902(12), or a statute permitting certification, unless the source of information or the method or circumstances of preparation indicate lack of trustworthiness. The term "business" as used in this paragraph includes business, institution, association, profession, occupation, and calling of every kind, whether or not conducted for profit.

(7) **Absence of entry in records kept in accordance with the provisions of paragraph (6).**—Evidence that a matter is not included in the mem-

oranda reports, records, or data compilations, in any form, kept in accordance with the provisions of paragraph (6), to prove the nonoccurrence or nonexistence of the matter, if the matter was of a kind of which a memorandum, report, record, or data compilation was regularly made and preserved, unless the sources of information or other circumstances indicate lack of trustworthiness.

(8) **Public records and reports.**—Records, reports, statements, or data compilations, in any form, of public offices or agencies, setting forth (A) the activities of the office or agency, or (B) matters observed pursuant to duty imposed by law as to which matters there was a duty to report, excluding, however, in criminal cases matters observed by police officers and other law enforcement personnel, or (C) in civil actions and proceedings and against the Government in criminal cases, factual findings resulting from an investigation made pursuant to authority granted by law, unless the sources of information or other circumstances indicate lack of trustworthiness.

(9) **Records of vital statistics.**—Records or data compilations, in any form, of births, fetal deaths, deaths, or marriages, if the report thereof was made to a public office pursuant to requirements of law.

(10) **Absence of public record or entry.**—To prove the absence of a record, report, statement, or data compilation, in any form, or the nonoccurrence or nonexistence of a matter of which a record, report, statement, or data compilation, in any form, was regularly made and preserved by a public office or agency, evidence in the form of a certification in accordance with rule 902, or testimony, that diligent search failed to disclose the record, report, statement, or data compilation, or entry.

(11) **Records of religious organizations.**—Statements of births, marriages, divorces, deaths, legitimacy, ancestry, relationship by blood or marriage, or other similar facts of personal or family history, contained in a regularly kept record of a religious organization.

(12) **Marriage, baptismal, and similar certificates.**—Statements of fact contained in a certificate that the maker performed a marriage or other ceremony or administered a sacrament, made by a clergyman, public official, or other person authorized by the rules or practices of a religious organization or by law to perform the act certified, and purporting to have been issued at the time of the act or within a reasonable time thereafter.

(13) **Family records.**—Statements of fact concerning personal or family history contained in family Bibles, genealogies, charts, engravings on rings, inscriptions on family portraits, engravings on urns, crypts, or tombstones, or the like.

(14) **Records of documents affecting an interest in property.**—The record of a document purporting to establish or affect an interest in property, as proof of the content of the original recorded document and its execution and delivery by each person by whom it purports to have been executed, if the record is a record of a public office and an applicable statute authorizes the recording of documents of that kind in that office.

(15) **Statements in documents affecting an interest in property.**—A statement contained in a document purporting to establish or affect an interest in property if the matter stated was relevant to the purpose of the document, unless dealings with the property since the document was made have been inconsistent with the truth of the statement or the purport of the document.

(16) **Statements in ancient documents.**—Statements in a document in existence 20 years or more the authenticity of which is established.

(17) **Market reports, commercial publications.**—Market quotations, tabulations, lists, directories, or other published compilations, generally used and relied upon by the public or by persons in particular occupations.

(18) **Learned treatises.**—To the extent called to the attention of an expert witness upon cross-examination or relied upon by the expert witness in direct examination, statements contained in pub-

lished treatises, periodicals, or pamphlets on a subject of history, medicine, or other science or art, established as a reliable authority by the testimony or admission of the witness or by other expert testimony or by judicial notice. If admitted, the statements may be read into evidence but may not be received as exhibits.

(19) **Reputation concerning personal or family history.**—Reputation among members of a person's family by blood, adoption, or marriage, or among a person's associates, or in the community, concerning a person's birth, adoption, marriage, divorce, death, legitimacy, relationship by blood, adoption, or marriage, ancestry, or other similar fact of personal or family history.

(20) **Reputation concerning boundaries or general history.**—Reputation in a community, arising before the controversy, as to boundaries of or customs affecting lands in the community, and reputation as to events of general history important to the community or State or nation in which located.

(21) **Reputation as to character.**—Reputation of a person's character among associates or in the community.

(22) **Judgment of previous conviction.**—Evidence of a final judgment, entered after a trial or upon a plea of guilty (but not upon a plea of nolo contendere), adjudging a person guilty of a crime punishable by death or imprisonment in excess of one year, to prove any fact essential to sustain the judgment, but not including, when offered by the Government in a criminal prosecution for purposes other than impeachment, judgments against persons other than the accused. The pendency of an appeal may be shown but does not affect admissibility.

(23) **Judgment as to personal, family, or general history, or boundaries.**—Judgments as proof of matters of personal, family or general history, or boundaries, essential to the judgment, if the same would be provable by evidence of reputation.

(24) [Transferred to Rule 807]

Rule 804

(a) **Definition of unavailability.**—
"Unavailability as a witness" includes situations in which the declarant—

(1) is exempted by ruling of the court on the ground of privilege from testifying concerning the subject matter of the declarant's statement; or

(2) persists in refusing to testify concerning the subject matter of the declarant's statement despite an order of the court to do so; or

(3) testifies to a lack of memory of the subject matter of the declarant's statement; or

(4) is unable to be present or to testify at the hearing because of death or then existing physical or mental illness or infirmity; or

(5) is absent from the hearing and the proponent of a statement has been unable to procure the declarant's attendance (or in the case of a hearsay exception under subdivision (b)(2), (3), or (4), the declarant's attendance or testimony) by process or other reasonable means.

A declarant is not unavailable as a witness if exemption, refusal, claim of lack of memory, inability, or absence is due to the procurement or wrongdoing of the proponent of a statement for the purpose of preventing the witness from attending or testifying.

(b) **Hearsay exceptions.**—The following are not excluded by the hearsay rule if the declarant is unavailable as a witness:

(1) *Former testimony.* Testimony given as a witness at another hearing of the same or a different proceeding, or in a deposition taken in compliance with law in the course of the same or another proceeding, if the party against whom the testimony is now offered, or, in a civil action or proceeding, a predecessor in interest, had an opportunity and similar motive to develop the testimony by direct, cross-, or redirect examination.

(2) *Statement under belief of impending death.* In a prosecution for homicide or in a civil action or proceeding, a statement made by a declarant while believing that the declarant's death was imminent, concerning the cause or circumstances of what the declarant believed to be impending death.

(3) *Statement against interest.* A statement which was at the time of its making so far contrary to the declarant's pecuniary or proprietary interest, or so far tended to subject the declarant to civil or crimi-

nal liability, or to render invalid a claim by the declarant against another, that a reasonable person in the declarant's position would not have made the statement unless believing it to be true. A statement tending to expose the declarant to criminal liability and offered to exculpate the accused is not admissible unless corroborating circumstances clearly indicate the trustworthiness of the statement.

(4) *Statement of personal or family history.* (A) A statement concerning the declarant's own birth, adoption, marriage, divorce, legitimacy, relationship by blood, adoption, or marriage, ancestry, or other similar fact of personal or family history, even though declarant had no means of acquiring personal knowledge of the matter stated; or (B) a statement concerning the foregoing matters, and death also, of another person, if the declarant was related to the other by blood, adoption, or marriage or was so intimately associated with the other's family as to be likely to have accurate information concerning the matter declared.

(5) [Transferred to Rule 807]

(6) *Forfeiture by wrongdoing.* A statement offered against a party that has engaged or acquiesced in wrongdoing that was intended to, and did, procure the unavailability of the declarant as a witness.

Rule 805

Hearsay included within hearsay is not excluded under the hearsay rule if each part of the combined statements conforms with an exception to the hearsay rule provided in these rules.

Rule 806

When a hearsay statement, or a statement defined in Rule 801(d)(2)(C), (D), or (E), has been admitted in evidence, the credibility of the declarant may be attacked, and if attacked may be supported, by any evidence which would be admissible for those purposes if declarant had testified as a witness. Evidence of a statement or conduct by the declarant at any time, inconsistent with the declarant's hearsay statement, is not subject to any requirement that the declarant may have been afforded an opportunity to deny or explain. If the party against whom a hearsay statement has been admitted calls the declarant as a witness, the party is entitled to examine the declarant on the statement as if under cross-examination.

Rule 807

A statement not specifically covered by Rule 803 or 804 but having equivalent circumstantial guarantees of trustworthiness, is not excluded by the hearsay rule, if the court determines that (A) the statement is offered as evidence of a material fact; (B) the statement is more probative on the point for which it is offered than any other evidence which the proponent can procure through reasonable efforts; and (C) the general purposes of these rules and the interests of justice will best be served by admission of the statement into evidence. However, a statement may not be admitted under this exception unless the proponent of it makes known to the adverse party sufficiently in advance of the trial or hearing to provide the adverse party with a fair opportunity to prepare to meet it, the proponent's intention to offer the statement and the particulars of it, including the name and address of the declarant.

Rule 901

(a) **General provision.**—The requirement of authentication or identification as a condition precedent to admissibility is satisfied by evidence sufficient to support a finding that the matter in question is what its proponent claims.

(b) **Illustrations.**—By way of illustration only, and not by way of limitation, the following are examples of authentication or identification conforming with the requirements of this rule:

(1) *Testimony of witness with knowledge.* Testimony that a matter is what it is claimed to be.

(2) *Nonexpert opinion on handwriting.* Nonexpert opinion as to the genuineness of handwriting, based upon familiarity not acquired for purposes of the litigation.

(3) *Comparison by trier or expert witness.* Comparison by the trier of fact or by expert witnesses with specimens which have been authenticated.

(4) *Distinctive characteristics and the like.* Appearance, contents, substance, internal patterns, or other distinctive characteristics, taken in conjunction with circumstances.

(5) *Voice identification.* Identification of a voice, whether heard firsthand or through mechanical or electronic transmission or recording, by opinion based upon hearing the voice at any time under circumstances connecting it with the alleged speaker.

(6) *Telephone conversations.* Telephone conversations, by evidence that a call was made to the number assigned at the time by the telephone company to a particular person or business, if (A) in the case of a person, circumstances, including self-identification, show the person answering to be the one called, or (B) in the case of a business, the call was made to a place of business and the conversation related to business reasonably transacted over the telephone.

(7) *Public records or reports.* Evidence that a writing authorized by law to be recorded or filed and in fact recorded or filed in a public office, or a purported public record, report, statement, or data compilation, in any form, is from the public office where items of this nature are kept.

(8) *Ancient documents or data compilation.* Evidence that a document or data compilation, in any form, (A) is in such condition as to create no suspicion concerning its authenticity, (B) was in a place where it, if authentic, would likely be, and (C) has been in existence 20 years or more at the time it is offered.

(9) *Process or system.* Evidence describing a process or system used to produce a result and showing that the process or system produces an accurate result.

(10) *Methods provided by statute or rule.* Any method of authentication or identification provided by Act of Congress or by other rules prescribed by the Supreme Court pursuant to statutory authority.

Rule 902

Extrinsic evidence of authenticity as a condition precedent to admissibility is not required with respect to the following:

(1) **Domestic public documents under seal.**— A document bearing a seal purporting to be that of the United States, or of any State, district, Commonwealth, territory, or insular possession thereof, or the Panama Canal Zone, or the Trust Territory of the Pacific Islands, or of a political subdivision, department, officer, or agency thereof, and a signature purporting to be an attestation or execution.

(2) **Domestic public documents not under seal.**—A document purporting to bear the signature in the official capacity of an officer or employee of any entity included in paragraph (1) hereof, having no seal, if a public officer having a seal and having official duties in the district or political subdivision of the officer or employee certifies under seal that the signer has the official capacity and that the signature is genuine.

(3) **Foreign public documents.**—A document purporting to be executed or attested in an official capacity by a person authorized by the laws of a foreign country to make the execution or attestation, and accompanied by a final certification as to the genuineness of the signature and official position (A) of the executing or attesting person, or (B) of any foreign official whose certificate of genuineness of signature and official position relates to the execution or attestation or is in a chain of certificates of genuineness of signature and official position relating to the execution or attestation. A final certification may be made by a secretary of an embassy or legation, consul general, consul, vice consul, or consular agent of the United States, or a diplomatic or consular official of the foreign country assigned or accredited to the United States. If reasonable opportunity has been given to all parties to investigate the authenticity and accuracy of official documents, the court may, for good cause shown, order that they be treated as presumptively authentic

without final certification or permit them to be evidenced by an attested summary with or without final certification.

(4) **Certified copies of public records.**—A copy of an official record or report or entry therein, or of a document authorized by law to be recorded or filed and actually recorded or filed in a public office, including data compilations in any form, certified as correct by the custodian or other person authorized to make the certification, by certificate complying with paragraph (1), (2), or (3) of this rule or complying with any Act of Congress or rule prescribed by the Supreme Court pursuant to statutory authority.

(5) **Official publications.**—Books, pamphlets, or other publications purporting to be issued by public authority.

(6) **Newspapers and periodicals.**—Printed materials purporting to be newspapers or periodicals.

(7) **Trade inscriptions and the like.**—Inscriptions, signs, tags, or labels purporting to have been affixed in the course of business and indicating ownership, control, or origin.

(8) **Acknowledged documents.**—Documents accompanied by a certificate of acknowledgment executed in the manner provided by law by a notary public or other officer authorized by law to take acknowledgments.

(9) **Commercial paper and related documents.**—Commercial paper, signatures thereon, and documents relating thereto to the extent provided by general commercial law.

(10) **Presumptions under Acts of Congress.**—Any signature, document, or other matter declared by Act of Congress to be presumptively or prima facie genuine or authentic.

(11) **Certified Domestic Records of Regularly Conducted Activity.**—The original or a duplicate of a domestic record of regularly conducted activity that would be admissible under Rule 803(6) if accompanied by a written declaration of its custodian or other qualified person, in a manner complying with any Act of Congress or rule prescribed by the Supreme Court pursuant to statutory authority, certifying that the record—

(A) was made at or near the time of the occurrence of the matters set forth by, or from information transmitted by, a person with knowledge of those matters;

(B) was kept in the course of the regularly conducted activity; and

(C) was made by the regularly conducted activity as a regular practice.

A party intending to offer a record into evidence under this paragraph must provide written notice of that intention to all adverse parties, and must make the record and declaration available for inspection sufficiently in advance of their offer into evidence to provide an adverse party with a fair opportunity to challenge them.

(12) **Certified Foreign Records of Regularly Conducted Activity.**—In a civil case, the original or a duplicate of a foreign record of regularly conducted activity that would be admissible under Rule 803(6) if accompanied by a written declaration by its custodian or other qualified person certifying that the record—

(A) was made at or near the time of the occurrence of the matters set forth by, or from information transmitted by, a person with knowledge of those matters;

(B) was kept in the course of the regularly conducted activity; and

(C) was made by the regularly conducted activity as a regular practice.

The declaration must be signed in a manner that, if falsely made, would subject the maker to criminal penalty under the laws of the country where the declaration is signed. A party intending to offer a record into evidence under this paragraph must provide written notice of that intention to all adverse parties, and must make the record and declaration available for inspection sufficiently in advance of their offer into evidence to provide an adverse party with a fair opportunity to challenge them.

Rule 903

The testimony of a subscribing witness is not necessary to authenticate a writing unless required by the laws of the jurisdiction whose laws govern the validity of the writing.

Rule 1001

For purposes of this article the following definitions are applicable:

(1) **Writings and recordings.**—"Writings" and "recordings" consist of letters, words, or numbers, or their equivalent, set down by handwriting, typewriting, printing, photostating, photographing, magnetic impulse, mechanical or electronic recording, or other form of data compilation.

(2) **Photographs.**—"Photographs" include still photographs, X-ray films, video tapes, and motion pictures.

(3) **Original.**—An "original" of a writing or recording is the writing or recording itself or any counterpart intended to have the same effect by a person executing or issuing it. An "original" of a photograph includes the negative or any print therefrom. If data are stored in a computer or similar device, any printout or other output readable by sight, shown to reflect the data accurately, is an "original."

(4) **Duplicate.**—A "duplicate" is a counterpart produced by the same impression as the original, or from the same matrix, or by means of photography, including enlargements and miniatures, or by mechanical or electronic re-recording, or by chemical reproduction, or by other equivalent techniques which accurately reproduces the original.

Rule 1002

To prove the content of a writing, recording, or photograph, the original writing, recording, or photograph is required, except as otherwise provided in these rules or by Act of Congress.

Rule 1003

A duplicate is admissible to the same extent as an original unless (1) a genuine question is raised as to the authenticity of the original or (2) in the circumstances it would be unfair to admit the duplicate in lieu of the original.

Rule 1004

The original is not required, and other evidence of the contents of a writing, recording, or photograph is admissible if—

(1) **Originals lost or destroyed.**—All originals are lost or have been destroyed, unless the proponent lost or destroyed them in bad faith; or

(2) **Original not obtainable.**—No original can be obtained by any available judicial process or procedure; or

(3) **Original in possession of opponent.**—At a time when an original was under the control of the party against whom offered, that party was put on notice, by the pleadings or otherwise, that the contents would be a subject of proof at the hearing, and that party does not produce the original at the hearing; or

(4) **Collateral matters.**—The writing, recording, or photograph is not closely related to a controlling issue.

Rule 1005

The contents of an official record, or of a document authorized to be recorded or filed and actually recorded or filed, including data compilations in any form, if otherwise admissible, may be proved by copy, certified as correct in accordance with Rule 902 or testified to be correct by a witness who has compared it with the original. If a copy which complies with the foregoing cannot be obtained by the exercise of reasonable diligence, then other evidence of the contents may be given.

Rule 1006

The contents of voluminous writings, recordings, or photographs which cannot conveniently be examined in court may be presented in the form of a chart, summary, or calculation. The originals, or duplicates, shall be made available for examination or copying, or both, by other parties at reasonable time and place. The court may order that they be produced in court.

Rule 1007

Contents of writings, recordings, or photographs may be proved by the testimony or deposition of the party against whom offered or by that party's written admission, without accounting for the nonproduction of the original.

Rule 1008

When the admissibility of other evidence of contents of writings, recordings, or photographs under these rules depends upon the fulfillment of a condition of fact, the question whether the condition has been fulfilled is ordinarily for the court to determine in accordance with the provisions of Rule 104. However, when an issue is raised (a) whether the asserted writing ever existed, or (b) whether another writing, recording, or photograph produced at the trial is the original, or (c) whether other evidence of contents correctly reflects the contents, the issue is for the trier of fact to determine as in the case of other issues of fact.

Rule 1101

(a) **Courts and judges.**—These rules apply to the United States district courts, the District Court of Guam, the District Court of the Virgin Islands, the District Court for the Northern Mariana Islands, the United States courts of appeals, the United States Claims Court, and to United States bankruptcy judges and United States magistrate judges, in the actions, cases, and proceedings and to the extent hereinafter set forth. The terms "judge" and "court" in these rules include United States bankruptcy judges and United States magistrate judges.

(b) **Proceedings generally.**—These rules apply generally to civil actions and proceedings, including admiralty and maritime cases, to criminal cases and proceedings, to contempt proceedings except those in which the court may act summarily, and to proceedings and cases under title 11, United States Code.

(c) **Rule of privilege.**—The rule with respect to privileges applies at all stages of all actions, cases, and proceedings.

(d) **Rules inapplicable.**—The rules (other than with respect to privileges) do not apply in the following situations:

(1) *Preliminary questions of fact.* The determination of questions of fact preliminary to admissibility of evidence when the issue is to be determined by the court under rule 104.

(2) *Grand jury.* Proceedings before grand juries.

(3) *Miscellaneous proceedings.* Proceedings for extradition or rendition; preliminary examinations in criminal cases; sentencing, or granting or revoking probation; issuance of warrants for arrest, criminal summonses, and search warrants; and proceedings with respect to release on bail or otherwise.

(e) **Rules applicable in part.**—In the following proceedings these rules apply to the extent that matters of evidence are not provided for in the statutes which govern procedure therein or in other rules prescribed by the Supreme Court pursuant to statutory authority: the trial of misdemeanors and other petty offenses before United States magistrate judges; review of agency actions when the facts are subject to trial de novo under section 706(2)(F) of title 5, United States Code; review of orders of the Secretary of Agriculture under section 2 of the Act entitled "An Act to authorize association of producers of agricultural products" approved February 18, 1922 (7 U.S.C. 292), and under sections 6 and 7(c) of the Perishable Agricultural Commodities Act, 1930 (7 U.S.C. 499f, 499g(c)); naturalization and revocation of naturalization under sections 310-318 of the Immigration and Nationality Act (8 U.S.C. 1421-1429); prize proceedings in admiralty under sections 7651-7681 of title 10, United States Code; review of orders of the Secretary of the Interior under section 2 of the Act entitled "An Act authorizing associations of producers of aquatic products" approved June 25, 1934 (15 U.S.C. 522); review of orders of petroleum control boards under section 5 of the Act entitled "An Act to regulate interstate and foreign commerce in petroleum and its products by prohibiting the shipment in such commerce of petroleum and its products produced in violation of State law, and for other purposes", approved February 22, 1935 (15 U.S.C. 715d); actions for fines, penalties, or forfeitures under part V of title IV of the Tariff Act of 1930 (19 U.S.C. 1581-1624), or under the Anti-Smuggling Act (19 U.S.C. 1701-1711); criminal libel for condemnation, exclusion of imports, or other proceedings under the Federal Food, Drug, and

Cosmetic Act (21 U.S.C. 301-392); disputes between seamen under sections 4079, 4080, and 4081 of the Revised Statutes (22 U.S.C. 256-258); habeas corpus under sections 2241-2254 of title 28, United States Code; motions to vacate, set aside or correct sentence under section 2255 of title 28, United States Code; actions for penalties for refusal to transport destitute seamen under section 4578 of the Revised Statutes (46 U.S.C. 679); actions against the United States under the Act entitled "An Act authorizing suits against the United States in admiralty for damage caused by and salvage service rendered to public vessels belonging to the United States, and for other purposes," approved March 3, 1925 (46 U.S.C. 781-790), as implemented by section 7730 of title 10, United States Code.

Rule 1102

Amendments to the Federal Rules of Evidence may be made as provided in section 2072 of title 28 of the United States Code.

Rule 1103

These rules may be known and cited as the Federal Rules of Evidence.

B

Selected Rules from the Federal Rules of Civil Procedure As Amended Through December 2006

Rule 26

(a) Required Disclosures; Methods to Discover Additional Matter.

(1) **Initial Disclosures.**—Except in categories of proceedings specified in Rule 26(a)(1)(E), or to the extent otherwise stipulated or directed by order, a party must, without awaiting a discovery request, provide to other parties:

(A) the name and, if known, the address and telephone number of each individual likely to have discoverable information that the disclosing party may use to support its claims or defenses, unless solely for impeachment, identifying the subjects of the information;

(B) a copy of, or a description by category and location of, all documents, data compilations, and tangible things that are in the possession, custody, or control of the party and that the disclosing party may use to support its claims or defenses, unless solely for impeachment;

(C) a computation of any category of damages claimed by the disclosing party, making available for inspection and copying as under Rule 34 the documents or other evidentiary material, not privileged or protected from disclosure, on which such computation is based, including materials bearing on the nature and extent of injuries suffered; and

(D) for inspection and copying as under Rule 34 any insurance agreement under which any person carrying on an insurance business may be liable to satisfy part or all of a judgment which may be entered in the action or to indemnify or reimburse for payments made to satisfy the judgment.

(E) The following categories of proceedings are exempt from initial disclosure under Rule 26(a)(1):

(i) an action for review on an administrative record;

(ii) a petition for habeas corpus or other proceeding to challenge a criminal conviction or sentence;

(iii) an action brought without counsel by a person in custody of the United States, a state, or a state subdivision;

(iv) an action to enforce or quash an administrative summons or subpoena;

(v) an action by the United States to recover benefit payments;

(vi) an action by the United States to collect on a student loan guaranteed by the United States;

(vii) a proceeding ancillary to proceedings in other courts; and

(viii) an action to enforce an arbitration award.

These disclosures must be made at or within 14 days after the Rule 26(f) conference unless a different time is set by stipulation or court order, or unless a party objects during the conference that initial disclosures are not appropriate in the circumstances of the action and states the objection in the Rule 26(f) discovery plan. In ruling on the objection, the court must determine what disclosures—if any—are to be made, and set the time for disclosure. Any party first served or otherwise joined after the Rule 26(f) conference must make these disclosures within 30 days after being served or joined unless a different time is set by stipulation or court order. A party must make its initial disclosures based on the information then reasonably available to it and is not excused from making its disclosures because it has not fully completed its investigation of the case or because it challenges the sufficiency of another party's disclosures or because another party has not made its disclosures.

(2) Disclosure of Expert Testimony.

(A) In addition to the disclosures required by paragraph (1), a party shall disclose to other parties the identity of any person who may be used at trial to present evidence under Rules 702, 703, or 705 of the Federal Rules of Evidence.

(B) Except as otherwise stipulated or directed by the court, this disclosure shall, with respect to a witness who is retained or specially employed to provide expert testimony in the case or whose duties as an employee of the party regularly involve giving expert testimony, be accompanied by a written report prepared and signed by the witness. The report shall contain a complete statement of all opinions to be expressed and the basis and reasons therefor; the data or other information considered by the witness in forming the opinions; any exhibits to be used as a summary of or support for the opinions; the qualifications of the witness, including a list of all publications authored by the witness within the preceding 10 years; the compensation to be paid for the study and testimony; and a listing of any other cases in which the witness has testified as an expert at trial or by deposition within the preceding four years.

(C) These disclosures shall be made at the times and in the sequence directed by the court. In the absence of other directions from the court or stipulation by the parties, the disclosures shall be made at least 90 days before the trial date or the date the case is to be ready for trial or, if the evidence is intended solely to contradict or rebut evidence on the same subject matter identified by another party under paragraph (2)(B), within 30 days after the disclosure made by the other party. The parties shall supplement these disclosures when required under subdivision (e)(1).

(3) **Pretrial Disclosures.**—In addition to the disclosures required by Rule 26(a)(1) and (2), a party must provide to other parties and promptly file with the court the following information regarding the evidence that it may present at trial other than solely for impeachment:

(A) the name and, if not previously provided, the address and telephone number of each witness, separately identifying those whom the party expects to present and those whom the party may call if the need arises;

(B) the designation of those witnesses whose testimony is expected to be presented by means of a deposition and, if not taken stenographically, a transcript of the pertinent portions of the deposition testimony; and

(C) an appropriate identification of each document or other exhibit, including summaries of other evidence, separately identifying those which the party expects to offer and those which the party may offer if the need arises.

Unless otherwise directed by the court, these disclosures must be made at least 30 days before trial. Within 14 days thereafter, unless a different time is specified by the court, a party may serve and promptly file a list disclosing (i) any objections to the use under Rule 32(a) of a deposition designated by another party under Rule 26(a)(3)(B), and (ii) any objection, together with the grounds therefor, that may be made to the admissibility of materials identified under Rule 26(a)(3)(C). Objections not so disclosed, other than objections under Rules 402 and 403 of the Federal Rules of Evidence, are waived unless excused by the court for good cause.

(4) **Form of Disclosures.**—Unless the court orders otherwise, all disclosures under Rules 26(a)(1) through (3) must be made in writing, signed, and served.

(5) **Methods to Discover Additional Matter**.— Parties may obtain discovery by one or more of the following methods: depositions upon oral examination or written questions; written interrogatories; production of documents or things or permission to enter upon land or other property under Rule 34 or 45(a)(1)(C), for inspection and other purposes; physical and mental examinations; and requests for admission.

(b) **Discovery Scope and Limits.**—Unless otherwise limited by order of the court in accordance with these rules, the scope of discovery is as follows:

(1) **In General.**—Parties may obtain discovery regarding any matter, not privileged, that is relevant to the claim or defense of any party, including the existence, description, nature, custody, condition, and location of any books, documents, or other tangible things and the identity and location of persons having knowledge of any discoverable matter. For good cause, the court may order discovery of any matter relevant to the subject matter involved in the action. Relevant information need not be admissible at the trial if the discovery appears reasonably calculated to lead to the discovery of admissible evidence. All discovery is subject to the limitations imposed by Rule 26(b)(2)(i), (ii), and (iii).

(2) **Limitations.**—By order, the court may alter the limits in these rules on the number of depositions and interrogatories or the length of depositions under Rule 30. By order or local rule, the court may also limit the number of requests under Rule 36. The frequency or extent of use of the discovery methods otherwise permitted under these rules and by any local rule shall be limited by the court if it determines that: (i) the discovery sought is unreasonably cumulative or duplicative, or is obtainable from some other source that is more convenient, less burdensome, or less expensive; (ii) the party seeking discovery has had ample opportunity by discovery in the action to obtain the information sought; or (iii) the burden or expense of the proposed discovery outweighs its likely benefit, taking into account the needs of the case, the amount in controversy, the parties' resources, the importance of the issues at stake in the litigation, and the importance of the proposed discovery in resolving the issues. The court may act upon its own initiative after reasonable notice or pursuant to a motion under Rule 26(c).

(3) **Trial Preparation: Materials.**—Subject to the provisions of subdivision (b)(4) of this rule, a party may obtain discovery of documents and tangible things otherwise discoverable under subdivision (b)(1) of this rule and prepared in anticipation of litigation or for trial by or for another party or by or for that other party's representative (including the other party's attorney, consultant, surety, indemnitor, insurer, or agent) only upon a showing that the party seeking discovery has substantial need of the materials in the preparation of the party's case and that the party is unable without undue hardship to obtain the substantial equivalent of the materials by other means. In ordering discovery of such materials when the required showing has been made, the court shall protect against disclosure of the mental impressions, conclusions, opinions, or legal theories of an attorney or other representative of a party concerning the litigation.

A party may obtain without the required showing a statement concerning the action or its subject matter previously made by that party. Upon request, a person not a party may obtain without the required showing a statement concerning the action or its subject matter previously made by that person. If the request is refused, the person may move for a court order. The provisions of Rule 37(a)(4) apply to the award of expenses incurred in relation to the motion. For purposes of this paragraph, a statement previously made is (A) a written statement signed or otherwise adopted or approved by the person making it, or (B) a stenographic, mechanical, electrical, or other recording, or a transcription thereof, which is a substantially verbatim recital of an oral statement by the person making it and contemporaneously recorded.

(4) *Trial Preparation: Experts.*

(A) A party may depose any person who has been identified as an expert whose opinions may be presented at trial. If a report from the expert is required under subdivision (a)(2)(B), the deposition shall not be conducted until after the report is provided.

(B) A party may, through interrogatories or by deposition, discover facts known or opinions held by an expert who has been retained or specially employed by another party in anticipation of litigation or preparation for trial and who is not expected to be called as a witness at trial, only as provided in Rule 35(b) or upon a showing of exceptional circumstances under which it is impracticable for the party seeking discovery to obtain facts or opinions on the same subject by other means.

(C) Unless manifest injustice would result, (i) the court shall require that the party seeking discovery pay the expert a reasonable fee for time spent in responding to discovery under this subdivision; and (ii) with respect to discovery obtained under subdivision (b)(4)(B) of this rule the court shall require the party seeking discovery to pay the other party a fair portion of the fees and expenses reasonably incurred by the latter party in obtaining facts and opinions from the expert.

(5) **Claims of Privilege or Protection of Trial Preparation Materials.**—When a party withholds information otherwise discoverable under these rules by claiming that it is privileged or subject to protection as trial preparation material, the party shall make the claim expressly and shall describe the nature of the documents, communications, or things not produced or disclosed in a manner that, without revealing information itself privileged or protected, will enable other parties to assess the applicability of the privilege or protection.

(c) **Protective Orders.**—Upon motion by a party or by the person from whom discovery is sought, accompanied by a certification that the movant has in good faith conferred or attempted to confer with other affected parties in an effort to resolve the dispute without court action, and for good cause shown, the court in which the action is pending or alternatively, on matters relating to a deposition, the court in the district where the deposition is to be taken may make any order which justice requires to protect a party or person from annoyance, embarrassment, oppression, or undue burden or expense, including one or more of the following:

(1) that the disclosure or discovery not be had;

(2) that the disclosure or discovery may be had only on specified terms and conditions, including a designation of the time or place;

(3) that the discovery may be had only by a method of discovery other than that selected by the party seeking discovery;

(4) that certain matters not be inquired into, or that the scope of the disclosure or discovery be limited to certain matters;

(5) that discovery be conducted with no one present except persons designated by the court;

(6) that a deposition, after being sealed, be opened only by order of the court;

(7) that a trade secret or other confidential research, development, or commercial information not be revealed or be revealed only in a designated way; and

(8) that the parties simultaneously file specified documents or information enclosed in sealed envelopes to be opened as directed by the court.

If the motion for a protective order is denied in whole or in part, the court may, on such terms and conditions as are just, order that any party or other person provide or permit discovery. The provisions of

Rule 37(a)(4) apply to the award of expenses incurred in relation to the motion.

(d) **Timing and Sequence of Discovery.**—Except in categories of proceedings exempted from initial disclosure under Rule 26(a)(1)(E), or when authorized under these rules or by order or agreement of the parties, a party may not seek discovery from any source before the parties have conferred as required by Rule 26(f). Unless the court upon motion, for the convenience of parties and witnesses and in the interests of justice, orders otherwise, methods of discovery may be used in any sequence, and the fact that a party is conducting discovery, whether by deposition or otherwise, does not operate to delay any other party's discovery.

(e) **Supplementation of Disclosures and Responses.** —A party who has made a disclosure under subdivision (a) or responded to a request for discovery with a disclosure or response is under a duty to supplement or correct the disclosure or response to include information thereafter acquired if ordered by the court or in the following circumstances:

(1) A party is under a duty to supplement at appropriate intervals its disclosures under subdivision (a) if the party learns that in some material respect the information disclosed is incomplete or incorrect and if the additional or corrective information has not otherwise been made known to the other parties during the discovery process or in writing. With respect to testimony of an expert from whom a report is required under subdivision (a)(2)(B) the duty extends both to information contained in the report and to information provided through a deposition of the expert, and any additions or other changes to this information shall be disclosed by the time the party's disclosures under Rule 26(a)(3) are due.

(2) A party is under a duty seasonably to amend a prior response to an interrogatory, request for production, or request for admission if the party learns that the response is in some material respect incomplete or incorrect and if the additional or corrective information has not otherwise been made known to the other parties during the discovery process or in writing.

(f) **Conference of Parties; Planning for Discovery.**—Except in categories of proceedings exempted from initial disclosure under Rule 26(a)(1)(E) or when otherwise ordered, the parties must, as soon as practicable and in any event at least 21 days before a scheduling conference is held or a scheduling order is due under Rule 16(b), confer to consider the nature and basis of their claims and defenses and the possibilities for a prompt settlement or resolution of the case, to make or arrange for the disclosures required by Rule 26(a)(1), and to develop a proposed discovery plan that indicates the parties' views and proposals concerning:

(1) what changes should be made in the timing, form, or requirement for disclosures under Rule 26(a), including a statement as to when disclosures under Rule 26(a)(1) were made or will be made;

(2) the subjects on which discovery may be needed, when discovery should be completed, and whether discovery should be conducted in phases or be limited to or focused upon particular issues;

(3) what changes should be made in the limitations on discovery imposed under these rules or by local rule, and what other limitations should be imposed; and

(4) any other orders that should be entered by the court under Rule 26(c) or under Rule 16(b) and (c).

The attorneys of record and all unrepresented parties that have appeared in the case are jointly responsible for arranging the conference, for attempting in good faith to agree on the proposed discovery plan, and for submitting to the court within 14 days after the conference a written report outlining the plan. A court may order that the parties or attorneys attend the conference in person. If necessary to comply with its expedited schedule for Rule 16(b) conferences, a court may by local rule (i) require that the conference between the parties occur fewer than 21 days before the scheduling conference is held or a scheduling order is due under Rule 16(b), and (ii) require that the written report outlining the discovery plan be filed fewer than 14 days after the conference between the parties, or excuse the parties from submitting a written report and permit them to report orally on their discovery plan at the Rule 16(b) conference.

(g) Signing of Disclosures, Discovery Requests, Responses, and Objections.

(1) Every disclosure made pursuant to subdivision (a)(1) or subdivision (a)(3) shall be signed by at least one attorney of record in the attorney's individual name, whose address shall be stated. An unrepresented party shall sign the disclosure and state the party's address. The signature of the attorney or party constitutes a certification that to the best of the signer's knowledge, information, and belief, formed after a reasonable inquiry, the disclosure is complete and correct as of the time it is made.

(2) Every discovery request, response, or objection made by a party represented by an attorney shall be signed by at least one attorney of record in the attorney's individual name, whose address shall be stated. An unrepresented party shall sign the request, response, or objection and state the party's address. The signature of the attorney or party constitutes a certification that to the best of the signer's knowledge, information, and belief, formed after a reasonable inquiry, the request, response, or objection is:

(A) consistent with these rules and warranted by existing law or a good faith argument for the extension, modification, or reversal of existing law;

(B) not interposed for any improper purpose, such as to harass or to cause unnecessary delay or needless increase in the cost of litigation; and

(C) not unreasonable or unduly burdensome or expensive, given the needs of the case, the discovery already had in the case, the amount in controversy, and the importance of the issues at stake in the litigation.

If a request, response, or objection is not signed, it shall be stricken unless it is signed promptly after the omission is called to the attention of the party making the request, response, or objection, and a party shall not be obligated to take any action with respect to it until it is signed.

(3) If without substantial justification a certification is made in violation of the rule, the court, upon motion or upon its own initiative, shall impose upon the person who made the certification, the party on whose behalf the disclosure, request, response, or objection is made, or both, an appropriate sanction, which may include an order to pay the amount of the reasonable expenses incurred because of the violation, including a reasonable attorney's fee.

Rule 33. Interrogatories to Parties

(a) **Availability.**—Without leave of court or written stipulation, any party may serve upon any other party written interrogatories, not exceeding 25 in number, including all discrete subparts, to be answered by the party served or, if the party served is a public or private corporation or a partnership or association or governmental agency, by any officer or agent, who shall furnish such information as is available to the party. Leave to serve additional interrogatories shall be granted to the extent consistent with the principles of Rule 26(b)(2). Without leave of court or written stipulation, interrogatories may not be served before the time specified in Rule 26(d).

(b) Answers and Objections.

(1) Each interrogatory shall be answered separately and fully in writing under oath, unless it is objected to, in which event the objecting party shall state the reasons for objection and shall answer to the extent the interrogatory is not objectionable.

(2) The answers are to be signed by the person making them, and the objections signed by the attorney making them.

(3) The party upon whom the interrogatories have been served shall serve a copy of the answers, and objections if any, within 30 days after the service of the interrogatories. A shorter or longer time may be directed by the court or, in the absence of such an order, agreed to in writing by the parties subject to Rule 29.

(4) All grounds for an objection to an interrogatory shall be stated with specificity. Any ground not

stated in a timely objection is waived unless the party's failure to object is excused by the court for good cause shown.

(5) The party submitting the interrogatories may move for an order under Rule 37(a) with respect to any objection to or other failure to answer an interrogatory.

(c) **Scope; Use at Trial.**—Interrogatories may relate to any matters which can be inquired into under Rule 26(b)(1), and the answers may be used to the extent permitted by the rules of evidence.

An interrogatory otherwise proper is not necessarily objectionable merely because an answer to the interrogatory involves an opinion or contention that relates to fact or the application of law to fact, but the court may order that such an interrogatory need not be answered until after designated discovery has been completed or until a pretrial conference or other later time.

(d) **Option to Produce Business Records.**— Where the answer to an interrogatory may be derived or ascertained from the business records of the party upon whom the interrogatory has been served or from an examination, audit or inspection of such business records, including a compilation, abstract or summary thereof, and the burden of deriving or ascertaining the answer is substantially the same for the party serving the interrogatory as for the party served, it is a sufficient answer to such interrogatory to specify the records from which the answer may be derived or ascertained and to afford to the party serving the interrogatory reasonable opportunity to examine, audit, or inspect such records and to make copies, compilations, abstracts, or summaries. A specification shall be in sufficient detail to permit the interrogating party to locate and to identify, as readily as can the party served, the records from which the answer may be ascertained.

Rule 34

Federal Rules of Civil Procedure Rule 34

Rule 34. Production of Documents and Things and Entry Upon Land for Inspection and Other Purposes

(a) **Scope.**—Any party may serve on any other party a request (1) to produce and permit the party making the request, or someone acting on the requestor's behalf, to inspect and copy, any designated documents (including writings, drawings, graphs, charts, photographs, phonorecords, and other data compilations from which information can be obtained, translated, if necessary, by the respondent through detection devices into reasonably usable form), or to inspect and copy, test, or sample any tangible things which constitute or contain matters within the scope of Rule 26(b) and which are in the possession, custody, or control of the party upon whom the request is served; or (2) to permit entry upon designated land or other property in the possession or control of the party upon whom the request is served for the purpose of inspection and measuring, surveying, photographing, testing, or sampling the property or any designated object or operation thereon, within the scope of Rule 26(b).

(b) **Procedure.**—The request shall set forth, either by individual item or by category, the items to be inspected and describe each with reasonable particularity. The request shall specify a reasonable time, place, and manner of making the inspection and performing the related acts. Without leave of court or written stipulation, a request may not be served before the time specified in Rule 26(d).

The party upon whom the request is served shall serve a written response within 30 days after the service of the request. A shorter or longer time may be directed by the court or, in the absence of such an order, agreed to in writing by the parties, subject to Rule 29. The response shall state, with respect to each item or category, that inspection and related activities will be permitted as requested, unless the request is objected to, in which event the reasons for the objection shall be stated. If objection is made to part of an item or category, the part shall be specified and inspection permitted of the remaining parts. The party submitting the request may move for an order under Rule 37(a) with respect to any objection to or other failure to respond to the request or any part thereof, or any failure to permit inspection as requested.

A party who produces documents for inspection shall produce them as they are kept in the usual course of business or shall organize and label them to correspond with the categories in the request.

(c) **Persons Not Parties.**—A person not a party to the action may be compelled to produce documents and things or to submit to an inspection as provided in <u>Rule 45</u>.

Rule 36. Requests for Admission

(a) **Request for Admission.**—A party may serve upon any other party a written request for the admission, for purposes of the pending action only, of the truth of any matters within the scope of Rule 26(b)(1) set forth in the request that relate to statements or opinions of fact or of the application of law to fact, including the genuineness of any documents described in the request. Copies of documents shall be served with the request unless they have been or are otherwise furnished or made available for inspection and copying. Without leave of court or written stipulation, requests for admission may not be served before the time specified in Rule 26(d).

Each matter of which an admission is requested shall be separately set forth. The matter is admitted unless, within 30 days after service of the request, or within such shorter or longer time as the court may allow or as the parties may agree to in writing, subject to Rule 29, the party to whom the request is directed serves upon the party requesting the admission a written answer or objection addressed to the matter, signed by the party or by the party's attorney. If objection is made, the reasons therefor shall be stated. The answer shall specifically deny the matter or set forth in detail the reasons why the answering party cannot truthfully admit or deny the matter. A denial shall fairly meet the substance of the requested admission, and when good faith requires that a party qualify an answer or deny only a part of the matter of which an admission is requested, the party shall specify so much of it as is true and qualify or deny the remainder. An answering party may not give lack of information or knowledge as a reason for failure to admit or deny unless the party states that the party has made reasonable inquiry and that the information known or readily obtainable by the party is insufficient to enable the party to admit or deny. A party who considers that a matter of which an admission has been requested presents a genuine issue for trial may not, on that ground alone, object to the request; the party may, subject to the provisions of Rule 37(c), deny the matter or set forth reasons why the party cannot admit or deny it.

The party who has requested the admissions may move to determine the sufficiency of the answers or objections. Unless the court determines that an objection is justified, it shall order that an answer be served. If the court determines that an answer does not comply with the requirements of this rule, it may order either that the matter is admitted or that an amended answer be served. The court may, in lieu of these orders, determine that final disposition of the request be made at a pretrial conference or at a designated time prior to trial. The provisions of Rule 37(a)(4) apply to the award of expenses incurred in relation to the motion.

(b) **Effect of Admission.**—Any matter admitted under this rule is conclusively established unless the court on motion permits withdrawal or amendment of the admission. Subject to the provision of Rule 16 governing amendment of a pretrial order, the court may permit withdrawal or amendment when the presentation of the merits of the action will be subserved thereby and the party who obtained the admission fails to satisfy the court that withdrawal or amendment will prejudice that party in maintaining the action or defense on the merits. Any admission made by a party under this rule is for the purpose of the pending action only and is not an admission for any other purpose nor may it be used against the party in any other proceeding.

Rule 37. Failure to Make Disclosure or Cooperate in Discovery; Sanctions

(a) **Motion For Order Compelling Disclosure or Discovery.**—A party, upon reasonable notice to other parties and all persons affected thereby, may apply for an order compelling disclosure or discovery as follows:

(1) **Appropriate Court.**—An application for an order to a party shall be made to the court in which the action is pending. An application for an order to a person who is not a party shall be made to the court in the district where the discovery is being, or is to be, taken.

(2) **Motion.**—

(A) If a party fails to make a disclosure required by Rule 26(a), any other party may move to compel disclosure and for appropriate sanctions. The motion must include a certification that the movant has in good faith conferred or attempted to confer with the party not making the disclosure in an effort to secure the disclosure without court action.

(B) If a deponent fails to answer a question propounded or submitted under Rules 30 or 31, or a corporation or other entity fails to make a designation under Rule 30(b)(6) or 31(a), or a party fails to answer an interrogatory submitted under Rule 33, or if a party, in response to a request for inspection submitted under Rule 34, fails to respond that inspection will be permitted as requested or fails to permit inspection as requested, the discovering party may move for an order compelling an answer, or a designation, or an order compelling inspection in accordance with the request. The motion must include a certification that the movant has in good faith conferred or attempted to confer with the person or party failing to make the discovery in an effort to secure the information or material without court action. When taking a deposition on oral examination, the proponent of the question may complete or adjourn the examination before applying for an order.

(3) **Evasive or Incomplete Disclosure, Answer, or Response.**—For purposes of this subdivision an evasive or incomplete disclosure, answer, or response is to be treated as a failure to disclose, answer, or respond.

(4) *Expenses and Sanctions.*

(A) If the motion is granted or if the disclosure or requested discovery is provided after the motion was filed, the court shall, after affording an opportunity to be heard, require the party or deponent whose conduct necessitated the motion or the party or attorney advising such conduct or both of them to pay to the moving party the reasonable expenses incurred in making the motion, including attorney's fees, unless the court finds that the motion was filed without the movant's first making a good faith effort to obtain the disclosure or discovery without court action, or that the opposing party's nondisclosure, response, or objection was substantially justified, or that other circumstances make an award of expenses unjust.

(B) If the motion is denied, the court may enter any protective order authorized under Rule 26(c) and shall, after affording an opportunity to be heard, require the moving party or the attorney filing the motion or both of them to pay to the party or deponent who opposed the motion the reasonable expenses incurred in opposing the motion, including attorney's fees, unless the court finds that the making of the motion was substantially justified or that other circumstances make an award of expenses unjust.

(C) If the motion is granted in part and denied in part, the court may enter any protective order authorized under Rule 26(c) and may, after affording an opportunity to be heard, apportion the reasonable expenses incurred in relation to the motion among the parties and persons in a just manner.

(b) Failure to Comply With Order.—

(1) **Sanctions by Court in District Where Deposition is Taken.**—If a deponent fails to be sworn or to answer a question after being directed to do so by the court in the district in which the deposition is being taken, the failure may be considered a contempt of that court.

(2) **Sanctions by Court in Which Action is Pending.**— If a party or an officer, director, or managing agent of a party or a person designated under Rule 30(b)(6) or 31(a) to testify on behalf of a party fails to obey an order to provide or permit discovery, including an order made under

subdivision (a) of this rule or Rule 35, or if a party fails to obey an order entered under Rule 26(f), the court in which the action is pending may make such orders in regard to the failure as are just, and among others the following:

(A) An order that the matters regarding which the order was made or any other designated facts shall be taken to be established for the purposes of the action in accordance with the claim of the party obtaining the order;

(B) An order refusing to allow the disobedient party to support or oppose designated claims or defenses, or prohibiting that party from introducing designated matters in evidence;

(C) An order striking out pleadings or parts thereof, or staying further proceedings until the order is obeyed, or dismissing the action or proceeding or any part thereof, or rendering a judgment by default against the disobedient party;

(D) In lieu of any of the foregoing orders or in addition thereto, an order treating as a contempt of court the failure to obey any orders except an order to submit to a physical or mental examination;

(E) Where a party has failed to comply with an order under Rule 35(a) requiring that party to produce another for examination, such orders as are listed in paragraphs (A), (B), and (C) of this subdivision, unless the party failing to comply shows that, that party is unable to produce such person for examination.

In lieu of any of the foregoing orders or in addition thereto, the court shall require the party failing to obey the order or the attorney advising that party or both to pay the reasonable expenses, including attorney's fees, caused by the failure, unless the court finds that the failure was substantially justified or that other circumstances make an award of expenses unjust.

(c) **Failure to Disclose; False or Misleading Disclosure; Refusal to Admit.**—

(1) A party that without substantial justification fails to disclose information required by Rule 26(a) or 26(e)(1), or to amend a prior response to discovery as required by Rule 26(e)(2), is not, unless such failure is harmless, permitted to use as evidence at a trial, at a hearing, or on a motion any witness or information not so disclosed. In addition to or in lieu of this sanction, the court, on motion and after affording an opportunity to be heard, may impose other appropriate sanctions. In addition to requiring payment of reasonable expenses, including attorney's fees, caused by the failure, these sanctions may include any of the actions authorized under Rule 37(b)(2)(A), (B), and (C) and may include informing the jury of the failure to make the disclosure.

(2) If a party fails to admit the genuineness of any document or the truth of any matter as requested under Rule 36, and if the party requesting the admissions thereafter proves the genuineness of the document or the truth of the matter, the requesting party may apply to the court for an order requiring the other party to pay the reasonable expenses incurred in making that proof, including reasonable attorney's fees. The court shall make the order unless it finds that (A) the request was held objectionable pursuant to Rule 36(a) or (B) the admission sought was of no substantial importance, or (C) the party failing to admit had reasonable ground to believe that the party might prevail on the matter, or (D) there was other good reason for the failure to admit.

(d) **Failure of Party to Attend at Own Deposition or Serve Answers to Interrogatories or Respond to Request for Inspection.**—If a party or an officer, director, or managing agent of a party or a person designated under Rule 30(b)(6) or 31(a) to testify on behalf of a party fails (1) to appear before the officer who is to take the deposition, after being served with a proper notice, or (2) to serve answers or objections to interrogatories submitted under Rule 33, after proper service of the interrogatories, or (3) to serve a written response to a request for inspection submitted under Rule 34, after proper service of the request, the court in which the action is pending on motion may make such orders in regard to the failure as are just, and among others it may take any action authorized under subparagraphs (A), (B), and (C) of subdivision (b)(2) of this rule. Any motion specifying a failure under clause (2) or (3) of this subdivision shall include a certification that the movant has in good faith conferred or attempted to confer with the party failing to answer or respond in an effort to obtain such answer or response without court action. In lieu of any order or in addition thereto, the court shall require the party failing to act or the attorney advising that party or both to pay the reasonable expenses, including attorney's fees, caused by the failure unless the court finds that the failure was substantially justified or that other circumstances make an award of expenses unjust.

The failure to act described in this subdivision may not be excused on the ground that the discovery sought is objectionable unless the party failing to act has a pending motion for a protective order as provided by Rule 26(c).

(e) **[Abrogated]**

(f) **[Repealed]**

(g) **Failure to Participate in the Framing of a Discovery Plan.**—If a party or a party's attorney fails to participate in good faith in the development and submission of a proposed discovery plan as required by Rule 26(f), the court may, after opportunity for hearing, require such party or attorney to pay to any other party the reasonable expenses, including attorney's fees, caused by the failure.

Model Standards and Guidelines for the Utilization of Legal Assistants

National Association of Legal Assistants, Inc.

The purpose of this annotated version of the National Association of Legal Assistants, Inc. Model Standards and Guidelines for the Utilization of Legal Assistants (the "Model," "Standards" and/or the "Guidelines") is to provide references to the existing case law and other authorities where the underlying issues have been considered. The authorities cited will serve as a basis upon which conduct of a legal assistant may be analyzed as proper or improper.

The Guidelines represent a statement of how the legal assistant may function. The Guidelines are not intended to be a comprehensive or exhaustive list of the proper duties of a legal assistant. Rather, they are designed as guides to what may or may not be proper conduct for the legal assistant. In formulating the Guidelines, the reasoning and rules of law in many reported decisions of disciplinary cases and unauthorized practice of law cases have been analyzed and considered. In addition, the provisions of the American Bar Association's Model Rules of Professional Conduct, as well as the ethical promulgations of various state courts and bar associations have been considered in the development of the Guidelines.

These Guidelines form a sound basis for the legal assistant and the supervising attorney to follow. This Model will serve as a comprehensive resource document and as a definitive, well-reasoned guide to those considering voluntary standards and guidelines for legal assistants.

I
PREAMBLE

Proper utilization of the services of legal assistants contributes to the delivery of cost-effective, high-quality legal services. Legal assistants and the legal profession should be assured that measures exist for identifying legal assistants and their role in assisting attorneys in the delivery of legal services. Therefore, the National Association of Legal Assistants, Inc., hereby adopts these Standards and Guidelines as an educational document for the benefit of legal assistants and the legal profession.

COMMENT

The three most frequently raised questions concerning legal assistants are (1) How do you define a legal assistant; (2) Who is qualified to be identified as a legal assistant; and (3) What duties may a legal assistant perform? The definition adopted in 1984 by the National Association of Legal Assistants answers the first question. The Model sets forth minimum education, training and experience through standards which will assure that an individual utilizing the title "legal assistant" has the qualifications to be held out to the legal community and the public in that capacity. The Guidelines identify those acts which the reported cases hold to be proscribed and give examples of services which the legal assistant may perform under the supervision of a licensed attorney.

These Guidelines constitute a statement relating to services performed by legal assistants, as defined herein, as approved by court decisions and other sources of authority. The purpose of the Guidelines is not to place limitations or restrictions on the legal assistant profession. Rather, the Guidelines are intended to outline for the legal profession an acceptable course of conduct. Voluntary recognition and utilization of the Standards and Guidelines will benefit the entire legal profession and the public it serves.

II
DEFINITION

The National Association of Legal Assistants adopted the following definition in 1984:

Legal assistants, also known as paralegals, are a distinguishable group of persons who assist attorneys in the delivery of legal services. Through formal education, training, and experience, legal assistants have knowledge and expertise regarding the legal system and substantive and procedural law which qualify them to do work of a legal nature under the supervision of an attorney.

COMMENT

This definition emphasizes the knowledge and expertise of legal assistants in substantive and procedural law obtained through education and work experience. It further defines the legal assistant or paralegal as a professional working under the supervision of an attorney as distinguished from a non-lawyer who delivers services directly to the public without any intervention or review of work product by an attorney. Statutes, court rules, case law and bar associations are additional sources for legal assistant or paralegal definitions. In applying the Standards and Guidelines, it is important to remember that they were developed to apply to the legal assistant as defined herein.

Lawyers should refrain from labeling those who do not meet the criteria set forth in this definition, such as secretaries and other administrative staff, as legal assistants.

For billing purposes, the services of a legal secretary are considered part of overhead costs and are not recoverable in fee awards. However, the courts have held that fees for paralegal services are recoverable as long as they are not clerical functions, such as organizing files, copying documents, checking docket, updating files, checking court dates and delivering papers. As established in Missouri v. Jenkins, 491 U.S.274, 109 S.Ct. 2463, 2471, n.10 (1989) tasks performed by legal assistants must be substantive in nature which, absent the legal assistant, the attorney would perform.

There are also case law and Supreme Court Rules addressing the issue of a disbarred attorney serving in the capacity of a legal assistant.

III
STANDARDS

A legal assistant should meet certain minimum qualifications. The following standards may be used to determine an individual's qualifications as a legal assistant:

1. Successful completion of the Certified Legal Assistant ("CLA") certifying examination of the National Association of Legal Assistants, Inc.;

2. Graduation from an ABA approved program of study for legal assistants;

3. Graduation from a course of study for legal assistants which is institutionally accredited but not ABA approved, and which requires not less than the equivalent of 60 semester hours of classroom study;

4. Graduation from a course of study for legal assistants, other than those set forth in (2) and (3) above, plus not less than six months of in-house training as a legal assistant;

5. A baccalaureate degree in any field, plus not less than six months in-house training as a legal assistant;

6. A minimum of three years of law-related experience under the supervision of an attorney, including at least six months of in-house training as a legal assistant; or

7. Two years of in-house training as a legal assistant.

For purposes of these Standards, "in-house training as a legal assistant" means attorney education of the employee concerning legal assistant duties and these Guidelines. In a ddition to review and analysis of assignments, the legal assistant should receive a reasonable amount of instruction directly related to the duties and obligations of the legal assistant.

COMMENT

The Standards set forth suggest minimum qualifications for a legal assistant. These minimum qualifications, as adopted, recognize legal related work backgrounds and formal education backgrounds, both of which provide the legal assistant with a broad base in exposure to and knowledge of the legal profession. This background is necessary to assure the public and the legal profession that the employee identified as a legal assistant is qualified.

The Certified Legal Assistant ("CLA") examination established by NALA in 1976 is a voluntary nation-wide certification program for legal assistants. The CLA designation is a statement to the legal profession and the public that the legal assistant has met the high levels of knowledge and professionalism required by NALA's certification program. Continuing education requirements, which all certified legal assistants must meet, assure that high standards are maintained. The CLA designation has been recognized as a means of establishing the qualifications of a legal assistant in supreme court rules, state court and bar association standards and utilization guidelines.

Certification through NALA is available to all legal assistants meeting the educational and experience requirements. Certified Legal Assistants may also pursue advanced specialty certification ("CLAS") in the areas of bankruptcy, civil litigation, probate and estate planning, corporate and business law, criminal law and procedure, real estate, intellectual property, and may also pursue state certification based on state laws and procedures in California, Florida, Louisiana and Texas.

IV
GUIDELINES

These Guidelines relating to standards of performance and professional responsibility are intended to aid legal assistants and attorneys. The ultimate responsibility rests with an attorney who employs legal assistants to educate them with respect to the duties they are assigned and to supervise the manner in which such duties are accomplished.

COMMENT

In general, a legal assistant is allowed to perform any task which is properly delegated and supervised by an attorney, as long as the attorney is ultimately responsible to the client and assumes complete professional responsibility for the work product.

ABA Model Rules of Professional Conduct, Rule 5.3 provides:

With respect to a non-lawyer employed or retained by or associated with a lawyer:

(a) a partner in a law firm shall make reasonable efforts to ensure that the firm has in effect measures giving reasonable assurance that the person's conduct is compatible with the professional obligations of the lawyer;

(b) a lawyer having direct supervisory authority over the non-lawyer shall make reasonable efforts to ensure that the person's conduct is compatible with the professional obligations of the lawyer; and

(c) a lawyer shall be responsible for conduct of such a person that would be a violation of the rules of professional conduct if engaged in by a lawyer if:

(1) the lawyer orders or, with the knowledge of the specific conduct ratifies the conduct involved; or

(2) the lawyer is a partner in the law firm in which the person is employed, or has direct supervisory authority over the person, and knows of the conduct at a time when its consequences can be avoided or mitigated but fails to take remedial action.

There are many interesting and complex issues involving the use of legal assistants. In any discussion of the proper role of a legal assistant, attention must be directed to what constitutes the practice of law. Proper delegation to legal assistants is further complicated and confused by the lack of an adequate definition of the practice of law.

Kentucky became the first state to adopt a Paralegal Code by Supreme Court Rule. This Code sets forth certain exclusions to the unauthorized practice of law:

For purposes of this rule, the unauthorized practice of law shall not include any service rendered involving legal knowledge or advice, whether representation, counsel or advocacy, in or out of court, rendered in respect to the acts, duties, obligations, liabilities or business relations of the one requiring services where:

A. The client understands that the paralegal is not a lawyer;

B. The lawyer supervises the paralegal in the performance of his or her duties; and

C. The lawyer remains fully responsible for such representation including all actions taken or not taken in connection therewith by the paralegal to the same extent as if such representation had been furnished entirely by the lawyer and all such actions had been taken or not taken directly by the attorney. Paralegal Code, Ky.S.Ct.R3.700, Sub-Rule 2.

South Dakota Supreme Court Rule 97-25 Utilization Rule a(4) states:

The attorney remains responsible for the services performed by the legal assistant to the same extent as though such services had been furnished entirely by the attorney and such actions were those of the attorney.

GUIDELINE 1

Legal assistants should:

1. Disclose their status as legal assistants at the outset of any professional relationship with a client, other attorneys, a court or administrative agency or personnel thereof, or members of the general public;
2. Preserve the confidences and secrets of all clients; and
3. Understand the attorney's Rules of Professional Responsibility and these Guidelines in order to avoid any action which would involve the attorney in a violation of the Rules, or give the appearance of professional impropriety.

COMMENT

Routine early disclosure of the legal assistant's status when dealing with persons outside the attorney's office is necessary to assure that there will be no misunderstanding as to the responsibilities and role of the legal assistant. Disclosure may be made in any way that avoids confusion. If the person dealing with the legal assistant already knows of his/her status, further disclosure is unnecessary. If at any time in written or oral communication the legal assistant becomes aware that the other person may believe the legal assistant is an attorney, immediate disclosure should be made as to the legal assistant's status.

The attorney should exercise care that the legal assistant preserves and refrains from using any confidence or secrets of a client, and should instruct the legal assistant not to disclose or use any such confidences or secrets.

The legal assistant must take any and all steps necessary to prevent conflicts of interest and fully disclose such conflicts to the supervising attorney. Failure to do so may jeopardize both the attorney's representation of the client and the case itself.

Guidelines for the Utilization of Legal Assistant Services adopted December 3, l994 by the Washington State Bar Association Board of Governors states:

"Guideline 7: A lawyer shall take reasonable measures to prevent conflicts of interest resulting from a legal assistant's other employment or interest insofar as such other employment or interests would present a conflict of interest if it were that of the lawyer."

In Re Complex Asbestos Litigation, 232 Cal. App. 3d 572 (Cal. 1991), addresses the issue wherein a law firm was disqualified due to possession of attorney-client confidences by a legal assistant employee resulting from previous employment by opposing counsel.

The ultimate responsibility for compliance with approved standards of professional conduct rests with the supervising attorney. The burden rests upon the attorney who employs a legal assistant to educate the latter with respect to the duties which may be assigned and then to supervise the manner in which the legal assistant carries out such duties. However, this does not relieve the legal assistant from an independent obligation to refrain from illegal conduct. Additionally, and notwithstanding that the Rules are not binding upon non-lawyers, the very nature of a legal assistant's employment imposes an obligation not to engage in conduct which would involve the supervising attorney in a violation of the Rules.

The attorney must make sufficient background investigation of the prior activities and character and integrity of his or her legal assistants.

Further, the attorney must take all measures necessary to avoid and fully disclose conflicts of interest due to other employment or interests. Failure to do so may jeopardize both the attorney's representation of the client and the case itself.

Legal assistant associations strive to maintain the high level of integrity and competence expected of the legal profession and, further, strive to uphold the high standards of ethics.

NALA's Code of Ethics and Professional Responsibility states "A legal assistant's conduct is guided by bar associations' codes of professional responsibility and rules of professional conduct."

GUIDELINE 2

Legal assistants should not:

1. Establish attorney-client relationships; set legal fees; give legal opinions or advice; or represent a client before a court, unless authorized to do so by said court; nor
2. Engage in, encourage, or contribute to any act which could constitute the unauthorized practice law.

COMMENT

Case law, court rules, codes of ethics and professional responsibilities, as well as bar ethics opinions now hold which acts can and cannot be performed by a legal assistant. Generally, the determination of what acts constitute the unauthorized practice of law is made by State Supreme Courts.

Numerous cases exist relating to the unauthorized practice of law. Courts have gone so far as to prohibit the legal assistant from preparation of divorce kits and assisting in preparation of bankruptcy forms and, more specifically, from providing basic information about procedures and requirements, deciding where information should be placed on forms, and responding to questions from debtors regarding the interpretation or definition of terms.

Cases have identified certain areas in which an attorney has a duty to act, but it is interesting to note that none of these cases state that it is improper for an attorney to have the initial work performed by the legal assistant. This again points out the importance of adequate supervision by the employing attorney.

An attorney can be found to have aided in the unauthorized practice of law when delegating acts which cannot be performed by a legal assistant.

GUIDELINE 3

Legal assistants may perform services for an attorney in the representation of a client, provided:

1. The services performed by the legal assistant do not require the exercise of independent professional legal judgment;
2. The attorney maintains a direct relationship with the client and maintains control of all client matters;
3. The attorney supervises the legal assistant;
4. The attorney remains professionally responsible for all work on behalf of the client, including any actions taken or not taken by the legal assistant in connection therewith; and
5. The services performed supplement, merge with and become the attorney's work product.

COMMENT

Legal assistants, whether employees or independent contractors, perform services for the attorney in the representation of a client. Attorneys should delegate work to legal assistants commensurate with their knowledge and experience and provide appropriate instruction and supervision concerning the delegated work, as well as ethical acts of their employment. Ultimate responsibility for the work product of a legal assistant rests with the attorney. However, a legal assistant must use discretion and professional judgment and must not render independent legal judgment in place of an attorney.

The work product of a legal assistant is subject to civil rules governing discovery of materials prepared in anticipation of litigation, whether the legal assistant is viewed as an extension of the attorney or as another representative of the party itself. Fed. R. Civ. P. 26 (b)(2).

GUIDELINE 4

In the supervision of a legal assistant, consideration should be given to:

1. Designating work assignments that correspond to the legal assistant's abilities, knowledge, training and experience;
2. Educating and training the legal assistant with respect to professional responsibility, local rules and practices, and firm policies;
3. Monitoring the work and professional conduct of the legal assistant to ensure that the work is substantively correct and timely performed;
4. Providing continuing education for the legal assistant in substantive matters through courses, institutes, workshops, seminars and in-house training; and
5. Encouraging and supporting membership and active participation in professional organizations.

COMMENT

Attorneys are responsible for the actions of their employees in both malpractice and disciplinary proceedings. In the vast majority of cases, the courts have not censured attorneys for a particular act delegated to the legal assistant, but rather, have been critical of and imposed sanctions against attorneys for failure to adequately supervise the legal assistant. The attorney's responsibility for supervision of his or her legal assistant must be more than a willingness to accept responsibility and liability for the legal assistant's work. Supervision of a legal assistant must be offered in both the procedural and substantive legal areas. The attorney must delegate work based upon the education, knowledge and abilities of the legal assistant and must monitor the work product and conduct of the legal assistant to insure that the work performed is substantively correct and competently performed in a professional manner.

Michigan State Board of Commissioners has adopted Guidelines for the Utilization of Legal Assistants (April 23, 1993). These guidelines, in part, encourage employers to support legal assistant participation in continuing education programs to ensure that the legal assistant remains competent in the fields of practice in which the legal assistant is assigned.

The working relationship between the lawyer and the legal assistant should extend to cooperative efforts on public service activities wherever possible. Participation in pro bono activities is encouraged in ABA Guideline 10.

GUIDELINE 5

Except as otherwise provided by statute, court rule or decision, administrative rule or regulation, or the attorney's rules of professional responsibility, and within the preceding parameters and proscriptions, a legal assistant may perform any function delegated by an attorney, including, but not limited to the following:

1. Conduct client interviews and maintain general contact with the client after the establishment of the attorney-client relationship, so long as the client is aware of the status and function of the legal assistant, and the client contact is under the supervision of the attorney.
2. Locate and interview witnesses, so long as the witnesses are aware of the status and function of the legal assistant.
3. Conduct investigations and statistical and documentary research for review by the attorney.
4. Conduct legal research for review by the attorney.
5. Draft legal documents for review by the attorney.
6. Draft correspondence and pleadings for review by and signature of the attorney.
7. Summarize depositions, interrogatories and testimony for review by the attorney.
8. Attend executions of wills, real estate closings, depositions, court or administrative hearings and trials with the attorney.
9. Author and sign letters providing the legal assistant's status is clearly indicated and the correspondence does not contain independent legal opinions or legal advice.

COMMENT

The United States Supreme Court has recognized the variety of tasks being performed by legal assistants and has noted that use of legal assistants encourages cost-effective delivery of legal services, Missouri v. Jenkins, 491 U.S.274, 109 S.Ct. 2463, 2471, n.10 (1989). In Jenkins, the court further held that legal assistant time should be included in compensation for attorney fee awards at the rate in the relevant community to bill legal assistant time.

Courts have held that legal assistant fees are not a part of the overall overhead of a law firm. Legal assistant services are billed separately by attorneys, and decrease litigation expenses. Tasks performed by legal assistants must contain substantive legal work under the direction or supervision of an attorney, such that if the legal assistant were not present, the work would be performed by the attorney.

In Taylor v. Chubb, 874 P.2d 806 (Okla. 1994), the Court ruled that attorney fees awarded should include fees for services performed by legal assistants and, further, defined tasks which may be performed by the legal assistant under the supervision of an attorney including, among others: interview clients; draft pleadings and other documents; carry on legal research, both conventional and computer aided; research public records; prepare discovery requests and responses; schedule depositions and prepare notices and subpoenas; summarize depositions and other discovery responses; coordinate and manage document production; locate and interview witnesses; organize pleadings, trial exhibits and other documents; prepare witness and exhibit lists; prepare trial notebooks; prepare for the attendance of witnesses at trial; and assist lawyers at trials.

Except for the specific proscription contained in Guideline 1, the reported cases do not limit the duties which may be performed by a legal assistant under the supervision of the attorney.

An attorney may not split legal fees with a legal assistant, nor pay a legal assistant for the referral of legal business. An attorney may compensate a legal assistant based on the quantity and quality of the legal assistant's work and value of that work to a law practice.

CONCLUSION

These Standards and Guidelines were developed from generally accepted practices. Each supervising attorney must be aware of the specific rules, decisions and statutes applicable to legal assistants within his/her jurisdiction.

ADDENDUM

For further information, the following cases may be helpful to you:

DUTIES:

Taylor v. Chubb, 874 P.2d 806 (Okla. 1994)

McMackin v. McMackin, 651 A.2d 778 (Del.Fam Ct 1993)

WORK PRODUCT:

Fine v. Facet Aerospace Products Co., 133 F.R.D. 439 (S.D.N.Y. 1990)

UNAUTHORIZED PRACTICE OF LAW

Akron Bar Assn. V. Green, 673 N.E.2d 1307 (Ohio 1997)

In Re Hessinger & Associates, 192 B.R. 211 (N.D. Calif. 1996)

In the Matter of Bright, 171 B.R. 799 (Bkrtcy. E.D. Mich)

Louisiana State Bar Assn v. Edwins, 540 So.2d 294 (La. 1989)

ATTORNEY/CLIENT PRIVILEGE

In Re Complex Asbestos Litigation, 232 Cal. App. 3d 572 (Calif. 1991)

Makita Corp. V. U.S., 819 F.Supp. 1099 (CIT 1993)

CONFLICTS

In Re Complex Asbestos Litigation, 232 Cal. App. 3d 572 (Calif. 1991)

Makita Corp. V. U.S., 819 F.Supp. 1099 (CIT 1993)

Phoenix Founders, Inc., v. Marshall, 887 S.W.2d 831 (Tex. 1994)

Smart Industries v. Superior Court, 876 P.2d 1176 (Ariz. App. Div.1 1994)

SUPERVISION

Matter of Martinez, 754 P.2d 842 (N.M. 1988)

State v. Barrett, 483 P.2d 1106 (Kan. 1971)

FEE AWARDS

In Re Bicoastal Corp., 121 B.R. 653 (Bktrcy.M.D.Fla. 1990)

In Re Carter, 101 B.R. 170 (Bkrtcy.D.S.D. 1989)

Taylor v. Chubb, 874 P.2d 806 (Okla.1994)

Missouri v. Jenkins, 491 U.S. 274, 109 S.Ct. 2463, 105 L.Ed.2d 229 (1989) 11 U.S.C.A. '330

McMackin v. McMackin, Del.Fam.Ct. 651 A.2d 778 (1993)

Miller v. Alamo, 983 F.2d 856 (8th Cir. 1993)

Stewart v.Sullivan, 810 F.Supp. 1102 (D.Hawaii 1993)

In Re Yankton College, 101 B.R. 151 (Bkrtcy. D.S.D. 1989)

Stacey v. Stroud, 845 F.Supp. 1135 (S.D.W.Va. 1993)

COURT APPEARANCES

Louisiana State Bar Assn v. Edwins, 540 So.2d 294 (La. 1989)

In addition to the above referenced cases, you may contact your state bar association for information regarding guidelines for the utilization of legal assistants that may have been adopted by the bar, or ethical opinions concerning the utilization of legal assistants. The following states have adopted a definition of "legal assistant" or "paralegal" either through bar association guidelines, ethical opinions, legislation or case law:

Legislation:

California	Illinois	Pennsylvania
Florida	Indiana	

Supreme Court Cases or Rules:

Kentucky	North Dakota	South Dakota
New Hampshire	Rhode Island	Virginia
New Mexico		

Cases:

Arizona	Oklahoma	Washington
New Jersey	South Carolina	

Guidelines:

Colorado	Idaho	Utah
Connecticut	New York	Wisconsin
Georgia	Oregon	

Bar Association Activity:

Alaska	Massachusetts	Ohio
Arizona	Michigan	Oregon
Colorado	Minnesota	Rhode Island
Connecticut	Missouri	South Carolina
Florida	Nevada	South Dakota
Illinois	New Mexico	Tennessee
Iowa	New Hampshire	Texas
Kansas	North Carolina	Virginia
Kentucky	North Dakota	Wisconsin

Selected Rules from the American Bar Association Model Rules of Professional Conduct

Rule 1.6

(a) A lawyer shall not reveal information relating to the representation of a client unless the client gives informed consent, the disclosure is impliedly authorized in order to carry out the representation or the disclosure is permitted by paragraph (b).

(b) A lawyer may reveal information relating to the representation of a client to the extent the lawyer reasonably believes necessary:

(1) to prevent reasonably certain death or substantial bodily harm;

(2) to prevent the client from committing a crime or fraud that is reasonably certain to result in substantial injury to the financial interests or property of another and in furtherance of which the client has used or is using the lawyer's services;

(3) to prevent, mitigate or rectify substantial injury to the financial interests or property of another that is reasonably certain to result or has resulted from the client's commission of a crime or fraud in furtherance of which the client has used the lawyer's services;

(4) to secure legal advice about the lawyer's compliance with these Rules;

(5) to establish a claim or defense on behalf of the lawyer in a controversy between the lawyer and the client, to establish a defense to a criminal charge or civil claim against the lawyer based upon conduct in which the client was involved, or to respond to allegations in any proceeding concerning the lawyer's representation of the client; or

(6) to comply with other law or a court order.

Rule 1.10

(a) While lawyers are associated in a firm, none of them shall knowingly represent a client when any one of them practicing alone would be prohibited from doing so by Rules 1.7 or 1.9, unless the prohibition is based on a personal interest of the prohibited lawyer and does not present a significant risk of materially limiting the representation of the client by the remaining lawyers in the firm.

(b) When a lawyer has terminated an association with a firm, the firm is not prohibited from thereafter representing a person with interests materially adverse to those of a client represented by the formerly associated lawyer and not currently represented by the firm, unless:

(1) the matter is the same or substantially related to that in which the formerly associated lawyer represented the client; and

(2) any lawyer remaining in the firm has information protected by Rules 1.6 and 1.9(c) that is material to the matter.

(c) A disqualification prescribed by this rule may be waived by the affected client under the conditions stated in Rule 1.7.

(d) The disqualification of lawyers associated in a firm with former or current government lawyers is governed by Rule 1.11.

Rule 1.18

(a) A person who discusses with a lawyer the possibility of forming a client-lawyer relationship with respect to a matter is a prospective client.

(b) Even when no client-lawyer relationship ensues, a lawyer who has had discussions with a prospective client shall not use or reveal information learned in the consultation, except as Rule 1.9 would permit with respect to information of a former client.

(c) A lawyer subject to paragraph (b) shall not represent a client with interests materially adverse to those of a prospective client in the same or a substantially related matter if the lawyer received information from the prospective client that could be significantly harmful to that person in the matter, except as provided in paragraph (d). If a lawyer is disqualified from representation under this paragraph, no lawyer in a firm with which that lawyer is associated may knowingly undertake or continue

representation in such a matter, except as provided in paragraph (d).

(d) When the lawyer has received disqualifying information as defined in paragraph (c), representation is permissible if:

(1) both the affected client and the prospective client have given informed consent, confirmed in writing, or:

(2) the lawyer who received the information took reasonable measures to avoid exposure to more disqualifying information than was reasonably necessary to determine whether to represent the prospective client; and

(i) the disqualified lawyer is timely screened from any participation in the matter and is apportioned no part of the fee therefrom; and

(ii) written notice is promptly given to the prospective client.

Rule 5.3

With respect to a nonlawyer employed or retained by or associated with a lawyer:

(a) a partner, and a lawyer who individually or together with other lawyers possesses comparable managerial authority in a law firm shall make reasonable efforts to ensure that the firm has in effect measures giving reasonable assurance that the person's conduct is compatible with the professional obligations of the lawyer;

(b) a lawyer having direct supervisory authority over the nonlawyer shall make reasonable efforts to ensure that the person's conduct is compatible with the professional obligations of the lawyer; and

(c) a lawyer shall be responsible for conduct of such a person that would be a violation of the Rules of Professional Conduct if engaged in by a lawyer if:

(1) the lawyer orders or, with the knowledge of the specific conduct, ratifies the conduct involved; or

(2) the lawyer is a partner or has comparable managerial authority in the law firm in which the person is employed, or has direct supervisory authority over the person, and knows of the conduct at a time when its consequences can be avoided or mitigated but fails to take reasonable remedial action.

Rule 7.3

(a) A lawyer shall not by in-person, live telephone or real-time electronic contact solicit professional employment from a prospective client when a significant motive for the lawyer's doing so is the lawyer's pecuniary gain, unless the person contacted:

(1) is a lawyer; or

(2) has a family, close personal, or prior professional relationship with the lawyer.

(b) A lawyer shall not solicit professional employment from a prospective client by written, recorded or electronic communication or by in-person, telephone or real-time electronic contact even when not otherwise prohibited by paragraph (a), if:

(1) the prospective client has made known to the lawyer a desire not to be solicited by the lawyer; or

(2) the solicitation involves coercion, duress or harassment.

(c) Every written, recorded or electronic communication from a lawyer soliciting professional employment from a prospective client known to be in need of legal services in a particular matter shall include the words "Advertising Material" on the outside envelope, if any, and at the beginning and ending of any recorded or electronic communication, unless the recipient of the communication is a person specified in paragraphs (a)(1) or (a)(2).

(d) Notwithstanding the prohibitions in paragraph (a), a lawyer may participate with a prepaid or group legal service plan operated by an organization not owned or directed by the lawyer that uses in-person or telephone contact to solicit memberships or subscriptions for the plan from persons who are not known to need legal services in a particular matter covered by the plan.

APPENDIX E

Glossary

A

admissible Material that may be considered by the jury or judge when rendering a verdict.

alternate juror A person who listens to a case as a member of the jury but who generally does not deliberate or vote unless one of the nonalternate jurors becomes unable to serve.

alternative dispute resolution (ADR) Processes other than court and jury trials utilized to resolve disputes.

answer A pleading from a defendant that replies to and defends against a complaint.

arraignment A preliminary procedure where the defendant is formally informed of the charges and his or her constitutional rights and enters a plea, usually of not guilty.

attorney work product Material prepared for litigation that is protected from disclosure due to the attorney-client privilege.

B

bench conference See side bar.

binding arbitration A proceeding where a nonjudge hears evidence in a shortened proceeding and makes a ruling that is binding on the parties.

boutique firm A specialty firm limited exclusively to one or two areas of practice.

Brady rule A rule derived from a U.S. Supreme Court case that requires a prosecutor to disclose to the defense evidence that is favorable to the defendant.

burden of proof The degree to which a party must prove its case in order to win.

C

case in chief The original opportunity a party has to present its case through witnesses and exhibits.

chain of custody A series of people and movements that caused an object to get from the incident to court, where it is presented as evidence.

Chinese wall Isolating an attorney or paralegal with a conflict of interest from the conflicting case so that the person with the conflict does not have access to the file or written or oral discussions about the case.

class action A lawsuit involving such a large number of plaintiffs who have suffered similar wrongs by the defendant(s) being represented that it would be inefficient to have many cases so that one person or a small group represents the class of injured people.

class representative The named and lead plaintiff who serves as a representative of the class in a class action suit.

clearly erroneous A standard of review that gives a very high level of deference to the trial court's ruling. Unless there was no support for the holding in the record, the trial court's ruling will stand.

coach To influence the content of a witness's testimony.

collective facts rule The rule that an opinion is admissible when there is no other way to describe an observation because the phenomenon is too complex or subtle.

comparative negligence The principle that reduces the plaintiff's recovery by the percentage of his or her fault.

complaint A pleading that starts a lawsuit, notifying the defendant of what he or she is being sued for and making demands for relief.

contingency fee A fee in which the amount, if any, is based upon whether a recovery is made on behalf of the client and the size of the recovery.

continuance A delay of a court date, usually of a trial or hearing. For example, "The case is continued for two weeks."

counterclaim A claim by the defendant against the plaintiff.

criminalist A person who investigates a crime either at a crime scene or in a crime lab.

cross-complaint A claim by a defendant against a co-defendant.

cross-examination Questioning of a witness by a party who is adverse to the one who called the witness.

CSI effect A jury's unreasonable expectation that science or technology should be presented in every case.

D

database A searchable collection of data. Sometimes a synonym of source.

date certain A date for trial that is fixed and definite, barring only the most dire emergency.

de novo A standard of review that gives no deference to the trial court's ruling. The appellate court decides the issue for itself, without regard for how the trial court ruled.

declarant The person whose statement a witness providing hearsay testimony is repeating.

deponent A person whose deposition is being taken.

deposition A hearing usually held outside of the courtroom to record the testimony of a witness or party.

direct examination Questioning of a witness by the party who called the witness to the stand.

double jeopardy Being placed at risk of life or liberty more than once for the same crime. The Fifth Amendment to the U.S. Constitution prohibits double jeopardy.

dyadic communication Two people talking to each other.

E

exculpatory evidence Material that tends to negate one or more elements of a crime.

F

fact finder The jury, or if the case is tried without a jury, the judge, serving the role of determining what happened in the incident or transaction that underlies the case.

foundation Evidence about evidence that establishes its admissibility, such as by showing that an item is what it purports to be.

G

gatekeeper The judge's role under the *Daubert* case, making sure that expert testimony will be helpful to the jury.

I

impeachment Attacking the credibility of a witness, often by showing prior inconsistent testimony or contradictions between the testimony and exhibits.

in camera Taking place before the judge in his or her chambers.

inadmissible Material that the judge or jury may not consider when rendering a verdict.

interrogatory A written question sent to a party that must be answered in writing, under oath.

J

judgment A legal document issued by the court at the end of the case that declares each party's legal obligations, such as owing the other party money.

jurisdiction The location where a case may be brought, such as federal court or state court.

M

material Having a logical tie to the facts that matter in a case.

medarb An alternative dispute resolution process that combines mediation and arbitration.

metadata Data about data, such as the author, time, and date of a file.

mini-trial An abbreviated trial conducted before paid jurors who render an advisory verdict. Also called summary jury trial.

mini-Miranda warning A warning that the "debt collector is attempting to collect a debt and that any information obtained will be used for that purpose."

motion in limine (pronounced lim'-in-ee) A request made in advance of trial for the court to rule on the admissibility of evidence; generally, such motions are to exclude evidence and to preclude mentioning the inadmissible evidence in front of the jury.

motion to suppress A request for the court to exclude evidence from a criminal trial based upon the defendant's constitutional or statutory rights, such as the Fourth Amendment right against unlawful search and seizure.

N

no-fault divorce Divorce granted because the marriage is irretrievably broken, without trying to determine which spouse is the root cause of the failure of the marriage.

nonbinding arbitration A proceeding where a non-judge hears evidence in a shortened proceeding and makes a ruling that has no legal force or effect on the case.

O

objection A request for the court to rule that a question is improper or that evidence should not be admissible.

offer of proof Placing excluded evidence on the record, outside the presence of the jury.

open-ended question A query that cannot be answered with a single word or phrase.

opening the door An attorney's action such as asking a question that makes it unfair for inadmissible evidence to be excluded, thereby requiring the court to admit the evidence.

order in limine (pronounced lim'-in-ee) Court directive not to refer to certain inadmissible evidence.

overbroad Beyond the appropriate scope. It can refer to discovery as well as statutes, constitutional law, or court orders.

overrule To rule an objection invalid and allow the question to be answered or to allow an exhibit or testimony into evidence over the objection.

P

parol evidence Evidence that a written contract was modified by something outside the four corners of the contract such as a verbal modification, or that a writing prior to the contract should be considered a part of it.

peremptory challenge An attorney's request, at his or her discretion, for the court to remove a potential juror. Also called peremptory strike.

plea bargaining A discussion between the prosecution and the defense regarding whether the defendant will plead guilty in exchange for a reduction in charges or prison time or for other considerations.

precedent How courts have previously addressed a legal issue.

prejudicial Causing the fact finder to focus on something other than the facts, such as emotion, in reaching a decision.

preponderance of the evidence When evidence for and against a contention results in the point being more likely true than not true.

primary law Material that is a direct source of the law, such as constitutions, statutes, cases, and rules.

pro se Representing himself or herself in litigation.

protective order A court order limiting or prohibiting conduct that would otherwise violate a right or be unduly burdensome.

published An object or document passed around or distributed to the members of the jury.

R

rape shield law A law designed to prohibit the admission of evidence regarding the sexual history of sexual assault victims.

reasonably calculated Any possibility that the question will result in the discovery of admissible evidence.

record Material that was compiled in the trial court, including transcripts of witness testimony, exhibits, and filings made in the trial court.

recross Questioning by an adverse party that follows redirect.

redirect An examination following cross-examination by the party originally calling the witness.

relevant Evidence that tends to make a fact in dispute more or less likely.

removal for cause The court's action to remove potential jurors from the panel because they are not qualified to serve on the case.

res gestae A hearsay exception that allows statements into evidence if they were made contemporaneously with the event they concern.

res ipsa loquitor Literally, the thing speaks for itself. A doctrine indicating that the occurrence of an injury by itself implies that the defendant was negligent in handling an item.

S

secondary sources Items that interpret, analyze, or summarize primary law but lack the force of law, such as treatises, encyclopedias, and law review articles.

self-authenticating Something that does not need foundation in order to be admissible.

side bar A conference at the bench among the attorneys and the judge conducted so that the jurors cannot hear the discussion. Also called bench conference.

skip trace A search for a person whose location is unknown.

source A searchable group of data. Sometimes a synonym of database.

special verdict form A questionnaire that the jury fills out in order to make specific factual determinations so that the verdict encompasses the answers to a series of questions.

spoliate To destroy, hide, or damage evidence intentionally.

standard of review A measure of how much deference an appellate court will give to a ruling of a trial court.

subpoena A court order to appear at a proceeding.

subpoena duces tecum A court order to appear and produce specified things, usually documents.

subsequent remedial measures Fixing a safety problem after it becomes apparent.

summary jury trial See mini-trial.

summons A notice that the defendant is being sued and has a limited amount of time to answer the suit.

sustained A ruling by the judge that an objection was proper and that the question should not be answered, or the evidence should not be admitted.

T

term of art A word or phrase that has a special meaning within the jargon of a profession, avocation, or other group.

testator The person signing a will and designating the disposition of his or her property upon death.

theme of the case The position of a party regarding the facts and its theory of why it should win the case.

tickler system A computer or card index system designed to provide advance notice of important deadlines.

U

ultimate issue A question the fact finder will be required to answer in order to return a verdict.

ultimate question of fact A key determination in a case regarding what happened.

V

venire The group of potential jurors from whom the jury is selected.

voir dire (pronounced v-'wah deer) The process of choosing a jury.

W

work product See attorney work product.

workers' compensation case A case in which employees injured on the job collect on the employer's insurance policy for injured workers rather than sue the employer.

Index